The American West
Frontier & Region

John W. Caughey

THE AMERICAN WEST

Frontier & Region

Interpretations by
John Walton Caughey

EDITED AND WITH AN INTRODUCTION BY
NORRIS HUNDLEY, JR. AND JOHN A. SCHUTZ

THE WARD RITCHIE PRESS · LOS ANGELES

To LaRee Caughey

Library of Congress Catalog Card Number 69-18265
Lithographed in the United States of America
by Anderson, Ritchie & Simon
Designed by Joseph Simon

CONTENTS

Introduction vii

Part I—THE WEST 3
The American West: Frontier and Region 5
Toward an Understanding of the West 11
The Spanish Southwest: An Example of Subconscious Regionalism 27

Part II—THE OLD SOUTHWEST 41
Louisiana: A Spanish Outpost, 1763-1783 42
McGillivray of the Creeks 72

Part III—CALIFORNIA 97
California and the Nation: A Tally of Two Histories 99
Gold is the Cornerstone: An Assay 108
Don Benito Wilson: An Average Southern Californian 114
Hubert Howe Bancroft 126
California in Third Dimension 135
The Local Historian: His Occupational Hazards and Compensations 154

Part IV—WESTERN JUSTICE 167
Their Majesties the Mob 171
A University in Jeopardy 191
A Plea to the Regents of the University of California 205
Trustees of Academic Freedom 209
The Practical Defense of Academic Freedom 221

Part V—CAUGHEY'S CREED 239
Unfinished Business 239
Our Chosen Destiny 241

Notes 256

Bibliography of Caughey's Writings 269

Index 279

ACKNOWLEDGMENTS

Part I. "The American West: Frontier and Region" was first published in *Arizona and the West,* I (1959), 7-12. "Toward an Understanding of the West" appeared in the *Utah Historical Quarterly,* XXVII (1959), 7-24. "The Spanish Southwest: An Example of Subconscious Regionalism" was originally published in Merrill Jensen, ed., *Regionalism in America* (Madison: University of Wisconsin Press, 1951), 173-186.

Part II. "Louisiana: A Spanish Outpost, 1763-1783" was excerpted from John W. Caughey, *Bernardo de Gálvez in Louisiana, 1776-1783* (Berkeley: University of California Press, 1934). "McGillivray of the Creeks" was taken from John W. Caughey, *McGillivray of the Creeks* (Norman: University of Oklahoma Press, 1938).

Part III. "California and the Nation: A Tally of Two Histories" is from the *California Historical Society Quarterly,* XL (1961), 193-202. "Gold is the Cornerstone: An Assay" appeared first in John W. Caughey, *Gold is the Cornerstone* (Berkeley: University of California Press, 1948), 291-299. "Don Benito Wilson: An Average Southern Californian" was originally published in the *Huntington Library Quarterly,* II (1939), 285-300. "Hubert Howe Bancroft" first appeared in the *American Historical Review,* L (1945), 461-470. "California in Third Dimension" appeared in the *Pacific Historical Review,* XXVIII (1959), 111-129. "The Local Historian: His Occupational Hazards and Compensations" is from the *Pacific Historical Review,* XII (1943), 1-9.

Part IV. "Their Majesties the Mob" was taken from John W. Caughey, *Their Majesties the Mob* (Chicago: University of Chicago Press, 1960), 1-25. "A University in Jeopardy" originally appeared in *Harpers Magazine* (Nov., 1950), 68-75. "A Plea to the Regents of the University of California" was published first as a pamphlet in 1950 and later reprinted under a different title in *Frontier,* Aug. 15, 1950. "Trustees of Academic Freedom" is from the *Bulletin of the American Association of University Professors,* XXXVII (1951), 427-441. "The Practical Defense of Academic Freedom" was originally published in the *Bulletin of the American Association of University Professors,* XXXVIII (1952), 244-260.

Part V. "Unfinished Business" is from John W. Caughey, John Hope Franklin, and Ernest R. May, *Land of the Free: A History of the United States* (Pasadena: Franklin Publications, Inc., 1967), 618-619. "Our Chosen Destiny" appeared first in the *Journal of American History,* LII (1965), 239-251.

INTRODUCTION

"The tradition of frontier vigilantism," John W. Caughey told a roomful of historians during an annual professional meeting, is much broader than many have thought. "In our day the vigilante impulse crops up in the resistance to desegregation. It appears at Philadelphia where a pressure group seeks to force the Plymouth Meeting to fire its librarian, at Houston where another group uses irresponsible charges to get rid of a superintendent of schools, and in Hollywood where a conspiracy of black-listers purges the employment rolls."[1]

Caughey was expressing his well known opposition to encroachments upon human liberty. He had condemned vigilante justice in speeches across the nation and was emphasizing in this address that justice arises out of law, equity, and the quiet of the courtroom. These sentiments are indicative of his philosophy, but they also reveal a relationship between Caughey the western historian and Caughey the fighter for civil rights and academic freedom.

In appearance Caughey does not resemble nor sound like a fighter, nor does everything he writes reveal him in that role. Slight of frame, mild mannered, speaking always in quiet, measured tones, he impresses many people as being what he is — a college professor. But he is not an ivory tower variety, as his friends and those who know him by reputation will readily attest. For they have all witnessed his battles with the University of California over academic freedom and fair standards of promotion, with the Los Angeles Board of Education over *de facto* segregation, with the state of California over capital punishment, with the Lyndon Johnson administration over American involvement in Vietnam, with the federal government over separation of church and state, and with the Los Angeles Dodgers over their land grab in Chavez Ravine. Important as these encounters have been in his life, they have not obscured his distinction as a leading western historian, and it is that aspect of his career we will emphasize here, though not to the exclusion of the other. Even if we should want to separate the two, it would be impossible.

Just as Frederick Jackson Turner's name is identified with the study of the frontier, Herbert Eugene Bolton's with the Spanish borderlands, and Walter Prescott Webb's with the great plains, so is John Walton Caughey's linked with California and the West to which he has devoted nearly forty years and most of a lifetime as a tireless editor and prolific researcher and writer. In more than twenty books, close to a hundred articles, and a shelf of book reviews, he has written and continues to write of the West from its beginnings to the critical issues of our day.

This concentration upon the West can probably be explained in part by Caughey's early life. He was born in Wichita, Kansas, in 1902, when that area of the state was still evolving from cattle ranches into tilled farms. From there his father, Rudolph Weyerhaeuser Caughey, a Presbyterian minister, took his wife, Emily Walton, and their children to Marion, Kansas, and then to Pawnee City and Lincoln, Nebraska, where young John gained even more intimate views of western life. He grew up in Lincoln, going to the local schools, enjoying the diversions of the nearby country, and joining with his parents in church life. Seated occasionally in the congregation was William Jennings Bryan, whose colorful antics in regional and national politics gave the young man an insight into the mentality of a prairie leader.

While maturing John had other opportunities to see the West, but he made his most significant move in 1919 when he went to Austin and the University of Texas. He was attracted to the university because of its excellent reputation, and, during the next four years, he enrolled in a wide variety of courses, with subject matter ranging from history to anthropology, from philosophy to sociology. Following graduation in 1923 with a major in English, he was unsure of his future career. For a time he took a job as a bookkeeper in Roswell, New Mexico, and then for almost two years he taught at the Schreiner Institute near Kerrville, Texas. Though his experience was rewarding and convinced him that he had chosen the right profession, he sensed that he would find even greater satisfaction working with more advanced students and engaging in research and writing. Such objectives, he knew, would be within reach if he became a college professor, but he had first to select a major educational interest and then a good graduate school. Both required serious decisions which took his thoughts back to his college years.

At the University of Texas he had enrolled in courses with Walter

Prescott Webb, who had only recently begun teaching there. Webb had not yet discovered those ideas which were to fire his imagination and lead to the publication of his epochal *Great Plains,* and perhaps this is the reason Caughey remembers him conducting rather uninspired discussions in European history. Still, history had a fascination for Caughey. Something in Texas' controversial past drew him to the state's history as well as to the larger story of America's westward movement. He was also attracted to Turner's essay on the "Significance of the Frontier," which had been published more than three decades earlier and had revolutionized American historical interpretation. Like so many students of his generation, Caughey had heard Turner's theories debated and pondered the influence of frontier social forces, but he was also excited by the challenging ideas of Herbert Eugene Bolton, a rising scholar at the University of California in Berkeley.

Bolton had taught at the University of Texas between 1901 and 1909 before going to the West Coast and, like Caughey, had become intrigued by the history of the early Southwest. Convinced that Turner and his disciples had an overly narrow view of what constituted the West, Bolton chided the Harvard historian for focusing almost exclusively on Anglo-American frontiersmen, particularly those of the Old Northwest, and forgetting that there were other "Wests" and other frontiersmen. The Dutch, Swedes, Russians, Danes, French, and the Spanish, insisted Bolton, had more often than not preceded the British advance by decades and even centuries. Instead of blazing trails into virgin wildernesses, Turner's frontiersmen usually found the groundwork already laid for their advance. For these and other reasons, Bolton concluded, American history was more than the history of the Thirteen Colonies, and to test his convictions he studied the Spanish explorers and settlers of the North American borderlands, an area stretching from the Carolinas to the Californias. He hoped to chronicle Spanish activities in much the same manner that Francis Parkman had narrated the rise and fall of New France. Although he never succeeded in Parkmanizing Spain's exploits, he did arouse a whole generation of scholars to the need for a broader approach to American history and made the Spanish borderlands a most popular area of historical research.

In the mid 1920's Bolton was in his prime, writing those articles and books which only added to his already impressive scholarly reputation, serving as chairman of the history department and director of the Bancroft Library, teaching hundreds of undergraduates, and turning out scores of students with graduate degrees. In the West he was easily the most distinguished historian, and Caughey, leaning to his ideas, decided in 1925 to apply for admission to the University of California. Though Caughey had some lingering doubts about his choice of history for advanced study, he was excited by the opportunity of working with Bolton and soon these doubts faded.

Joining Bolton's "round table" of graduate students, Caughey spent Thursday nights sharing the findings of research and helping unravel the story of Spain's northward march of empire. At first his own area of special interest was New Mexico, whose borderlands became the subject of his master's thesis. Then, acting upon Bolton's advice, he focused on the Old Southwest, completing in 1928 his doctoral dissertation, "Louisiana under Spain, 1763-1783."

With Bolton's encouragement Caughey then secured a fellowship from the Native Sons of the Golden West and spent a year in Spain collecting material that would serve as the basis for several books and articles. On his return to California in 1929, he faced the disheartening prospect of finding a teaching position during the unsettled times of the depression. Fortune was with him, however, when the authorities of San Bernardino Junior College, impressed by his qualifications, offered him a job. He received classes in sociology, political science, and history. Though it was not an unusual load of class preparation and lecturing, it absorbed even his leisure hours, leaving little time for research and writing.

In searching for a position more favorable to his interests Caughey made inquiries at the Los Angeles campus of the University of California and learned of a temporary opening in American history. An offer went out and, in 1930, he seized the opportunity to enter UCLA, as he likes to say, "through the back door." The job turned into a permanent one, and for the next two score years his life was bound closely with UCLA's. The school was new, having only recently exchanged its status as an undergraduate college for that of a university, and was experiencing growing pains. The library had to be developed, course offerings enriched, and a graduate program established. During the busy years of the 1930's and 1940's Caughey joined the fights to secure for UCLA an autonomous position within the University of California system and to win promotion criteria emphasizing merit. The last one, though university-wide in importance, arose from his own experience in the history department. A backlog of promotions had embittered some younger men like Caughey who were aggravated by the premium placed on seniority rather than scholarship. When he failed to win advancement after authoring three or four well received books and numerous articles, he finally went in desperation to the department chairman and sought an explanation. "What does one have to do to get promoted around here?" A nervous laugh broke the silence, and then this disappointing reply as the chairman ushered him from the office. "Just wait your turn. There are several who have been around here longer than you." Such rebuffs served only to spur his demand for reform.

Nor was Caughey afraid to speak out when he believed a colleague was being treated unfairly. During an incident involving an assistant professor whose contract had not been renewed, Caughey urged the Academic Senate to instruct the Committee on Privilege and Tenure to hold a hearing. Earlier the committee had refused because the assistant professor did not possess tenure. To Caughey, also an untenured faculty member, the committee's reply missed the point. "Presumably the supplicant had some privileges," he reasoned, "even if he had no tenure."[2] The Senate was finally convinced and ordered a hearing. But the committee found no irregularity in procedure and no reason to prevent termination of employment. "We saved the principle," Caughey later noted, "but lost the man." In retrospect, his concern for principle in his professional relations has been preeminent, and it has furthered his goal of academic excellence as a teaching scholar.

A measure of his devotion is the large number of students he has helped shepherd toward graduation. His courses on the American West and California are taken yearly by hundreds of students who are drawn to his classes by his reputation as a scholar and his relaxed, conversational way of lecturing. As a speaker he refrains from dramatic outbursts, preferring a manner similar to that of his admired teacher, Herbert Bolton, who avoided the spectacular, according to Caughey, and offered instead "a down-to-earth exposition, a straight-forward narrative, together with his observations on the meaning."[3]

As a teacher Caughey is perhaps most effective with graduate students who appreciate his modest, undogmatic manner and firm dedication to scholarship. He lets seminar topics range widely, reflecting his own varied interests and his broad concept of western history. Though everyone participates equally, and the criticism, like the papers presented, depends on the quality of the students, Caughey usually saves his analyses for last. These he delivers quietly, revealing his own mastery of the field and leaving the good student with a warm feeling and the careless researcher with uneasiness. The subtlety of his remarks is astonishing. More than one student has later remarked: "While he was speaking, I felt that I had done a reasonably good job. But, when I later reflected on his comments, I realized that he had destroyed my paper."

In Caughey's hands the seminar is a center of research in which the theories of a dissertation or thesis can be tested, evaluated, and refined. His objective always is publication, not for the sake of getting one's name into print, but for the knowledge it will give the scholarly world. His frank insistence that publication is the most important, though not the only, measure of scholarly productivity is an admonition that many former members of his seminar have taken to heart. Some of those winning doctorates under his supervision are now well known historians. They include John Baur, Edwin Bingham, Bernard Bobb, Edwin Carpenter, Glenn S. Dumke, Emmett Greenwalt, Werner Marti, Ernest R. May, A. Russell Mortensen, and R. K. Murdock, as well as Leonard Pitt, William Rice, Andrew Rolle, Raymond A. Rydell, Merlin Stonehouse, K. Ross Toole, and Hyman Weintraub. As a group, his former students have authored dozens of books, and nearly every year new studies lengthen the shelf of titles. In addition to writing, most hold professorships in distinguished colleges and universities, and two have risen (or fallen) into leading administrative positions in California's state college system.

Though Caughey himself emphasizes the scholar's obligation to publish research, he has never neglected other aspects of academic life. Over the years he has given freely of himself, participating in public lectures and forums, serving as department chairman, and acting as historical consultant to motion picture and television studios, to the *Encyclopedia Britannica,* the California Department of Justice, the state Landmarks Commission, the city of Los Angeles, and to numerous state and civic organizations. He has worked as well with the American Historical Research Center, the American Association of University Professors (as a vice president), the American Civil Liberties Union of Southern California (as a member of the board), and the Doris Duke American Indian History Study project (as director). For thirty-one years he was associated with the *Pacific Historical Review*, serving as staff member, associate editor, and, from 1947 to 1968, as managing editor. Under his guidance, the *Review* became a major source of articles and reviews concerning the West and the lands bordering the Pacific area. He has also served as literary editor of *Frontier*, general editor of the "Chronicles of California," editorial consultant for *Arizona and the West*, member of the editorial board of *The American West*, regional editor of *American Heritage*, contributing editor to the section on Latin American bibliography in the *American Historical Review*, and a fellow of the Rockefeller Foundation, the American Council of Learned Societies, and the Historical Society of Southern California. These activities, together with his scholarly research and his spirited defense of academic freedom during the University of California loyalty oath controversy of the 1950's, brought him that most coveted of achievements — the acknowledged respect of his colleagues in the historical profession. In 1958 they elected him president of the Pacific Coast Branch of the American Historical Association and, in 1964, they elevated him to the presidency of the Organization of American Historians. This last represented a double honor, for his election was accompanied by a new name for the organization (formerly the Mississippi Valley Historical Association) which mirrored its national membership, something Caughey had sought for years.

These honors are symbolic of Caughey's prodigious scholarship which seems to reflect a steady, quiet pace of writing. He does not give the impression of working in short, highly productive bursts of energy, but rather of operating for long hours at a consistently even speed. The result has been a four-foot shelf of publications which can be approached in many ways, depending on what phase of his career is being examined. Obviously his early interests followed those of Bolton in the Spanish borderlands and the dividends included two books and nearly half a dozen articles. The first of the books, a revision of his doctoral dissertation, appeared in 1934 and focused on the careers of Louisiana's Spanish governors, particularly on the dramatic life of Bernardo de Gálvez, governor between 1777 and 1783, who deployed Spanish forces in significant battles of the American Revolution. By capturing key British posts in the Old Southwest and provisioning American revolutionaries, Gálvez assured American claims to vast western territory when the peace treaty was finally written. Indeed, as Caughey clearly emphasized, the United States acquisition of the southern trans-Appalachian area was due more to Gálvez' military victories on the Gulf Coast than to American military prowess.

Though Gálvez was unaware of it, his victories had no lasting benefits for Spain. As the new republic gained quickly in strength, the settlers of the two countries clashed in the borderlands and competed for the allegiance of southeastern Indians in a campaign of bloodshed and intrigue. Most prominent among the Indians was a wily, half breed named Alexander McGillivray. Son of a Creek-French mother and a Scotch father, he had lived as a youth in the British colonial towns of Charleston and Savannah before returning to his mother's people as a tribal leader. Caughey's interest in this gifted man was aroused by the discovery of some unusual letters in the Archives of the Indies at Seville. A glance at these documents convinced him that much more could be told about this unique personality and, in 1938, he published *McGillivray of the Creeks,* a fascinating volume containing a biographical sketch and more than two hundred letters of the Indian leader and his contemporaries. Together they describe in rich detail the frontier problems of the United States, Britain, and Spain during the post-Revolutionary decade. But more than this, the narrative and documents underscore the diplomatic talents of the remarkable McGillivray, who displayed astonishing loyalty and devotion to his Indian people. For a generation he devised strategy to shield the Creeks from the encroaching whites by playing off the invaders against each other. Eventually disease, plots, and the force of numbers defeated him, but not before he had won the respect and admiration of his white adversaries.

Even before the publication of McGillivray, Caughey's interests had begun to shift from the Tombigbee to the Pacific Coast. He was motivated partly by the vagaries of the academic marketplace, since his position at UCLA depended upon his willingness to teach courses on the history of the Pacific slope of North America. In accepting the post, he was faced with the additional obligation of providing students with accessible reading materials, a major problem in an age of limited library budgets, expensive duplication, and few mass circulated paperbacks. Aside from the multivolume history of Hubert Howe Bancroft, which Caughey rightly considered "a group of local histories rather than a regional study," no one had produced a historical analysis that could be assigned to students. In 1933, Caughey overcame this difficulty with the publication of his *History of the Pacific Coast,* a pioneer work and the first of many textbooks which would make his name known to generations of students. Ranging in subject matter from the Indians of ancient Mexico to the changing West of the early twentieth century, but emphasizing California and the years before 1846, the book presented an engaging study of exploration and settlement.

It became a stimulant also for Caughey who now shifted his teaching and research interests to California's past. The state had always been popular among historians, yet none had written a single-volume narrative which gave adequate attention to the state's cultural and intellectual life while also tracing its past from pre-discovery to the twentieth century. When Caughey published his study in 1940, critics hailed its outstanding merit. Literary-historian Lawrence Clark Powell, himself a distinguished author, described the history as exceptional "in its range, balance, scholarship, and felicity of expression."[4] The book, now in its second edition, with a third on the way, enjoys wide public use, a practice due not only to its graceful style and illustrations, but also to its comprehensive, annotated bibliography of some forty pages. In later years, when Caughey and his wife, LaRee, prepared a children's history of California (which was promptly adopted by the state as a fourth grade text), they reached more students than any previous California historian.

Through the 1940's Caughey's interest in California deepened, and his list of publications lengthened with his graphic studies of Hubert Howe Bancroft, the Gold Rush, E. Gould Buffum, R. R. Taylor, Walter Gardner, and Benjamin Wilson. The life of Bancroft, appearing in 1946, represented the first full-length study of the West's most versatile and significant early historian. Book collector, author of a massive thirty-nine volume history of the Pacific slope, and owner of the largest publishing house in the West, Bancroft was a formidable subject for any biographer. Yet Caughey's "mastery of Pacific Coast history" and "informed insight," in the opinion of critics, had produced an admirable portrait of the man and his activities.[5]

In 1948, less than two years after publishing the Bancroft volume, Caughey had researched and written *Gold is the Cornerstone.* The haste was necessary because of the approaching centenary of the gold rush, and he had been commissioned to assay the significance of that famous event. It had, in Caughey's opinion, awakened national and world interest in California and laid the foundation of the future state's prosperity. Opening his narrative with the discovery at Coloma, Caughey describes the spread of gold fever, the various routes and "by-ways" taken by the "forty-niners," and the life and mining techniques in the diggings. Since the gold rush had never before been discussed so broadly, the book represented a pioneering effort, and its success encouraged him to follow it with edited journals, letters, and other descriptive eyewitness accounts.

The nineteen fifties took Caughey abruptly out of the relative quiet of classroom and library, bringing him personally into the history of California and the West and influencing sharply his later writings. This development had its immediate beginnings in the Cold War. That conflict with its polarization of world power between the United States and the Soviet Union aroused an almost hysterical demand for loyalty that shook the country's very institutions. Now sadly referred to as McCarthyism, the witch-hunt with its concomitant demand for conformity spread across the nation and penetrated deep into American life.

In such a climate of opinion schools came quickly under scrutiny by watchdog groups, both governmental and self-appointed. The fear of Communism on college campuses upset rationally minded people who became unusually sensitive to news of controversial speakers, publications, and rallies. Adding to the tension were the loyalty investigations, like those at the University of Washington where, in 1949, two admitted Communist party members were dismissed. These disclosures in turn alarmed many Californians who petitioned their state legislature to conduct its own investigations. Urged on by Senator Jack B. Tenney, a notorious red baiter, the legislature studied ways of determining the loyalty of university employees, an action which frightened the Regents of the University of California. Fearing possible state encroachment on their authority and alarmed themselves by alleged disloyalty on the campuses, the Regents instituted a test oath and made it a condition of employment.

For Caughey and his colleagues the Regents' oath seemed to be a political test because it forced them to deny membership in the Communist Party, at the time a legal organization. More than this, they believed it violated the state constitution, unfairly singled out university employees, and, most importantly, jeopardized academic freedom, since refusal to sign the oath, for any reason, resulted in dismissal. In effect, the oath allowed the Regents to break contracts of employment, thus violating tenure and interfering with matters of university discipline customarily left with the faculty.

The furor arising from the oath and the jockeying for advantage by both faculty and Regents is too complicated a story to be told here.[6] Suffice to say that, with few exceptions, faculty members condemned the measure, but the threat of dismissal forced most to sign it. Caughey and thirty others refused to be coerced and, on August 25, 1950, were summarily fired. Ironically, their dismissal occurred in spite of an investigation by Academic Senate Committees on Privilege and Tenure which had found them to be competent scholars, objective teachers, and non-Communists. Such evidence caused many of the Regents to acknowledge that Communism was no longer their concern. "The real issue," admitted Regent Fred Jordan, "has nothing to do with Communism, the Loyalty Oath or anything else." The fundamental question was simply "whether this faculty is to be permitted to select its own members and govern itself without encroachment or interference by the Trustees [Regents] of the State University."[7]

On this issue Caughey knew where he stood and he launched a vigorous speaking and writing campaign to inform the public about the crisis in the university. While admitting that he was no Communist and that "only the loyal deserve faculty posts," he denounced the Regents' oath because of the threat it posed to academic freedom.[8] The University of California, he noted, was regarded among the most distinguished in the land. It had achieved that position due to its great faculty, who were chosen "on the basis of character, competence, and performance." Though he conceded the process of selection was fallible, he was certain that "the only trustworthy and effective means of building and maintaining a proper faculty is by reliance on the expert judgment of scholars. The alumni may be the best judges of football coaches," he observed wryly, and "the Regents may be better connoisseurs of capital investments. But just as we rely on the lawyers to decide who shall be admitted to the bar and on the doctors to say who may practice medicine, the only sound procedure is to have the scholars in the several disciplines decide who shall constitute a university faculty." Only in this way, he believed, could a university ever hope to escape outside pressures and engage in its primary function — the search for truth.

In Caughey's opinion, no one — not even a Communist — should be dismissed from a faculty unless found guilty of sacrificing "scholarly integrity" or of "incompetence, gross neglect of duty, or grave defect in character."[9] And, he insisted, the judge in these matters should be the faculty itself, not a Board of Regents applying a "political test which could easily become a precedent for further narrowing of the base of eligibility for the faculty." "Firing Communists on sight," he feared, could easily "spread, and it has, to suspected Communists, rumored members of Communist fronts, 'Communist thinkers' (whatever that may mean), and to many others not even remotely connected with Communism." In short, the worth of a scholar must be judged from the evidence of his research and teaching; guilt by association, labels, and symbols are no substitute for due process.

Caughey had other objections to the Regent's oath, as his essays indicate, but none can explain the personal bitterness which he suffered on account of the controversy. During the first four months following his dismissal, he and his family lived on a handout from CRUG, the Committee for Representative Government at UCLA. He then received grants from the Rockefeller Foundation for eight months and from the American Council of Learned Societies for nine months. For the next seven months he had no income. All the while he and his fellow nonsigners were denounced as "visionaries," "dupes," and purveyors of "foreign despotism" by most politicians, by every major newspaper in California save the *San Francisco Chronicle,* and by scores of self-appointed guardians of "Americanism." Even more distressing was the about-face of some colleagues whose hostility towards them increased as the popular attack broadened to include the university itself. "Forget your principles and think of the University's welfare," was their strange advice.

The denunciations decreased significantly in April 1951, when the California Third District Court of Appeal ruled that the Regent's oath violated the state constitution and was a threat to academic freedom. Most of the Regents, tempered now by changes of mind and personnel, favored withdrawal of the oath, but a minority pressed for a review by the state Supreme Court. A year and a half later the high court finally handed down a decision in *Tolman* v. *Underhill* which pleased no one. Ignoring the district court's eloquent contention that intellectual freedom was at stake, the court found the Regent's oath unconstitutional on the narrow legal grounds that it represented an unwarranted invasion of the legislature's police powers. In fact, the state had already exercised its authority in the field of loyalty legislation a year earlier when it had enacted the Levering Oath, a measure later added to the California constitution and required of all state civil defense workers and public employees, including university professors.

The new state oath brought little joy to Caughey or other liberal minded people. Upon reflection, however, he considered it an amelioration of conditions and counted the blessings. For one, it did not mention the Communist or any other party by name, even though it required disavowal of organizations advocating the overthrow of the government (and he had always held that only the loyal should hold university positions). For another, its broader application made it less of a Jim Crow device than the Regents' oath which singled out university personnel. Finally, it was state law not the Regents' fiat.[10] Nevertheless, he doubted the oath's wisdom and constitutionality and began working with others for a climate of opinion that would favor the elimination of all such tests. His patience was rewarded more than fifteen years later when the California Supreme Court, in December 1967, struck down the state's loyalty oath as an infringement on the freedom of association guaranteed by the United States Constitution.

Caughey's experiences as a member of a minority intensified his already sensitive feelings for the rights of others. In the 1930's he had criticized the wretched living conditions of migratory agricultural labor and, during World War II, he had expressed shock at the treatment of America's Japanese citizens. But his suffering during the oath controversy probably explains as much as anything else his plunge into the civil rights battles of the 1950's and 1960's. The infringements upon liberty, he wrote in *In Clear and Present Danger,* had threatened the foundations of our civilization. Leaders, special groups, and governmental agencies everywhere were investigating opinion and denying to others what they claimed for themselves. Through loyalty checks, blacklists, and special oaths, the nation was dividing into paranoid camps, in which conformity or ignorance seemed the only escape. While Caughey believed the Supreme Court under Earl Warren's leadership had reaffirmed some freedoms, he also noted with disappointment the popular hostility which greeted the court's long overdue pronouncements. Recent decisions, he observed in 1958, "drew an edgy comment from President Eisenhower indicating his disapproval, a blast from former President Truman, a chorus of abuse from the South predisposed against the court because of the desegregation order, and more criticism than praise from northern congressmen and editors."[11]

As Caughey reflected on the almost hysterical demand for loyalty in the 1950's, he was struck by its similarity to earlier examples of mob action. Too often, he believed, Americans had been denied the right of due process and robbed of their jobs, property, and often their lives by people taking the law into their own hands. "To gang up and discipline an alleged wrongdoer is an ancient and deep-seated impulse," he admitted. But it is an impulse running "counter to a principle on which all governments insist, that trial and punishment for crime are the business of the state and solely of the state."[12] To emphasize his convictions, Caughey assembled over fifty examples of the vigilante process in American history and published them in 1960 under the provocative title, *Their Majesties the Mob*. Labeling the book a "brief for due process," he unhesitatingly concluded that, "whatever the temptation to escape the technicalities of legal justice by substituting direct action, the wiser course is to handle all such cases through the regular courts."[13]

Confirming Caughey's faith in the judicial process had been the Supreme Court's 1954 decision in *Brown* v. *Board of Education* which outlawed segregation in the nation's schools. Delighted with the decision but disappointed with its slow implementation, John Caughey and his wife LaRee enlisted in the fight for the establishment of equal opportunity for all Americans. Together they authored scores of briefs, letters, articles, and pamphlets denouncing the evils of segregation, especially as practiced in their home town of Los Angeles, and calling on their local board of education to implement the ruling by the Supreme Court. Los Angeles had never segregated its schools in the southern fashion but, like many other northern and western cities, its schools had become just as black and white as those in the South. Primarily responsible, they believed, was the city's segregated ghetto housing which simply mirrored itself in the neighborhood schools. Joining with the American Civil Liberties Union of Southern California, they fought for open housing and other methods of integrating the local schools.

Although the state board of education had acknowledged that learning was impaired by segregation, the Caugheys' pleas went largely unheard. Of course, many whites for racist or other reasons vigorously opposed ameliorative action, and they had the support of the powerful California Real Estate Association. Many others, however, were apathetic, inured by freeways which allowed them to pass through neighborhoods without seeing the occupants and to live out their lives in their own suburban areas, ignorant — or pretending ignorance — of a problem that somehow was not theirs. To acquaint these people with the situation and to arouse the conscience of the community, the Caugheys published in 1966 *School Segregation on Our Doorstep,* a small book detailing five years of frustrated attempts to awaken Los Angeles school officials to the problem in their midst. This was followed in 1967 by *Segregation Blights Our Schools* which drew on a survey conducted, largely as a result of their protests, by the Los Angeles Superintendent of Schools. That survey, a racial and ethnic census, dramatically demonstrated in its columns of figures the advanced stage of the city's segregation. Approximately 86% of all Negro pupils were in schools in which they predominated, while about half the city's Mexican-American pupils were in schools that were predominately Mexican-American.

Despite the Caugheys' educational campaign and the publicity given their efforts by local radio and television, they have candidly acknowledged only negligible success. But the stiff opposition has only caused them to redouble their efforts.

These efforts on behalf of civil liberties obviously aroused the prejudices of many people and created enemies for the Caugheys. Their numbers multiplied significantly in 1965 when John Caughey joined with John Hope Franklin of the University of Chicago and Ernest May of Harvard University to publish *Land of the Free,* certainly the most debated textbook of the 1960's. Prepared as an eighth grade American history text and written specifically to tell a more balanced story of all Americans, regardless of color, the volume received an almost unanimous endorsement from scholars and was adopted by numerous school boards across the country. "It occurred to me," explained Caughey, "that if we couldn't integrate the class, the least we could do was integrate the curriculum."[14] But the book's inclusion of material on ethnic minorities and its acknowledgement that the United States had not always acted from the purest of motives evoked a bitter attack, especially in California where extremist groups have often had an influence out of all proportion to their numbers. Heightening their anxiety and increasing the pressure of their tactics was California's practice of allowing a single agency, the State Board of Education, to select books for the entire state.

Because Caughey was the only author resident in California, he bore the brunt of what became a bitter campaign of villification — phone calls in the middle of the night, vicious letters, slanderous film strips circulated among right wing groups, and abuse by radio and television commentators. The loyalty oath issue was revived, charges of "thought control" levelled, and veiled insinuations of Communism made. One critic announced that "there could not be a book more pleasing to Communists." To which Caughey promptly replied, "Not being a Communist, I can't answer that one."[15] On another occasion a father denounced the book because it mentioned people he had never heard of, while still another parent vowed that he would burn the history rather than let his child read it; others asserted that "its criticisms of the United States will give pupils a guilt complex." The Junior Chamber of Commerce of Monrovia, California, outdid most critics when it solemnly proclaimed that the book did not measure up to the Jaycee Creed. Equally incensed was a Los Angeles woman who assailed the history because it cited only the American Dental Association as an information source on water fluoridation.

So the pot boiled. While his critics often lost their tempers, Caughey remained outwardly placid. "Criticism of texts is by no means new," he declared in a characteristic rejoinder. "It goes back at least to Moses and the Ten Commandments. The children of Israel, as all remember, promptly sent him up Mount Sinai again for a new edition." On another occasion with a twinkle in his eye, he told an audience of reporters and journalists, "*Land of the Free* is the most controversial California book since *The Grapes of Wrath,* perhaps even since Upton Sinclair's *I, Governor of California, and How I Ended Poverty*. My colleagues and I achieved this distinction without using any four-letter words and without promising to overturn the capitalist system." Agreeing with him in a left-handed way was an outspoken dentist from Sierra Madre. "The book," he proclaimed, "is not pornography — it's worse!"

There were moments of crisis, however, which seemed to lack any trace of humor, as when the State Curriculum Commission began wavering under the intense pressure. After it had unanimously recommended adoption of the book to the State Board of Education and secured the board's approval of its recommendation in May 1966, the commission took the unprecedented step of asking a panel of three historians to reexamine the volume. The fact that many scholars and teachers had spent nine months in careful evaluation seemed not to matter. Caughey was understandably annoyed. "Prior to adoption," he declared, "asking for expert advice would have been altogether proper; indeed, the commission had received evaluations from several equally expert historians. At this post-adoption stage the impression was that this panel had been hired as censors to decide what changes were to be made. One phrasing, in fact," he dourly noted, "was that they were hired 'to revise the book.' "

Fearful of censorship, Caughey and his fellow authors fell back on a set of principles which they had devised for just such an eventuality. "These," they announced, "would be our buckler and our shield — shield against pressures from without and buckler against caving in on our own." The ground rules they drew up for themselves were simple and direct:

1. They would correct outright mistakes.
2. They would eliminate unfairness.
3. They would make other improvements, where feasible and appropriate to the intended use of the book.

As it turned out, Caughey's fears were shortlived, though a few anxious moments still remained. One of the most vexing problems concerned the book's references to W. E. B. DuBois, an outspoken Negro leader of the turn of the century, who had urged his people to insist on their equal rights. The panel of historians demanded that DuBois be identified as a Communist, something he did not become until the advanced age of ninety-three. Caughey and his fellow authors refused to make the identification. "In a full-scale biography," they reasoned, "this strange epilogue to a distinguished leader's long career would certainly be included. In our survey of United States history this detail seemed to us a most improper addition, disconnected, out of step with DuBois' overall behavior, and misleading as to his character."

Despite their explanation, the authors were pressed to make the change. The Curriculum Commission accepted the panel's report and good friends, some close to the publishers, advised emphatically that, unless DuBois were labeled a Communist, "the book was dead." Reluctant to deny to minority youngsters a text to which they could relate for the first time and equally determined not to identify DuBois as a Communist, the authors decided to "remove the fulcrum on which the demand rested." They rewrote the section in which DuBois appeared, but, instead of mentioning him by name, they described his advice to Negroes by focusing on the Niagara Movement, *Crisis* magazine, and the NAACP, in all of which he had been prominent.

With the DuBois episode out of the way, the Curriculum Commission reaffirmed its approval and the board finally released the contract on January 20, 1967. Though sporadic attacks on *Land of the Free* continued, the decisive battle had been won.

Despite such absorbing contests, Caughey still found time to reflect on certain themes and characteristics of western history. In his presidential address to the Pacific Coast Branch of the American Historical Association in 1958, he emphasized the value of literature to the historian seeking "to have real people walking the pages of his writing" and to avoid "figures that are cardboard and a picture that is flat."[16] Literature, especially that classified as creative writing, offered the historian another perspective or "third dimension" allowing him to probe "matters of the spirit and issues of human conflict." Taking California as his example, he suggested how historians in general and western historians in particular could distill a richer understanding of the past "through the eyes and the emotion" of such writers as John Steinbeck, William Saroyan, Mary Austin, and Robinson Jeffers. To dramatize his conviction that "the student of history neglects at his peril the works of literature," he and LaRee prepared an anthology of California history and literature. Published four years later as *California Heritage,* it won immediate classroom and popular use.

Caughey had also been meditating upon the American West as a general field of historical inquiry. His deliberations were published in many places, particularly in the *Utah Historical Quarterly* and *Arizona and the West,* the latter a sprightly new journal for which he wrote the lead article of the first issue.[17] The West, he observed, has too often been considered merely as a frontier, the meeting place of civilization and wilderness, the stomping ground of Indian, trapper, and cowboy. But it has another face — the face of "a section or, more honorably, a region differing from the rest of the nation in many incidentals and in some essentials." Though the explorations of Columbus, DeSoto, and Coronado opened the frontier, the settlements in the Caribbean, Mexico, and along the Atlantic coast called regions into being which had the character of outposts of Europe. As the frontier advanced, regions developed in the Piedmont, the Kentucky-Tennessee area, along the Mississippi, and in the Far West. Instead of looking to Europe, most of the inhabitants of these areas looked to the American East. But the people soon realized — as had those who had looked to Europe — that the "facts of geography and of human circumstances" forced upon them "a recognition that their region could not be forced into the exact pattern" that existed elsewhere. Thus, as westerners were called upon to modify much of what they had borrowed, a significant measure of regional distinction was achieved.

Going beyond Turner and adopting an attitude similar to Webb's *Divided We Stand,* Caughey applied his analysis to the twentieth century West and argued for its existence as a special region. "It is distinctive or possibly bizarre, and this quality arises partly from the geography and partly from its history." Both have combined to provide the West with "a composite of problems and opportunities more or less peculiar to it." "The challenge of water and hydroelectric development, the special relevance of forest, park and conservation policies, and the remoteness of Washington and Wall Street are just a few of the considerations that suggest the West is still with us, alternatively as a problem or a force."

To Caughey the recent West was above all a minority region, suffering from political and economic discrimination. Lack of an adequate voice in Congress and unfair prices, like those specifying "slightly higher west of the Rockies," "F.O.B. Detroit," and "Pittsburgh plus," have been historic signs of injustice. Because discrimination still existed, Caughey urged westerners "to rise above provincialism, cultivate an essential unity of the West, and strive for at least a measure of solidarity" so as to eliminate such practices. As a first step in this direction, he recommended history as a unifying force. "The time is at least ripe for a discovery of the regional history," he observed, since "such a discovery would be of the greatest possible assistance toward achieving throughout the West a sense of regional unity. Indeed, it may be a prerequisite."

Whether writing about regional or ethnic minorities, or fighting for academic freedom and fair standards of promotion, or analyzing the history of western America, or insisting on local autonomy for UCLA, or opposing capital punishment, or questioning the role of the United States in Vietnam, or walking in civil rights demonstrations in the South, Caughey has time and again demonstrated his willingness to be counted. His true measure, however, is best seen in the rightousness of the causes he has advanced. And here a word must be said about his wife.

LaRee Caughey is her husband's closest confidant and a charming, vivacious woman whose bubbling personality complements John's more reserved and shy manner. She is a woman who has made her husband's interests and battles her own; indeed, he has made some of her battles his. More to the point, she is a force in her own right, the author of popular children's stories, education chairman of the American Civil Liberties Union of Southern California, and collaborator with John in many publications, especially those promoting school desegregation and advocating literary history. On some occasions her talent for phrasing has helped him acquire the graceful style characteristic of his writing.

Actually Caughey's ready acknowledgement of his wife's editorial eye has boomeranged. As a young instructor, he thanked her in a preface for aid "more than secretarial." "Thereafter," he recalls with that kind of humor which can come only long after a disturbing event has passed, "I had a devil of a time persuading anybody that any of my writing was my own."

A time for persuasion came unexpectedly. "As though it were yesterday," he recently told a group of friends, "I recall one time in 1940 in the *Pacific Historical Review* office when we needed about half a column of copy in a hurry. I sat down and batted it off, pulled the sheet out of the typewriter, and handed it to the editorial assistant, Bill Rice. He began to shake his head, his jaw dropped, and then he said, 'I didn't think you could do it. I thought Mrs. Caughey did all your writing.' "[18] It was this reputation, Caughey thinks, which helps explain why it took him so long to win promotion, eleven years in obtaining the associate professorship and seven more in attaining the professorship. "On the basis of the books that came out over my name," he observes with a wink, "I'm sure that LaRee would have made the grade five or six years before I did."

Sometime later Caughey set the record straight by acknowledging his wife's actual role. "My version of it," he noted, "is that I do not have a ghost writer and never have had. But I do have — and I want the whole world to know it — I do have the best ghost rewriter that ever was. And an alter ego who is more than an inspiration to me in the business of standing up and being counted."

As far as the American West of the past and present is concerned, John Caughey is certainly one of those who must be "counted." Part of the evidence can be found in the following essays which have been selected to reflect his special interests as well as his understanding of the West in its larger setting. The first few selections, though written more recently, underscore his regional approach and demonstrate his conviction that western history embraces far more than just frontier history. Most of the remaining essays, published over the years, are illustrative of particular western regions and topics that have constant and absorbing interest. And the final selection, his presidential address to the Organization of American Historians, not only reveals him as a sensitive observer of today's events, but also displays how his reading of American history has made him both an optimist and an activist.

Part I

THE WEST

THE WEST

The West in American history began with the Indian, then with the explorations of Cabrillo and Coronado in the sixteenth century and the settlements of Virginia and Quebec after 1600. Its history has been characterized by successive stages of development as men rushed ever deeper into the continent — into the Old Southwest, the Piedmont of the Atlantic coast, the Mississippi Valley, the Pacific slope, the Rocky Mountains, and the Great Plains. Operating like a spearhead, a confrontation pitting men and environment against each other, it provided adventure and escape, while offering and molding a new life.

The West as frontier and region, as interrelated forces of movement and settlement, is how John W. Caughey conceives of this process of adjusting older habits of life to new conditions. He thinks of the land itself as always a primary challenge to the pioneer because of its diversity and ruggedness, its vast distances and extremes of climates, its barrenness and riches. But the land had to await the people, who arrived in successive waves, starting before recorded time with the families of Indians. These waves seem to reflect the interaction of man and his inventions, enabling him to reach beyond the mountain barriers, the rivers, and the plains. The advance was slow until the middle of the nineteenth century, when improved transportation and the vigor of the youthful United States were responsible for accelerating the movement of people. Though the West was sparsely settled by 1890 and the frontier drawing to a close, the modern post-frontier twentieth century has seen a continuation of the population rush, the adapting of eastern institutions to western conditions, and an interplay of climate, science, and technology to create a regional way of life. An evaluation of these later developments, Caughey believes, is essential to an understanding of western history. Unless historians are willing to think in broader terms, then their history is "likely to be nothing but 'cowboys and Indians' and what they have to say is likely to be antiquarian and sterile."[1]

Western historians, like the area they describe, reflect some of the region's peculiarities. For one thing, they are uncertain about the value of their specialty in the broader outlines of history and they often label themselves professors of American history or something else rather than admit being *western* American historians. Caughey, in attacking this apologetic mood, urges his colleagues to "develop backbone. . . . The history of the West need not continue to be the least prestigious field."

To a large extent the problem is the lack of unity among westerners. What the West faces is that it is a group of wests. Living with similar problems but often standing apart from each other, they spar over water allocation and federal money, while treating one another like colonial areas. The result has been a competitive spirit, with less cooperative action than might be expected from people experiencing common difficulties. It is reflected in the lack of a coherent regional history of the present West. Local histories are attempting to fill the gap; local historical journals are tying the history of subregions together. But a regional history has yet to be written. Ironically, the West is being drawn more into national and world culture and politics than it is to itself, finding unity in commercial services, radio and television programs, syndicated newspapers, chain stores, and the manufactured styles of Hollywood, New York, or Paris.

Inherent in western development, moreover, is this attachment to other regions. The roots of local culture are often shallow; transplanted people yearn for old patterns of life. For those who have lived long enough in the present West there is the undeniable affect of open sky, arid land, and the expanse of desert and mountains upon them, but they adjust slowly. This process of change has taken place since the westward movement began centuries ago. It has constantly provided challenges to pioneers in each area and time period, forcing modification of an older way of life. In John Caughey's estimation, the West remains a challenge, not losing its intensity in our day.

THE AMERICAN WEST: FRONTIER AND REGION

The phrase "American West" is transparent. It calls to mind a select part of the United States, a directional part with a character of its own, which in turn has been important to the nation as a whole.

The United States began as a string of settlements along the Atlantic seaboard. Step by step, the American people and nation advanced across the continent. Throughout it was the lot of the West to be the particular growing point and thus the place where one can see most readily how the United States increased and became what it is. This experience is not altogether peculiar. Other nations have expanded but in few if any has so much of the dynamics of growth been mustered in a movement north, south, east, or west. Here is something distinctively American.

The West has two faces. In one it is the frontier. That is how most people have visualized it: the youngsters playing cowboy and Indian, eminent men from Hitler to Eisenhower reading "westerns," and the rest of us at our television sets. There is more to the pioneer epoch than these contacts suggest, more even than can be extracted from James Fenimore Cooper, Ned Buntline, Owen Wister, and Zane Grey. The frontier is an avenue for adventure and escape, a plunge into the unknown or at least the unfamiliar, leaving behind the comforts and security of home. Viewed more discerningly, it is the drama of the bearers of civilization advancing upon the wilderness.

In its other face the West is a section or, more honorably, a region differing from the rest of the nation in many incidentals and in some essentials. This profile has had much less popular notice and considerably less scholarly attention. The textbook accounts, a reasonably accurate barometer, dwell almost exclusively on the frontier, and several are frankly labelled as "frontier history." A case can be made, however, that the West as region has been as influential as the West as frontier. Western regionalism made early appearance. Since space was not inexhaustible, the frontier eventually would diminish and disappear, whereas the region could persist and become increasingly significant. Nevertheless, the regional face of the West is much less familiar; even many Westerners often seem not to be aware of it.

America quite clearly began as a frontier opened by Columbus and continued by such pioneers as De Soto and Coronado in the Spanish borderlands, Cartier and Champlain on the St. Lawrence, John Smith and company at Jamestown, and the Pilgrims at Plymouth. As settlement developed along the fringe of the Atlantic, a region came into being which had the character of an outpost of Europe. The location, to be sure, was about as far to the eastward as could possibly be in North America; yet it was a Western outpost, or, if you please, an American West. Out of this semantic haze the reality shows through that America began not only as a frontier, but with the regional characteristics that from that time on are properly called Western. At the start America was West, and only later came to have a section with qualities to fit the designation East.

From that time, the West has been on the move. Traders and explorers and missionaries often advanced more rapidly, but by the late seventeenth century the frontier settlement was entering the Piedmont, the upland part of Virginia and her neighbors. A century later it was crossing the Appalachians. As the nineteenth century opened it was filling the Mississippi Valley. Shortly after that it entered Texas and then sent smaller contingents to Oregon and California. As of the 1860's farmers, cattlemen, and miners were carrying it into the Plains and the Rockies, and later it would beckon in Alaska.

The West as region likewise marched across the continent. At one time it was in the Piedmont, then in the Kentucky-Tennessee region, soon along the Mississippi, and later in the farther West.

Perhaps the most striking thing is that every spot in the United States had this sort of beginning. The moving frontier passed over every inch of the land, and every part of the country at the outset had the flavor of the West. Every American, wherever he is, can know that his particular part of the nation began in this way.

Partly because the West was constantly being transplanted from one soil to another, it changed mightily in the process. The march of time also was a powerful modifier. In a society so dynamic as that of the United States, the conditions and the challenge of one era would not be a mere replica of those of another. Thus it was one thing to go over the Wilderness Road with Daniel Boone, quite different a century later to join the rush to the Black Hills. In the 1940's it was not the same to go down the Santa Fé Trail or over the road to Oregon. The West, to take another example, asked one thing of the national government in the 1790's, posed a different problem in the 1840's, something else again in the 1880's, and with the twentieth century continued to amend its definition of the ideal in federal relations. Local peculiarities made the history of the West complex, but not to the extent of obscuring this persistent characteristic of change.

The changes, furthermore, were often exceedingly sharp and for the West as a whole. Much of the periodization of Western history thus is implausibly neat. Until about 1690 the English frontier was in the Caribbean islands and the tidewater belt. Then it began to move into the more remote foothill country. At about the same time a series of inter-imperial wars began, and for the next couple of generations Piedmont settlement had to share the spotlight with the long drawn out contests with the French and the Spaniards.

That epoch in turn was followed by another encompassing roughly the last third of the eighteenth century, the generation of the American Revolution, the first settling west of the Appalachians, and a series of crises concerning American claims and policy in the district as far west as the Mississippi. It took a little longer to clear American title in the heart of the continent, but through the Louisiana Purchase in 1803, the War of 1812, the treaties with Britain in 1815 and 1818, and John Quincy Adams' treaty with Spain in 1819, the United States came into undisputed possession east of the Mississippi and throughout the tremendous area drained by its Western tributaries.

Another three decades witnessed continued spectacular population increase in the Mississippi Valley proper, and along with that vigorous growth a sudden blossoming of the Rocky Mountain fur trade, other trade with Santa Fé, Hawaii, and California, missionary enterprise in Hawaii and Oregon, migration to Texas and the West Coast, and expansionism which by 1848 gave the United States sovereignty all the way to the Pacific.

That era closed as abruptly as it had opened, and was succeeded by another in which the dominant Western types were the prospector and miner, the prairie and plains farmer, the stockman of the open range, the stage driver and wagon freighter, the railroad builder, the Indian fighter, and the architect of state government.

As of about 1890 these types, and the activities they represented, ceased to be the leading factors in Western life. The West continued to feature raw-products output, but now with increasing attention to specialty crops, lumber from the Northwest, and copper and oil. Reclamation gained increasing support. Tourists and health-seekers were solicited, real estate promotion was stepped up, some urban growth was registered, and there were attempts to develop industry. Later, with the impact of the automobile and airplane, the Great

Depression, wartime industrialization, and far-reaching applications of science and technology, the West moved into a still more modern era.

Being in motion in time and space, through discrete time zones and contrasting environments, the West came to have a neatly stratified history. It is a convenient and remarkable feature, but no more noteworthy than the continuities that unite all these Wests, early and late, Atlantic seaboard, midcontinent, and Pacific slope.

There are other characteristics. As the popular interpreters remind, the West has abounded in haphazard violence. To participate successfully or just to survive, its people repeatedly have had to display the outdoor virtues. The West has demanded suffering and endurance — that is how we remember the pioneer women and children. More fundamentally the West has featured action and its theme has been growth and development. Its leaders include soldiers and politicians, but its real heroes are the promoters of colonization such as Stephen F. Austin and Brigham Young, Theodore Judah and his successors who built the Pacific Railroad, George Chaffey and the other pioneers in water and power development, industrialists such as Donald Douglas and Henry J. Kaiser, all those who had a hand in building the Boulder and Grand Coulee dams, A. P. Giannini who created the Bank of America, David Starr Jordan who launched Stanford University, and Oppenheimer and company who constructed the first atomic bombs. Material progress has been the big thing in the West; yet its people have cherished aspirations to culture, some of which have been fulfilled.

Beginning as a raw-products area supplying fish and furs, the West went on to emphasize tobacco and forest products, and at later stages corn and pork, sandalwood, sugar, gold and silver, wheat, beef, oil, gas, uranium, and so on. After generations of striving, the West has a modest industrial plant. The regional output, however, is predominantly extractive, and the West continues to be the kind of colony that the mercantilists before Adam Smith would have hailed as ideal.

The West always has been and probably always will be a minority section. In the seventeenth century when the settlements were strung out along the edge of the Atlantic from Guiana to Labrador, the pioneers then called the colonists were only a handful as compared to the people of the mother countries. When the Piedmont was the West, its occupants were much fewer than those of the Tidewater. By 1850, though there had been rapid progress in occupying the Mississippi Valley, the center of population had not crossed the Appalachians, and by 1950 the Western half of the nation contained less than a quarter of the total population. To be a minority is a very real handicap. Absentee government, absentee ownership, economic colonialism — these are a few of the disadvantages.

The ingredients of Western history may be set down as three: the land, the people, and the institutions. The environmental factor has not always been dominant; but for the frontier period in particular when life was close to the land, it was momentous. On the whole, the West has had a well-favored setting — almost, though not quite, the best that there is on the globe. Yet there have been drawbacks. The pioneers encountered some lands that were pestilential, others that were thorny, swampy, impassably rugged, or arid. The richness of the land often was disguised and not immediately exploitable. Whole stretches seemed to call for revamping, and the frontiersmen started in on this work, girdling trees and clearing the eastern forest land, breaking the prairie sod, and killing off the buffalo. More ambitious remaking of the environment had to wait for higher technologies. Meanwhile, several centuries of Western history ran their course, with the land as a very strong conditioning factor in practically every activity that was carried on.

A land so diversified may be thought of as calling for a population as richly varied. The people of the American West, it must be granted, have been cosmopolitan. Even of the first residents, the Indians, this can be said, because they were of many strains, spoke a great variety of languages, and differed radically in skills, habits, and customs, area by area across the continent. Colonization likewise was cosmopolitan. Over vast stretches Spain, France, or Russia pioneered, and in other important spots the Netherlands or Sweden opened the work. Into English America many non-English were welcomed, Scotch-Irish and Germans in particular, together with Negroes as diverse as the Europeans. In the nineteenth and twentieth centuries, immigrants came in still larger numbers and from almost every land.

The first major demonstration run of the melting pot is attributed to the Piedmont frontier. Other frontiers, agricultural and particularly mineral, held special attraction for immigrants, and although frontier conditions have receded into history, the most recent censuses continue to show the percentage of foreign-born higher in the West than in the East. Of Indians in the United States, a substantial majority live in the West; of Scandinavians the Northwest has most, of Orientals the Far West, of Mexicans the Southwest. Having a multiple-origined population is not an exclusive property of the

West. Therein the region merely shares an important characteristic of the United States as a whole, but in a degree that exceeds the national average.

Alongside this entrance of the foreign-born came a still larger immigration from what used to be called the States, meaning the older and more Eastern part of the United States. At every given moment since at least as far back as the middle of the colonial period, a majority of Westerners were of this derivation. Of all the population facts about the West, this is probably the one of greatest significance.

Receipting for all these recruits, the West was exposed to equally diverse cultural influences. Over the long pull, the ways of the dominant group have the best chance of survival, and this is how it worked out in the American West. Yet every entering group had opportunity to introduce its tested and favorite customs and institutions, some of which found favor. Indian contributions, for instance, are visible as the pioneers on the Atlantic seaboard learned the local techniques of food production, as the hunters who first entered Kentucky and Tennessee dressed like Indians and copied their woodsmanship, and as the Rocky Mountain fur men borrowed even more of Indian ways. In the Pueblo area Spanish colonists incoporated many Indian culture elements and passed them on to their successors.

The American fur trade, as its vocabulary reminds, owed much to the methods that the French had worked out. The American cowboy had greater indebtedness to Spanish experience, and here too the vocabulary was accepted along with the equipment. The Spanish land system, mining law, and water law had partial adoption into the procedures of the American West. The log cabin is credited as a Swedish introduction, and other elements of wide diversity can be traced to other foreign or minority participants.

Throughout most of the West's history the animating social purpose appears to have been to recreate in the new environment the life that was familiar and remembered. For the first colonists this meant trying to achieve a reasonable facsimile of England in America. For most subsequent Westerners it meant trying to reproduce the essentials of the American East. Other Westerners meanwhile were trying to inject something cherished from Germany or Sweden or Italy or the Orient, and on this account the West's aspect and its institutions could never be an exact replica of the East.

The facts of geography and of human circumstances also forced upon Westerners a recognition that their region could not be forced into the exact pattern that served the East. They responded by trying to devise methods and institutions more properly attuned to Western needs. The invention might be merely a new combination of old elements, or it might be just a slight twist given an old device or idea. That was the degree of newness in most Western constitutions. Sometimes, as with the revolver or the reaper, it was a matter of enthusiastic welcome for an Eastern idea. At other times, as with the Fresno scraper, the Stockton gangplow, the Oregon system, or the oil-burning locomotive, Western originality is directly attested.

Out of this effort to develop a pattern of behavior appropriate to the realities, the West came to have distinctiveness. On the successive frontiers the peculiarities were readily apparent; in the region especially of later date, the evidences often were more subtle. Always the distinctiveness was relative, and always it ran counter to the ruling aspiration to integrate more and more with the nation.

It is in this context watchmen and writers, noting the recedence of frontier conditions, have announced the disappearance of the West. In terms of the ideal of Americanness, this has the lineaments of a most patriotic thought. But in so far as conditions and problems persist that are peculiarly or especially Western, a pragmatic argument can be advanced that more, rather than less, regional consciousness should be good for the West and good for the country. The pinch of freight rates and discriminatory pricing, the challenge of water and hydroelectric development, the special relevance of forest, park, and conservation policies, and the remoteness of Washington and Wall Street are just a few of the considerations that suggest the West is still with us, alternatively as a problem or a force.

TOWARD AN UNDERSTANDING OF THE WEST

The West is not shown neatly bounded on any official map, but it is a geographical reality. It begins about halfway across the states that are piled up from Texas to the Dakotas. It extends on through a baker's dozen of states to the coast and Alaska, with one to grow on in Hawaii. Even if Alaska and Hawaii are regarded as thrown in for good measure, this is a big area — half the United States.

Lots of people outside this area think they live in the West. There are all the youngsters everywhere who get into boots and stetsons and strap on their sixshooters. And there is the whole population from Ohio to Iowa who call their region the Midwest. In an antiquarian sense they are right, but of course in accuracy they should reckon that they live in the Middle East.

It is the legitimate West that I propose to deal with — the part of the United States beyond the halfway point on the road to the Pacific — the West of the Plains and Rockies, the Great Basin, and the Pacific Coast.

The outside world began to hear of this land in the sixteenth century with the reports of Coronado and Cabrillo and Drake. Late in the eighteenth century another wave of reporting began, initiated by mariners who sailed to the Pacific Coast. Pike and Lewis and Clark made dramatic penetrations across country, and before long other visitors emerged with glowing reports — Moses Austin from Texas, Josiah Gregg from Santa Fé, Marcus Whitman from Oregon, and Richard Henry Dana from California. To the fever and ague sufferers in Missouri, Antoine Robidoux carried tidings of California's healthgiving climate, while John C. Frémont waxed lyrical over the Eden-like valley of Bear River and the flower-bedecked plains of the San Joaquin.

A trifle later the West had promoters who were even more dedicated. Some, such as James M. Hutchings, the first worshipper of Yosemite, had no visible ulterior motive. Others had railroads in need of customers, towns to boom, or lands to sell. Successive mining strikes gave the West the aura of a great bonanza, and there were bonanzas also in wheat and cattle. The Mormons, meanwhile, found the most ulterior motive of all: they set it up as a religious duty to move west. By 1890, through these channels and others, several million souls had been lured to the Plains and Rockies and beyond, and they were sufficiently distributed that the Director of the Census could announce that the frontier of free land was so much broken into that it had disappeared.

After 1890 the lure of the West became even more seductive and more scientific. Chambers of commerce and convention bureaus solicited tourists and businesses. The automobile put the open spaces within reach. Hollywood glamorized the appeal. During World War II draft boards saw to it that thousands of young men saw the West first. Now this same West has a population of forty or forty-five million.

With this growth in population an increasing number of persons knew something about the West just from living in it. As travel became easier, other millions paid it the honor of a visit. Some of these outsiders came specifically to make written report: this was true of Bayard Taylor in the Gold Rush, of Henry Villard in Colorado a decade later, of Horace Greeley another ten years later, and of many other journalists and sociologists. Fictionists by the score have also spread information about the West. Irving, Bennett, Twain, Helen Hunt Jackson, Hough, Norris, Wister, Vardis Fisher, Steinbeck, Stegner — these and others worked in a great deal of the real West, and there is some of it in Ned Buntline, Zane Grey, and Raymond Chandler.

Historians also have helped to make some things about the West common knowledge. Topics such as the Lewis and Clark expedition and the building of the Pacific Railroad are recognized as part of United States history and have been so treated; other episodes such as the Mormon exodus to Utah, the Santa Fé Trail, and the San Francisco fire have been so ably presented in state history that they are well known.

The most characteristic historical study of the West has been narrowed down to relatively small particulars. Thanks to Herbert Eugene Bolton we can follow Anza's marches from campsite to campsite. Thanks to Dale Morgan we can go with Jedediah Smith almost step by step on his travels. LeRoy Hafen has done as much for the Old Spanish Trail. For many a town we can be told who opened the first store; who built the first house, and just where.

At the other end of the scale the West has tempted free-hand generalizers to offer interpretations or single themes upon which the whole history of the West could be strung. Hubert Howe Bancroft, for instance, though having to work with a foreshortened view because he was writing in the seventies and eighties, saw what had happened in the West as the last and most glorious chapter in the transit of civilization from Greece to Rome to western Europe, to the Atlantic seaboard, and at last to the edge of the Pacific. The Frederick Jackson Turner thesis on the significance of the frontier, though based almost entirely on studies of the Piedmont and trans-Appalachian frontiers, was extended by Turner and more especially by his disciples as the masterkey for comprehension of the farther West.

In 1931, with special reference to the Plains segment of the West, Walter Prescott Webb argued what amounted to a doctrine of geographical determinism. This new region, he held, was such a contrast to the land between the Atlantic and the ninety-eighth meridian that it blocked settlement for a generation and then forced radical change in institutions. This thesis was sharply contested by certain scholars, and James C. Malin offered a constructive amendment by applying the concept of possibilism, extending his view to the West at large. Henry Nash Smith, meanwhile, pointed out that Americans had habitually looked at the West through the rose-colored spectacles of great expectations. A footnote might add that a fair number of these myths and dreams came true.

In 1957 Webb extended his view to the West at large, seized upon aridity as the supreme fact west of 98° and, again with strong tinge of geographical determinism, concluded that the history of the region has comparable dryness and emptiness.

Before exploring theory, however, we might do better to explore the West and its history.

To begin with, it had better be stressed that this is a land where the environment has to be taken into account. It may be lavish in resources, but unlike a South Sea island with its coconuts and breadfruit, it does not automatically nourish. The mark of the land is strong on its history, and the facts of geography are these:

First, it is a big country, a land of distances, of remoteness. The problem of transportation has always been uppermost for those who wanted to use or develop the West.

Second, it is a rugged land, a land of sharp uplifts, canyons, and gorges, a region complex in topography and with a great deal of exposed geology. The multiplicity of landforms — the alternation of plains, mountains, basins, mesas, valleys — complicates the transportation problem.

It also sets up a broad diversity of climates. The isothermal lines climb the mountains more rapidly than they do the degrees of latitude. Zones of climate ranging from subtropical to arctic may be only a few miles apart, and the precipitation on one side of a mountain range often is much greater than on the other side.

The West is a land of extremes. It has the highest and the lowest points in the United States. From the scorched depths of Death Valley one used to be able to look up more than 15,000 feet to the highest point in the United States. This is no longer allowed, but one can stand there and imagine Mount McKinley towering another 5,000 feet above Mount Whitney. Day after day the West reports the highest and lowest temperatures. It has the highest and the lowest annual rainfalls. This diversity is also shown within many of its parts: in Alaska or Idaho or California, for example. Parts of the West fall all along the scale from hyperhumid to arid. The parts where it rains all the time and the parts where it never rains sort of balance each other off, and sometimes have been made to do precisely that. This is part of the secret of the existence of Los Angeles. At the downtown weather station the average annual rainfall is only fifteen inches, but within a forty-mile radius of the city hall there are locations where the average reaches forty inches. For the greater part of the West the classification that fits is subhumid or semiarid. And that of course spells a contrast to the humid East.

To the eye of a stranger the West often looks utterly desolate. Parts of it are bleak; yet on closer inspection the West repeatedly has proved ever so much richer than the first inventory showed. It has or had great deposits of gold, silver, copper, sulphur, petroleum, and uranium. It offers nine-tenths of the nation's hydroelectric potential and now has the nation's best stand of timber. In variety of crops it surpasses the East. Two of its states consistently lead the other forty-seven in total value of agricultural output, though the East as a section continues to have a substantial over-all lead.

There was a time, nevertheless, when the West carried as large a population as the East. This was in the days when people lived closer to the land and were more directly dependent on the local resources. That was before the coming of the white man, when the peak density of Indian population was in the upper Rio Grande Valley, along the northwest coast, and in California. Other factors such as the unwarlike character of some of the tribes were partly responsible, but the population count is also a testimonial to the resources of the western half of the continent.

The West of our day also represents very clearly the interaction of man and society upon the land. The contemporary West, in other words, is also the product of its history. That history is long and varied. It is characterized by drastic changes, period by period, and within it there are local peculiarities both of omission and commission. On closer scrutiny, however, an unmistakable regional unity shows through.

Throughout the West history begins with an Indian prologue (for Alaska and Hawaii add Eskimo and Polynesian). For lack of conventional records we lump this whole fifteen- or twenty-thousand-year period as prehistoric, but from the anthropologists we have learned a great deal about the patterns of living that evolved. We also have some awareness of the carry-over of influence on later developments.

Then followed what is often dismissed as a second prologue — the opening of the West by agents of European imperialism. Throughout most of the West, it was these agents who were first on the scene: Spaniards working north from Mexico as far as Nebraska and Nootka, the French from Canada advancing west and southwest all the way to the Rockies, Drake to a Nova Albion (New England) in California, other Britishers leading the way to Hawaii and the Pacific Northwest, and Russians in the Aleutian Islands and southward.

Clearly these activities of the sixteenth, seventeenth, and eighteenth centuries were not prehistoric; many of them have been recorded much more meticulously than has the later American pioneering. These Europeans gave the American West an early start. Two of its states were named before any of the "original thirteen" and one, New Mexico, was colonized before Jamestown. These Europeans came to take possession and to settle as well as to explore. Especially in the belt from Louisiana and Missouri through Texas, New Mexico, Arizona, and California, they implanted customs and institutions that greatly influenced what followed. Through Mexico in the Greater Southwest, the Hudson's Bay Company and Russian-American Company in the Northwest, and the Hawaiian monarchy in its realm, these regimes that we call "foreign" had continuing importance in the nineteenth century.

With the nineteenth century, the people of the United States took over as the dynamic force. Ships from Boston had already touched along the Northwest Coast, and Lewis and Clark, Pike, Long, James, and Frémont entered from the east as official explorers. The fur men searched out every possible beaver stream. Traders opened shop in Santa Fé, Hawaii, and California, missionaries went to Hawaii and Oregon, and later a sprinkling of settlers moved into Oregon, California, and Utah. By 1848, with the military and the diplomats functioning in the final moves, the United States fulfilled its Manifest Destiny by taking possession all the way to the Pacific.

Even when these events are brought between the covers of a single book, there is a tendency to fragment this history by isolating the Oregon missions, or to treat the Santa Fé Trail as though it had no relation to the fur trade. On the other hand, a book on the fur trade necessarily ranges most of the West, and a biography of Kit Carson or John Marsh or James K. Polk has to have a wide spread.

As of about 1848, the West passed over a historical divide. The fur trade, the Santa Fé trade, the hide trade, the Oregon missions, and Manifest Destiny became closed chapters. Jim Marshall's gold discovery in the Sierra foothills ushered in a new era which would be characterized by the prospector for gold and silver, the cattleman of the open range, the farmer more gradually advancing the agricultural frontier, the stage driver and wagon freighter, their superior the railroad builder, the regular and volunteer Indian fighters, and the architects of state government. Here is an epoch readily distinguishable from the early nineteenth century, but again these are historical elements that are widely distributed over the West.

Once again western history hangs together as well as it did in the days of the mountain men and Manifest Destiny. Cattle raising on the open range flourished in California before it did in Texas and spread not only over the Plains but into the grasslands of the Rockies, Great Basin, and Northwestern Plateau. Rölvaag and Cather found prairie farmers in the Dakotas and Nebraska; Vardis Fisher found their counterparts in Idaho, Frank Norris in California, and Dorothy Scarborough in Texas. So it went with other components of the real West of the late nineteenth century.

And once again an epoch came to an abrupt end and gave way to a new one. The Director of the Census may have exaggerated the disappearance of the frontier, but as of 1890, give or take a few years, the era of the gold and silver rushes, the open range, the stage lines, the Indian wars, and the railroad builders did come to a close.

In the generation after 1890 the cattle industry stabilized with improved stock and closed range. Wool and wheat growing also solidified, but a more spectacular change was in agricultural specialty lines such as orange and apple growing in the Southwest and the Northwest. Lumbering scored heavy gains. The West experienced a health rush and the tourist business boomed. These are elements in the picture, but a simpler description for the period from 1890 to the 1920's is to say that the West lived by the railroad.

The East in these years piled up many ton-miles and passenger-miles on its railroads, but continued to have coastal shipping, lake steamers, and river barges as active competitors. There were ships plying the west coast, but everywhere else in the West the railroad was the one carrier. It determined where people should live and what they might produce for market. The railroad was the prime giver of value to land. It brought the tourists and the new settlers. A generation ago, to give one example, we all would have come to this Salt Lake City convention by rail.

The railroad clearly enriched the West of this generation, but it exacted a price. Many a westerner felt that he lived by the railroad, as a puppet of the railroad, and for the railroad. In a few eastern states an occasional politician might give major attention to railroad regulation as La Follette did in Wisconsin. In almost every western state or territory at the turn of the century it loomed up as the prime issue.

The West of later date has no single feature that so dominates the scene. Ours is the automobile age and also the air age, but not to the exclusion of the railroads and the pipelines. It also is the age of the engineer, with display performances in San Francisco's bay bridges, the causeway now building across Salt Lake, the elaborate highway systems, and the tremendous dams such as Boulder, Shasta, Bonneville, and Grand Coulee. The crop list bears close resemblance to that of a few decades ago, but agriculture is increasingly mechanized and scientific. And as the place names Geneva, Fontana, Hollywood, Hanford, and Los Alamos may suggest, the West at last has something to show in industrial capacity.

In resumé, its sharply stratified character may be the most spectacular feature of the history of the West: the Indian period, followed by an epoch of European contact and limited occupation; then the early nineteenth century invasion by American explorers, traders, missionaries, and empire builders; another era dominated by miners, farmers, cattlemen, Indian fighters, and railroad builders; then a generation dedicated to making the most of the railroad, but with attention also to the tourist, the health seeker, real estate speculation, and developing the eastern markets; and next our own more sophisticated generation, with a more far-reaching application of science to the problems of production, processing, and transportation.

The history of the West has other characteristics. It is full of adventure, of the haphazard violence so dear to the creators of "westerns." It includes many instances of suffering and endurance — that is how we remember the women and children of the covered-wagon migrations. It has its sordid and lamentable parts — the Chinese massacres at Los Angeles, Tacoma, and Rock Springs; the harsh treatment of the Wobblies and the migratory farm laborers; the wartime concerntration of the Japanese-Americans; and the misuse of the land that produced the Dust Bowl. Our history is full of accidents, some of which were happy — among them the opening of the market for furs in China, most of the gold discoveries, and the introduction of the navel orange and Russian wheat.

For the eastern half of the nation, especially through the early stages, much of the history is written properly in terms of state and local development and state and local politics. That was how it was throughout the colonial period and the tendency persisted. In early nineteenth-century New York, for instance, the government that mattered most was certainly that of the state. Who built the Erie Canal? And in the South to 1860 the addiction to states' rights was not just an argument for use in Washington, but was in line with the habit of looking more to state legislatures and executives than to those of the nation.

In contrast, westerners from the beginning have been acutely conscious of the federal government. The White Father in Washington has not always remembered them, but they have known that their regional interest as often as not would rise or fall by virtue of federal action or inaction. Parts of the West only now are reaching the point where state government has more prestige, and a shift from the United States Senate to a governorship is thought of as a step up.

Americans in the West before 1848 looked to the federal government to extend United States sovereignty to the Pacific. The West from 1850 to 1890 counted on Uncle Sam to underwrite transportation improvements, to quiet the Indians, to clarify land titles, and to admit to statehood. The federal government was beseeched to purchase silver or in other ways inflate the currency as a means of relieving western debtors. It was asked to bar oriental immigration, to regulate the railroads, to proceed with reclamation projects, to give federal aid for highway construction, to move more rapidly in flood control, to eliminate the freight-rate differential against the West, and to give western industry a fair chance.

The stages in federal relations reflect the evolution of the West. All told it is a more persistent thread and a bigger one in our regional history than in that of the East.

The West quite patently is a region that has depended heavily on imports. Throughout recorded time its most valuable import has been people: Spanish soldiers and settlers, French-Canadian voyageurs, Indians pushed out of the American East, pioneer settlers from the older states, Chinese and Japanese, other immigrants fresh from Europe, later comers from Canada and Mexico, and millions more from all the more easterly sections of the country.

All these people brought with them as much as they could of their institutions and culture. In this way and in others the history of the West is rooted outside its borders and particularly in the older part of the United States. Thus the West claims a share in the colonial heritage and sees the Founding Fathers, the Bill of Rights, Jefferson and Marshall, the Fourteenth Amendment, and many other elements of the nation's history as components without which the history of the region would be incomplete.

From the beginning, Americans who came west have been consumed with the desire to make their new home a reasonable facsimile of the old one in the East. Some of the effects have been pathetic: only after repeated failures were the pioneers willing to concede that eastern methods of farming just would not work in western Dakota or eastern New Mexico or even in southern California. Some of the consequences are ridiculous. I cite but one: by enslaving ourselves to it, my wife and I manage to have a quarter-acre of green lawn where Nature strongly prefers chaparral and salvia. Some imported institutions are as obviously misfits.

To such an extent have we Americanized or "easternized" the West that most people from the East soon are able to feel at home. Belatedly we have shown a little more wisdom about adjusting our ways to fit the peculiarities of the environment.

The West has been chided for various deficiencies, among them an alleged lack of wars and warfare. As a matter of fact, soldiers were the chief participants in many early western activities. Wars or threats of wars contributed to the Louisiana Purchase, the annexation of Texas, the Oregon Treaty, the Mexican Cession, and the annexation of Hawaii. The American military were deployed in far-flung exercises in the Mexican, Mormon, and Civil wars, and from 1865 to 1890 the chief occupation of the United States Army was in the Indian wars in the West.

As it happened, many a military operation in the West ended up as an exhibition of "brinksmanship." Again and again westerners worked themselves up to a warlike pitch but stopped at the brink, or just over the brink. For example, in 1846 General Armijo in New Mexico prudently decided not to resist the entrance of General Kearny's Army of the West. That same year at San Pascual the southern California rebels showed their mettle, but as soon as they could they found a friendly general to whom they could capitulate with honor. Meanwhile, at Santa Clara the principal northern California battle was fought. Chronicler Pickett reports heavy cannonading that did "considerable damage" — to the wild mustard stalks. He also reports two men wounded, but later in the same letter enters this correction:

> I am just informed that the wounded men on our side were not touched by the enemy, as they at first supposed and so reported, but hurt them-

selves in the oak bushes. And it is even doubted whether the Californians recd. any injury. The fight lasted several hours. And the treaty which was made half way between the Mission and the oaks, in sight of the two armies, lasted nearly one whole day.[1]

In the Mormon War the Saints found that it was more effective to concentrate on burning Johnston's supply trains rather than on pitching into his troops. The Confederates who invaded the Mesilla Valley and Arizona countermarched rapidly enough to evade the California column, and at Glorieta in New Mexico, when Union and Rebel forces came face to face, Colonel Chivington executed a brilliant flanking movement and butchered six hundred mules. Such was the decisive action that turned Sibley's army back. The Indian wars of the next quarter century were much bloodier, even though the Indian habit insofar as it was possible was to avoid battle whenever it promised to be too costly. By 1890 those wars had run their course.

From the Spanish-American War through the first two World Wars and the Korean War, the West has been as much involved as any other part of the country and presumably would be also in a third World War. As in Civil War days the situation of westerners has been that they had to go away to do their fighting, which is awkward but certainly the lesser evil.

Alas, the West owes much to war. The Civil War made a number of San Franciscans rich, chiefly because they could buy in the East for currency and sell in the West for gold. The Civil War made possible the passage of the Pacific Railroad Bill. The two big booms in west coast shipbuilding were strictly wartime. That also is how the West got the bulk of its steel industry and most of its airplane, missile, and electronics industries. The uranium rush was triggered by defense demands, and so it has gone with many other features of the western economy.

All this may sound as if the West would have an impressive indebtedness to Mars, but on balance these war-generated profits probably were considerably below the national average. In steadily mounting federal taxes, most of which are for wars already fought or for wars that may come, the West has paid out considerably more than its grand total of war profits, and since 1898 it has suffered its share of the casualties. Perhaps it could be argued that the West has received whatever values a military past has to offer. No sane westerner would long for a greater military involvement for his region in the past or in the future.

The history of the American West, nevertheless, is not most effectively told in terms of officers and soldiers. Nor is it most effectively told in terms of politicians, although some of its elected representatives have been of utmost importance. I think, for instance, of Hiram Johnson of the Lincoln-Roosevelt League of political reformers in California and of George Norris, whose major monument, TVA, is not in the West but symbolizes a method of transcendent value to the region.

Our emphasis more characteristically goes to men such as Stephen F. Austin, who shepherded the early migration to Texas; Brigham Young, who directed the settlement and the early economic development of Utah; Theodore Judah and his successors, who built the Pacific Railroad; George Chaffey and his genius in water and power development; banker William Ralston, who built San Francisco, and A. P. Giannini, who created the Bank of Italy; to an industrialist like Henry J. Kaiser or Donald Douglas; to David Starr Jordan for the creation of Stanford University; to all those who planned and built Grand Coulee Dam; and to Oppenheimer and company for what they produced at Los Alamos.

The booster spirit has taught us to revere whatever can be registered on a rising graph or chart. At rare intervals we entertain doubts whether more people, more production, more loans, more sales on credit are really good for the country. Yet it is hard to see how anyone can take stock of the American West since 1848 and not see growth and development as the dominant characteristic. More than for New England, more than for the South, that has been the case, and if historians have so interpreted they are hardly to be criticized.

Sometimes the emphasis on colossal material growth is so great that it is assumed that the West has no culture. On every frontier the first necessity has been to solve the problem of making a living, and refinements could only be achieved a bit later. The homesteader's shack or the sheepherder's camp was not the most likely spot for artistic or intellectual flowering, nor was the mining camp, the track-layer's camp, the logging camp, or the army post.

Yet the West does have a cultural history, some of it on the level of simplicity as in Mormon hymns and cowboy ballads, some of it reflecting a striving for improvement as in the early school systems and the initiation of the Hollywood Bowl concerts, some of it more ambitious as in the performances at Red Rock and the conferences at Aspen, some of it unmistakably topnotch as in the attainments of our physical scientists.

In things cultural we continue to take inspiration from the East —

which may be why we show such enthusiasm for the San Francisco Forty-Niners and Giants and the Los Angeles Rams and Bums, and why in higher education we try to achieve an Amherst or Oberlin of the West, a western Columbia or Chicago. Perhaps we do not altogether measure up to the attainments of the schools in the Ivy League and the Big Ten, but much of the gap that once separated us has been closed, and the West is working vigorously to continue its improvement.

Throughout, the western economy has been mainly extractive. The role of the West has been to supply raw products which, with a minimum of processing, were sent off to market. First it was furs, then sandalwood from Hawaii and cowhides from California. Later it was gold and silver; wheat and beef; salmon from the west coast and Alaska; sugar from Hawaii, Utah, and Colorado; lumber; wool; wine; fruits and vegetables; oil and gas.

Many pioneer communities dabbled in manufacturing, essentially on a subsistence basis — wagon-making for local use; bricks or bread or harness — again for the locality. With cigar-making and printing and engraving, San Francisco became something of an emporium for the region. But manufacturing for export from the region is a phenomenon of no more than the present and the immediate past. The commodity list proves the recency: moving pictures, airplanes, oil machinery, Indian curios, sports attire, plywood, plastics, electronics. Important though this industry is, the basic output of the region still is in raw products. It is, in other words, still the kind of colony that mercantilists before Adam Smith would have commended as ideal.

Not only has the economy of the West been persistently colonial, the plain truth is that the West is also a minority section. It always has been and it probably always will be. As such it naturally and inevitably has been discriminated against.

Political discrimination is easy to document. For a time the West may have had more "sons of the wild jackass" in the Senate than its population rated, but reapportionment of the House never has kept pace with the shift of population westward. The West was underrepresented when it consisted of the western townships of Massachusetts and later when it was in the western counties of Virginia. The later instances are as glaring; Congress, for example, sat out the whole decade of the twenties without reapportioning. Except for Nevada, which was rushed into the electoral college, and Texas, which was in position to strike a good bargain, every part of the West has had reason to complain about unreasonable delay in admission to statehood. Utah had earned admission long before 1896. Hawaii is the current example; even with Alaska as an icebreaker her ship of state may not make port.[2]

Economic discrimination has been and is more crippling. Much of it is applied without malice. There was a Wall Street before the American West as we know it took shape; eastern financial dominance grew of its own accord, and the subordinate position of the West in money matters thus came about in a way that seemed natural and inevitable. The industrial headstart of the New England-Middle Atlantic-Great Lakes axis likewise set the stage for the absentee ownership and out-of-area management of so much of western industry. A similar explanation holds for the concentration in the Northeast of ninety per cent or more of the wholesale drug business and the underwriting of insurance.

In part, however, the discrimination against the West has been more overt. It is written into our tariff law. It has been put into our code on patents and particularly on the licensing of patents. It appears in pricing systems, such as "slightly higher west of the Rockies," "F.O.B., Detroit," and "Pittsburgh plus." By these devices a transportation charge often fictitious was and is collected from customers in the West.

Even more damagingly the discrimination is embedded in the freight schedules. These schedules are unbelievably complex. It would take a whole battery of electronic brains to calculate how much the West has been gouged, but the evidence is overwhelming that there is a differential. Take any manufactured item — sugar, automobiles, shoe-leather, or television sets. Spot a factory or a distributor in the Northeast and another in the West. Then spot a customer equidistant from these two suppliers. The freight rate from the West almost invariably will turn out to be appreciably higher than the rate from the East. This is not the whole story of discriminatory freight rates, but it will illustrate.

Curiously, westerners have shown relatively little awareness that they are cast in this subordinate role. In part, no doubt, the colonialism is not felt because it is concealed. A great deal of it comes in the form of indirect taxes and hidden charges. Western climate and scenery doubtless distract from the hard realities. And many a westerner is blissfully unaware that it is costing him politically and financially to live in the West.

Another good reason is that comparatively few westerners have much realization that the West is a region. The main lines of communication drain eastward instead of focussing on a regional metropolis. Several of the cities that mean most to the West are not in it: New York and Washington, but also Minneapolis, Omaha, St. Louis, New Orleans, and Chicago. The West has never been organized as a political unit, much less as an independent confederacy. It has no flag, no shibboleth such as states' rights, no feeling of cultural and intellectual mission like that of New England. It has never gone to war on its own account, much less had a great defeat to cherish as a lost cause.

When the history of our nation is being told, the western half of the continent gets very little space. In school histories Webb found that the average allotment was no more than six or seven pages in a hundred. He might have added that in standard college texts the percentage is even smaller. The West crops up in a chapter on Manifest Destiny and another on growth and problems, 1865-90, and 5 per cent of the total wordage is about the maximum. In Turner's writings the fraction devoted to the area west of 98° is even less. The general works on the American frontier give the area more space: Paxson 42 per cent, Branch 29 per cent, Riegel 46 per cent, Clark 36 per cent, Billington 42 per cent. The striking thing is that all these writers seem to have felt that most of America's frontier history — most of its western history — took place short of the Mississippi in what is now the far-eastern and middle-eastern half of the country.

At the level of state and local history, however, the West has been very well served. The Pacific Northwest, for instance, in the works by Bancroft, Shafer, Fuller, Winther, Johansen, and Gates has a shelf of general surveys that compares favorably with those on the Old Northwest. With its long roster of distinguished historians from Castañeda and Villagrá to Gregg and Garrard to Fergusson and Hammond, New Mexico can compete with any eastern state. And on Utah contributions in the last few years by Mortensen, Mulder, Brooks, West, O'Dea, Morgan, and Arrington are something of which any state would be proud.

Some corners of the West have less to show, but there is good news from Arizona, which is going to launch a new historical quarterly, from Idaho, which has just done so, and from Alaska, which is going to reward its best historian with a seat in the United States Senate.

But a history of the West as a region — a history geared toward explaining the West that is ours today — has not been achieved or even attempted. And the outline for such a history, the general contour of what it would include, seems to have eluded the grasp even of eminent historians who have dealt with the West.

Friends and foes agree that the West does differ from the eastern half of the United States. It is distinctive or possibly bizarre, and this quality arises partly from the geography and partly from its history. The West offers a challenge which is a composite of problems and opportunities more or less peculiar to it.

For any such western problem our standard practice is to do one of two things: either we try to get the nation, perhaps through the federal government, to work out a solution, or in our particular subregion we try to get one state, perhaps through the state government, to tackle the problem. These are natural impulses. But the nation has other worries; the power center of that government is far away, and three-fourths of its citizens and voters are not of the West and cannot be expected to have full understanding or full sense of crises in its problems. The state to which we turn is western, but often is too small or too synthetic to be competent for the task. The authorities who subdivided this land are partly to blame. They did their work mostly at the drawing board by putting straight lines on the map, and all too often the units they produced were artificial. We love these states and we will keep them, but that does not mean that they fill the bill in serving the region.

For the West challenges on a broader front. To make the most of the water that is available, to attain peak efficiency in hydroelectric power development and distribution, to achieve a viable reclamation program, to eliminate the discriminatory freight rates, to give western industry an even chance, and so on down the line, the regional approach has far more to recommend it than the alternatives of state or nation on which we have been depending.

In the light of the hardcore sectionalism that has flourished in one or two other parts of the United States, an appeal for that kind of westernism would seem unpatriotic. Regionalism, however, need not be antisocial; in fact, rightly channeled it can inure to the benefit of the nation as well as the region. To achieve it we need to rise above provincialism, cultivate an awareness of the essential unity of the West, and strive for at least a measure of solidarity.

Many a western pioneer operated notebook in hand because he was acutely aware that he was making history. Many later westerners have seen the light and realizing that there is such a thing as western history have devoted themselves unstintingly to its study — usually, it is true, on topics that take in considerably less than the whole West. The time is at least ripe for a discovery of the regional history. Such a discovery would be of the greatest possible assistance toward achieving throughout the West a sense of regional unity. Indeed, it may be a prerequisite.

Some things about such a history can be forecast. The whole is sure to be greater than the sum of its parts, the history of the West as a region something more and more significant than the totalling of the state histories. Also it should be simpler. In the history of the region, many of the purely local peccadillos would fall away and some of the nonentities who have to be noticed in lesser works would be eclipsed. Other matters would fall into perspective; the relationship to the nation should become much more apparent; and the over-all importance ought to stand out more clearly. Such is the intriguing prospect that lies beyond frontier history of the conventional sort and western state and local history as it has been practiced.

THE SPANISH SOUTHWEST AN EXAMPLE OF SUBCONSCIOUS REGIONALISM

There are regions in the United States — New England, the South, and the Great Plains, for example — which have fixed and obvious boundaries and therefore exactness of meaning. But the term Southwest, with or without the adjective Spanish, is by contrast a variable which has meant almost all things to all men. Prudence therefore suggests that anyone proposing to talk about this region should begin by searching for a definition.

The political approach is not of much help, since there is no Southwestern unit intermediate between the states and the nation, nor has there been such a unit since the brief appearance of the Comandancia General de las Provincias Internas of the seventeen-seventies and eighties. And, although there is a Southwest to and for which Nature does certain things differently than for other parts of the United States, its geographical boundaries are blurred rather than sharp and ordinary maps do not make it clear.

Another possible approach is through appeal to authority. In recent years the term Southwest has been bandied about by a multitude of persons who should know. Charles F. Lummis, Lansing

Bloom, Erna Fergusson, and company have given vigorous endorsement to the principle that the Southwest is New Mexico-centered. The Texas State Historical Association issues a journal called the *Southwestern Historical Quarterly,* but is content to have it pure Texas. J. Frank Dobie, in his course and syllabus on the life and letters of the Southwest, starts with Texas, but is willing to expand as far as the trail herds went. In the "Southwestern Historical Series," Ralph P. Bieber, LeRoy Hafen, and Arthur H. Clark took a stance in Missouri and looked south and west, chiefly down the Santa Fé Trail into New Mexico, but incidentally at Colorado, Arkansas, Texas, northern Mexico, and California. The editors of *Look,* in their series of picture books on American regions, marked off a Southwest beginning in Texas and stopping in Arizona. The Rockefeller Foundation, the host "once removed" of this conference, has compromised on a dual answer to the question. It has chartered a research program at the Huntington Library on a transmontane, trans-Rocky Southwest, and another at the University of Oklahoma on a Southwest bounded by the thirty-seventh parallel and the Gulf, the Mississippi and the Continental Divide.

By implication, at least, W. P. Webb in *Divided We Stand* and E. G. Mezerik in *The Revolt of the South and the West* point to a much larger Southwest. They discuss a common plight and a unity of interest for the historic South and the western half of the nation. They come, therefore, virtually to the conclusion that the Southwest is that part of the United States — about three-fourths — which is not the favored Northeast.

Still another approach, to which I as a historian turn by instinct, is to look for definition by history.

The first fact encountered is that the southern half of the United States, along with much more land south of the border, came into history through the visits of early sixteenth-century explorers, men such as Ponce de León, Ayllón, De Vaca, De Soto, Coronado, and Cabrillo. Likewise, it was the Spaniards, a century or two later, who first occupied much of this territory.

In the late eighteenth century, when the United States emerged as a nation, these lightly garrisoned Spanish provinces were its neighbors both on the south and on the west. Furthermore, thanks to the reforms of the enlightened Charles III, these were provinces of a revitalized Spanish Empire, an empire less fabulous than it had been a quarter-millennium earlier in the golden age of the conquistadores, but now reaching its greatest territorial extent. In 1789, in fact, when Washington was inaugurated President, the United States was confronted by the reality of a Spanish Southwest that began at the Georgia-Florida frontier, swept through the Creek Indian country to the Tennessee, thence to the Ohio and the Mississippi, and wound up north of Nootka on the Pacific. Spanish title and control thus spread over most of what we now call the South and over the entire trans-Mississippi West, an area that closely approximates the Webb-Mezerik South and West.

As soon as there was a United States and even before, the Americans and their governments betrayed an irresistible impulse to encroach upon these sparsely settled borderlands. Emboldened by the distresses of Europe and heartened by the vigor of American growth, diplomats challenged Spanish rights in the Old Southwest and, in the Treaty of San Lorenzo in 1795, picked up clear title as far as the thirty-first parallel and the Mississippi. In its pattern of Spanish retreat and American advance, this treaty set a motif that was to be repeated with variations all across the continent — in West and East Florida; in Louisiana, where Napoleon arranged a brief interregnum; in Oregon, contested also by Russia and Britain; in Texas, the Mexican Cession, and the Gadsden Purchase.

The expansion into the territory of Spain (and her legatee, Mexico) was relentless and rapid. Mid-nineteenth century saw it accomplished, the final steps taken in the brash certitude of Manifest Destiny. The territorial enlargement of the United States, mostly by taking over lands that once were Spanish, is a fact of great significance. The corollary may be even more important: that for the United States there has always been a Spanish Southwest.

Throughout the vast area once held or claimed by Spain, more or less of a Spanish heritage is discernible today. It may be in place names, in vocabulary, in the choice of sites for settlements, in law or customs, in agricultural methods, or in actual population. Over much of the area the reminders of Spain have worn thin. They are most in evidence in the states adjacent to the Mexican boundary from Texas to California.

Out of this apparent jumble of geographic, political, didactic, and historical fact, a Southwest emerges, which, as I see it, stretches from central Oklahoma and Texas to southern California. Much of Colorado, Utah, Nevada, and northern California belong, so that it embraces the lower left-hand quarter of the parallelogram that is the United States. Geometrically, at least, this is an incontrovertible Southwest. In other respects as well it constitutes a genuine region.

A number of the traits most characteristic of it penetrate farther afield; many, for example, are shared with the states and territories of northern Mexico. But there remain other traits, some of them Spanish in derivation, which are the core of Southwestern regionalism.

As a setting for analysis of these regional characteristics, a rapid review of Southwestern history seems in order.

In the beginning, of course, throughout the hemisphere were the Indians, their civilization wonderfully diverse, remarkably provincial. Ethnology, however, discerns a regionalization in culture areas, each characterized by pervading similarities and by contrasts to the traits and patterns of other areas. Of the dozen or fifteen such areas in pre-Columbian America, two account for most of the territory here labeled Southwest: the California-Great Basin area reaching from central and northern California to the Great Salt Lake, and the Pueblo-Southwestern, its center with the Pueblo Indians, but raying out to Utah, Colorado, Texas, Chihuahua and Sonora, Baja and southern California. The pre-Columbian civilization of this southwestern quarter of the present United States thus was distinguishable from that to the north and the east. In the Pueblo center, it had the highest population density of the entire United States. Presumably if Indian culture was to exert any influence on post-Columbian America, some carry-over of its regionalism would be entailed.

The first intrusion of Europeans into this region came three-quarters of a century before Jamestown and a century and a quarter before the earliest entry in the history of Wisconsin. Álvar Núñez Cabeza de Vaca showed the way. Cast ashore on the Texas coast after a thwarted attempt at settlement in Florida, he was servant, almost slave, to the Indians, rose to be a trader and a medicine man, and finally traipsed across the continent and got back to civilization (in the form of a band of Indian-hunting Spaniards) on the west coast of Mexico. His tales of the north led to a probing by Friar Marcos and Estevanico and to more extensive *entradas* by Cabrillo, Alarcón, and Coronado, while De Soto and Moscoso, working out of Florida, advanced to the eastern margin of the area. With these first recording agents, the history of the Southwest begins. The reports taken back to Mexico, however, could not compete with the actual riches of the Aztec and Inca lands, and consequently occupation was deferred until considerably later.

When Spanish occupation did occur — after 1598 in New Mexico, 1687 in Pimería Alta, 1697 in Baja California, 1718 in Texas, and 1769 in Alta California — the age of the conquistadores had given place to empire-building of quite a different sort. Imperial authority had made itself paramount. Advance into a new province was determined, not by a rugged-individualist, gold-hungry *adelantado,* but by a calculating government. This later advance, in every instance, was more for the sake of erecting defenses for Mexico and the Caribbean than because of the intrinsic attractions of the new lands. The settlements began as frontier garrisons; they were staffed by government employees, particularly soldiers and missionaries. The most fundamental procedure was the effort to Christianize and civilize the Indians into useful citizens of the Spanish Empire, but beyond that, imperial policy did not call for building up much more than a token occupation of these northern borderlands.

At their maturity they had approximately these contours: in religion, orthodox Roman Catholic, though with some admixture of Indian belief and practice; in government, loyal to and dependent upon the orders and appointees of the king; in economy, practicing simple Spanish agriculture supplemented by whatever could be carried over from Indian methods; and in society, achieving a blend of Spanish and Indian customs. Nowhere in the course of the American westward movement did there develop settlements so unified in religion, so subordinate to imperial or national authority, or so committed to the principle of the preservation and incorporation of the Indians.

Except for the brief experiment of the Comandancia, these colonies were individually run by military, civil, and religious officers directed by the viceroy at Mexico City. Up to the end of the Spanish epoch (in 1821) they were only incidentally brushed by foreign contacts — a St. Denis (French, 1715) in Texas, the Mallet brothers (French, 1739) in New Mexico, a horse-trading Philip Nolan (1785) in Texas, an otter-hunting William Shaler (1804) in California, a courtly Rezanov (Russian, 1805) in California, and an inquisitive Zebulon Montgomery Pike (1806) in New Mexico. By the end of the Spanish epoch there were third-generation Spaniards in California, fourth- and fifth-generation Spaniards in Texas, and ninth- or tenth-generation Spaniards in New Mexico.

The onset of the Mexican period cut off effective control from the old viceregal capital, but of course a strong momentum of Spanish custom carried on. The abandonment of the old restrictive system and the breakdown of the supply lines from Mexico opened doors to foreign trade. Russians and English had some success in California, but it was chiefly American enterprisers who seized the opportunity:

Boston droghers in California, and Missouri merchants on the trail to Santa Fé. Commercial annexation of California and New Mexico to the United States was achieved by these men. They were soon joined by the leather-shirted mountain men who poured across the unmarked boundary in quest of beaver pelts, and by thousands of pioneer settlers moving into Texas and a much smaller number venturing all the way to California.

In 1836 the Texas Americans raised a lone-star flag and defied Mexican rule. A decade later a handful of California Americans made similar use of a one-star flag, though in theirs the star was eclipsed by a bear. Meanwhile in 1844 the voters of the United States had given James K. Polk what he interpreted to be a mandate for expansion. The lame-duck Congress and President acted on the annexation of Texas, diplomatic pressure yielded clear title in the Pacific Northwest, and the Mexican War permitted Polk to square out the nation with the seizure and retention of New Mexico and California and their intermediate environs. The advance to the Pacific encompassed the new Zion of the Mormons and brought them back into the jurisdiction of the United States, which in these few years had increased its territorial holdings by more than 60 per cent.

The American century began with many problems of adjustment to the new regime. Texas and California had a few thousand and New Mexico a larger number of residents of Spanish persuasion who, at least in the two latter provinces, were covered by treaty guaranties. The Anglo-Americans already on hand and those who came in '49 and the fifties, notwithstanding the democratic and tolerant qualities that F. J. Turner imputes to the frontier, too often took a hostile and discriminatory attitude toward these older residents.

Out of what probably would have been a process of gradual change and development, the Southwest was shaken by the discovery of gold in California in 1848. A rush ensued that quickened interest in the entire Southwest. Soon the Westerners were clamoring for a mint, for immediate settlement of Mexican land titles, for prompt Indian control, for a transcontinental wagon road, and for a railroad to the Pacific. Within the next few years these things and much more were accomplished. Mining of gold and also silver spread to Nevada and Colorado, in lesser degree to Arizona and New Mexico, and up the Rockies to Alaska. Mining boomed California cattle raising, prompted a great development of wheat farming, created a market for Pacific Coast lumber, gave excuse for the forced runs of the clipper ships, justified improvement of the steamer service by Panama, led to transcontinental stage lines and the Pony Express, and was an argument for federal support of Pacific railroads.

In Texas and Indian Territory, meanwhile, southern plainsmen began to farm the prairies, while in Utah the Mormons resorted to irrigation to make a garden in the desert. Without benefit of theocratic leadership, California made important additions to its irrigated lands, and New Mexico continued to utilize the dams and ditches inherited from its Indian and Spanish epochs. From Texas the range cattle industry spread west as well as north. Throughout the Southwest, too, the buffalo hunter was busy, and the United States Army was fighting Indians and trying, at first without much success, to point the moral of reservation life.

By 1890, when the frontier is supposed to have made its disappearance, the Southwest was "filled" with perhaps two million inhabitants. The last Indian war had been fought, the open-range phase of the cattle industry was over, the railroad builders had practically completed their mission, San Francisco felt itself an old metropolis, and Los Angeles was clearing its head after the orgy of its first great real estate boom. By this date admission to statehood was a completed process in the Northwest as well as throughout the East; yet, in the Southwest, of the eventual eight states only four were functioning. In the studied judgment of their peers, Oklahoma had too many Indians, New Mexico too many Spaniards, Utah too many Saints, and Arizona not enough of any sort of people to be entrusted with statehood.

Came the twentieth century and, in time, statehood, the automobile, the truck and tractor, the refrigerator car, the airplane, and the radio. Factors such as these facilitated development of an agriculture in several parts of the Southwest specializing in perishables for rapid delivery to eastern markets. Several of them cut down the time lag, if not always the cost, of maintaining contact with the rest of the world. Joined with the warmth and sunshine of the region, they encouraged the habit of looking to the Southwest as a sanatorium. With dude ranches, Indian tours, parades, fairs, expositions, excursions, rodeos, frontier days, national parks and monuments, desert spas, and Hollywood, they have greatly enlarged the tourist crop.

The twentieth century has seen the Southwest far outstrip the rest of the nation as an oil producer. This has been the period of gargantuan dam building, huge and intricate projects for carrying water to parched lands and thirsty cities, and equally stupendous projects for hydroelectric generation and transmission. In such matters, as well as in harbor improvement, highway construction, and bridge building, twentieth-century engineers have put their mark on the Southwest.

Stimulated by the experiences of two world wars, the Southwest has redoubled its efforts to develop industry. In motion-picture making, airplane manufacture, and Indian curios it has gained great success. In shipbuilding it earned temporary acclaim. In the making of such things as furniture, garments, and tires, it has done at least moderately well. During the forties two great steel plants rose at Geneva and Fontana, California. The uncertainties that attend their future illustrate the complications that absentee ownership, branch plants, patents and licenses, freight rates, interest rates, and federal interference cast athwart the aspirations of the Southwest for an industrial development of its own. But, whatever the control, industrial expansion has gone forward.

The new agriculture, the new industry, the expanded service trades, catering to tourists as well as residents — these are the elements largely responsible for the rapid population growth of the Southwest in the decades since 1890. The current estimates run to approximately twenty-five million.

In this Southwest it is possible to identify a number of distinguishing characteristics. The people, for example, at least if taken en masse, are distinguishable from those of any other quarter of the United States. First, by reason of history and propinquity, it is the part of the United States preferred by those of Spanish extraction or background. In number of Mexicans, Los Angeles is second only to Mexico City. Arizona and Texas have large contingents, and New Mexico has so many whose language is Spanish that its legislature is still bilingual.

Second, the Southwest has at least four-fifths of the Indians surviving in the United States. In part this is due to the system of Indian removal which shunted Southeastern Indians into what is now Oklahoma. In part it is traceable to the large and flourishing Indian groups of pre-Columbian times. Spain's well-intentioned program of preserving the Indians may have helped in New Mexico and California. More important, doubtless, was the fact that American settlement of parts of the Southwest, particularly in New Mexico and Arizona, was delayed until the United States Indian Office was functioning with effectiveness for the protection of the Indians.

Of Orientals, likewise, the Southwest has the most. In still other respects, the region has a cosmopolitan population.

Probably more significance attaches to the fact that for more than a century a regional characteristic has been large volume of immigration. Some have come in response to superficial attractions, such as the dry warmth and the stars of Hollywood. Others have surrendered to the blandishments of our chambers of commerce and our realtors. A substantial number came because of the vaunted pleasures and comforts of Southwestern life. Still others saw job opportunity or business opportunity and came aswarming. Literally, therefore, the people of the Southwest have not yet had very much time to get acquainted with each other or to figure out, in all instances, how best to make use of the region.

The Southwest is something of a paradox of oldness and newness. It has a large number of first Americans and some towns that date back far beyond Columbus. Two of its states, California and New Mexico, got their names sooner than any others of the forty-eight except Florida. The colonization of the Southwest began a long time ago; yet the major impact of American development of the region has been felt only recently, chiefly indeed in the twentieth century. In these circumstances it is not surprising that the Southwest showed high receptivity to technological improvements: in the seventies and eighties to the railroad, the six-shooter, the Winchester, and the windmill, and more recently to the automobile, the airplane, the aqueduct, the high-tension line, and the junior college.

For a long time it has been customary to speak of the colonialism of the Southwest. With payrolls of its frontier agents the Spanish Empire was willing to subsidize its colonies in this area. When the United States took over, it did some subsidzing through its Indian program and its grants for transportation improvement. The Southwest made relatively modest response in the form of direct taxes paid to the federal treasury, but it poured out a wealth of raw products — gold, silver, buffalo hides, beef, wheat, wool, etc. — which added greatly to the national wealth. The part of the public domain located in the Southwest was also an asset to the nation, and particularly to the national government.

In our day, new sorts of federal contribution have been devised: aid in education, road building, and harbor improvement; expenditures for the national parks; federal planning and leadership in water and power development; and federal outlay for research. Statistically, however, these additions are far more than counterbalanced by the exploits in the Southwest of the Collector of Internal Revenue. Meanwhile the Southwest has greatly stepped up its raw-products output, especially in oil, oranges, cotton, fruits and vegetables, fish, and copper. With the continuing export of wheat, beef, and wool, this smacks of economic colonialism, notwithstanding the concurrent flowering of a certain amount of manufacturing.

Economic colonialism, in the sense of exploitation of the region's resources for the benefit of interests nearer the seat of government, certainly is still a fact. The Webb-Mezerik analysis, though spread on a broader canvas, applies to the Southwest. It points to discrimination through the tariff system, patents and patent-leasing, interest rates, freight rates, pricing, absentee ownership, and absentee management. The facts appear to be as stated. That there is a measure of well-being in the Southwest in spite of this exploitation is variously attributed to the obtuseness of its people; to the vast resources of the region, especially in fertile soil, minerals, and oil; and to the ingenuity with which production has been widened and built up.

When I first came to the Southwest, I was most impressed by its vastness and openness, not to say emptiness. "This is the country," the saying ran, "where you can see farther and see less. . . ." There are spots in the Mojave Desert and Nevada and the Navajo country where the adage still holds, but for much of the Southwest its truth has deteriorated on both counts. There are more people, buildings, and enterprises to see, and through industrial fumes the visibility is impaired. But the Southwest is still big, and it is still remote. Not so isolated as once perhaps, no longer the "Too Far West," but still handicapped by the cost in time and money of its regional logistics. Much has been done to shrink distances. The Southwest would like to see still more accomplished.

The major fact about the Southwest undoubtedly is that it is subhumid. Limited water supply, more than any other one factor, sets the ceiling on agricultural development, on industrial capacity, and on the population that can be supported. As concerns the water problem, one may generalize that the easy things came first and have been done (the Pueblo ditches from the Rio Grande, the artesian wells in the Pecos Valley, the initial diversion of Colorado River water into the Imperial Valley); the hard things took a little longer but also have been done (the Owens Valley Aqueduct, the Salt River project, the Moffat Tunnel waterway, and San Francisco's Hetch Hetchy); the impossible tasks were postponed, but several have been tackled and some have been finished (Boulder Dam, the Los Angeles Metropolitan Aqueduct, and the Central Valley project). Ahead lie mostly still more impossible projects, such as piping the Mississippi to Los Angeles, squeezing the salt out of the ocean, or making rain.

Water is the Southwest's biggest problem. Except on a partial and localized basis, no other region can make that claim.

In the United States of our time, so many forces are nationwide in their impact that regionalism cannot be a matter of absolute differences. All parts of the country listen to the same commentators and advertisers, read the same columns and news dispatches, see the same films and comics. All have participated in the last several wars and elections. All have a share in federal policy-making and in the national debt. Our society, furthermore, is fluid and we are highly foot-loose individuals. Rolling about by automobile, bus, train, and plane, we see to it that no section has a chance to gather much moss of provincialism.

In the light of these circumstances, the measurable distinctiveness of the Southwest in its population, its high incidence of technological advance, its economic colonialism, its specialized pursuits, its handicaps of size and remoteness, and its critical shortage of water constitutes it beyond cavil as a region.

Peculiarly, the inhabitants of this area seem to be relatively innocent of regionalism. Whereas millions proclaim "I am a Texan," or "I am a Californian," almost no one boasts "I am a Southwesterner." Why, I do not know. Perhaps because the phrase is too much of a mouthful. Perhaps because the Southwest is not and never has been a political unit, an officer-electing unit, a taxing unit. Perhaps because it has had several local literatures instead of one that was as integrated as New England's. Perhaps because no single newspaper has ever spread its tentacles through the region as has "The World's Greatest Newspaper" in the Midwest. Perhaps because the Southwest has never been embattled as was the South.

I submit that greater consciousness of regionalism would help the Southwest. It might help in combating the ogres of exploitation from the Northeast, as has been suggested. More certainly it would help in meeting the region's internal problems. A united front in preserving the natural beauty of the Southwest, in readying it as a vacation land, and in welcoming tourists would be good business and better hospitality. The habit of outdoor living, to which the climate of much of the region invites, suggests the utility of a regional approach to domestic and public architecture and to apparel design. Conservation of timber, of which the region is short, of arable soil, and of minerals, which are not inexhaustible, is frequently of moment to much more than the immediate locality or even the state. The water problem in particular will almost have to be faced as one for the region instead of as an assortment of little problems susceptible of local solution or neglect.

Whether the utility of the regional approach will eventually create an effective Southwestern regionalism is another matter. The loyalties to the several states are already deeply ingrained. Some have as much as four hundred years of history back of them. Yet the state lines throughout the Southwest are, every one of them, artificial. And the hyperloyalty of a synthetic Californian, recently arrived from the Midwest, may indicate that, with proper conditioning, an equivalent devotion to the Southwest could be engendered in the course of much less than four centuries. The regional publishing now occurring at Norman, Dallas, Albuquerque, Stanford, and Berkeley, and the regional studies in progress at Oklahoma and the Huntington Library connote a scholarly recognition of the reality of the Southwest as a region. It may be that a grass-roots recognition will follow.

Part II

THE OLD SOUTHWEST

THE OLD SOUTHWEST

The Peace of Paris of 1763 ended in America a war of eight years and allowed European powers to redraw the map of the frontier. Britain received much of the Old Southwest, the Ohio Valley, and Canada, while Spain succeeded to French Louisiana. The vast lands between the Appalachian Mountains and the Mississippi River were inhabited by Indians who were disturbed by these clashes of empire, and Britain, in order to pacify the area, limited American colonization by the Proclamation of 1763.

For Spain the territory of Louisiana was annexed as a buffer zone, a necessary expense of empire in establishing a line of frontier defense. At first her vigorous monarch, Charles III, was preoccupied with reorganizing the royal administration in Spain and it was not until 1766 that he sent to Louisiana the distinguished gentleman scholar, Antonio de Ulloa, as the colony's first Spanish governor. During the next twenty years Ulloa, O'Reilly, Unzaga, and Gálvez adapted Spanish institutions to the rule of Louisiana. The governors were often handicapped by lack of money, armed forces, and appropriate authority, but they succeeded remarkably well in winning French loyalty and laying the foundations for enlightened rule. Gálvez, in particular, was extraordinarily capable as a political and military leader. During the American Revolution he extended aid to the British colonists and led a Spanish army against British positions in Florida.

The Peace of Paris of 1783 removed Britain from Florida and that part of the Old Southwest she had claimed as well as from the Thirteen American Colonies. It made the United States and Spain, in turn, the chief rivals for control of the southern frontier. Through the Revolution Americans had in great numbers already entered the territory of the future states of Kentucky and Tennessee. Some had dared venture as far west as the Mississippi River and south into the disputed boundary lands of Florida. Their increasing numbers were obviously unsettling Spanish officials in Louisiana who tried to discourage further colonization and trade by bribing settlers and Indians.

This American penetration also disturbed the Creeks and their great leader, Alexander McGillivray. This half breed Indian was loyal to the British during the Revolution and was offended by the peace treaty in which Creek territory passed unceremoniously to the United States. Under McGillivray the Creeks had a leader who was determined to make them a powerful, respected force in the Old Southwest. To achieve this goal, he hoped to exploit Spain and her desire for a buffer against American encroachments. His plans proceeded well for half a decade. When Spain became distracted in Europe by rivalry with Britain and the French Revolution, she left McGillivray without the military support to wage a prolonged war against the American settlers, and the weakening of Spanish interest in the Creeks forced McGillivray to seek American help. Those negotiations marked the beginning of the end of Creek power in the southeast.

The following essays emphasize the effect of conflicting European imperialism in the exploitation and settlement of the West. McGillivray, like many another Indian leader, rises momentarily to challenge European penetration of his homeland only to die prematurely just as his policies begin to fail.

LOUISIANA: A SPANISH OUTPOST, 1763-1783

The traditional view has been that Spain . . . recognized Louisiana as a "white elephant" and that, when Carlos III couched his reluctance to accept in the polite protest, "My cousin is losing altogether too much," he really meant "My cousin is giving me something that will cost me altogether too much." Though corroborated by Spain's delay in taking charge of Louisiana after the cession, this interpretation has been something of a paradox in view of Carlos' full appreciation of the northern borderlands as a buffer to insulate Spanish America. . . .

Recent research in the diplomatic archives vindicates Spanish perspicacity. As early as 1760, it now appears, Carlos had broached the matter thus to the French ambassador, "I must arrange with France after the peace for Louisiana by means of some exchange." In subsequent negotiations France, mindful of the strategic value of Louisiana to Spain, proffered it as a bribe for Spain's agreement to the Family Compact, for a Spanish loan to France, and for Spain's prompt entrance into the war against England. Then in the peace negotiations the offer was renewed, but more as a peace bribe than as recompense for Florida. The purpose of the cession as finally made was to reconcile Spain to an early peace with England and to English possession of the Gulf Coast east of New Orleans. Thus is recorded history made more logical — both France and Spain looked askance at Louisiana as an expensive colony, but both nations recognized its strategic value as a part of the barrier against the English which Spain was erecting along the northern fringe of her American empire.[1]

Nevertheless, Spain was in no hurry to take possession; the cession was kept a secret, and a lack of zeal is evident in the assumption of Louisiana's expense. . . . Eventually Spain moved to possess her new colony. As its governor, Carlos III appointed one of the most distinguished of his subjects, Antonio de Ulloa, "who had made himself illustrious in the republic of letters, and who was one of the brightest ornaments of Spain in the eighteenth century by his scientific labors and travels, and by his long and useful services as a naval officer and an administrator."[2]. . .

Ulloa was appointed governor of Louisiana at the zenith of his career. But his actual arrival, on March 5, 1766, was not at all auspicious; he was ushered into the colony by a severe thunderstorm. This may not have been prophetic of the trouble that lay ahead of him, but certainly the habitants recalled it later as an ill omen.

In person Ulloa was mild and unimposing, not of the prepossessing type whose every attitude carries conviction of power. His retinue was correspondingly unimpressive; a mere handful of soldiers, about ninety in all, travel worn and drenched by the rains, forming an escort utterly inadequate for a triumphal entry. The impression was rather that the Spanish nation had reached senility and could take only a faltering hold upon Louisiana. On the very day of his arrival Ulloa gave offense by brusquely refusing a request of the Superior Council, thus wounding the pride of those petty functionaries and setting to smoulder the fires of discontent that were eventually to drive him from the colony.[3]

Ulloa's difficulties in Louisiana were largely the result of misunderstandings. Had the colonists known the governor's actual instructions, they might have been less apprehensive of the change, for Spain apparently realized that Louisiana presented a new problem in colonial administration to which Spain's customary methods were hardly applicable. Ulloa, therefore, was directed to alter existing conditions as little as possible. Local laws and customs were to continue. The colony was not to be integrated with the rest of Spanish America, but was to be directly under the king. These instructions, however, were not fully announced in New Orleans. Had Spain provided an adequate escort, the colonists would have had a more wholesome respect for Spanish power. Had Ulloa's great reputation preceded him into Louisiana, the colonists might have excused some of his vagaries.

But none of these foundations was properly laid. The colonists deplored the coming of the Spaniards. They expected in Spanish rule a blight to their prosperity and happiness. Their disapproval of the imposition of Spanish control was ingrained, and could only be overcome by the exercise of consummate tact on the part of the new governor, by promises and proof that as Spanish colonists they would be better off than they had been under France, or by a great display of force that would quell rebellious spirits, over-awe malcontents, and win the admiration of the populace. Unfortunately Ulloa was not endowed by nature or equipped by his king to win the allegiance of the colonists by any of these methods. His cold reception offended him, and the more he saw of New Orleans and its inhabitants the more contemptuous he became. The creoles felt this and closed the doors of their hearts against reconciliation through the personality of the governor. Nor were they inclined to listen to his promises.[4]

Ulloa's two and a half years in Louisiana were fraught with perplexing problems. The first was how to control the colony with a handful of soldiers, the ninety with which he arrived being reduced by death and desertion to seventy-nine. At first blush Spain seems open to harsh criticism for providing her representatives with a force so inadequate. But there was an understanding with France which led Spain to believe that the French soldiers stationed in Louisiana could be induced to enter the services of Spain, thereby saving unnecessary transportation charges for both governments.[5] Ulloa invited the soldiers to enlist under the Spanish flag, but in spite of the urging of their officers, they were practically unanimous in declining. Perhaps the chief reason for their refusal was that Ulloa reduced the pay of Spanish soldiers from thirty-five to seven livres a month. This action was in consonance with his instructions, "not to change existing conditions in Louisiana" (seven livres having been the regular pay of French soldiers), and it put the soldiers of the two nations on an equal footing. Notwithstanding these theoretical advantages, the actual results were the refusal of the French troops to enter the Spanish service, and almost mutinous discontent on the part of the Spanish troops. . . .

The depreciated paper currency of the colony was another grave problem. Though recognized officially by the French government at three-fourths of its face value, this currency actually circulated at about one-fourth. Ulloa's policy was probably a more liberal one than the French government would have followed. He proposed to make the paper legal tender at 65 per cent, and he tried to buy up a supply at 75 per cent, but the people clamored for assumption at par. . . . Commercial regulations also occasioned commotion. Under France, New Orleans had exported large quantities of furs, mostly to the mother country. There had also been much trade with New England, particularly the importation of meal. After the English established themselves at Natchez and Manchac, contraband trade became so common that the phrase, "going to Little Manchac," was coined to denote smuggling. According to Ulloa's original instructions Louisiana was to have no commerce with the rest of Spanish America, but, by a decree of May 6, 1766, the Spanish government permitted such trade under certain conditions. On September 6, [Philip] Aubry [the retiring French governor] made public announcement of Spain's new requirement that French ships have their passports and price lists approved by Ulloa before discharging their cargoes. English merchants could trade under the same restrictions. Although this regulation was designed to protect the inhabitants from exploitation by the merchants, or perhaps because that was its effect, it was severely criticized by the merchants of New Orleans and by the captains of vessels then in the river.[6]. . .

In 1768 Ulloa received another commercial decree from the Spanish court restricting the colony's commerce to Spanish ships and certain Spanish ports.[7] Strictly enforced, this measure would have wrought havoc with most of the trade of the colony; for example, with the lumber exports directed almost entirely to the French islands, and with the imports of slaves from Sainte Domingue. Trade with Spain, furthermore, had no prospect of satisfaction; Spain had little use for furs, one of the leading Louisiana exports, and could get indigo, sugar, and lumber from other colonies more advantageously than from Louisiana.[8]. . .

As a counterirritant to his disputes with the French colonists,

Ulloa had the Indian problem. Notwithstanding the economic advantages which the English traders enjoyed, the French had cultivated the friendship of many Indian tribes on both sides of the Mississippi. The French method, emphasizing the trader and annual presents, differed radically from the Spanish mission-presidio system. In Louisiana Spain perforce adopted the French method. Soon after Ulloa's arrival he was visited by delegates from tribes as far away as eighty leagues. Everything possible was done, by Spanish and French alike, to ingratiate these Indians toward their new masters. That he might have first-hand information upon which to base his actions toward the Indians, Ulloa, in company with Aubry, made an extended tour through Lower Louisiana in the summer of 1766. He held conferences with the Indians, examined sites for forts, and surveyed trade possibilities, spending some time at Natchitoches investigating communications with Texas and New Mexico.[9]. . .

Handicapped by the inadequacy of his military retinue, Ulloa was unable to take formal possession of Louisiana. On his arrival the Superior Council requested that he exhibit his powers, but he declined. By word and by action (in preferring to deal with the French governor, Aubry) he offended the Superior Council. A royal order to suppress the Superior Council and to appoint in its place an assessor and two secretaries, one French and one Spanish, threatened to add injury to insult for the councilors.[10] An anomalous situation ensued; Ulloa financed the colony, but his orders became effective only as they were announced through Aubry. At Balize on January 20, 1767, Ulloa and Aubry prepared a document whereby possession was taken for Spain, and the Spanish flag was hoisted there. Nevertheless, it is evident that this was not considered a complete transfer, for a year later Aubry wrote to his government, "I am still waiting for the arrival of the Spanish troops, without which it is absolutely impossible that Ulloa should take possession of the colony."[11] Spain was dilatory, however, in sending additional troops to Ulloa. . . . This delay unquestionably made possible the insurrection of October, 1768.

Allusion had already been made to several reasons for discontent with the Spanish régime in Louisiana. A half-century of intermittent warfare on the Texas frontier had accentuated antipathy toward Spain, even though not toward the Texans. Ulloa's alienation of the troops, the nonredemption of the paper currency, the interference with free trade and smuggling, the snubbing of the Superior Council, the devious method of government through Aubry, the refusal of Ulloa to exhibit his powers — all these contributed to diminish Spanish prestige. Another list of grievances can be ascribed to Ulloa's personality. . . . By one report a charming conversationalist, combining sparkling wit and deep learning, by another he is described as peevish, haughty, excitable, tactless, unsympathetic.[12] His wintering at Balize offended New Orleans' civic pride. His marriage to the Peruvian Marchioness d'Abrado still further antagonized the populace. Her beauty excited the jealousy of the Louisiana women. Her intimacy with her cortège of Peruvian girls provided the wherewithal for gossip. Their marriage by Ulloa's chaplain created another scandal.[13]

Intrigue and agitation fanned the smouldering discontent into open rebellion. Idealistic motives doubtless played a great part in producing the insurrection, yet it is worth noting that almost without exception the leaders in the movement to purge Louisiana of the Spaniards had some personal grievance. By diligent propaganda their feelings of righteous indignation had been disseminated to most of the people of Lower Louisiana, and to assure their success they circulated a few exaggerations and misrepresentations. Ulloa was charged with threatening certain Acadians with slavery; with forcing the inhabitants of New Orleans to go six miles out of town to punish their slaves, merely because his wife was shocked by the cries of the blacks; with threatening to reduce the French to a diet of tortillas. . . .

The actual insurrection was worthy of comic opera. First, a petition was circulated, which more than five hundred signed, demanding Ulloa's banishment, restoration of former privileges, and freedom of trade. Then, on the night of the 27th, the guns at the gate of New Orleans were spiked. The next morning, the petition having been presented to the Superior Council and referred to committee, the membership of the council was increased by the addition of half dozen of the insurgents. In the afternoon Villieré entered New Orleans with a mob of four hundred Germans, Acadians, and other agriculturists. Seeing that "all was in a state of cumbustion," Aubry advised Ulloa to take refuge on the Spanish frigate anchored in the river, and Ulloa gathered up his family and his official papers and followed this advice. . . . He dropped down to Balize, waited a few days for favorable weather, and sailed for Cuba on November 16. . . . On December 4 he wrote a detailed report from Havana, and on February 14, 1769, he arrived in Spain to report in person to the king.[14]

Meanwhile, the more radical leaders of the insurgents were anxious to follow up the advantage gained through the departure of Ulloa. First, they made sure that he was really gone. Supposing that he had fortified himself at the mouth of the Mississippi, they sent a party of one hundred and thirty or forty men in four boats to dislodge him. The party went down fourteen leagues, but, hearing that Ulloa had gone, it returned to New Orleans.

The insurgents also dispatched three men to represent to the French court the causes and aims of the revolution. Their sailing was delayed; after a false start on December 17 their vessel had to return to Balize for repairs and did not set out again until January 19. When they finally reached France, information about the insurrection had preceded them through Spanish channels. Consequently — though the result might easily have been the same without any delay in their passage — France declined to interfere in a problem which she regarded as belonging entirely to Spain. . . .

Confusion was the chief characteristic of the situation in Louisiana during the ten months following Ulloa's departure. Aubry, who had opposed the expulsion, became the nominal head of the colony. There were a number of flare-ups of the revolutionary impulse . . . , but general support for the defiance of Spain seems to have waned as the months passed, and even the rebellious leaders modulated their radicalism. . . . American revolutions, in their full form, . . . seem to pass through two stages. The English colonists were fighting at first for their rights as Englishmen and later for independence. The Spanish Americans, likewise, rallied first to the slogan, "Old King or None," and later shortened it to "No King." The Louisiana revolt did not get past the first stage. Expulsion of the Spaniards was the aim of the movement, and restoration of French control its highest goal. Some of the more volatile spirits, it is true, did propose the expulsion of Aubry and the French troops and the erection of a Creole Republic. . . .

Reports of the insurrection reached France, as has been described, but the French government seems not to have taken official cognizance of them. Grimaldi, on the part of Spain, remonstrated with France for this flagrant indifference to the insult to Spain. In the latter country, however, the Council of the Indies pondered the problem. There were two alternatives. Spain might let the erring child depart in peace, or might vindicate her honor by a vigorous repression of the revolt. The Council of the Indies recognized once more the cost of maintenance of Louisiana; it saw the expense of resuming control. But it realized the usefulness of the barrier against the English and the advisability of avenging the insult to Spanish honor. Hence, for reasons of policy, the most important of which had to do with the effect that would be produced on the rest of the Spanish colonies, the Council settled on the suppression of the revolt and the establishment of Spanish control.[15]

Responsibility for the task was assigned to Don Alejandro O'Reilly, one of the many Irish Catholics driven by persecution at home to service under a foreign but sympathetic monarch. He was forty-seven years of age when sent to Louisiana. Most of those forty-seven years had been devoted to military service for Spain, . . . Austria, . . . France, . . . [and] for Spain again in the war with Portugal and in the Seven Years' War. At the close of this last-named war he was given an opportunity to drill the Spanish army in Austrian tactics, and was sent to Havana to restore the defenses of Cuba. Returning to Spain, he had the good fortune to save the life of Carlos III in the Madrid riot of 1765. . . .

Although probably not any more distinguished than Ulloa, O'Reilly was of a different fiber. Whereas Ulloa was preeminent in scholarship, only incidently a naval commander, and deficient in tact, O'Reilly was Spain's foremost military figure, and as capable an administrator as a general. He became dictator of Louisiana. Comparison of the achievements of these two men, nevertheless, is bound to be unfair to Ulloa. For in contrast to the ninety soldiers that had composed the first Spanish force of occupation, O'Reilly brought 2056 of the flower of the Spanish army. Even had the Louisianians been without dissent in their opposition to Spain, they could have mustered no more than 1800 men.[16]. . .

On August 17, 1769, the Spanish fleet of twenty-four sails anchored at New Orleans. At five o'clock the next afternoon the flagship fired a signal gun and the Spanish troops poured out of the ships. With splendid precision they marched, two thousand strong, to their appointed posts on opposite sides of the square. Then the artillery of fifty pieces and the cavalry contingent stationed themselves on the side of the square next to the river, and opposite the French troops drawn up in front of the church. Suddenly the sailors on the Spanish ships shouted, "*Viva el Rey, Viva el Rey, Viva el Rey,*" and the Spanish troops replied with gusto. While the echoes were still ringing, the guns of the ships thundered a salute. The fifty cannon on the square roared out an answer, augmented by the simultaneous discharge of the Spanish muskets. The reverberations announced the landing of General O'Reilly. . . .

An imposing escort of Spain's finest soldiers, in smart uniforms and bearing silver maces as the symbol of his authority, preceded the general, and behind him came the other officers in their full regalia. With the greatest pomp, made even more impressive by the general's slight limp, they advanced to the flagpole near which were gathered Aubry and the other prominent colonists. At O'Reilly's request Aubry read aloud the proclamations of the French and Spanish monarchs concerning the transfer. O'Reilly received the keys of the town. As the French flag was lowered and that of Spain raised, the French soldiery shouted "*Viva el Rey*," the Spaniards responded, and another salute was fired.

O'Reilly then went to the cathedral, exchanged cordial greetings with the Vicar-General, and received his blessing. They entered the church, where a *Te Deum* was sung as conclusion to the ceremony of taking possession.[17]. . .

The second step was taken without any ostentation. The general invited the twelve foremost leaders in the insurrection to gather at his quarters on the morning of August 21, and then quietly arrested them. He acquainted them at once with his purpose to have them tried according to (Spanish) law as the king had ordered, and introduced the judges who would hear the defenses and decide the verdict.[18] The general forebodings roused throughout New Orleans by this preliminary of retribution for the revolt were allayed by . . . [a] proclamation of amnesty for all participants in the uprising other than the twelve under arrest. . . .

The issue of the trial hinged on whether Louisiana had become a Spanish colony and whether the colonists owed allegiance to Spain. If the answer to these questions was affirmative, the accused were technically guilty of treason. . . . The question is a delicate one, though the principles of international law apparently support the prosecution. Nevertheless, the court's verdict, pronounced on October 24 by O'Reilly, though determined by his legal advisors, the judge and the assessor, was a surprise. The defendants were declared guilty of treason; five were condemned to the gallows and six to prison, the twelfth defendant having died before the trial ended. . .; the property of the twelve was confiscated.[19]. . .

In most accounts of O'Reilly's administration the tragic episodes of the trial and executions are unduly emphasized. His vindication of Spain's honor was significant, yet the subsequent acts of his administration, though less spectacular, were more important to the colony. The punishment of the leading insurrectionists quelled the revolutionary impulse; but O'Reilly's later conduct mollified the French creoles and won their loyalty to Spain. In addition, O'Reilly sketched the plans and laid the foundations for Spain's activities in Louisiana for the next thirty years.[20]. . .

His first concern, of course, was to serve the interest of his sovereign — to make Louisiana subservient and profitable to the king. This dominant motive did not exclude all others, but they were subordinate to it. He was anxious, for example, to bring prosperity and contentment to the Louisianians for their own sakes but more especially because he knew that the king would have a better, more loyal, more profitable colony under such circumstances. Consequently we find him recommending and instituting many reforms for the benefit of the populace. A third compelling motive, subordinate again to the service of Carlos III, was his constant concern to prevent encroachments by the English, to exclude them from commerce in Lower Louisiana, to prevent their intrusions into Spanish Illinois and the Arkansas region, to forestall any occasion for English aggression because of undue Spanish activity east of the Mississippi. A true picture of O'Reilly would show him devoted primarily to the interests of his king, but not unconcerned about the welfare of the colonists, and always on the alert against the English. . . .

Spain's first intention had been to alter Louisiana as little as possible, to hoist the Spanish flag in place of the French but in all other respects to leave the colony virtually French. Ulloa's reports on the inefficiency of some of the French methods, followed as those reports were by the insurrection, persuaded the court that a change of policy was advisable. O'Reilly was directed, therefore, to reorganize the institutions of Louisiana, establishing "that form of political government and administration of justice prescribed by our wise laws, and by which all the states of his majesty in America have been maintained in the most perfect tranquillity, content, and subordination."[21]

For the political reorganization of New Orleans O'Reilly applied the orthodox Spanish pattern, which called for an indigenous local government, officered by resident landowners responsive to local interests, and supported by local sources of revenue.[22] The Superior

Council of the French régime, in disrepute because of its activities in the insurrection, was abolished and a *cabildo* erected in its stead. . . .

Inasmuch as the province had been accustomed to French legal practices, O'Reilly attached to the proclamation creating the cabildo, another indicating the salient features of Spanish law. This statement, which came to be known as the "Code O'Reilly," was substantially an abridgement of the *Recopilación de Leyes de las Indias*. With the French Black Code it was declared the law of the colony.[23] French and Spanish law were not very different from each other, both being derived largely from Roman law. The change in Louisiana was drastic, however, because a system of enforcement was set up where the absence of enforcement had been conspicuous. "O'Reilly," Aubry wrote with a measure of accuracy, "enforced all those wise and beneficient laws of which the impotence of our government had prevented the observance for several years."[24]. . .

In addition to the purely local officials such as those of the cabildo, Spanish political theory recognized another class, the provincial officers. These were ordinarily *peninsulares* (Spanish-born Spaniards) appointed by the crown or the governor and detached as much as possible from local ties and support. Their attachment, it was hoped, would be to the crown rather than to the colonists. In Louisiana an exceptional circumstance dictated departure from this pattern. Frenchmen, it was conceded, were better fitted to govern the parishes and to deal with the Indians than were any Spaniards available. All the parishes, therefore, were placed under French lieutenants, and a French commandant was appointed for the Natchitoches district. Only in the Illinois district did a Spaniard receive an important provincial commission from O'Reilly.[25]. . .

O'Reilly's reform of trade regulation represents probably the most drastic change that he produced in the colony. The change was not so much the introduction of new theory as the tightening of enforcement. Both France and Spain, and for that matter, all Europe, stood committed to the mercantilist theory, and their trade regulations aimed at an exclusive policy. Under France this control had been so very loose that the greater part of the trade fell to ships from the English colonies. In Ulloa's term as governor some changes were announced, but Ulloa's authority, even when supplemented by Aubry's, was not sufficient to secure enforcement. O'Reilly had enough soldiers to command respect for mercantilism.

He forbade commercial intercourse with foreign ports and with the rest of the Spanish colonies, Havana excepted, and limited the trade with Spain and Havana to Spanish ships. Envisioning the danger of contraband trade with Mexico from Natchitoches and Opelousas, he recommended that the officials at these posts should be relieved "with sufficient frequency so that they would not have time to corrupt themselves with illicit gains."[26] He banished from the colony two Genevans, the Duraldes brothers, and likewise three Jews because their stocks of diamonds, watches, and jewelry far exceeded the capacity of the local market and were intended apparently for smuggling into Vera Cruz and Campeche, where these merchants had correspondents. . . .

While O'Reilly remained, smuggling was distinctly on the wane, yet it is a mistake to think that trade with the English was done away entirely, or that the interruption was of long duration. At least one Anglo-American merchant, Oliver Pollock, was not expelled from New Orleans. He had ingratiated himself with O'Reilly by refusing to profiteer on a shipload of flour when New Orleans was suffering a shortage, offering it instead to the governor at the latter's price. Reporting the transaction to the king, O'Reilly recommended that Pollock be allowed free trade at New Orleans thenceforth.[27]. . .

Although enough of a soldier to believe that laws should be rigorously enforced, O'Reilly was not fully in sympathy with mercantilism. He recognized the vital necessity of foreign trade for Louisiana. The colonists needed flour, wine, tools, arms, ammunition, and clothing, in return for which they could export lumber, indigo, tobacco, and furs. O'Reilly therefore recommended to the court that free trade in certain specified commodities be allowed between Louisiana and Havana as well as the ports of Spain. His friend [Antonio María] Bucareli, who was Captain General of Cuba, endorsed this recommendation, and the court accepted it.[28]. . . O'Reilly, it would appear, was interested not merely in securing a more profitable trade for Spain and in stamping out the English trade with the colony but also in promoting the prosperity of Louisiana.

Anthropologists have directed attention to the tendency for continuity of certain cultural traits in a given area, notwithstanding the intrusion of a new racial element. The Indian policy in Louisiana might be cited as an example. Because the local tribes had become accustomed to control by traders and had acquired an insistent craving for the trade goods, there was no attempt to establish missions. Perhaps it is just as well, for these Indians were of the aggressive, warlike sort that had not proved very susceptible to mission control. Moreover, after their experiences with French traders, they were certainly spoiled for the mission system. At any rate, Spain followed the line of least resistance by continuing the French system.[29] The experiment, for experiment it was for Spain, had been launched by Ulloa, who had held parleys with the Indians of Lower Louisiana, assuring them that Spain would grant annual presents just as the French had done.

O'Reilly continued this deviation from the customary Spanish method. One of his first moves was to convene an Indian council[30] at New Orleans, in which he tried his hand at French Indian diplomacy. He called together the chiefs of all the tribes within a radius of seventy leagues of New Orleans. At eleven thirty on the morning of the appointed day nine chiefs, accompanied by interpreters and a number of warriors, presented themselves at O'Reilly's house. They found the general seated under a canopy in front of his house, surrounded by offices of the garrison and some of the principal citizens of New Orleans. Laying down their weapons at O'Reilly's feet, the chiefs saluted him with *banderas* (small painted sticks with fans of feathers), which they waved around their heads, tapped four times against their breasts, and then presented to O'Reilly. A pipe was lighted and circulated to everyone in the council, and O'Reilly participated in this ceremony, "not to depreciate their customs." Finally, each chief gave his hand to the general, "their principal sign of friendship." . . .

Medals bearing the royal image were then conferred on the nine chiefs. After the medals had been kissed by the chiefs, O'Reilly drew his sword, touched each one on the shoulder and breast, made the sign of the cross above their heads, and embraced and shook hands with them all. There were also presents for them. So astounding was the ceremony that the usually immobile faces of the chiefs lighted up with pleasure and surprise. Their awe-struck admiration was renewed in the afternoon when they witnessed a spectacular sham battle staged by the Spanish soldiers. Superior showmanship captivated the Indians just as it had impressed the French colonists at the possession-taking formalities. The chiefs departed with such manifestations of gratitude and admiration as the interpreters and the French officials still in the colony had never before seen. O'Reilly's actions at the council are reminiscent of Bienville, or of Frontenac at Lake Ontario; they are a far cry from those of the typical Spanish missionary.

Winning the support of the Indians along the lower Mississippi required merely a transfer of the affection already felt toward the French. For other tribes, particularly for those along the old Red River border, a conversion was required. Hatred of the Spaniards, inculcated by the French traders, must be transmuted into friendliness. Here in the Red River region lived the *Norteños,* the Indians of the North, who had been such an abomination to the Texas colony. Athanase de Mézières — a Frenchman who possessed the double advantage of friendship with the Indians and familiarity with the French system, and in whom, moreover, the Indians would see living proof that the accession of Spain meant continued friendly interest on the part of the Louisiana whites — was made commandant of Natchitoches. "By this," O'Reilly reported to his government, "I hope to obtain for the presidios of Mexico [i.e., those of Texas] a quietude which they have not hitherto enjoyed, and to make it very difficult for anyone to introduce illicit trade at these posts."[31]. . .

In Upper Louisiana the Indian problem was in one respect the reverse of that at Natchitoches. In the Red River region there was a lacuna in the list of friendly tribes, a gap which De Mézières was expected to fill by winning over the Norteños. In Spanish Illinois, on the contrary, there was a plethora of friendly tribes, many of them residing in English territory east of the Mississippi.[32] Now Spain was glad to have the friendship and the trade of these tribes, but she did not care to give England legitimate cause for complaint about undue Spanish influence among them. The commander at St. Louis therefore had to walk circumspectly. In the instructions which O'Reilly sent to that officer he enjoined him to take special precautions against offending the English. Presents were not to be given to tribes east of the Mississippi, and the Indians in Spanish territory were to be urged not to molest the English and not to interfere with their navigation of the river. The commandant was to regulate strictly, however, the commerce of Spanish Illinois. All traders and hunters had to be licensed by him, and on returning to St. Louis were to make a report.[33]. . .

Spain had accepted Louisiana because she saw in it the means of insulating the rest of Spanish America against the English. Acquisition of the province, it is true, made possible the abandonment of the struggling outposts on the old Louisiana-Texas border, and in accordance with one of [the Marqués of] Rubí's recommendations for a general reorganization of the northern frontier that retrenchment was undertaken;[34] but a new frontier had been acquired, and new frontier problems were the price for relief from old ones. If Louisiana was to be a barrier at all, it was necessary to stop the English at the Mississippi. A threefold resistance was organized by O'Reilly: penetration of English traders and settlers into Louisiana and commercial intercourse across the Mississippi were forbidden; a line of forts was built along the river; and a citizen militia was created. . . .

O'Reilly instituted other reforms. He established titles to agricultural land and set the requirements for "homesteading." He investigated the church in Louisiana and recommended provision for eighteen priests. When he left for Havana in March, 1770, he had reënforced Spain's formal title to the province by transforming it, so far as was possible, into a Spanish colony.[35] The Hispaniolizing of Louisiana was never to be completed, but O'Reilly made a good beginning and succeeding governors augmented his efforts. . . .

Unzaga's governorship of Louisiana was to a very marked degree a continuation of O'Reilly's control, modified in many particulars, however, by the personality of the new governor. [Luis de] Unzaga [y Amézaga] was a native of Málaga. Since 1735 he had been serving in the Spanish army, the first eight years in Spain, Italy, and Africa, and the last twenty-six in America, where he had risen to the rank of colonel of the Regiment of Havana. In 1769, when O'Reilly set out for Louisiana, he brought Unzaga along to be governor of the province, a capacity in which the latter served for approximately seven years.[36]

Introduced to the Louisianians as a protégé of O'Reilly, subordinate to the latter's orders until his departure, Unzaga, nevertheless, was in sharp contrast to his chief. As an older man, he might have been expected to be less impetuous; in addition, he seems to have been by nature milder, more conciliatory. These qualities fitted him well to serve as a mollifying influence upon the French creoles. He was not exactly an antidote for O'Reilly, for that was not needed. O'Reilly's good work in Louisiana was not entirely unappreciated at the time, though later generations have lost sight of it. But Unzaga carried on the work he had started, the work of reconciling the creoles to Spanish rule; and, because of his gentler nature, he did it more effectively, perhaps, than O'Reilly himself could have. . . .

Early in Unzaga's administration there was danger that war between Spain and England might arise out of the Falkland Islands dispute, and the British commanders, Gage and Haldimand, laid plans for an attack on Louisiana, should war eventuate.[37] On June 8, 1770, Unzaga reported that Pensacola had been reënforced by one thousand men; and the governor of Havana, being appraised of this reënforcement, informed his government of the danger of an English attack on Louisiana or Havana. O'Reilly recommended that one hundred men and additional military supplies be sent to Louisiana. This was done and Unzaga was ordered to defend Louisiana as best he could with the small force of regulars and with the militia; but if attacked by a strong force, he was to retreat to Mexico. . . . Though the fires of war were all ready to be kindled, the match flickered out: the Falkland Islands dispute was settled amicably; Louisiana and the English colonies might relax their vigilance.[38]

Religious contentions impinged upon the consciousness of the colony much more forcefully than apprehension of an English attack. . . . Soon after the establishment of Spanish domination, . . . Father Cicilo [Cyril de Barcelona] penned virulent tirades to his superior denouncing the ignorance, laziness, and corruption of the Louisiana Capuchins. Father Dagobert, it must be admitted, was an easy-going old fellow, well liked by the people, but not a strict shepherd, blissfully ignorant of the finer points of Catholic doctrine, and inclined to be overconfident of God's forgiving grace — at least, Father Cirilo thought such confidence unwarranted. Father Dagobert and his fellow-priests lived in luxurious comfort, set the best table in New Orleans, and were ministered to by black wenches, whose morals Father Cirilo questioned. But Bishop [Santiago José] Echevarría, on the advice of Unzaga, resolved to continue Father Dagobert as vicar-general. . . .

Unzaga hesitated to offend either faction in this clerical squabble. Father Cicilo got the impression from conferences with him that the governor was opposed to the French Capuchins and anxious for the removal of Father Dagobert. But, as Father Cicilo's diatribes grew more and more caustic, Unzaga asserted himself in favor of the French Capuchins. Political considerations doubtless had great influence on his decision. Father Dagobert was very popular with the Louisianians and his expulsion would have disaffected the colonists, though probably not so seriously as some maintained. Yet the governor's arguments took cognizance chiefly of the scurrility of the persecution and the imprudence of Father Cirilo.[39]. . .

The bishop [of Santiago de Cuba] accused Unzaga of indolence in the matter and asked the captain general of Cuba to remonstrate with him. Unzaga defended his original position in a long letter to the captain general, and justified himself further in a letter to [Julián de] Arriaga, minister of the king. Finally the whole question was submitted to the king, who supported the bishop, but without censuring Unzaga, and recommended that harmony be attained by mutual concessions. Thus the matter blew over.[40]. . .

Inasmuch as the king did not pronounce judgment against either party in this dispute, it may suffice, by way of conclusion, to indorse Unzaga's statement, "I know how difficult it is to come to a correct appreciation of the true merits of men of that sacred calling, when they choose to quarrel among themselves." More interesting possibly than the altercation was Unzaga's fearlessness in opposing the bishop . . . and the boldness with which he argued for liberal policies.

> It is not always that the laws made for one region can be safely adapted to another. . . . You should take into consideration the difficulty which there is in eradicating practices, usages and customs. . . . The people here will remain quiet as long as they are gently treated; but the use of the rod would produce confusion and ruin. Their dispositions are the result of the happy state of liberty to which they have been accustomed from the cradle, and in which they ought to be maintained, so far as is consistent with the laws of the kingdom.[41] . . .

Under Unzaga justice was administered in accordance with the forms outlined by O'Reilly. Some cases were tried before the alcaldes; others were taken to the governor's court. In this latter court, Unzaga, not being a lawyer by profession, relied largely on the advice of Don Cecilio Odoardo, his *assessor* or *auditor*.[42] Court procedures embodied some peculiarities. Witnesses did not ordinarily appear in court, but their sworn depositions were introduced as evidence. The defendant in a criminal case, likewise, had an examination in jail instead of a "day in court," and his confession or protestation of innocence was entered in the record. Torture was applied to some suspects who were reluctant to testify. Capable counsel was provided, however, even for negroes charged with crimes against whites.[43]. . .

All evidence possible was collected in criminal cases. But where the evidence was clear the court acted rapidly. For example, Juan Baptiste Cezaire Lebreton was murdered on the night of May 31, 1771. The next morning the court appointed two doctors to examine the body. Testimony was taken from all who knew anything of the murder, and suspects were jailed. When it was seen that the accusations of the various witnesses were corroborated by several independent bits of evidence, an accused Negro was tortured on the rack, a confession was extracted, and along with it the implication of a partner in his crime. Under torture this second Negro confessed. Just three weeks after the murder these two slaves were hanged, and their heads and hands were cut off and nailed up on the public roads. An accomplice received one hundred lashes and her ears were cut off, and another was tarred and feathered and ridden on a pack animal. . . . Punishment was prompt, versatile, and rigorous, but not without a touch of compassion — or perhaps, since the slave was merely a piece of property, it would be more nearly correct to say that the court tempered justice with business acumen.[44] . . .

However rigorous Unzaga was in the enforcement of local laws in Louisiana, he was discreet enough to close his eyes to brazen infractions of Spain's commercial regulations for the colony. Although O'Reilly had obtained some modifications in Spain's exclusive policy and had recommended still further liberality, he was too much a military man not to enforce the restrictions until they were repealed. The effect was to stifle Louisiana's trade. For the colony's available exports, chiefly furs and peltries and lumber, there was little demand in Spain and Havana. France, England and the English colonies, however, provided ready markets, while West Florida abounded in depots where manufactured goods were offered in exchange. English ships on the Mississippi were handier still. The Spanish restrictions ran counter to economic law, and through the connivance of Unzaga the latter triumphed. With his tacit consent trade with the English recovered from its temporary lethargy. The English converted two large vessels into floating warehouses and employed them exclusively in the contraband trade, and practically the entire sum that the Louisianians mustered annually to pay for imported goods found its way into English hands.[45] . . .

Under Unzaga's administration the policy that O'Reilly had outlined for the Natchitoches district began to bear fruit. Although De Mézières never received from the Spaniards the full confidence that he deserved, he made a success of the tasks assigned him. In

1770 he went to Cadodacho and held conferences with the chiefs of the Taovayas, Tawakoni, Yscanis, and Kichai (Tribes of the North), as a result of which, in the following year, treaties were concluded with these tribes as well as with the Cainiones and Tonkawa. After coercing these tribes into submission by cutting off their trade, it was now advisable to retain their friendship by extending to them the system of bonded traders. Unzaga gave de Méziéres permission to appoint the traders. Governor [Juan María de] Ripperdá of Texas appreciated De Mézières's service to Texas in pacifying the Norteños without destroying their hostility toward the Apaches. He objected, however, to the penetration of traders into Texas on the ground that this trade indirectly supplied the Apaches with arms and ammunition. But the traders were not withdrawn.[46]. . .

That the Natchitoches district flourished under Unzaga's governorship is borne out by the census report of February 16, 1776. Population had risen from 800 to more than 1000. There were sizable herds of horses, cattle, and hogs. Some indigo was raised and much tobacco. But economically the Indian trade was the leading business, its profits being computed in deerskins and bear oil. The fort had been rebuilt and was in good condition. De Mézières's particular pride, however, was the splendid parochial church which he had been instrumental in building.[47]. . .

Peace and prosperity went hand in hand also in Spanish Illinois. French Illinois, of course, had been a rich colony, at least agriculturally; so rich, in fact, as to deserve the name "the Garden of New France." Farm products such as flour, corn, pork products, and tobacco supplemented the fruits of the chase such as furs, hides, bear hams, bear oil, and venison as export commodities. With the cession to England, many of the French settlers joined the trek across the river to what turned out to be Spanish Illinois. There they found conditions quite as favorable as those they had left, and in a short time they were living in comfort. Francisco Vallé, the richest habitant of Ste. Geneviève, raised quantities of provisions and had 100 Negroes besides hired white help.[48] . . . An official report for 1770-1771 gives Ste. Geneviève a population of 605, including slaves, and St. Louis, 497.[49]. . .

The English settlements on the east bank of the Mississippi, especially those in the Natchez and Manchac districts, were increasing even more rapidly than the settlements in Spanish Louisiana. The English government did nothing to encourage the populating of this region, but the New England and to a lesser extent the other

Atlantic Coast colonies contributed individualistic immigrants.[50] In their coming Unzaga saw a menace to Spanish control west of the river. "If they possess these establishments fronting on the kingdom of Mexico without any other interposition than the Mississippi River, they will introduce to us commerce in time of peace and armies in time of war."[51]

With the outbreak of the American Revolution this chronic concern of Unzaga's became acute. Ordered "to investigate with all discretion and secrecy . . . ," he launched a number of inquiries, including the sending of a ship to Philadelphia, "ostensibly to look for flour, but also to endeavor to discover their designs."[52] The reports that he received were alarming, and a survey of the defenses of Louisiana was not reassuring. He wrote that there were "neither troops to defend the colony, nor forts to contain them, nor means to march on land.". . . His conclusion was that, if he were attacked, he would follow the advice that had been given him in 1770 and fall back to Mexico.[53]

The state of war in the English colonies also forced Unzaga to face certain problems of neutrality. Various Revolutionary leaders, encouraged by Spain's hints of interest in the colonial cause, importuned the governor of Louisiana to lend assistance to the Revolutionists. They buttressed their requests for arms and military supplies with embarrassing arguments and uncomfortable predictions. In May, 1776, for example, Charles Lee, then second in command to Washington, pointed out that, if Great Britain subjugated the colonies, the Spanish West Indies and even Mexico itself would be at the mercy of Great Britain. If, on the contrary, the colonies won independence, Spain would have nothing to fear from them as neighbors. "The genius of the people, their situation and their circumstances, engage them by preference in agriculture and free trade, which are most suited to their interests and inclination."[54]. . .

Ungaza preferred not to commit himself. He conferred with George Gibson, who brought Lee's letter, and, encouraged by Oliver Pollock, of whom more later, even went so far as to have Gibson arrested (temporarily) to allay suspicion long enough for Lieutenant Linn to start north with nine thousand pounds of powder for the Revolutionists.[55] But when Gibson made certain pointed inquiries about Spanish policy and his own attitude, the governor put him off without an answer and referred the queries to the court.[56] Unzaga was uneasy about Louisiana's exposure to attack but he was not convinced that the surest defense of the province was through aiding the Americans.

Of one thing he was convinced, however, and that was his desire to retire from the governorship. Poor health, advanced age, and impaired eyesight handicapped him in his work, and after forty-one years in American service he was homesick for his native Málaga. His reiterated requests for permission to retire were answered eventually not with the coveted recall but with promotion to the captaincy general of Caracas. . . . By the end of 1776 three Spanish governors had administered Louisiana. Each one had played a part: Ulloa in bringing on the insurrection, O'Reilly in establishing and formulating Spanish control, Unzaga in reconciling the colonists to Spanish rule. The stage was set for the new governor, Bernardo de Gálvez. . . .

The young man to whom Unzaga relinquished his office on January 1, 1777, had come to the colony just a few months earlier as commandant of the troops in Louisiana. He had been introduced, of course, by the usual formal notice, [but] . . . more illuminating is the postscript that O'Reilly subscribed in his own hand: . . . "He is an individual whom I esteem highly, and his uncle, the minister of the Indies, is my particular friend, wherefore I will thank you for any attentions you can show him."[57] The word "wherefore" probably should be underlined, for his family connections were worth much to Bernardo de Gálvez; they were possibly an even greater advantage than his dynamic and attractive personality. He was not only the nephew but also the favorite protégé of José de Gálvez, formerly visitor-general of New Spain and now minister of the Indies; and this in an age when nepotism was a virtue rather than a scandal. José de Gálvez, enjoying power second only to that of King Carlos himself, showered favors on all his relatives, but the greatest honors went to his elder brother, Matías, who was elevated to the viceroyalty of New Spain, and to Matías' son Bernardo.[58]

When he came to New Orleans, Bernardo de Gálvez already had a long service record. In the war with Portugal in 1762 he served as lieutenant, after which his uncle obtained for him a captain's commission in the Regiment of Corunna. He came to New Spain as part of his uncle's *entourage* in the visitation of that viceroyalty. In April, 1769, he was attached as captain and second in command in an expedition against the Apaches on the frontier of Nueva Vizcaya. In reporting this appointment to José de Gálvez, Lope de Cuellar stated quite frankly, "I hope that you will recognize my motives to provide the greatest satisfaction for Don Bernardo, and to manifest to your excellency my constant recognition."[59] Protesting against Cuellar's "excess of gratefulness or kindness," José de Gálvez remarked that his nephew showed "promise of valor and leadership," but because of his extreme youth had not yet acquired "steadiness and experience." He questioned, therefore, the wisdom of ranking him ahead of the seasoned and distinguished soldier, Lieutenant Diego Becerril. But though he deplored the "excessive honor" bestowed upon his nephew, he did not countermand it, and Bernardo not only continued in this capacity but was soon made commander of the Nueva Vizcaya and Sonora frontier.[60]...

As commandant of this frontier Gálvez led several major expeditions against the Apaches. On the first of these, in the fall of 1770, he demonstrated the qualities of leadership that he possessed. With about one hundred and thirty-five frontier soldiers and Indian allies he set out from Chihuahua in mid-October. Not until they reached the Pecos River were the elusive Apaches located, but by this time supplies had run short, the men were discouraged, and prudence seemed to dictate an immediate return to Chihuahua. But on the morning of November 2, after all were on horse, the young commander spoke to his soldiers and Indians "more or less in this tone":

"My comrades: the time has come to deliver the final blow and to give proof of our constancy. Cold and ice! already I have seen the light-heartedness with which you know how to endure them. Hunger! which is worse than all inclemencies of weather, we have known, not through my fault, but because Heaven with much water destroyed our provisions. Our enemies do not know the day or the month when we expect to encounter them; to return to get provisions would be to give time for the Indians to give us the slip, after which, it is my feeling, it will be impossible to catch them.[61]..."

Having given this challenge, Gálvez struck spurs to his horse and started to ford the Pecos. With one accord his men followed, shouting "that they would follow until they died; that they would eat horses, and after that stones, and would never forsake him." ... The Indians had no chance to resist. Some avoided death by surrendering; others sought to escape by jumping into the river, but Gálvez, setting an example which his soldiers followed, plunged his horse into the stream to attack the Indians in the water, "where they perished miserably between the two elements." ... Six months later, after Gálvez had led a second successful expedition against the Apaches — an expedition notable because for the first time Apache captives (from the preceding foray) were persuaded to accompany the Spanish troops as guides and auxiliaries. . . . Tidings of this good treatment had penetrated to the tribes and impelled them to propose to Gálvez a cessation of hostilities throughout *Apachería*.[62]

Congratulations were premature, however, for peace did not prevail. . . . The Indians ran off a herd of horses and mules; they were overtaken by a corporal and fourteen men, but in the clash which followed ten of these men lost their lives and four were wounded. . . . In November of the same year Gálvez attempted to lead another expedition into the land of the Apaches, this time toward the Gila region, but, receiving "a heavy blow on the chest" when thrown by his horse, he found it almost impossible to continue the campaign.[63] Even before this accident the visitor-general had asked that his nephew be relieved and allowed to return to Spain.[64]. . . The viceroy acquiesced. . . .

An impartial estimate of Gálvez' work on the Chihuahua frontier must recognize that he was not so successful toward the last as earlier. It must recognize, however, that he was handicapped in the fall of 1771 by impaired physical condition, chiefly the result of wounds of battle. It must reckon also with the foe, for whose fortitude and skill Gálvez expressed unfeigned admiration.[65] Viewed as a whole, Gálvez' frontier defense compares very favorably with that of more experienced men to whom Spain intrusted this knotty problem. Certainly it brought him to the attention of the court; unmistakably influences of this frontier training seem apparent in the way that he met military and Indian problems in Louisiana; and when later he became the viceroy of New Spain, the jurisdiction of that office was extended again over the frontier because of his knowledge of the problem. . . .

Soon after his return to Spain, Gálvez obtained a leave of absence from Spanish service, went to France, and enrolled in the Regiment of Cantabria "to perfect himself in military science." He earned promotion to the rank of lieutenant in this organization and then returned to Spain in 1775.[66] As captain of infantry under O'Reilly in that same year, he was a member of the unfortunate landing party at Algiers and received another severe wound. By way of reward he was made a lieutenant colonel and attached to the military school at Ávila. Then in 1776 he came to Louisiana as colonel of the regiment.

He had hardly time to familiarize himself with the duties of this position before new responsibilities were thrust upon him. A royal order of September 19, 1776, instructed him to succeed Unzaga as acting governor of the colony.[67] On January 1, 1777, he took over the office. . . .

His administration began with a prospect of hearty approval from the Louisianians, because new commercial regulations arrived almost simultaneously permitting trade with France and the French colonies, on condition merely that it be conducted through two duly appointed French commissioners, that a 5 per cent export duty be paid, that guards be put on the ships to prevent smuggling, and that the ships load only at New Orleans.[68]. . . The new regulations, even if strictly enforced, would have diverted much of Louisiana's trade from the English to the French. Governor Gálvez went further, interpreting the convention liberally, making the inspections of cargoes perfunctory, and permitting French ships to load anywhere on the river instead of just at New Orleans, with the result that the French commissioners could report, as early as March 30, that trade between Louisiana and the French islands was waxing prosperous.[69] . . .

In the meantime Gálvez obligingly . . . closed his eyes to the English smuggling, and trade [continued] . . . "on its ancient footing," greatly to the satisfaction of all concerned. Commerce with the English, however, enjoyed only a temporary revival. By a series of proclamations in . . . 1777, Louisiana was given freedom of commerce with Yucatan and Cuba, the export duty at New Orleans was reduced to 2 per cent, and permission to import Guinea Negroes was given once more to the French.[70] The result was complete destruction of British trade. "The British flag," the French commissioners reported on July 18, 1778, "has not appeared on this river for more than three months. . . . The duties to be paid by our ships . . . are reduced every day. . . . The whole trade of the Mississippi is now in our hands."[71] As a consequence of the new Spanish commercial policy as interpreted by Gálvez, English contraband trade with Louisiana was almost extinguished even before Spain's entrance in the war against Great Britain in 1779 put a final stop to it.

Gálvez sought to encourage agriculture as well as commerce. The Spanish government had agreed to make annual purchases of tobacco to the amount of $800,000 in the hope of stimulating the Louisiana planters and of acquiring a cheap supply for the tobacco monopoly in Mexico and for sale to France.[72] Gálvez convened a meeting of the planters to deliberate upon a fair price, and they agreed upon seven livres a pound for leaf tobacco and ten for tobacco in *carottes*. A proclamation to that effect was issued on June 15, 1777.[73] After having made arrangements with the viceroy of New Spain about prices, methods of grading, packing, shipping, etc., Gálvez promised to buy the entire crop of the colony.[74] The French commissioners were very optimistic about the future of tobacco culture in Louisiana. "Enjoying a better climate than Maryland and Virginia," they wrote, "Louisiana, on account of its extent and fertility, could furnish the world with tobacco." Although production fell considerably short of this rosy estimate, the export to Mexico in 1777 sold for more than 50,000 pesos.[75]

The strongest deterrent to tobacco culture and to agricultural development in general was a shortage of labor. When the government urged, for example, the cultivation of hemp and flax, the colonists of Upper Louisiana replied "that they were going to make all possible efforts" but could not "expect a large crop," and petitioned the king to "make easier for them the method by which they might acquire some Negro slaves."[76] The king ordered that Negroes be supplied them on credit. And on November 21, 1777, Gálvez published a proclamation authorizing the introduction of Guinea Negroes. The embargo against Negroes from the islands, however, was expressly reaffirmed.[77]

A census taken shortly after Gálvez became governor revealed that population had increased but slightly since the close of the French period.[78]... For the sake of prosperity and strengthened defenses Louisiana needed more white settlers. Spain redoubled her efforts to attract settlers by promises of paternalistic protection. Advertising was the first artificial stimulant employed. French coasting vessels were requested to broadcast the inducements of Louisiana to the inhabitants of the French West Indies. . . .

Immigrants received actual assistance as well as invitations. By order of the governor families were to be located in the most suitable places, were to receive plots of ground five arpents in frontage, as well as rations of maize during the first year at the rate of a barrel a head for adults and half a barrel for children. In addition each family was given "an axe, a hoe, a scythe or a sickle, a spade, two hens, a cock, and a pig of two months, with which they may easily found and establish a household which will provide them a living, or may even make their fortune."[79] . . .

Meanwhile, English and American refugees from the disturbances of the American Revolution had discovered and occupied a site in

Spanish territory about sixty miles northwest of New Orleans. These refugees "formed a small village," Gálvez wrote, "to which they gave the name of Gálveztown [villa de Gálvez], asking me not to change the name, since in consideration of their having gathered at this refuse during my governorship they wished by the said name to give indication of their gratitude and a notice of the period of its foundation."[80]. . .

Almost five hundred settlers from Málaga arrived in 1779. Francisco Bouligny conducted them to Bayou Teche, a region already occupied by a few Acadians. A settlement called New Ibera was founded. The new immigrants were treated even more liberally than their predecessors. They received cattle and money, as well as lands, implements, and houses.[81] The new settlers, at the instigation of the government, made serious attempts to raise flax and hemp, but finding the culture difficult they concentrated on cattle raising, an industry for which the region was ideal. The populating of Louisiana proved an expensive undertaking. In 1779, for example, the Louisiana Division of Immigration and Indian Affairs expended 128,568 pesos instead of the 40,000 allowed by the royal budget, and the excess was due chiefly to the influx of settlers.[82]. . .

Other developments in Gálvez' civil administration cannot be taken up in detail, but one deserves special mention. Some of the Spanish officers at New Orleans quite understandably succumbed to the charms of the creole beauties. Jacinto Panis, the adjutant major, implored the king's permission to marry Margarethe Wiltz, widow of Joseph Milhet. . . . Likewise Estevan Miró, sergeant major of the battalion and future governor of the colony, sought and received the king's permission to marry Marie Céleste Elénore de Macarty. Following the good example of his brother officers, Governor Gálvez married Félicie de St. Maxent d'Estréhan, the widow of Jean Baptiste Honoré d'Estréhan.[83]

By all accounts they were a very happy couple; certainly the marriage enchanced Gálvez' popularity and political appeal as well as his financial standing. The Louisianians were flattered that their governor selected a daughter of the colony to be his wife. Nor was the charm and winsomeness of Doña Félicie of merely local appeal; she won just as enthusiastic approval in Mexico City and was one of the chief factors in her husband's great popularity there as viceroy.

In administering the domestic affairs of Louisiana, Gálvez deserves credit for a few outstanding accomplishments. The various measures by which the commerce of the colony was taken out of

English hands and turned over in large part to the French constituted an important reform. As superintendent of immigration he brought about a more enduring improvement. His most noteworthy service to Spain, however, was the intangible one of captivating the creoles by his policies, his marriage, and his personal charm. . . .

Throughout the years in which he sought solutions for Louisiana's domestic problems, Gálvez was rendering important though unostentatious assistance to the patriots in the American Revolution. In view of the spectacular campaigns of George Rogers Clark, and of the inconspicious but momentous work of Oliver Pollock, the two Americans most instrumental in securing the trans-Alleghany region for the United States, it would be folly to claim for Gálvez entire credit for the success of the Revolution in the West. It is justifiable, however, to include him with Clark and Pollock in a triumvirate to which the honors are due. Much of Gálvez' assistance was given before Spain had entered the war against England.

Of course, Spain took a lively interest in the Revolution from the start. Her Louisiana officials in particular were directed to submit in full and frequent reports whatever echoes of the struggle reached them. Her policy, nevertheless, was not very clearly defined; and Unzaga, lacking specific instructions, was in a quandary about how he ought to treat the various Tories and Rebels with whom he came in contact. In all probability he would have followed a policy of strict neutrality had it not been for the influence of Oliver Pollock, an Irish-American who deserves further introduction.

In Louisiana Pollock had the initial advantage of a personal friendship with O'Reilly. He had met the general at Havana, being introduced by Father Butler, and their mutual Irish extraction and Pollock's mastery of the Spanish language had done the rest.[84] Their friendship was cemented, after both had come to New Orleans, by the American's generosity in relieving the danger of famine there. Pollock's favorable position continued after O'Reilly's departure. "It is notorious," General [James] Wilkinson stated some years later, "that Mr. Pollock's connection with the Spanish officers, at New Orleans, was the most intimate, and his influence boundless, from the administration of Governor O'Reilly to that of Governor Miro."[85]. . .

From the outset of hostilities between England and her colonies Pollock was an ardent partisan of the latter. . . . He has been likened to Robert Morris and called the western Financier of the Revolution. He faced herculean tasks in establishing American credit at New Orleans so that there would be financial support for the three major American activities in the West: the supply service, Willing's expedition, and Clark in Illinois. . . .

The exploits of George Rogers Clark are a familiar story.[86] Weary of the constant danger of British-Indian attacks on the trans-Alleghany settlements of Virginia, Clark had journeyed to the state capital to get permission to strike at the root of the trouble. On January 2, 1778, Governor Patrick Henry gave him a colonel's commission and secretly authorized him to raise a force of three hundred and fifty men for an attack on Kaskaskia. . . .

On the night of July 4 they took Kaskaskia by surprise. While one division surrounded the town, Clark and the rest of the troops entered the open gate of the fort, captured in his bedroom the Frenchman Rocheblave, commander for the English, and without firing a shot secured the town's submission. By daylight all the inhabitants were disarmed. . . .

Vincennes was the next objective. Doubting his ability to take the place by force, Clark resorted to a ruse. "I pretended," he admitted later, "that I was about to send an Express to the falls of the Ohio for a Body of Troops to Join me at a certain place in order to attact it."[87] The French of Kaskaskia, not knowing there were only ten men at the falls, were anxious to save their neighbors and kinsmen from injury. Father Gibault offered to go in person to persuade them to accept American control. Clark consented; and so did the people of Vincennes. Thus, without a single life being lost, Clark had secured control of the region north of the Ohio. . . .

A great deal of Clark's success is attributable to his intrepid leadership and to the fortitude of his followers. His men endured many hardships; they got along at times on very short rations; they suffered for lack of clothing, being "often barefoot, and at times almost naked."[88] But there is an irreducible minimum of food and clothing that soldiers must have. . . .

Virginia had sponsored his expedition, but her resources were so depleted by the burden of supplying Washington's army that she could give to Clark little more than moral assistance. The French creoles of Illinois helped considerably by donating supplies; the Cahokians contributed one-fifth of their live stock, and the people of Vincennes furnished powder for the assault on the fort.[89] But Clark's chief reliance was upon Pollock and Gálvez at New Orleans. . . . During September Pollock sent Clark goods amounting to

$7200, and just before the attack on Vincennes five hundred pounds of powder and some swivels were received.[90]

Not only did Clark receive essential supplies from Pollock and Gálvez; he also depended on them for credit to meet most of the bills of his commissary department. This financial support enabled the Americans to retain control of the territory north of the Ohio. Clark did not begrudge Pollock recognition of this essential aid. "The invoice Mr. Pollock rendered upon all occasions in paying those bills," he declared, "I considered at the Time and now to be one of the happy circumstances that enabled me to keep Possession of that Country."[91]. . .

To meet Clark's drafts proved to be Pollock's most difficult problem. . . . His first recourse was to the governor of Louisiana, and Gálvez was generous in putting government funds at his disposal. . . . These funds, Pollock testified later, were received "as very secret service money" for the use of the United States but chiefly on his own credit, and they were delivered usually at night by Juan Morales, Gálvez's private secretary.[92] Liberal though Gálvez was in advancing government funds, American needs could not have been met if Pollock had not made use of his personal fortune and credit. He did so without stint so long as he possessed either, and he succeeded in paying Clark's drafts at par in New Orleans when Continental currency was worth only twelve cents on the dollar in the East.[93]. . .

While Spain was still neutral, Gálvez played an important part in the American Revolution. He facilitated American shipping by sea and up the river. He cooperated with Pollock in sending essential supplies to Washington's army and to the army of the West. In conjunction with Pollock he was the financial backer of the expedition that won the Northwest. To assistance from New Orleans is largely attributable the establishment of American control west of the Alleghanies. American appreciation of Gálvez' help was expressed several times but never more happily than when Pollock, because of Gálvez' services dating from January, 1777, expressed a desire to have his portrait made for Congress.[94]. . .

In relation to the history of the United States, it suffices perhaps to know that this assistance was given, but in relation to the history of Louisiana the motive for the aid is of importance. Most emphatically the aid was not an end in itself. Had this been so we would be compelled to label it a quixotic action — the purposeless encouragement of a revolution that was to be an inspiration for the revolt of the Spanish colonies. Rather it was a by-product of Spain's persistent policy of opposing the English along the Mississippi frontier. In the Revolutionary War Spain saw an opportunity to make a new application of the *divide et impera* principle, a principle that she had occasionally used with good effect in Indian control. This was the spirit that prompted Gálvez to assist the Americans. . . .

At the end of the war Louisiana found herself the beneficiary of a relaxation in trade regulation. . . . [Gálvez] convinced the court that Louisiana's existence as well as her prosperity depended upon a trade that Spain was totally unable to provide. England or the United States could furnish it, but to grant to either of these nations privileges in Louisiana would nullify the gains of the war. Instead, Spain should turn to her Catholic and absolutist ally, France, and countenance commerce between Louisiana and her former mother country.[95]. . .

Acting upon Gálvez advice Spain announced that for a decade Louisiana and West Florida would be permitted to trade with France and under certain conditions with the French West Indies. There were a few minor qualifications, such as a 6 per cent duty on imports and exports and a 2 per cent duty on exports to other Spanish colonies, but the privilege of direct trade with a foreign nation was absolutely unprecedented in Spanish colonial practice.[96]

Immediately after the cessation of hostilities Gálvez returned to Spain. In the correspondence incident to his departure are some indications of the cordial relationship existing between him and the people under his jurisdiction. He took this opportunity to thank the Louisianians for urging the king to honor him with the title of Viscount of Gálveztown. Of the "gold fleur-de-lis on field of blue" that the king had approved for his coat of arms he was especially proud. . . . Gálvez was in Spain from September, 1783, until October, 1784. During these months Spain was formulating the policies that were to prevail on her new Mississippi and Florida frontiers. The questions of recognition of the United States, of the Florida boundary, of the use of the Mississippi, of American immigration into Spanish territory, of relations with the Southeastern Indians — these were some of the problems arising. Through his experience Gálvez was well fitted to give advice on these questions, and he was called upon frequently.[97]

Late in 1784 Gálvez returned to America, coming to Havana as captain general of Cuba and retaining also the governorship of

Louisiana and the Floridas. He was at Havana only a short while.[98] ... Upon the death of his father, Matías de Gálvez, he was sent to Mexico City to succeed him as Viceroy of New Spain.... Together with his wife and their three children he arrived at Vera Cruz on May 21, 1785,... and... was received at Mexico City on January 17.[99]

McGILLIVRAY OF THE CREEKS

The London *Gentleman's Magazine* in August, 1793, carried an unusual obituary notice. Its columns headed "Marriages and Deaths of Considerable Persons" were ordinarily reserved for the blue-bloods of royalty and nobility and for those most distinguished in politics, war, or wealth. In this issue its mark of distinction was accorded a young Indian chief who had died at far-away Pensacola in the Spanish province of West Florida; a young half-breed, who in the tongue of his mother and his people was called Hoboi-Hili-Miko, the Good Child King, and in the language of his father and historians, Alexander McGillivray.

To the best of our knowledge no likeness of McGillivray exists. Tradition, as Pickett was able to discover it eighty-five years ago, described him as "tall, rather slender, and of a constitution by no means robust." Several observers mention the gravity of his bearing and the immobility of his expression, typical Indian traits, so it seemed to them. He was noted for unbounded hospitality and for sparkling conversation whenever his interest was aroused. "He is decent," said caustic Fisher Ames, "and not very black." Long, tapering fingers, with which he could write at prodigious speed, piercing eyes, and an abnormally broad and high forehead are the other features that must suggest the rest of the portrait.[1]...

Among the indisputable facts about McGillivray are several indictive of the handicaps under which he labored. He was not endowed with all the heroic attributes. His health was persistently bad. His letters are interspersed with references to gout and rheumatism, splitting headaches, and confinement in bed for weeks on end. Once he wrote that he was afraid that he would lose all his fingernails. On another occasion he received from his friend the Governor at New Orleans a package of Olvenza's famous powder, a venereal specific. The incontestable fact that much of his ill health was traceable to social disease may deprive him of certain sympathy. Others will find it all the more to his credit that he achieved in spite of serious physical handicaps. He was often so weakened that he could not mount a horse, so stiffened by rheumatism that he could not grasp a quill, so racked by pain that he could not enter into conversation or exercise his full powers in the administration of tribal business.

In practically all Indian tribes, chiefs were chosen by some sort of merit system, though often in conjunction with what amounted to hereditary nomination of eligible candidates. Hence it followed, since military and religious power were the abilities considered most valuable, that few chiefs in aboriginal America could not boast at least one of these qualifications; for example, Joseph of the Nez Percés, Gerónimo of the Apaches, and Caupolicán of the Araucanians are well-known warrior chiefs, and Montezuma of the Azetecs was a typical priest-chief. But McGillivray possessed neither martial prowess nor supernatural power. The fact that the Creeks accepted him as head of their nation demonstrates at once the sagacity of the tribe and the remarkable qualities of McGillivray which led to such a departure from precedent. . . .

McGillivray made early discovery that he did not possess the military virtues. Having found himself out (and herein lies one of the secrets of his success) he seems to have wasted no time or energy in trying to remake himself along more warlike lines. Actual military operations he left to others, such as Red Shoes, Mad Dog, or Milfort, while he concentrated upon affairs of state.

Most historians affirm that McGillivray's worst handicap was his mixed parentage. A single writer applauded the union of civilized and savage strains in McGillivray as "the most felicitous compound of the kind ever seen,"[2] but the general opinion is that this was a serious drawback. No apologist has denied that he came of a Scotch father and a French and Indian mother. There has been a tendency to attribute some of his shortcomings to a mestizo's inevitable emotion instability and psychic dualism.

Our language contains several words that may be applied to a person of mixed blood: half-breed, half-blood, half-caste, hybrid, mestizo, miscegenate, mongrel. Not one is complimentary. The implication is obvious. The tendency with regard to McGillivray has been, naturally enough, to commiserate him for the bad luck of his racial admixture. Yet the sociologists, to the best of my knowledge, have found no tangible proof that the offspring of mixed unions are physically or mentally inferior. Such persons, however, often encounter very serious social difficulties. Had McGillivray attempted to live in an Anglo-American community, it is altogether likely that he would have found his Indian blood and characteristics a handicap. He chose instead to live in the Creek Nation where a different set of mores functioned. . . . In Creek society he was on the same footing as everyone else. Accepted as a normal person, he had full opportunity to live his life, an equal among his peers. . . .

Alexander's father, Lachlan McGillivray, had been one of the later agents in making available to the Creeks the benefits of Old World civilization. As a youth he had migrated from Scotland, arriving at Charleston with the traditional one shilling in his pocket. The frontier naturally beckoned him. He fell in almost immediately with a group of fellow Scots in deerskin attire who were about to set out with a pack train for the Indian country. There his first venture in private trade was to barter his jackknife for pelts. With this capital and with the wages for his work, Lachlan bought trade goods on his own account, and persisted in the business to which chance opportunity had led him. Hard work and thrifty and canniness in trade were then the sure road to success. By the time the American Revolution broke out, Lachlan had pyramided his shilling and jackknife into a very respectable fortune. He had liquid assets that enabled him to retire to Scotland, he had other wealth in the Creek Nation, and in addition there was $100,000 in real property which the patriots of Georgia confiscated. The date of Lachlan's migration to America is not precisely known. Evidence points, however, towards 1738, the same year that William Johnson left Ireland for the Iroquois country of western New York. The coincidence is appropriate, because the two men developed along parallel lines. Both became wealthy. Both came to live among the Indians, the one at Mount Johnson on the Mohawk River, the other at Little Tallassie on the Coosa. Both earned the respect and confidence of the Indians. Both had Indian wives and half-breed children whom they proudly acknowledged. Both rendered signal service to Britain in the French and Indian War, Johnson at the head of the Mohawk forces at Crown Point, McGillivray in keeping the Creeks from going over to the French side. Johnson, to be sure, attained the greater fame. He was knighted in 1755. . . . Lachlan's only approach to such glorification was when James Adair strongly recommended him for the superintendency of the southern Indians and dedicated to him his *History of the American Indians,* which appeared in London in 1775.

Lachlan McGillivray passed on several things to his son. First of all he gave him his name. This may seem a very obvious thing to have done. Yet in Anglo-American society, even in the colonial period, racial prejudice had great weight. Any man who was openly a squaw-man and who accepted his half-breed children lost a certain amount of caste. One wonders, for example, what remonstrances Lachlan's mixed marriage elicited from his ministerial and Calvinist cousin, the Reverend Farquhar McGillivray of Charleston.

The plantation at Little Tallassie was another tangible legacy from his father.[3] This site, near the ruins of the old French Fort Toulouse, became Lachlan's headquarters soon after he moved into the Creek Nation. As a trader he was, of course, heartily welcomed by the Indians. The red men as a race have been just as consistent in welcoming those who brought them the boon of trade as in resisting the farming folk who came to encroach upon their hunting grounds. Lachlan subsequently became a planter as well as a trader, but the Creeks did not object, because his agriculture seemed to be an afterthought, a whim that he indulged as a sideline to the fur trade. Little Tallassie was no Mount Vernon. It included the "Apple Grove" which Lachlan set out. There came to be a complement of Negro slaves, and its masters enjoyed many of the amenities of life as did other country gentlemen of the Old South. The Indian town of Otciapofa, however, was always hard by, and the plantation never entirely lived down its trading post past. . . .

Alexander's mother was the famous Sehoy Marchand. Her French name harked back to the early days of Fort Toulouse.[4] This outpost thrown into the Indian country four hundred miles upstream from Mobile had been established primarily for the control of the Creek trade. Yet unlike its contemporary outposts in the Mississippi Valley and west of the Great Lakes, it had at first a definite military and missionary tinge. . . . That Toulouse began with soldiers and Jesuits instead of mere traders is a fact of considerable moment in the McGillivray genealogy. Thus was the stage set for the convergence of the French and Indian lines of his family tree. One of the first officers at the fort, a certain Captain Marchand, fell in love with a belle of Otciapofa and took her to wife. Sehoy was their daughter.

When Lachlan McGillivray reached the banks of the Coosa, Fort Toulouse was a crumbling ruin, and Captain Marchand was long since dead. His daughter Sehoy was blossoming into the full beauty of womanhood. Such descriptions of this maid as have come down to us are tantalizingly vague. One of the exasperations of historical study is that the analyst, while preserving the lifeless important, have let slip through their fingers the illuminating and personable trivia. We can chance it that Sehoy was brunette. How copper-hued is another matter. Sparkling, vivacious, bewitching are adjectives customarily bestowed upon her, but perhaps on no surer foundation than that her father was French.

For lack of a direct description, and on the principle of "like mother like daughter," we may insert a sketch of one of Sehoy's daughters, "a pretty girl, clad in a short silk petticoat, her chemise of fine linen clasped with silver, her ear-rings and bracelets of the same metal, and with bright-colored ribbons in her hair."[5] These words of Milfort's betray a truly Parisian interest in clothes, but Milfort fell in love with the girl, too, and made her his wife.

Sehoy had exerted much the same charm over Lachlan McGillivray. As to how they met, the nature of the courtship, and the particulars of the marriage ceremony, the records are distressingly blank. In all probability there was an Indian wedding ceremony. Sehoy's family connections were so powerful that no struggling young trader would antagonize them by flouting tribal customs. A second strong probability is that the marriage did not occur during the first months of Lachlan's residence among the Creeks. At the outset he was too poor to have been able to finance the marriage "purchase" from Sehoy's clansmen and clanswomen. . . .

Proper courtship was by proxy. The man sent his talk, together with some presents, to the lady of his choice. If she looked with favor upon the proposal, the proxy asked the consent of her clanspeople: her maternal uncles and aunts and her brothers. Her father of course had no voice in the matter since he was not a member of her clan. Lachlan doubtless proposed in this fashion, employing some woman friend as his proxy since he had no clanswoman in the nation. . . .

The actual marriage ceremony was engagingly simple. Before the proper witnesses the groom broke an ear of corn and gave half to his bride, or they exchanged reeds which were kept as a sort of marriage certificate. It was customary, too, for the groom to give his bride a piece of venison, and for her to give him an ear of corn. An essential part of the ceremony was performed by the girl's uncle, who conducted the couple to the bed that had been prepared for them and said, "This is your bed. Lie in it." Except for dancing and feasting this was the entire ritual. For a month, however, the groom was not supposed to have much to do with his new in-laws, or to be with his wife during the daytime.[6]

Such a marriage was binding — until the Green Corn Dance. Then, if either party was dissatisfied, the match could be called off. Neither Lachlan nor Sehoy exercised this option. By all reports they were a happy couple all the years of Lachlan's residence among the Creeks.

From the historical standpoint the culmination of Lachlan's and Sehoy's idyllic romance was in the birth of Alexander. This great event did not excite enough immediate attention to insure the recording of the day or month. There has even been gross miscalculation of the year, which was in actuality 1759. . . . But notwithstanding this apparent neglect, Alexander was not dismissed as just another papoose, for during her pregnancy Sehoy had dreamed of paper and ink and quills, a forecast, it seemed, that her son was to be an extraordinary Creek.

According to tribal customs a father had little to do with the upbringing of his children, or more properly his wife's children. Lachlan may have taken a Scotch interest in his young son, but the meager evidence that exists indicates that Alexander in his childhood was almost entirely under his mother's supervision. Her oversight was probably supplemented by that of the *tawa,* or maternal uncle, who was the proper person to inject the masculine note into child training. . . .

The Creeks had no formalized education. They had no schools. Yet the opinion that children were allowed to grow up unrestrained, undisciplined, and untutored is largely due to the surprise of white visitors over the sparing of the rod. As a matter of fact these little savages were made aware of the inexorable thou-shalts and thou-shalt-nots of the society in which they were to live. They learned to use the tools which their race had found indispensable. What more should we ask of elementary education? . . .

Alexander's report cards are not on file. But if we may judge by his later record, he did not lead the class in archery, and while he may have been manager of the boy's ball team he doubtless was not its playing captain. Similar reasoning suggests that these were happy years, because a short time later when a choice offered, Alexander unhesitatingly returned to the scenes of his childhood.

In Alexander's fourteenth year, according to the traditional chronology, his father prevailed on Sehoy to permit her son's being sent off to school. Sometime in 1773, then, he left the nation for Charleston. It was the same year that a better known band of "Indians" descended upon a tea ship in Boston harbor.

Charleston was then three years past its centennial. It was the one "city" south of the Potomac, the metropolis of the lower South, and had a population of perhaps eleven thousand. A materialist would stress its unpaved streets, foul and ill-smelling, its unsanitary neglect of sewage, its annual epidemics of smallpox. Reverend Jedidiah Morse in his *American Geography* (1789) came nearer catching the spirit of the place, "In no part of America," he wrote, "are the social blessings enjoyed more rationally and liberally than in Charleston. Unaffected hospitality, affability, ease in manners and address, and a disposition to make their guests welcome, easy and pleased with themselves, are characteristic of the respectable people of Charleston." Charleston was the logical place for young Alexander's schooling, the more so since his cousin, Reverend Farquhar McGillivray of the Presbyterian church, had agreed to be his tutor.

It is a temptation to dwell on the sociological readjustments that Alexander must have had to make. Going off to school is an experience to any youngster who has a home to leave. For Alexander it must have been a much sharper transition. He stepped from one plane of civilization to another. The actual distance was only a few hundred miles, but he left behind the language of his youth, the customs, conventions, and usages to which he was accustomed. His cousin's utmost kindness could not have eliminated all the bewildering confusion.

Greek and Latin, English history and literature are listed as the studies Alexander pursued. How assiduously is not known; his letters seem not to contain a single Latin phrase or a classical or literary allusion. But he did become a very skillful penman, perhaps with the assistance of some preliminary instruction from his father, and he attained a literary style that could not have been based exclusively upon Indian models of conversation and oratory. For a brief period he was at Savannah in the countinghouse of Samuel Elbert, subsequently a governor of Georgia. This work proving distasteful, study was resumed at Charleston.

Again it was interrupted, and this time permanently, by the Revolution. Lachlan McGillivray was an ardent loyalist. The Georgia patriots honored him by placing his name at the head of the proscription list, whereupon Lachlan and his son went home, the one to Scotland, the other to the land of the Creeks. Father and son corresponded as occasion offered, and there is mention of yearly presents, yet one suspects that Lachlan was not anxious to take his half-caste son with him to Scotland. On the Coosa, however, Alexander was most welcome. Because of his mother's position in the powerful Wind clan he was eligible to be a lesser chief, and this rank was promptly accorded him.

The British soon commissioned him colonel and made him one of their agents to maintain the loyalty of the Creeks. It was a congenial task, especially in view of his animosity toward the Americans who had proscribed his father and many intimate friends, and who had confiscated family property valued at more than $100,000. As colonel and Indian agent he was one of the chief factors in securing the British unfaltering support from the Creeks during the war.

His presence with Indian auxiliaries helped delay the fall of Pensacola in 1781.[7] The next year he arrived in the Chickasaw country just after Colbert had seized several Spaniards in reprisal for the punishment of the leaders in the Natchez rebellion. Colbert was hazy as to methods but not at all reticent. He talked very freely to his prisoners and boasted about his plans. McGillivray's first act was to advise Colbert to hold his tongue. Then he drew up a "Parole of Honour," whereby the prisoners were permitted to go to New Orleans on their pledge that the nine Natchez prisoners would be set free. He also penned a vigorous letter to the governor of Louisiana, stressing the humanity and consideration of Colbert's procedure, and protesting against "a matter that is prevalent in West Florida, particularly at Mobill, that is offering Great rewards to Indians for the Heads of particular Men in the Indian Country." In this affair he demonstrated more sagacity and incisiveness of mind than any of the other leaders.[8]

McGillivray's work and that of the Southeastern Indians was only incidental in the war, which was won and lost on more distant battlefields. He was merely one of many Creek chiefs, and his reputation purely local. The period of the Revolution, in fact, may be regarded as essentially an apprenticeship for the work that was to engage him subsequently. . . .

McGillivray's work will be best understood if displayed in relief against the background of Creek tribal history. . . . In his day the Creeks occupied the western part of the modern state of Georgia and the northern part of Alabama. For Indian neighbors they had the Seminoles on the southeast, the Choctaws and Chickasaws to the west, and the Cherokees on the north. Their land was fairly extensive, but Creek title to it was clouded by the white's habit of divorcing ownership and sovereignty. A land map would properly show a block of Creek territory as large as a modern state. Political maps assigned the area to England up to 1783 and afterwards to Spain and the United States.

In the late eighteenth century the Creeks are estimated to have numbered about 5,000 gunmen. If anything, the figure is too large. Later figures are smaller and so are earlier ones. Even the least of the American states possessed greater man power. But in comparison with the northern tribes this was a large number; the Creeks in fact were as numerous as any north of Mexico. . . .

The Muskogean group, consisting of the Creeks and their immediate neighbors, is sometimes dignified by the title Confederation. Yet as an effective governmental unit it fell far short of the famous Six Nations of the Iroquois League, and still farther short of the Aztec and Inca Empires. Except briefly under the genius of McGillivray, this so-called Confederation had never functioned. In fact, rather than emphasizing the Confederation, a nearer approach to the truth would be to think of the Creek Nation as consisting of several score tribes, usually called towns, which were regarded as the largest natural units. The old Greek conception of confederacies as a sort of artificial superstructure on the natural units, the city-states, is a very close parallel.

In many other particulars, cultural development among the Creeks had stopped at a rather low level. They practiced agriculture, raising fair crops of maize, squashes, and pumpkins. From the whites on their borders they had acquired a mild interest in cattle raising. Yet these "civilized" pursuits were secondary to hunting. The hunt, of course, had a special significance because of the trade value of deerskins and other peltries. It also contributed the major portion of the food supply. A clue to its volume is to be found in the division of labor between the sexes. The men, according to several eighteenth century observers, rode about, stretched out at their ease, amused themselves with a pipe or a whistle, engaged in the ball play or in various dances, went on war parties, and hunted. Squaws' work, on the other hand, included "cultivation of the soil and almost every other domestic drudgery.". . .

Nevertheless, the Creeks were not entirely devoid of Southern chivalry. "You may depend upon my assertion," said . . . [an] early visitor, "that there is no people any where who love their women more than these Indians do, or men of better understanding in distinguishing the merits of the oppositive sex, or more faithful in rendering suitable compensation." . . . Two tribal customs made women especially influential. One was that the care and control of pre-adolescent children was in their hands. The other was that, although women had practically no place in religious or governmental ceremonies, descent was in the female line and so also was reckoned eligibility for office. Thus McGillivray was eligible for a chieftaincy at Otciapofa through the fact that his mother was a member of the Wind clan.[9]. . .

For the Creeks the Treaty of Paris marked the end of an epoch, an epoch in which the bow had given way to the gun, the canoe to pack animals, the earthenware bowl to the copper kettle, the stone knife to one of steel, and in which simple aboriginal tastes had been supplanted by a preference for European shirts and blankets, a penchant for glass beads, ribbons, and other foreign gewgaws, and a craving for hard liquor. French fur traders had been largely responsible. The French would be missed more than the Spaniards.

Fortunately for the Creeks, England recognized responsibility as well as opportunity in her newly acquired monopoly of eastern North America. The famous proclamation line of 1763, beyond which settlers were not to go "for the present," was primarily a device to protect the Indians. England appointed capable superintendents to handle Indian affairs, Johnson in the north and Adkins and Stuart in the south, and there was sufficient competition among her merchants to keep trade goods at reasonably low prices. No better proof is needed of England's good treatment than the loyalty of the Southeastern Indians to her throughout the Revolutionary War. The American patriots did not succeed in detaching any important Indian groups, nor did Spain a little later when she entered the war against England.

The outbreak of the Revolution ushered in a new period of international rivalry in the Southeast. Spain made the recovery of the Floridas her principal American war aim, overshadowed only by the desire to recapture Gibraltar. The brilliant campaigns of Bernardo de Gálvez won the Floridas and set the stage for Spanish efforts to extend control over the Indian country at least as far north as the Tennessee. The treaties terminating the war necessarily took into account these Spanish conquests on the lower Mississippi and in the Floridas, because they had made England's position east of the Mississippi untenable. England accordingly partitioned that vast area between Spain and the United States, with some measure of injustice shunting the lion's share toward the latter.[10]

Thus it happened that the Creeks in 1783 found themselves between a new pair of neighbors: in the Floridas and Louisiana the Spaniards, who had never satisfactorily supplied the trading needs of the Indians; in Carolina and Georgia, the Americans, whose trading capacity was unproved but whose land hunger was notorious. The Creeks faced a double predicament. England had abandoned her erstwhile allies without making any provision for the trade that was so essential to them. She had also signed away the Indian territory with no regard for tribal titles. With one or the other of their recent adversaries the Creeks must arrange for a satisfactory trade and recognition of Creek sovereignty. In tribal history so serious a problem was unprecedented. . . .

Even before England had completed the formalities of signing away her claims to the Creek country and its adjacent gulf and Atlantic coasts, McGillivray began to put out feelers to see if Spanish trade and support could be secured. There were several reasons why a Spanish connection seemed preferable to an American one: most of these reasons are brought out clearly in McGillivray's early letters to the governors of Pensacola and New Orleans. A personal reason had to do with the persecution of his father and many of his friends by the patriots in the states. Under the circumstances it was easier to turn to the other recent enemy, Spain, than to the Americans.

The restlessness of the American frontiersmen and their propensity for encroaching upon the land of the Indians was a most powerful argument against the United States. McGillivray had no confidence that the American government would be able to restrain these land-hungry backwoodsmen. Spain, on the other hand, might see that it was worth her while to assist the Creeks to preserve their lands from unsurpation by these Americans. For Spain's possessions in America were similarly endangered, and her logical defense was to strengthen the Indian nations as buffer provinces against the expanding Americans. . . .

From the standpoint of convenience, Pensacola was the most eligible town through which to supply the Creek Nation. McGillivray had geography in mind when he asserted that for protector of the Creeks no other power was "so fitting as the Master of the Floridas."

Later, it developed that the Americans could supply better trade goods and on better terms than could Spain. But in 1783 there was no positive assurance that this would be the case. American manufactures were entirely inadequate, and there was no guaranty that England would continue to permit the United States to acquire by importation the necessary goods for supplying the Creeks.

But the decisive circumstance seems to have been an arrangement entered into with William Panton.[11] When it appeared that the British were soon to evacuate St. Augustine, the one remaining channel for the Creek supply of English goods, McGillivray approached Panton to urge him to stay and to keep up the Indian trade. Panton agreed, but only on condition that McGillivray associate himself with the trading company and guarantee that it would be safeguarded.

The connection thus established was to prove momentous to both men. One immediate effect upon McGillivray was to deepen his prejudice against the Americans, for Panton had also suffered at the hands of the Georgian patriots and was most vindictive against them. His quaint outburst to [Estevan] Miró that the Americans could not bribe him, not even "Washington himself, had he the thirteen United States in his Belly,"[12] was typical of his spirit. Panton, moreover, saw for himself a financial opportunity if the Creeks became partial to Spain. . . .

McGillivray visited Pensacola in September, 1783. To judge from Governor O'Neill's[13] report of their conversation, he simply requested the establishment of a trade and tendered his services to enlist the friendship of the Creeks. Three months later, when he learned of the signing of the definitive treaty between England and Spain and of the retrocession of the Floridas to Spain, he renewed his petition [in a series of letters]. . . . This time he made the request much more emphatic. . . . McGillivray's letters bore fruit. O'Neill and Miró were ordered, in pursuance of McGillivray's suggestion and their own recommendation, to hold a meeting with the Creeks at Pensacola and with the other Southern tribes at Mobile. They looked upon McGillivray as the principal representative of the Creeks. His earlier letters had not made the claim in just that form. He signed himself merely "A Native and chief of the Creek Nation.". . .

There is no gainsaying that McGillivray's authority was still in the process of growth at the time of the Congress. On the other hand, it must be observed that the English commission as colonel, which he had held for almost eight years previously, raised him above the level of the average chief, that he did not lay claim as yet to absolute power in the nation, and that the Creeks of their own volition designated him their spokesman and principal representative in the negotiation of the treaty.

In two particulars the treaty fell short of McGillivray's hopes. The Spaniards refused to guarantee the Creek territories in full, and agreed merely to protect the Creeks in so far as their lands fell within the Spanish limits. Secondly, they declined to install Panton in the Indian trade at Pensacola and Mobile. That privilege had already been promised the New Orleans firm of Mather and Strother. . . Panton was confirmed in his trading privileges at St. Marks of Apalache, which was all that McGillivray could obtain for him at this time. . . .

In order to attend the Congress of Pensacola, McGillivray had declined a Georgian invitation to Augusta and Savannah. But though the Spaniards carried off first honors in the competition for the support of the Creeks, the Americans did not give up their hopes of persuading the Indians to shift sides.

The Congress of the United States acted in the spring of 1785, appointing five men, the first in a procession of Indian commissioners, to try to negotiate a peace and to cement it by a commercial treaty. Three of these men, Hawkins,[14] Pickens,[15] and Martin,[16] actually undertook to treat with the Creeks. First and last there were a dozen United States commissioners who had dealings with McGillivray. A few of them were miscast as Indian commissioners, but almost without exception they were men who had already distinguished themselves or who were to go on and attain distinction in some public capacity. . . . Yet in the correspondence that they exchanged with McGillivray the advantage lay all with the half-breed. It was he who wrote with most vigor, he who analyzed the issues with greatest clarity, he who determined the course of most of the negotiations, he who had his way in the diplomatic exchanges. . . .

The experiences of the commissioners of 1785-86 indicate clearly the extent to which McGillivray was the factor preventing American success in these negotiations. The commissioners invited the Creeks to meet at Galphinton on the Ogeechee. In his reply,[17] McGillivray applauded the American desire to put matters "on an equitable footing" with the Indian nations but deplored the long delay about making this move. Meanwhile, he added, the Creeks, in view of Georgia's vengeful attitude, had sought and obtained the protection of Spain and the promise of a free trade through the

Floridas; they had determined to use force against the encroaching Georgians, but in deference to the request of the commissioners he would call off the proposed attacks. After remarking that he "could wish that the people of Cumberland shewed an equal good disposition to do what is right," and mentioning their written acknowledgment that they had begun the hostilities, he concluded by censuring the commissioners, though most deferentially, for selecting a horse thief as their messenger. . . .

The Spanish authorities praised McGillivray for the loyalty he had shown to the Treaty of Pensacola by his refusal to meet with the Americans. But when he took the next logical step in the expression of his loyalty, they were slightly taken aback. At a special meeting of the Creeks in March, 1786, the question of American aggressions was considered, and the chiefs decided to resort to arms to expel the invaders from the lands of the nation. McGillivray promptly reported this determination to the governors of St. Augustine, Pensacola, and New Orleans, and called for "the speedy Interposition" promised at Pensacola. This was interpreting the treaty rather loosely, since the war was defensive only on the theory that all land grants since the one to Georgia in 1773 were defective . . . [and] Spain might have insisted upon being consulted before a war was started to expel the Americans.

The governors, however, did not stand on formality. [Vizente Manuel de] Zéspedes at St. Augustine praised "the moderation unexampled among Indians." . . . Pending definite orders from his superiors, he promised that he would issue the customary amounts of powder and ball for "hunting," and larger quantities to those whom McGillivray accredited.[18] O'Neill also began to furnish military stores at once. . . . Miró, however, foresaw embarrassment if the United States learned that Spain was furnishing the Creeks arms and ammunition. . . . He advised O'Neill not to send any written promises to McGillivray. In the meantime, the normal issue of power and ball "for hunting" continued. . . .

The enthusiasm with which the Creeks were waging war against the Georgians and the Cumberland settlers was a . . . valid cause for Spanish uneasiness. With the Indians so manifestly on the aggressive, issuance of arms and ammunition was less logically justifiable as a measure to protect them against American invaders. Spain, furthermore, had no real interest in the aggrandizement of the Creeks; all she wanted was that they should hold their own against the Americans. Now that they were doing considerably more than that, it appeared that Spain had been unnecessarily generous and that economy was indicated.

Early in January, 1788, McGillivray learned from Miró that Spanish support was to be diminished. He immediately wrote to Zéspedes, whose interest had always seemed warmer. Mentioning the recent successes of the Creeks, "My Warriors are Victorious in every quarter over the americans, the people of Cumberland are drove over the Ohio river & the State of Georgia now lays at our Mercy," he expressed his astonishment and regret at Miró's action, remarked that the Creeks were engaged in a war not entirely their own, and requested a prompt answer from the captain general so that he would know what to say to the chiefs when they assembled in April.[19]. . .

Curtailment of military supplies did not occasion an immediate crisis, because Georgia and Cumberland had been partially paralyzed by the attacks just delivered. In Georgia, furthermore, a contention raged over whether Congress had any right to interfere in its conduct toward the Indians. But in view of the uncertain Spanish support, McGillivray returned equivocal answers to two emissaries from Cumberland and to Pickens and Mathews, who proposed a settlement of the Georgia issue. He promised the latter that hostilities would be suspended but insisted on evacuation of the Creek lands as a necessary preliminary to peace. Meanwhile, he appealed again to Miró and to Spain for renewed support. . . .

Succor came from an unexpected quarter. A young man arrived on the Florida Coast, announcing tht he had been sent out from England by a charitable society which had heard of the distress of the Creeks and sent a present of powder and ball for their relief. McGillivray accepted without hesitation. Subsequently, when he was called to task by the Spaniards for having broken faith with them, he insisted that there was nothing out of the way in an Indian accepting gifts from anyone who wanted to present them. . . . Governor O'Neill, in his impatience, was ready to credit two most improbable charges. The first was that when McGillivray and Panton met at Apalache . . . , they determined to invite this assistance from the Bahama Islands. The second was that McGillivray planned to unite with this stranger and his few followers in making an attack upon Pensacola.

The real backers of the expedition were Lord Dunmore, better known as the last colonial governor of Virginia but at this time governor of the Bahama Islands, and a certain John Miller . . . of the firm of Miller and Bonamy of Nassau. Miller had a grudge against Spain for certain damages incurred during the investment of Nassau in 1782 and another grudge against Panton, Leslie and Company.[20]

As their agent, Miller and Dunmore selected William Augustus Bowles, a young adventurer who had plied the trades of soldier, painter, actor, and gambler. What particularly recommended him for this enterprise was that, after he had been drummed out of the loyalist garrison of Pensacola during the Revolution, he had gone off to live with the Lower Creeks and Seminoles. He knew the country and the Indian tongue and could promise that Miller's goods would be warmly received. The idea was to win the good will of the Indians by presents and then gradually to wean them away from Panton and the Spaniards.

McGillivray went to the Lower Towns to see this "stranger," and discovered to his surprise not a stranger but his old associate Bowles, whom he had known at Pensacola. McGillivray was ready to accept him as what he purported to be, but in spite of persistent questioning he could not elicit much information about Bowles's designs or backers. He was happy to hear, however, that Bowles planned to return to the Bahamas for additional Indian presents. Thus the matter rested, and McGillivray returned home. . . .

No sooner had he begun to feel a trifle easier about the American danger because of the arms and ammunition that Bowles supplied than he had a new problem to face, that of regaining the confidence of the Spaniards. Gradually additional information came to light about Bowles and the purpose of his expedition. Colonel [Thomas] Brown, formerly the Indian superintendent in Florida for the English, wrote a long letter to Zéspedes, telling him all that he had been able to learn at Nassau. O'Neill took declarations from several traders, and investigators sent by Zéspedes to the Mosquito Coast discovered still other facts. But though it became clear that the project was directed especially against Panton and his trade, McGillivray was insistent that Bowles should not be harmed: "Having had some personal acquaintance with him when in Garrison at Pensacola last war, I can't treat him as a felon, but will give him wholsom advice & dismiss him."[21]

When Bowles got back to Florida in November, 1788, he brought a few horseloads of ammunition, a few small brass cannon, and just enough cloth to trade for food for the thirty-odd men of his expedition. The Indians were grievously disappointed that his bold promises of presents were so skimpily fulfilled. Not long after they landed, twenty-six of his men deserted and surrendered themselves to the Spanish commandant on the St. Johns. They said that they did so because they learned that Bowles planned to use them in an attack on one of Panton's stores. McGillivray suggested that the wet weather discouraged them. Bowles later asserted that his men were lazy and cowardly and that their story was fabricated to curry Spanish favor. At any rate, Bowles's party fel to pieces, McGillivray and the Indians turned against him, and early in 1789 he left the nation.

McGillivray was worse off for Bowles's coming. The small presents received were more than offset by the bitter suspicions that were aroused and by O'Neill's persistent efforts to undermine his authority over the Creeks. . . .

In the meantime, McGillivray had to carry on a correspondence with various American commissioners. A truce with the Cumberland people gave him a brief breathing spell on that frontier. Commissioners Pickens and Mathews were joined by a United States delegate, Richard Winn, but they got no further than to appoint a meeting for the spring of 1789. Fortunately for McGillivray, the American commissioners were merely marking time until the Constitution should be adopted, when the new government was expected to handle Indian affairs with a firmer grasp. . . .

The commissioners were prompt to notify McGillivray when the new government took effect. "We are now governed by a President who is like the old King over the great water," they wrote. "He Commands all the Warriors of the thirteen great fires."[22]. . . McGillivray, however, did not meet these commissioners in June. He excused himself by saying that the Lower Creeks, in view of recent hostilities, strongly advised that negotiations would be useless. A more potent factor probably was the receipt of a new promise of active support from Governor Miró. . . .

At New York in July, Washington, Knox, and Congress gave serious attention to the Creek problem. Knox prepared for the president a long analysis of the possible alternatives, of the probable expenses of a war to chastise the Creeks, and of the steps advisable to settle the issues amicably. Washington incorporated most of Knox's ideas in a message to Congress, which approved it, and on August 29, they were restated in the instructions to Lincoln, Griffin, and Humphreys, who were to proceed at once to Rock Landing on the Oconee, there to treat with the Creeks.[23]. . . They came post haste to Savannah and hurried to the frontier where they arrived just in time for the meeting.

The sequel was farcical. There were the customary formalities, including the ceremony of the black drink. The proposed treaty was read, and McGillivray asked permission to discuss it with the Indian chiefs. He entered objections to the boundary proposed and to the assumption of sovereignty, but the commissioners would make no concessions. . . . McGillivray was insistent that the commissioners make concessions to the Creeks, and Humphreys as insistently refused. At length McGillivray put an end to the wrangling by decamping with his followers. He did not bother to excuse himself or to serve notice of his departure. . . . The commissioners retraced their steps with what grace they could muster. Lincoln hurried on to New England without tarrying at New York to offer any explanation of the report of the expedition. That report most emphatically put the blame upon McGillivray. . . .

Except for the importunate clamorings of the land speculators the winter of 1789-90 was uneventful. As a bid for the active support of her neighbors in her western pretensions, Georgia had made the now famous Yazoo grants. The speculators who held these grants approached various prominent individuals to seek to draw them in. . . . No one, however, was more assiduously courted than McGillivray. His name on the list of directors of a company would serve as a guaranty against Indian attacks and would do much to stimulate land sales. But he turned a deaf ear, protested when his name was used, and reminded these land speculators that the areas in question were claimed by Spain or possessed by the Indians.

This land speculation was directly responsible for the journey of Marinus Willett to the Creek Nation.[24] He came as a special envoy from Washington with a letter from the former commissioner and then United States Senator Benjamin Hawkins. Hawkins mentioned the incredulity with which the report of Lincoln, Griffin, and Humphreys had been received, and his and some others' belief that the commissioners were really at fault. He introduced Willett as a gentleman of honor and urged McGillivray to accept his invitation to come to New York to settle a firm and favorable peace. . . .

The coming of so distinguished a man as Willett was itself an argument in favor of McGillivray's going to New York. Another consideration which Willett probably mentioned and which certainly was stressed at New York was that Spain and England seemed to be on the verge of war over the Nootka question. In such a war Panton's trade would almost certainly break down and Spain might find it impossible to get arms and ammunition to the Creeks, which would leave them in a most embarrassing predicament.

Willett chose rather to emphasize the Yazoo companies and the contest between the United States and Georgia for control of these western lands. To put it badly, he represented that Washington was so anxious to perfect the title of the national government to these lands and to get in ahead of Georgia that he was willing to concede unusually favorable terms to the Creeks. There was diplomatic verbiage, to be sure. Washington was represented as motivated by "justice and humanity," and as the true friend of the Indian. McGillivray doubted Washington's pure magnanimity . . . and believed the president's real end was to restrain the malevolence of the northern and eastern states against the southern. He went to New York because he believed that the situation held promise of advantage for the Creeks. . . .

Willett, McGillivray, and their entourage formed a veritable pageant. Through the wilderness, past Stone Mountain, and Pickens' home at Seneca, they traveled, McGillivray and several others on horseback, twenty-six chiefs and warriors in three wagons, and Willett riding in a sulky. All along the way the delegation was greeted with great interest and McGillivray was feted by the more prominent citizens. . . . From Elizabethtown Point they boarded a sloop for New York, where the newly organized Society of St. Tammany met them in full regalia and escorted them up Wall Street to Federal Hall where Congress was in session, then to the president's house, and finally to the City Tavern, where Governor [George] Clinton and Secretary of War Knox were hosts at dinner. . . .

Negotiations were opened by informal conferences between McGillivray and Henry Knox. When all was ready to draw up the final treaty, Knox was given a regular appointment as commissioner, the Senate at the same time being asked to take note of the secret articles that were to be a part of the convention. The treaty was concluded on August 7, and the ceremonies of signing took place a week later.[25]

The actual treaty was something of a compromise. McGillivray said of it that it was not exactly what he wanted, but about as good a treaty as could be gotten under the circumstances. . . . McGillivray held out against an acknowledgment of American sovereignty except over the parts of the nation that were within the limits of the

United States. The effect of this provision was to make the ultimate disposition of the Creeks depend upon the settlement of the disputed boundary between the United States and Spain. . . . Similarly the boundary laid down between the Creeks and the citizens of the United States was not entirely satisfactory. McGillivray had to relinquish that part of the disputed area on which the Georgians had already settled. To move them out would have been practically impossible. On the other hand, Georgia did not get the boundary set as far west as she had claimed, and the Indians gained a valuable hunting area on the Altamaha. Financial compensation was included for the territorial claims that the Creeks surrendered. Knox strove hard to get an American trade authorized, but McGillivray was true to Panton and would only consent to an arrangement for an emergency trade in case an English war closed the existing channels. . . . Other provisions were of less significance, with the exception of a secret commission of McGillivray as a brigadier with a salary set at $1200 a year. . . .

The Treaty of New York set a precedent in American treaty-making. Frequently thereafter the United States followed the policy of bringing Indian chiefs to the seat of government, partly for the sake of impressing upon them the nation's size, wealth, population, and power.

But though it was "ratified with the signature of Washington and McGillivray," the treaty fell far short of the latter's prediction. The Georgians, naturally enough, fulminated against it as a betrayal of the state, an admission that Georgia had been in the wrong in the entire controversy with the Creeks, and a questionable exercise of the powers entrusted to the central government by the new Constitution. . . . In Congress, Representative James Jackson of Georgia bellowed forth a denunciation of the treaty, which, he said, had "spread alarm among the people of Georgia," had ceded away "three million acres of land guaranteed to Georgia by the Constitution," . . . and, worst of all, had contained secret articles.[26] . . .

The Spaniards and Panton set about immediately to nullify the treaty. Several months passed before they succeeded in getting a complete copy of the treaty as published. . . . Working upon the Indians, . . . they insinuated that McGillivray had been too much influenced by a desire to recover his family property and by the flattery of the Americans. They also took McGillivray to task for the concessions he had made or was said to have made.

His replies were adequate to the occasion. . . . He summed matters up with his customary acumen when he wrote that the Georgians should have been satisfied with the substantial concessions made to them and should have thanked O'Neill and Miró, except for whose urgings he would not have made such sacrifices to "rebellious vagabonds." He mentioned the bitter criticisms that were being made of him and Knox and even of Washington. "I signed the death sentence of the Company of the Yazoo," he continued, "and if our allies and western protectors do not help us greatly, I shall have to accept the title of Emperor of the West, which was offered me on my journey to New York, and which I then refused. On the contrary, I want some rest after so long drawn out a dispute with my neighbors.[27]

Two circumstances, however, militated against his peaceful enjoyment of the results of his statecraft. Throughout the winter his health was very poor. All January he was confined to his fireside as the consequence of a scalded leg, following which his old enemies, rheumatism and fever, took him in charge. It was soon apparent, also, that underneath their surface cordiality the Spaniards were intriguing to undermine his authority over the Indians. They conducted what was virtually a whispering campaign against him and persuaded a substantial minority of the Indians that the Treaty of New York ought not to be put into full effect. . . .

[To combat this hostility McGillivray traveled to New Orleans to visit the new governor, Baron de Carondelet, who was principally responsible for the aggressive tone of Spanish policy.[28] Their conference resulted in the Treaty of 1792, in which some issues of sovereignty, trade, and defense were settled.]

At Mobile on his way home from the conference with the governor, McGillivray contracted a violent fever which did not leave him for a long time. He got back to Little Tallassie early in October, but was still not entirely recovered. "On my first Coming home," he wrote later, "I had so much to do that I could not leave it soon & the Cursed Gout seizing me has laid me up these two months nearly. Every periodical attack grows more Severe & longer in Continuance. It now mounts from my feet to my knees, & am Still Confind to the fire side."[29]. . . . At eleven o'clock on the night of February 17 [, 1793] McGillivray died. . . .

Alexander McGillivray was a striking figure and with all his imperfections was cast in heroic mold. His contemporaries recognized him as a man of parts — head and shoulders above his countrymen and "the very soul of the Creek Nation." Even when he ventured out of the Indian country, as on the trip to New York, he still made a favorable impression. What he could have accomplished on a larger stage and with more substantial forces at his command is a tantalizing question. But it is beside the point, for he was definitely of the Creeks, and his talents peculiarly appropriate to their problems.

Part III

CALIFORNIA

CALIFORNIA

Assigned the task of teaching Pacific Coast history, John W. Caughey had early in his career been confronted with the problem of working up new courses and relating the subject matter to world developments. When his blend of regional and national history seemed appropriate for the study of the coast, and he had published his *History of the Pacific Coast,* he turned to the challenge of interpreting California's past. Here local pageantry, folklore, and a diversity of civilizing elements complicated research, organization of his materials, and writing. Almost every problem connected with the state's growth involved an appreciation of local history and an understanding of contemporary national and international events.

Of necessity Caughey had to be interested in local history, in the activities of Don Benito Wilson, Charles F. Lummis, and William Heath Davis; concerned about Indian lore and diggings, the missions and their secularization, land claims of Indian and conqueror, and the development of family life and customs. But he realized the hazards of becoming immersed in local matters. The most deadly of those perils, he believed, was provincialism — the inability to see the forest for the trees. With an uneasy feeling always present whenever he concentrated his attention on local affairs, he was on guard against the pitfalls of such investigations.

Thus his history of California appropriately begins by emphasizing the impact of the gold rush on the future state's emergence "from comparative obscurity to . . . cynosure of world-wide attention." That dramatic event, Caughey notes, "could not have come at a more opportune time," because it gave restless peoples everywhere an escape to adventure. The gold rush attracted more than two hundred thousand people, qualified California for statehood, and advertised its climate and resources. From that day until this the magic of California's name has drawn millions of people across the plains and deserts. The diversity of population, as during the gold rush, has given the state strong minded, picturesque, and gifted citizens, and always some celebrities.

Though California as a state is younger than Virginia and Massachusetts, its history is older and its population today is greater. While it can count but two United States presidents (and one of them Iowa born), one vice president, and three defeated presidential candidates, in a future count it may well surpass any state on the Atlantic seaboard. Its uniqueness, says Caughey, is its rapid growth; its immediate rise from obscurity to world-wide interest in a year; its continued phenomenal expansion decade after decade. Though California's history has reflected national trends, science and the machine have strongly determined the character of its living standard. The transformation of a semiarid land into a hospitable place to live is itself a miracle of technology. Californians may not always realize that their neighboring states have similar patterns of development, but they are well aware of geographic distances, the cost of importing water across miles of desert, the burden of transportation rates, the variety of agricultural and industrial problems.

To tell the story of California, John Caughey often depended upon others, many of whom were his graduate students and professors. Their names and their contributions to the state's history are infused into his narrative. No single historian, however, wins Caughey's regard in a greater degree than does Hubert Howe Bancroft whose multivolume histories and vast library he treasures. Like other historians who have researched in the Bancroft Library, he expresses his admiration for this industrious man who gathered together such vast information about the West.

Caughey's own *California* was published in 1940, revised and republished in 1953, and is currently undergoing revision. Long admired for its balanced presentation and beauty of language, it follows Herbert Eugene Bolton's theories of interpretation by tracing Spanish colonization from the Caribbean and Mexico into the Pacific area, providing proper emphasis for topographical factors in determining the pattern of settlement, and by pausing appropriately to review the culture of the Indians. The narrative passes easily through the era of exploration, missions, and initial settlement, sketching a story that involves Spain and Mexico in the management of a frontier colony. Then it discusses California as a market for New England traders and as an object for exploration by the mountain men. The slow process of penetration is interrupted by the Mexican-American War, annexation, and the discovery of gold. If *Gold is the Cornerstone,* as Caughey insists, so also is the willingness of the gold seekers to stay in California and make it their home. Then the riches from wheat, corn, fruit trees, cattle raising, and real estate drew even more people. Each decade saw a spread of settlers across the state so that expanding railroads, cheap land, disappointment, social conflict, good climate, great resources, and adventurous people together played parts in forming its spirit and character.

The new technology has made possible industry, jobs, and homes for the successive waves of population. While advances in communication have drawn the state closer to the East, thus minimizing the harmful affects of distance from centers of power, new industries like synthetics, assembly plants, space research, and electronics have given California a production and manufacturing base that rivals most eastern states. At the same time, California has retained the entertainment industry, its glamour as a vacation land, and its diversified agricultural production. The state in mid century, in Caughey's final chapters, may be faced with social and political crises, but the industrial activity, population expansion, and restless progress continue unabated. The closing lines of his *California* may illustrate best his theme: "The essence of California history has been change upon change. The legacy which past generations hand on to those of the present and the future is not a matter of a perfected solution to all possible problems. Rather, it is a record of persistent development, of techniques that have worked and that, with alert attention, may keep on working. Beyond that it is a challenge to pick up where the past has left off and build a still better California, perhaps improved in things material, and certainly made more satisfying to the mind and the spirit."

CALIFORNIA AND THE NATION: A TALLY OF TWO HISTORIES

As Californians we are, of course, citizens of the United States. In a special sense we consider ourselves heirs of the English nation and people, heirs too of medieval man and medieval institutions, heirs of the Greeks and the Romans. By virtue of immigration and by transfer of ideas we feel an affinity and an indebtedness to modern Europe. We and our ways are somewhat derived from Asia and

Africa. In other particulars our civilization has been influenced by the America that was before Columbus, and even by the far-flung area of the Pacific. In short, if we take full account of our backgrounds as well as of our current outlook, we are citizens of the world.

A case can be made that the only kind of history to study is world history. We need to consider the human race in its entirety. We need to acquaint ourselves with the people of the world in their interrelations. We can profit by studying the features that are analogous. We will find some things that are common in human experience, even when there is isolation.

Few of us have the languages to take on this full assignment. The sources and the literature of world history are overwhelming. The setting is so extended and so diverse that even with the advantages of modern transportation we cannot learn it adequately. The complexity of the subject is enough to defeat most efforts.

Consequently, the practice of historians usually is to settle for a more modest sample. Usually it is a sample chosen for its inherent attractions, and often without concern for its tie-in with universals. Nevertheless, whatever segment we select is a sample. And each such sample is susceptible upon examination of being classified as random or selective, warped or true, representative or misleading, discriminative or nonsensical, illustrative or exceptional, a sample of convenience or one that can be honored as "scientific."

One fetish that has grown up among historians is to hold that a dash of antiquity hallows the subject or sample chosen. By this token the study of Old World history is adjudged a cut above that of New World history. (Here I do not press my opinion; I merely report.) By the same token a historian is often thought to be on better ground if he attempts an appraisal of the governorship of Gaspar Portolá rather than that of Edmund G. (Pat) Brown.

Another even more widespread assumption is that, of any two samples of world history, the one that is larger is presumably to be preferred. Thus, if a college student has time for but one course in European history, he is almost always advised to choose one that embraces the whole continent rather than one that is narrower.

That is not exactly the way it works on this side of the Atlantic. The history of the New World has far less patronage than the history of the United States. But the proposition that the history of our nation is more to be esteemed than the history of any of its parts has almost universal endorsement. Indeed, it is a proper question to ask why I say *almost* universal endorsement. The qualifier is there because, tonight at least, I am about to maintain that this broad proposition is not necessarily so.

As an alternative sample, a citizen of the United States, and of the world, might profitably choose to study his own state and its history. Especially if that state is California. The majority of my professional colleagues would dismiss this suggestion as unfashionable, heretical, and arrant nonsense. This I know without asking them.

There is, of course, one formidable argument against my counterproposition. California is only one part of the United States, and the United States as a nation is something more than the sum of its parts. If one could know everything about United States history, he would be closer to apprehending the history of the world than if he merely knew everything about California history.

My proposition has to be a bit more modest. On a portal-to-portal basis — in a given period of study time (say half a lifetime) — one who concentrates on California's history might make as much progress toward understanding the aspirations, experiences, and achievements of mankind as if he had elected the history of the United States.

There are some obvious conveniences. The locale is smaller and closer at hand. The climate is better. The cast of characters is more compact. The source materials are not all right here. I remember Herbert Eugene Bolton saying, "I am an American historian (and he might as accurately have said, "I am a California historian"), therefore I have to do my research in foreign archives." On the whole, however, the materials for the study of California history are handier.

A half dozen arsenals of research materials are already assembled: the Bancroft Library, the Huntington Library, the State Library, the UCLA Library, the California Historical Society collection, the Los Angeles Public Library, the Stanford Library, the Mason collection at Claremont, the Southwest Museum. True enough, some important collections got away — the William Robertson Coe collection (and the first Coe professorship) to Yale, and the Morse collections of Bret Harte and Mark Twain materials. A dozen or a hundred private collectors are amassing other significant holdings.

The Huntington Library, the California Historical Society, and the University presses regularly add to the publications available.

Western-lore, Dawson, Howell, Ward Ritchie, Clark, and several other private presses enter this same friendly competition. The Huntington Library makes grants in aid of research on California topics. And a small army — not so large as a regiment, but not so small as a corporal's guard — keeps slogging away at the study and writing of the history of our state. Anyone who wants to pursue this branch of historical study can count on company and on help.

Are there tangibles in California history that we can measure in relation to corresponding ones of the United States? Let us begin with size. Our unseen host tonight, Charles F. Lummis, called our land "the Right Hand of the Continent." A cutout of California overlaid on the corresponding part of "the Left Hand of the Continent" spreads from Charleston, South Carolina, to Cape Cod, and with depth enough to cover the Tidewater, the Piedmont, and the Appalachians. This is the Cisappalachia that Clarence W. Alvord used to talk about. Here we have "the Colonies" save only Georgia, Maine, and perhaps New Hampshire. Here we have the arena of the Revolution, except for Benedict Arnold's march on Canada and George Rogers Clark's conquest of Illinois.

There are Americans who still feel that not much of importance has transpired in the United States outside this main stem along the Atlantic Coast. It is the America of John Smith and the Pilgrim Fathers, of Washington, Franklin, Adams, Hamilton, Jefferson, Calhoun, Webster, the Roosevelts, the Kennedys, Marshall, Holmes, J. P. Morgan, Harvard, Princeton . . . This list could go on indefinitely. Even if we do not accept all the contentions of eastern provincialism, here is proof that such an area is large enough to contain much historical substance.

Since history is made by people more than by space, population may give us a better clue. California is now pressing on the sixteen million mark; may indeed have passed it. When did the United States reach that size? The answer is in the presidency of Martin Van Buren, shortly after the Panic of 1837. In all probability it was in the first half of 1838.

Does that mean that $h_c = h_{us} - (1838\text{-}1961)$? That the history of California is equal to the history of the United States to 1838? I have put this question to student after student. Not yet have I found one who would say yes.

I believe I know why. These historians I have been trying to pin down know a great deal about the history of the United States. They have in mind the sufferings and endurance of the first colonists. They call to mind the hard work of wresting the land from the Indians and of subduing the wilderness. They remember the ingenuity shown in making a living an ocean removed from Europe. They think about the lessons that colonials learned in politics and government. They think of the winning of independence and the establishment of a new government, a makeshift one in 1775, a formal constitutional one in 1781, and another on an improved order in 1789. With territorial expansion to the Mississippi in 1783, to the Rockies in 1803, and southeastward as far as Key West in 1819, the nation was halfway toward its present dimensions. Within this span of years is all that we associate with Washington, Franklin, Jefferson, Monroe, and Jackson.

This is the history, furthermore, that absorbed the attention of such giants among historians as Francis Parkman and Henry Adams, Charles M. Andrews, Herbert Osgood, Lawrence H. Gipson, Thomas J. Wertenbaker, Carl Bridenbaugh, and the younger A. M. Schlesinger.

What loyal American can admit that California history might equal all that? And yet, perhaps what this formidable United States record demonstrates is that when in the course of human events, a people had risen all the way to 16,000,000, the accrued history can be a respectable quantum.

Perhaps there are better measures than square miles and round numbers of population. Suppose we try it on a crassly materialistic basis. What was the accumulated wealth of the United States in 1838 as compared to that of California today? Compare the inventories, US 38 and Cal. 61, in buildings, in roads and other transportation facilities, in plant and equipment. Compare the gross annual product, expressed in commodity dollars, from agriculture, from the forests, from mines, from industry. What was the volume of business transacted? What was the annual expenditure for government? I shall not burden you with exact statistics on any of these points, but the answer to every one of these questions would be that the United States holdings and output in 1838, by each of these measures, was less, much less, or even trivial, compared to that of California in 1961.

On a more elevated level, what is the comparison in library holdings? California has times over more books stacked up on its shelves. (They're having to burn them up in Sacramento.) In educated men? California is far ahead. In emancipated women? We may wonder whether by modern standards there were any in the

United States in 1838. Certainly America was not a community property state. In emancipated Negroes? The United States then had most of the way still to go. In care of the sick, the insane, and the criminal? The United States then was exceedingly primitive. Even with capital punishment still practiced, we are times over more humane. As concerns respect for the rights and liberties of individuals, we are not letter perfect, but our rating clearly should be better than that of the slave-holding and Indian-removing nation of 1838. Perhaps there are more reliable cultural indexes: how many eminent men of science, what art exhibits, what musical performances, what patronage of the arts, what caliber of schools and colleges, what percentage of literacy? Here too the competition is one-sided.

Shifting criteria abruptly, let us compare the worldwide awareness of the United States in 1838 and of California in 1961. It is hard to reconstruct how obscure and insignificant the United States was on the world scene in the early nineteenth century. That is as difficult to realize as it is easy to note how widely known and sometimes heralded California is today.

Reputations of course can be false. Let us climb back to something we can measure with more confidence of significance. What is the comparison of the state of historical scholarship on the United States in 1838 and on California in 1961?

Suppose an immigrant, landing in 1838, had wanted to Americanize himself quickly. What histories and biographies would an alert bookman have recommended to him? And how would that reading list compare with the best California reading list that could be assembled for citizen No. 2,525,252, who is due to knock on Los Angeles' door any minute?

The new American might have been referred to Parson Weems' *Washington,* preferably the 5th edition (1806) because it introduces the cherry tree anecdote; or to John Marshall's five-volume *Washington* (1804-1807), ponderous, dull, and plagiarized; and for good measure to the twelve volumes of Jared Sparks' blue-pencilled edition of the *Writings of George Washington* (1834-1837).

With Francisco Palou's *Vida . . . de . . . Junípero Serra* (1787), Maynard J. Geiger's *Serra* (1959), and any dozen of Bolton's documentary volumes, the new Californian can get off to a much better start. These books offer adulation better reasoned, compendiousness far better assembled, and source materials meticulously rendered and wisely interpreted.

Our new American might have been happier with original narratives such as John Smith's *True Relation* and William Bradford's *Plimmoth Plantation.* With original narratives California is well supplied also. Miguel Costansó's diary of the Portolá expedition had been published in Mexico in 1770. William Shaler's circumstantial description of the California he saw as a sea otter man came out in 1808. And Richard Henry Dana's *Two Years Before the Mast* issued just two years after the magic date of 1838. Reaching on to the present we could regale our new recruit with Patrick Breen's Donner diary, the *Shirley Letters,* a surfeit of Gold Rush narratives, and not quite countless others.

For outright histories, our immigrant in 1838 could have chosen from David Ramsay's *History of the American Revolution* (1789), Mercy Warren's *History of the Revolution* (1805), Jedidiah Morse's *Annals of the American Revolution* (1824), and Noah Webster's *History of the United States* (1787). Much more probably, an alert advisor would have pushed George Bancroft's *History of the United States,* the first two volumes of which had appeared in 1834 and 1837. It was, as Bancroft himself said, "intended for the unlettered portion of the community." Throughout the generation to come, and, indeed, longer than that, Bancroft's *United States* was regarded as the ideal presentation and exactly the interpretation most likely to mold good Americans. One drawback, however, was that Volume I came forward only as far as 1660, and Volume II only to 1689. Our eager student of the history of his new home would have to wait until 1885 for the volume that would carry the story to Washington's inauguration.

Had this same immigrant chosen California in 1838 a small shelf of books might have been laid out for his inspection. Among them would certainly have been Miguel Venegas' *Noticia de la California* (1757). It is still reckoned the starting point for histories of California, and, incidentally, it was even more plagiarized than the works of Weems, Marshall, Ramsay, or Warren. As Charles E. Chapman pointed out, and before him Fidel Fita y Colomé, the real author of this work was another Jesuit, Andrés Marcos Burriel.[1]

Along with the Burriel-Venegas work might have been offered Johann Jakob Baegert's *Nachrichten von der Amerikanischen Halbinsel Californien* (1771) and Francisco Javier Clavigero's *Storia della California* (1789). These three works are in as many languages, but then all Europeans are great linguists, so that would not matter. They deal, it is true, only with Baja California, somewhat of a shortcoming, but their terminal dates at least were much closer to the present than George Bancroft's 1689.

A year later, in 1839, we could have provided our imagined student a history of California in English, the one by Alexander Forbes. And as early as 1836 he could have had a copy of the first book published in California, the famous *Tablas para los niños que empiezan a contar.*

Of course, in tarrying with the published California history available in 1838 I am violating our first principle — that the valid comparison is for the period of the build-up of the first sixteen millions of population. For California on this improved basis we then have the spacious shelf of Hubert Howe Bancroft's *Works,* thirty-nine volumes of them, with a certain amount of depreciation claimed on the parts somewhat remote from California. The fashion has been to depreciate this Bancroft on other grounds as well. That is a whole subject in itself. In our present context it may suffice to remark that, whereas George Bancroft is read now only by antiquarians and specifically those interested in the history of American historiography, our Bancroft is still the foundation for every working library on the Far West, still consulted, still read (in parts), still relied on, and sometimes cited.

The great Bancroft history may be garnished with the four volumes by Theodore H. Hittell (1885-1897), the five edited by Zoeth S. Eldredge (1915), and the shelf of ten engineered by the Powell Publishing Company (1929-1931). In their companion volumes in 1921 and 1922, Charles E. Chapman and Robert G. Cleland were able to draw on source materials that had eluded the late nineteenth century businessmen historians, particularly the resources of the Spanish and Mexican archives. Add then the research contributions of Herbert E. Bolton and Henry Raup Wagner and a host of others carrying on to today's busy scholars such as Dale L. Morgan and John H. Kemble, Fred Rogers and W. W. Robinson, and we have a wealth of published history that far outshines the best and the total on the United States as of 1838.

History, as everyone knows, is a comparatively late-blooming art form. If we take literature as our trace element, surely the United States to 1838 will fare better. Now we can include Benjamin Franklin's *Autobiography,* the war of the pamphlets that preceded the Revolutionary War, the panegyrics of Thomas Paine and Philip Freneau, the novels of James Fenimore Cooper, Washington Irving's *Sketchbook* and several of his other works, and the early poems of Edwin Bryant. Edgar Allen Poe's prize-winning tale, "MS Found in a Bottle," was in print, as was also *Nacoochee,* his first volume of poetry. Ralph Waldo Emerson had already earned reputation as an essayist and a lecturer, combining the two talents in his Phi Beta Kappa lecture at Harvard in 1837 on the American Scholar. This is by no means the complete list of literary people of merit productive by 1838.

Can California match it? Dana and Dame Shirley give us a start. Ambrose Bierce, Prentice Mulford, Bret Harte and a bit of Mark Twain, John Muir, Frank Norris, Jack London, Mary Austin, William Saroyan. John Steinbeck, Robinson Jeffers, and company are a real gold mine of talent. Quite possibly I have omitted a favorite writer: Edwin Corle, George Stewart, Idwal Jones, Oscar Lewis, Aldous Huxley, Robert Louis Stevenson, Helen Hunt Jackson, Will Irwin — this list is by no means exhaustive. My preference goes to them above the Irving-Cooper-Bryant group.

Long since, I am sure, partisans of the Left Hand of the Continent are muttering unfair, unfair. By ringing in on the California side the century and a third from 1838 to 1961 there is a rigging of the contest. With automation, mechanization, the internal combustion engine, the Fourteenth Amendment, schools for writers, schools for historians, federal aid for education, tax-exemption inducements for patronage of the arts, government initiative and financing for public improvements, rampant urbanism, and other powerful catalysts for development on all fronts, of course California as of 1961 can outscore the United States of 1838.

To that accusation there is only one answer. All this I must admit, all this and more. This is the reason above all others why California history shines. Because it is longer, the history of California to sixteen million is richer than the history of the United States to the first sixteen million. It also has far better relevance to the world we live in. What kind of preparation for our era is it to know nothing about the industrial revolution in America, about life with the automobile and the airplane, the telephone and the nuclear bombs? What kind of preparation for world citizenship is it to have the story end with the United States ensconced as it was in 1838 in comfortable isolation, walled in by the Atlantic and the Rockies and protected by the untested paper blockade of the Monroe Doctrine?

This brings me back full circle to the question we started with — for the purpose of apprehending world history, what are the relative merits of focussing on the history of California or on an equivalent helping of the history of the United States. I have not presented a run-down on all possible elements in such a study. I have deliberately omitted one in which California is often charged with a great deficiency — war. It is true that we have had next to no fighting right here in California — San Pasqual and the Modoc campaign, it is true, but as more typical we might cite the Battle of the Old Woman's Gun and in World War II the Battle of Los Angeles. For a peace-loving nation, the United States, in contrast, has had an inordinate number of wars, and this element of alleged "superiority" over California is not demolished by pointing out that the biggest of these wars came after 1838, among them the Mexican War, the Civil War, the Spanish-American War, the first two World Wars, and the Korean War. I have omitted war from the comparisons, but I have not deliberately selected the elements that would be most favorable to California. I have not made detailed comparisons in the history of science, the history of education, power from petroleum, electrification, or use of what we call the mass media.

In certain quarters I can well imagine that this tally of two histories might seem to have the color of being un-American. That is not my intention. I have the highest respect for what was accomplished in the formative period of the Revolution and its immediate aftermath. I am not purposely un-American, just pro-Californian. And though I have cast much of my talk in a vein of let's choose one or the other, the conclusion I would like to stress ought to be able to stand alone. It is that the California sample of world history, extending from a prehistoric setting and primitive society, through great variations, to the high modernity of the present, is a reasonable, appropriate, and possibly even an adequate make-ready for Californians, Americans, and worldlings entering upon the New Frontiers of the 1960's.

GOLD IS THE CORNERSTONE: AN ASSAY

Of all the localities in the world that have been favored with great gold rushes, California is unique in having used hers as a springboard to a rapid and a gratifyingly consistent development. How this happened is worth inquiring.

The irreverent, it must be admitted, sometimes ask whether the gold of California did not do more harm than good. Anyone who follows the boulder-strewn trail of the dredger, visits the gaping holes and barren debris piles of the hydraulickers, and contemplates the unsightly dumps of the hard-rock mines will be conscious of some of the damage done. Add then the muddying of the streams that made the salmon stop running, the silting of the lower rivers that slowed and then stopped the river boats, the devastation of farm lands by floodwaters and tailings.

The Indians of the Sierra foothills were early victims, first in having their sources of food supply laid waste and then in the "wars" of extermination. Marshall got no profit from the discovery and Sutter lost his all. On the sea routes, shipwreck, cholera, and Panama fever claimed victims; on the overland routes, cholera, mountain fever, traffic accidents, and Indian attacks. In the mines, mishaps and illness afflicted the gold seekers, and another untold number went to their graves. The gold rush, it must be admitted, was responsible for more bereavements, more broken homes, than the War with Mexico.

For many forty-niners, perhaps for the majority, the proceeds of gold hunting turned out to be a paltry return on the investment of time and capital that went into getting to California and working the mines. Farm wagons burned in Death Valley, the carcasses of oxen strewn along the Humbolt, ships rotting in San Francisco Bay — these were tangible reminders of the vast outlay required to deliver the labor force of the diggings.

In the next hundred years, to be sure, two billion dollars' worth of gold was to come out of the California gold fields, the first part in a torrent, the rest more gradually and regularly. Even allowing for the cost of production hinted in the saying, "It takes a gold mine to work a gold mine," the two billion dollars total is impressive — impressive until one recalls that the ultimate fate of this metal was to be sterilized and buried at Fort Knox.

Still others deplore the gold rush on moral grounds. The miners, they say, were rowdy; their epoch a field day for liquor dealers, gamblers, and harlots. Standards of conduct got out of hand at the very outset, making it an uphill fight to bring them to the level of the East. Speculative instincts were overstimulated, and the California spirit came to be too strongly implanted in the get-rich-quick patter.

Admittedly the gold rush led Californians to hasty decisions where longer tussling with the problems might have produced a better solution. Admittedly also, California's present material success is to a large extent the result of fertile soil, climate, position, and ingenuity not directly derived from its golden beginning. Nevertheless, there are tangible proofs that gold was the touchstone that set California in motion on the course that made her what she is today, and that her gold did things for the West at large and the Pacific basin that otherwise would not have been done for a generation or perhaps at all.

Gold mining itself provides clear examples. In July, 1849, roused by a shipment of 1,200 ounces of California gold that reached Port Jackson, a party of Australians sailed by way of New Zealand and Pitcairn for San Francisco. After a trying experience with an unreliable teamster, they got to the southern diggings, where by trial and error and by observation they learned how to pan and cradle and where to look for dirt that would be worth washing. One of these men, E. H. Hargraves, more observant than the rest, was struck by the geological resemblance to a locality in New South Wales. His companions scoffed at the idea of going back there to do their mining, but Hargraves on reflection became more and more convinced that he was correct. He wrote to friends in Sydney on the subject, and then, as Bidwell had gone from Coloma to the Feather in 1848, he went home to Australia.[1]

February, 1851, found him across the Blue Mountains in New South Wales, with pick, pan, and trowel, riding off with a black boy to discover Australia's gold. Arrived at a California-looking spot, he scratched the gravel off a schistose dyke, which ran across a dry creek, dug a panful of earth, and announced to his companion that he would now wash out the gold. Sure enough it was there. He continued his prospecting, proving to his own satisfaction that the gold deposits were extensive and rich.

Then, instead of rushing into secret production, as might have been the California way, he went to Sydney, sought out the colonial secretary, broke the news to him, and asked for official recognition as the discoverer, and a suitable reward. Although the secretary was reluctant to believe, he did admit that if Australia proved to be a gold country it would stop England from sending any more convicts and would stop the drain of men to California. Hargraves now publicized his discovery assiduously, accepted appointment as commissioner of crown lands, and returned to the diggings to show others how to use pan and cradle, but without stooping to steady mining. A grateful government rewarded him with a donation of £10,000, with which he went to England and wrote a book about his experiences. For the mining methods employed, as well as for the discovery, Australia was clearly indebted to California.

In February, 1858, a Hudson's Bay Company ship arrived at San Francisco with $800,000 in gold from the Fraser River. From the city and from the mining camps a horde of gold seekers promptly sailed for the new El Dorado. According to one count, 23,428 Californians set out in less than six months. The Hudson's Bay Company factor and governor, James Douglas, succeeded in imposing a system of government and a mining code, but the Californians far outnumbered all other exploiters of these diggings. Naturally they brought with them the full pattern of mining method.

Colorado's 1858 rush, with its slogan of "Pike's Peak or Bust," drew a lesser complement of Californians, but the state was represented in the Cherokees, who had panned the first gold when they were California-bound in 1850, and some of whom now returned to prospect the Cherry Creek district more thoroughly. These sands disappointed, but a rich vein of quartz near Central City and placers with scale gold the size of watermelon seeds revived the excitement in 1859. Here also, mining techniques benefited from the California experience, and the life of the camps tended to reproduce that of the farther West of a decade earlier.

To the mining frontier of Baja California, Sonora, and Sinaloa, California shipped thousands of prospectors and tens of thousands of dollars' worth of mining equipment in the 'fifties and 'sixties. On Bill Williams Fork in Arizona in 1861, it was deserters from the California Column who started the mining rush. In eastern Washington, Californians participated in prospecting along the Columbia and the Snake, and they made the advance to the Clearwater and the Salmon, Alder Gulch, Grasshopper Creek, and Last Chance Gulch largely an eastward-moving frontier. On the Stikine, in the Klondike, and on the beach at Nome a few veterans of forty-nine were still active, while the use of California practices was a stronger carryover.

From the early 'fifties, California gold hunters had carried their prospecting across the Sierra to the drearier wastes of the Great Basin. Returns at first were modest, but as the miners worked up Gold Canyon toward Mount Davidson the color increased. There in the spring of 1859 partners Peter O'Riley and Patrick McLaughlin made a real strike, on which a shiftless, loud-mouthed Virginian,

Henry Thomas Paige Comstock, horned in and subsequently gave his name to the mine and lode. The Riley-McLaughlin gold mine was cluttered with a heavy dark substance that settled with the gold. They thrust this bothersome "blue stuff" indignantly aside, but after a while a Californian took a sample across the Sierra to the assayer at Nevada City. When he reported that it contained to the ton $1,595 in gold and $4,791 in silver, eager Californians began to swarm across the mountains.

Most of them arrived too late to do much mining in 1859, but they forthwith staked out claims, incorporated mining companies, and began to peddle stock. Silver mining, they soon found, was not the same as washing gold. Elaborate machinery, capital, and technical knowledge were requisite. The tested arrastre was put to work, to which veterans of silver mining in Mexico added patios and adobe furnaces. Germans, also from California, introduced the "barrel" process, and the California stamp was an early import.

In 1860, no fewer than 10,000 Californians stampeded to the Comstock. For supplies and equipment they depended on California. San Francisco banks and merchants, in turn, became heavy investors in the Washoe mines and, with Comstock silver as the coveted prize, they embarked on an era of speculative investment that made William Ralston a multimillionaire and then broke his bank, elevated William Sharon to be King of the Comstock, built fabulous fortunes for James G. Fair, John W. Mackay, and their partners Flood and O'Brien — Californians all. Adolph Sutro with his tunnel, George Hearst and John P. Jones — these were other Californians who rose to stardom on the Comstock.

The lode drew from all mining countries. It was a German named Deidesheimer who introduced a method of square cribbing that made it possible to work the vast ore body of the big bonanza. Cornish miners deserve credit for demonstrating how to work the lower levels. Yet the history of the Comstock has many reminders of the influence of California and the indebtedness to the arsenal of men and methods built up there.

In matters other than mining the boost that the golden era gave to California is equally unmistakable. The sudden influx of enough persons to justify statehood and the prompt erection of such a government were a start. San Francisco, placid hamlet of 812 souls at the time of the discovery, soon became the largest city west of the Missouri, a hive of commerce and industry, and the metropolis of the entire West and much of the Pacific.

Transportation facilities, demanded by the gold miners and financed out of their earnings, spread up and down and across the state. Because of the gold, San Francisco became the terminus of the mail steamers instead of just a way point on the line to Oregon. Gold gave force to the earlier arguments that the federal government should speed the mails across continent by stage and should improve upon that facility with a railroad. California's mineral wealth and its population mounting toward the half-million mark were most powerful considerations in its favor, and the line eventually built led to Sacramento and San Francisco. But it was called the Pacific Railroad, it bound the entire West to the nation, and it opened a window upon the Orient.

From a geographical curiosity that even informed persons might locate rather hazily on the map, gold lifted California to immediate and worldwide fame. Thereafter no one would be in doubt. From this moment, too, great and spectacular things would be expected of California. In the long run, the black gold of petroleum, the orange gold of the fruit growers, the silver screen of the movies, and the brass of the real estate boomers might overshadow the genuine article, yet no one can say what these industries and the tourist trade would have amounted to had there not been the initial impetus of the golden beginning.

Even in the realm of the intellectual and the artistic it was an inestimable boon that California started rich. The standard frontier experience was that there should be a starving time, a period in which every ounce of energy had to go into scraping together the bare essentials, with no possibility remaining for more ambitious strivings. In California the Spaniards had done most of the starving. Then the gold rush rolled up an early surplus, some of which went to the encouragement of letters and the arts, schools, and churches. Within a very few years San Francisco had a bookstore that was better stocked than any other west of the Alleghenies. It was also a center of writing and publishing to a degree that would have been absolutely impossible except for the gold. In educational facilities, in libraries, in graphic arts, and in the sophisticated pleasure of the theater the acceleration that gold imparted is equally to be seen. The momentum of leadership thus provided is one of the state's choicest heritages.

DON BENITO WILSON: AN AVERAGE SOUTHERN CALIFORNIAN

Capricious is the fate that decides for what a man shall be remembered: Benjamin Franklin for his kite, George Washington for his cherry tree, Paul Revere for his midnight ride, James Ohio Pattie for his prophylactic peregrination, and the hero of this sketch, Benjamin Davis Wilson, for the mountaintop observatory that perpetuates his name. Published history, as formulated by Don Benito's self-estimate[1] and conventionalized by Hubert Howe Bancroft's interpretation, adds that he was a California pioneer of 1841, an inglorious captive at Rancho El Chino, a doughty Indian fighter and grizzly-bear hunter,[2] and the first mayor of Los Angeles.[3]

Manuscript materials in various California repositories, and especially in the B. D. Wilson Papers[4] at the Huntington Library, reveal other facts about Don Benito, possibly more significant than those on Bancroft's classic list. His varied experiences in the fifties, sixties, and seventies exemplify the multiple phases of the transition through which southern California was moving. He appears, not as an exceptional leader, but as a prominent, respected, and moderately successful citizen, an average southern Californian.

Wilson's earlier activities may be briefly summarized.[5] A native of Tennessee, born in 1811, he had gone as a young man to New Mexico, where for eight years he was a beaver trapper and trader. In 1841 many of the Americans around Santa Fé, alarmed because of a rumored Texan expedition against New Mexico, deemed it prudent to move on to California. They did so by the Old Spanish Trail north of the Grand Canyon, traveling much of the distance in company with the regular caravan of New Mexican traders and driving along a flock of sheep as their principal food supply for the journey. Wilson insists that it was only by accident that he stayed in California. China was his destination, but failing several times to make connection with a China ship he settled down in southern

California, married a daughter of the country, Doña Ramona Yorba, turned ranchero at Jurupa (near present San Bernardino), and became a genuine *Californio*. He is accorded much of the credit for leading the Americans out of action in the test of strength between Micheltorena and Alvarado at Cahüenga in 1845, and after his capture at Chino he was a conciliatory factor at the conclusion of the American conquest.

In common with most southern Californians Wilson was but slightly involved in the stirring events of '48, '49, and '50. He was little disturbed by the persistence of military government after the Treaty of Guadalupe Hidalgo. The discovery of gold did not take him north, and the forty-niners who came by southern trails passed on quickly to the gold fields. It was the north also which drew up the constitution of 1849 and exulted over California's admission to statehood. Even Don Benito's term as the first mayor of Los Angeles was more honorary than arduous. Southern California was yet to feel the full impact of Americanization.

Wilson's correspondence in the fifties yields several bits of biographical data. His first wife having died, on February 1, 1853, he married Margaret Hereford, widow of Dr. T. A. Hereford and a relative of the famous Missouri Sublettes. By his will on June 10 of that year Wilson named his wife Margaret as his principal heir and her son Edward as lawful heir, share and share alike, with Mary and John, the children of his first marriage.[6] He had previously purchased a half interest in Rancho San José de Buenos Ayres (now the site of Westwood and the Los Angeles campus of the University of California), where in partnership with W. B. T. Sanford he engaged in raising cattle and sheep. At this time he was also subordinate Indian agent for southern California, in which capacity he exhibited a rare understanding and compassion for the much-abused natives. Subsequently, his one request to Bancroft was that the historian should give him credit for urging the settling of the Indians on reservations at the old missions.[7] His principal duties seem to have been to reconnoiter with his chief, E. F. Beale, for suitable reservation sites, to hold Indian councils, and to supervise the supplying of the Indians, particularly at the Tejon Reservation. Numerous inquiries came to him for information about the Indians of southern California, and at least one of his reports was published.[8]

In 1854, despite Beale's eloquent and repeated advice that Wilson owed it to his daughter to give her the educational advantages which only San Francisco or the East could afford,[9] he decided that his children would be better off in the country. He purchased a country seat thus described in a letter to his elder brother in Mississippi:

> I am so comfortable here and enjoy such fine health with all my family in fact, no Country can be more healthy than this, now for me to breake up here and to go to the Atlantic States I feel certain that I never could find another place so healthy and affording so many comforts, here besides the finest climate in the world we produce every species of grain and fruits in the greatest abundance As a proof I will just give you a list of the different fruits on a place I bought a few days since there is on the farm growing Grapes pears Oranges appricots Amonds peaches apples English walnuts cherries figs Olives Quinces plumbs & other fruits of the smaler kinds two numerous to mention now those fruits all grow so luxurant that we dont know which grows the best the above perchase I made is one of the most beautiful places that heart could desire fine water and land and about 30 acres in fruits of the kinds just mentioned above this place lies about seven miles from this town.[10]

The description is of Huerta de Cuate, formerly the home of that Scottish don, Hugo Reid, who was also an authority on the Indians of Los Angeles.[11] From Reid's widow Don Benito purchased this diminutive rancho of 128 acres. Further improved, and rechristened Lake Vineyard, the hacienda became his permanent home. By purchase from the original grantee, Manuel Garfías, Wilson acquired the adjoining rancho San Pascual, later disposing of an undivided half interest to Dr. John S. Griffin. By purchase from other rancheros and from homesteaders, and through the use of scrip, bounty lands, and lien lands, Wilson came into ownership of much of the land once possessed by Mission San Gabriel. With Phineas Banning and others he acquired title to a 2,400-acre parcel of Rancho San Pedro. The exact extent of his broad holdings is not easily determined because, like his neighbors, he often held "one-third of an undivided fourth,"[12] or some other such fraction. In addition to the San Bernardino, Westwood, and San Pedro properties, his domain was approximately: Pasadena and South Pasadena, San Marino, Alhambra, and San Gabriel.

Having decided upon Lake Vineyard as his home, Wilson was ready to dispose of his town house, a capacious two-story structure in a ten-acre orchard and vineyard (where the Los Angeles union station now rises). Public-spirited citizens acquired the property for the Sisters of Charity, who operated it as a school and orphanage. There are various descriptions of this place, but none more graphic than that by William the gardener. "Sire," he wrote, "I am sorry to learn you fine Resident be sold. it has bless my so much to ynpruf you Resident to wan of the finest in Los Angeles."[13] As such it brought $8,000.[14]

In the same year, 1856, Don Benito represented the Democratic party and the counties of Los Angeles, San Bernardino, and San Diego in the State Senate. The major issue was choice of a United States Senator. His constituents volunteered much advice, expressed confidence in the success of "Our Party," and predicted that Wilson's "known conservative and moderate grounds in politics" would give him an influence such as few, if indeed any other, members could attain.[15] More illuminating than the legislative record are the opinions expressed on various political issues. In 1853 he approved in principle the separation of San Bernardino from Los Angeles County, though with Don Bernardo Yorba's Rincón and Sierra ranchos and the Santa Ana Valley left in Los Angeles County. "I think it just," he wrote, "when any portion of the community wish to be separated to govern themselves to accede to their wishes."[16] Later, he was ready to apply this same principle to the state as a whole. The Rev. S. H. Willey inquired as to the prevalence of state-division sentiment,[17] and in 1859 Archibald Gillespie broached the matter of a loan of $300 so that he could come south and join his erstwhile foe, Don Andrés Pico, in working for the separation of the southern counties.[18] If the Civil War had not occurred, Pico's proposed Territory of Colorado might have eventuated.

Meanwhile, Don Benito was arranging sheep drives to Sacramento,[19] was adding to the buildings at Lake Vineyard,[20] was seeking Senator Gwin's assistance in getting his land titles unscrambled and confirmed,[21] was soliciting a federal appropriation for harbor improvement at Wilmington,[22] was experimenting with sugar-cane production,[23] was employing an expert vineyardist and wine maker,[24] was borrowing money at rates as high as three per cent a month,[25] and was patronizing a portrait painter ready to be paid in "cattle Horses or any Kind of Stock."[26]

The sixties witnessed a considerable expansion of the market for Wilson's wines. His San Francisco agent reported: "The reputation of B. D. Wilsons wine, Los Angeles, is becoming more popular every day."[27] From San Francisco his wines were shipped to Sacramento and Washoe, to Boston, New York, Chicago, and Philadelphia, and even to Japan. California wines were thought to be very much improved by the voyage round the Horn. There was the hazard, however, that the pipes would spring leaks, or that the sailors would draw off part of the wine and substitute water, and a frequent complaint was that unscrupulous eastern dealers adulterated the California wines.[28] Nor was it easy to remit eastern money to California. Particularly if the payment was in currency, it often seemed advisable to invest in commodities for shipment to San Francisco.[29]

Marketing of most of the wine, and likewise of lemons and oranges, was through commission houses in San Francisco, where the wine had to compete with that from the Napa and Livermore valleys and the fruit with oranges from the islands and limes from Sicily. Payment was partly by drafts or certificates of deposit but largely by return steamer shipments of groceries, sugar, seed potatoes, hoes, plow points, furniture, staves, cultivators, soap, clothing, and even a pair of spectacles — the last with assurance that they could be sent back and exchanged if they did not fit.[30] San Francisco, it appears, was not merely the financial metropolis of the West, but the retail emporium as well.

Civil War issues obtruded upon Wilson in several ways. He and Banning supported the Union cause by donating a large tract at Wilmington for the erection of Drum Barracks, the base of operations for the California Column and for restraint of the "secesh" element in southern California. Yet Wilson's sympathies were known to be with the Confederacy. That he severed relations with Hobbs, Gilmore & Co. in San Francisco was largely because Hobbs, as a "black Republican," seemed to be discriminating against him.[31] Incidentally, the B. D. Wilson & Son wine cellar that he thereupon opened in San Francisco was not a great success, principally because its location at First and Market Streets was too far from the business center on Front Street.[32] To him as a Southern sympathizer a Sacramento pastor could write without reserve that all his fellow preachers had "gone off from the platform of truth, and followed the crowd in making the church of the living God a theatre for political debate," that he had had to bear "any amount of obloquy, and all manner of opposition," that "many prominent men, with their numerous and ignoble laquies," were bending every effort to break up his church and drive him out, and that he was seriously contemplating a removal to Los Angeles.[33] A few months later Wilson was almost of a mind to move from Los Angeles.[34] The cotton lands of Sinaloa beckoned, while the success of Union arms was a propulsive force. He did not go to Sinaloa, but to the end of his days he remained a staunch Democrat. In 1877 his subscription to the Los

Angeles *Star* was immediately forthcoming when the new editor wrote that the paper was now "emphatically democratic."[35]

Agricultural development went on apace in the postwar years, particularly when Lake Vineyard was managed by Don Benito's son-in-law, J. De Barth Shorb. There was experimentation with new crops — for example, mulberry trees, set out by the thousand for the sake of the state bounty. Additional water was developed for irrigation. The crops of wheat, barley, and alfalfa were large. Pears and walnuts brought good prices, and quantities of oranges and lemons were shipped to San Francisco: by 1876 Wilson was buying orange boxes by the carload.[36] Wine and brandy, however, were the principal products: in a protest of rail freight rates in 1876, Shorb set the annual Lake Vineyard shipments to the Atlantic seaboard at 500 tons.[37]

Wilson's miscellaneous activities in these later years reflect the changing trends in southern California. The decade-long effort to get Uncle Sam to return the Drum Barracks property was a personal rather than a community project. Not so was the pressure exerted for increased appropriations for harbor improvement at Wilmington. The rivers and harbors bills in the late sixties and seventies provided sums up to $150,000 for this work. The postwar excise taxes on brandy were also of immediate concern to all vineyardists. Much of Wilson's correspondence relates to dealings with the "revenuers" and to efforts to get the brandy tax modified.[38]

In 1865 and 1866 Wilson was actively interested in the Los Angeles Pioneer Oil Company. His son, when forwarding a case of lamp oil from San Francisco, urged, "You had better 'strike ile' soon for it commands a good price";[39] but though the wells near Wilmington were sunk to 75,110, and 200 feet they produced only water and gas. In 1874, after surveying the experiences of the several oil companies in southern California, Wilson's son-in-law advised the state geologist: "As a question of financial importance to the individual or State at large, the petroleum interests of this State can never amount to anything. To obtain oil at all a large sum has to be expended; and when obtained nothing can be done with it that will give profit to the manufacturer."[40]

A venture more immediately successful was the Los Angeles & San Pedro Railroad Company, of which Wilson was a director. Construction was proposed as early as 1861 but not actually carried through until 1869. The primary function of this line was to operate boat trains connecting with the steamers to San Francisco. Yet its employees were eligible for passes on the Central Pacific — Union Pacific,[41] and it was an effective pawn in bringing the Southern Pacific to Los Angeles.

As state senator again, from 1869 to 1872, Wilson was urged by his constituents to get legislative permission for Los Angeles "to issue her bonds to Erect a fine school building at Corner of Spring & Second streets" — a site that in 1870 had been thought too far out of town for the meeting of the first Teachers' Institute. With not a vacant seat in the public schools and with "a large influx of inhabitants" expected, this expansion was represented as "a stern necessity." Moreover, the argument was made that other cities in the state, notably San José, were far ahead of Los Angeles in schools, and finally there was the perennial plea that "the taxation will never be felt."[42]

A few "childless taxpayers" were against this bond issue of $20,000; on the proposed "no fence" law there was greater unanimity. This bill provided that orchardists, vineyardists, and grain raisers were not under obligation to fence their land, but that stock raisers were responsible for any damages caused by their loose cattle. The general demand for this act is a clear sign of the passing of the "cow counties." In the words of J. W. North, of Riverside:

> It is a contest between advancing civilization and obsolete barbarism. Every friend of improvement should unite and make the law general for the entire State. The development of the latent resources of the State would be twice as rapid if men did not have to expend more than half their capital in making fences for other peoples stock. The owners of Stock that are allowed to grase on our grain fields, do nothing to improve the country; they simply prey upon the products of others. The State ought to see that its true interest is to end this state of things at once.
>
> To show how this works in new settlements like ours. A poor neighbor has put in ten acres of Wheat. He must now expend near three hundred dollars to fence it; to guard against other peoples stock. If others were obliged to take care of their own stock he could put in fifty acres more. In that manner the developement of the State is retarded, by those who do nothing to improve the State. If our Legislature are as wise as they should be they will end this matter at once by a general law, that shall not leave enterprising people at the mercy of an ignorant representative. Do not fail to do all you can to secure this end, & oblige Yours truly,[43]

In the opinion of others, civilization would be more rapidly advanced by the "5% Act," a measure authorizing Los Angeles County to bond itself to the extent of five per cent of its assessed valuation to subsidize the Southern Pacific to build to Los Angeles. "There is more talk by the people general about the no fence law than any other proposed measure before you," wrote Wilson's neighbor, L. J. Rose, "whereas I feel more intress in the Rail Road Bill and hope that circumstances may be favorable for you to do something."[44]

Both measures passed. The no-fence law immediately resulted in a slump of sixty per cent in cattle prices, whereupon Shorb began to buy and built up the Lake Vineyard herd to one hundred head.[45] That such a herd was reckoned large is a commentary on how far southern California had gone since Don Benito's early days as a ranchero. On the positive side, the no-fence law stimulated planting and horticulture and was basic in the agricultural boom of the succeeding decades. Early fruits of the "5% Act" were not sweet without alloy. The Southern Pacific did not reach Los Angeles until 1876. Rates were set at "all the traffic would bear," and Angelenos protested without avail or tried to fall back upon a freight-and-passenger steamer to San Francisco.[46] As one purchaser of Wilson's brandy remarked, "The greatest drawBack to buying in Lower Cal. [i.e., southern California] is the *enormous ft.* and so *much difference* between *your place & San Fran.*"[47] Genuine relief was not forthcoming until the 1880's, when the Santa Fé injected a competitive element into transcontinental transportation. Wilson, interestingly enough, had been one of those who had actively urged a railroad on the 35th-parallel route.[48]

Because of Wilson's prominence in business and politics and because of the conspicuous success of his farming operations at Lake Vineyard, he was frequently asked for information about southern California. Could a New Yorker with an invalid wife and with capital of $1,000 buy enough land in oranges, lemons, olives, or walnuts to warrant his coming? Could he obtain "a subordinate position," on a farm where these fruits were cultivated, till he learned "how to avoid failures"?[49] Another New Yorker had been reading Nordhoff's *California* and wanted to know if all that he found there was true. "What is the population of those Southern Counties? Is the population Spanish, Yankee or French, or is it mixed? Is the people hospitable and liberal towards strangers? What is the price of land in your County? . . . please tell me too if there would be a chance for me to earn my living and the living of my family besides farming, because I am an educated man. I have been through a course of College studies, I can teach the English, French and Latin Linguages if it was necessary."[50] Still another wanted to know the price of unimproved land and of vines and young orange trees for setting out, whether the summers were not extremely hot, and what prospect "for a competent industrious and Steady young Dr. to Settle in Los Angeles."[51] Would anyone care to exchange California property for coal-and-iron lands, in eastern Tennessee, "which at the particular time are hard to dispose of but will ultimately be verry Valuable"?[52] How satisfactory was Chinese labor? The editor of the Waco (Texas) *Daily Reporter* asked for a few seeds of the "Australian Gum or Ucalyptus Tree."[53] And Professor Ezra S. Carr requested "one or two good specimens of the Orange, Lemon, Citron and Olive," which the Pacific Mail Company would transport free of charge to the "Arboretum, and orchard of specimen fruits," of the University of California at Oakland.[54]

Since the Wilson Papers consist principally of in-letters it is easier to tabulate questions than answers, but two of the latter, penned by Shorb, are probably fair samples. The first relates expecially to the Chinese as laborers; the second is a general appraisal of southern California as a place in which to live.

Mr. C. Cooper Spencer Lake Vineyard, May 8, 1870
Dear Sir

At the request of my Father-in-law Mr. Wilson to reply to your letter of enquiry regarding the adaptability of Chinese labor to viticulture and other farm labor, I am happy to report that my experience with this labor has been eminently satisfactory.

In the cultivation of these vineyards which I have leased for a term of years I soon discovered the necessity of employing a more intelligent class of labor than that supplied by the old Mission Indian or Sonorenans from Mexico: and hence last fall brought a number of Chinamen from San Francisco to make my vintage. They were not selected men, and I believe none of them had ever worked on a farm before, in a very few days however they learned the nature of the work and done it with more care and exactness than either the Indians or Mexicans of experience. In gathering grapes they did more and required less overseeing than the labor already referred to. The distillation required much care and watchfullness here too they proved a success.

When the pruning season commenced, a work requiring good judgement and ordinarily several years of experience to thoroughly understand, I had some difficulty in teaching them the principles of pruning upon which your grape crop so much depends, but was rewarded on the third day by finding they then understood what they were doing and from that time on had no trouble whatever: the vines they pruned shewing more skill and judgement than those by the other pruners who had pruned for years.

In the management of horses, ploughing &c I have had no experience with them, but judging from their capacity in acquiring more difficult knowledge so rapidly I believe they would prove capable of doing any and all work appertaining to the cultivation of the soil and growth of the vine, tree, bottom sugar cane, tobacco and the cereals. In all subsequent work since pruning, such as summer screening, in the use of the hoe, pick or shovel, planting & replanting vines and trees they have been equally as satisfactory.

I have had experience in working our own negros East before the war, and in this county men of nearly all nationalities in various kinds of works and enterprises, and I believe as a class the Chinese are superior to them all, certainly more reliable and must eventually furnish the labor for all agricultural enterprises throughout the world. . . .[55]

Mr. Herman Glass Jany 9th 77
Rochester, N. York
Dear Sir

Your favor of the 26th ultimo to my father-in-law Mr. Wilson has been received and at his request I cheerfully answer you. The pamphlet issued by the Chamber of Commerce of Los Angeles which we sent you answers many of your questions more in detail than is possible in a letter.

We have no extremes of heat and cold as understood by an Eastern man, although the mercury sometimes rises to 100° in Summer during our hot days which never continue more than three days in succession and then only for a few hours during the day, followed always by nights cool and so pleasant as to require a blanket for comfort at night. It must also be remembered that our heat is not similar to the Eastern heat for it is dry and a temperature here at 100° is not as oppressive as the Eastern heat at 85° or 80°. Our coldest spells rarely ever sends the mercury to 35°, although occasionally we have frosts in the lowlands not however occasioning damage to any extent. But once for the past 40 years has any serious injury been done by frost. We do not irrigate as a rule to raise any grain crop, if only one crop is expected. We irrigate the orange, lemon, lime &c. but never the vines.

The uncultivated lands produce the very best natural grasses in the world, which when dried on the lands are then in their best condition for fattening cattle, owing to the large quantities of seed, rich in oils. I would refer you to my Article in the pamphlet for my views on the question of our orange [production] being overdone.

Hops are grown with marked success. There is no question as to your health being improved by living in California at least at any point from Point Conception south to Arizona on the Sea Coast, it is all a healthy country. In point of business, any one with 15 to $20,000 capital with good judgement can always do well here. If he has a taste for agricultural life, he can invest a portion in a home sett out more land in trees costing in all say $5000.00 and loan the balance out; which can be done in A1 securities at 1¼ to 1½ pc per month U. S. gold coin, which would enable a man of ordinary tastes to live and improve his property which in a few years would yield him a competency and independence.

I am really at a loss to state the objectionable features of this Country, except for the general farming interests (raising small grains) and not providing irrigation facilities. We have some years of dry seasons which reduces the yield per acre and at times the farmers lose their seed as an extreme case, but there is not in any portion of Los Angeles County, as much probability of loss of crops as the most favored sections of the Eastern States. In other words we produce year after year better crops and that with less than one half the labor.

The charge of mosquitoes, fleas &c is untrue. We have of course mosquitoes near the ocean sloughs that head in fresh water springs. We have no more fleas than you have East with the same care and cleaniless. The grass does dry up on the uncultivated lands in the dry season and at first it is not an agreeable feature to an Eastern eye.

The social conditions in many of the small settlements have not been what was desirable: but of late years a good and most respectable class of families are settling around us who are building handsome homes; churches school houses &c. and are fast becoming wealthy in happiness and properties. . . .[56]

The Wilsonian enthusiasm for southern California has the hallmark of sincerity, even though by a strict economic interpretation it might be listed under advertising and promotion. For by the seventies Wilson had added to his many other activities that of real-estate subdivider and promoter. Through the Lake Vineyard Land and Water Association he was offering thousands of acres of improved and irrigable land, attractively subdivided into town lots and orchard tracts. Advertisements appeared in newspapers, magazines, pamphlets, and correspondence. The boxed statement on the Association's letterhead[57] is a fair summary of the advertising material: "The Lands of the Lake Vineyard Land and Water Association are located in the heart of the great Fruit Belt of Los Angeles County, and are peculiarly adapted to Semi-Tropical Fruits. The scenery is varied and rugged. Water supply is unlimited, and the water right is vested in the land. Title perfect. School houses and churches convenient. The Southern Pacific Railroad passes directly through this tract. . . ." As a sample response the following is offered:

Hon. D. B. Wilson — Littleton No. Ca. July 30th, 1877
Dear Sir,

I have for a long time had a desire to settle in California chiefly on account of the climate. For 4 years I have studiously & Carefully examined all the books maps &c relating to it as well as having recd numerous letters from prominent men in various sections of the State & have come to the conclusion that Los Angeles, Alameda & Sonoma are the best counties in the State (all things considered) taking them in the order named and around about San Gabriel & Town of Los Nietos the favored points of your county. Now what can 40 acres of the 6000 you advertise be bought for the amt of 1st payment & *time* on the balance & about what cost could a plain cottage with hall & 2 rooms single story be built for there? I have a wife & 4 children we all have our health, have had large means, but ruined by the late war. I know your section has suffered this year but with your facilities for Irrigation dont care for rain. I suppose you have good society & good drinking water. . . .[58]

Wilson was also ready to employ the time-honored device of donating building sites to developers whose enterprises would enhance the value of the rest of his holdings. Throughout 1876, for example, he was in correspondence with Mrs. Jeanie Spring Johns, proprietress of the Eagleswood Park Hotel, Perth Amboy, New Jersey. To her Wilson offered a ten-acre site on the Oak Knoll ridge on which Mrs. Johns would engage to build a "Sanatarium-hotel of great attractiveness and comfort." She continued:

I should expect to arrange with a good physician as resident, and should bring with me an accomplished head nurse familiar with the Swedish Movement etc. a tried French cook, who can get up wonderful dinners at an hour's notice, and a black butler who has been for fourteen years in our family. . . .

I should bring —

About six thousand dollars' worth of furniture, carpets, etc.

A good library for the hotel guests.

Paintings by European and well known American artists, to the value of from twenty to thirty five thousand dollars.

Eight or ten Health Lift machines costing three hundred dollars each.

I agree to spend ten thousand dollars on the Sanatarium-Hotel and necessary outbuildings, as stable, laundry, bowling alley etc. and shall probably spend nearer twenty thousand. . . .[59]

Sad to relate, the Perth Amboy property proved not only unsalable but also unacceptable as collateral for a loan.

Many other illustrations of southern California's transition could be drawn from Wilson's correspondence. He came to be addressed less frequently as "Don Benito Guilsa" and more often as "the Hon. B. D. Wilson." His daughter María Jesús, by contraction of her middle name, became "Sue." Cattle, sheep drives, bear hunts, and Indian fighting gave place to orange shipments, wine marketing, oil and railroad promotion, and real-estate subdivision. The old order did not disappear immediately; as late as 1870 son John and Charles E. Beane of the *News* fought a duel with rifles at thirty paces, John sustaining a flesh wound in the arm but behaving coolly and manfully,[60] and in 1872 the superintendent of the Los Angeles schools in submitting his resignation caustically remarked: "I find I am in the wrong country to rise. My Kind dont seem to flourish in this Country."[61] Yet the trappings of civilization were increasingly in evidence: "piano lessons for Nannie and Ruth,"[62] and an urgent suggestion from Wilson's son-in-law that he seek rest and relaxation by "making the tour of Europe."[63]

In all this development Don Benito played an important, respectable, and representative part. Greatness is something which only a rash biographer would claim for him. Quiet, unobtrusive, generous to a fault, and without benefit of extensive schooling, he was not cast in heroic mold and certainly was a less striking figure than many of his contemporaries. Abel Stearns was a larger landowner, Benjamin Hayes was a greater force in local politics and Senator Gwin on the national stage, Phineas Banning dominated the scene at Wilmington, and Rose and Shorb excelled as practical farmers. To none, however, did Wilson have to yield in adaptability to a changing environment. He made a physical reality of the Greeley suggestion, "Go West, young man, and grow up with the country." And, doing so, he was not only typical of southern California in its transition, but also representative of the more generalized process whereby the American West was lifted from rough frontier to the threshold of civilization.

HUBERT HOWE BANCROFT

In the historiography of western America no name is writ larger than Hubert Howe Bancroft. He was the first determined collector of the materials on this half continent and the first to undertake to chronicle its history comprehensively and exhaustively. The library that he established is the chief depository of such materials and for a generation has been the area's fountainhead of historical research. Similarly the thirty-nine massive volumes of his *Works* stand today, a full half century after their publication, as the fundamental reference on this vast subject matter and the best reference on a good fraction of the topics which comprise it. Basic to these achievements he had a long career as an individual and a businessman reasonably representative of the West in the gold rush and post gold rush generations.

Despite these claims to fame Bancroft has never had a biographer. In a volume entitled *Literary Industries,* published in 1890, he put on record a partial narrative of his life and in *Retrospection* in 1912 he added a few other particulars. There have been fragmentary comments about his collecting, about the launching of his first book, about his method of authorship,[1] but no full-scale treatment. The reason, I believe, is twofold. In common with most of us, Bancroft fell short of perfection. Some of his defects were seized upon, and it came to be the fashion to disparage him not only for these shortcomings but in all that he had done. The result was to becloud his eligibility for biographical attention. An even greater deterrent was the bulk of his published works. These include not only the seven and a half foot row of *Native Races* and *History of the Pacific States,* but three other sets, a number of individual books, and a sheaf of pamphlets — in all some sixty-odd volumes, the majority of them solid and weighty.[2] Their ponderousness tended to ward off prospective biographers and, it must be admitted, considerably retarded the present writer.

In his eighty-five years Bancroft was, among other things, businessman, publisher, collector, historian, essayist, and philosopher. Self-made and largely self-tutored, in each of these lines he was a pioneer, breaking new ground. His life thus was complex as well as long, not easily encompassed at book length, much less in a brief paper.

Bancroft was born in 1832 at Granville, Ohio, an offshoot and a transplanting of Puritan New England. His schooling stopped short of college, and at sixteen he began clerking in a Buffalo bookstore. In 1852, as a belated Argonaut, he went to California, experimented as miner, teamster, and clerk, and wound up with six or eight thousand dollars. A trip back east to the States made him homesick for California, and in 1856 he went west again and opened a bookstore in San Francisco. The beginning was simple. It was a one-salesman shop, and the proprietor acted as nightwatchman, janitor, and general handyman. Yet within a few years it became San Francisco's leading book mart, and for a generation it continued to be the foremost institution of its kind west of Chicago, employing more than three hundred persons, overflowing a five-story building, and active in book publishing and job printing as well as in merchandising.[3]

So prosperous was the business that Bancroft could travel extensively and in his late thirties could think seriously of retiring. Actually he did not sever his connections with business, but he began to give his chief attention to the pursuit of history.

Somewhat earlier — in 1859, to be precise — he had begun to collect Californiana.[4] Gradually his search widened to a world-wide canvass for materials on the western half of North America from Panama to Alaska. In this search he had the good fortune to be first in the field. Yet the real basis of his success lay in his philosophy of collecting. He believed in collecting for content rather than for externals of format. He believed in sweeping in every item that seemed to have even slight bearing on his subject. He had high regard for newspapers, and this before most historians had discovered them. He went after manuscripts, preferring the originals but if necessary resorting to copies and abstracts. He created historical materials by taking dictations from hundreds of pioneers and old-timers. He argued, oftentimes successfully, that it was a patriotic service to put materials in his collection. He was a sturdy beggar and a good borrower, but he drew heavily on his financial resources to buy from dealers, out of catalogues, and at auctions. At the time of its sale to the University of California, Reuben Gold Thwaites appraised the collection at more than $300,000.[5] It has since appreciated in value at least tenfold; and Director Herbert E. Bolton has said that with $10,000,000 and twenty years in which to spend it the collection could not be duplicated or satisfactorily replaced.[6]

As his library grew, Bancroft felt repeated urges to make some use of it. He considered publishing selected original narratives. He toyed with the idea of a Pacific states cyclopedia. He also thought of establishing a newspaper patterned after but improving upon the London *Times*. Fortunately his decision took another direction. In his words, "I would strike at once for the highest, brightest mark before me. . . . History-writing I conceived to be among the highest of human occupations, and this should be my choice."[7]

He was never in doubt about what history to undertake. It would be that of his field of collecting, the Pacific states, a modest one twelfth of the earth's land surface. He proposed, furthermore, a straightforward, frontal, factual attack upon this vast subject matter. He would attempt comprehensive and exhaustive treatment and leave philosophical theorizing to others. In freshness and in significance his opportunity as a historian was even more magnificent than as a collector.

From the outset he realized that he was undertaking more than any one man could do. In businesslike fashion he therefore hired assistants, employing first and last some six hundred persons to help in the production of his works. After much experimenting and at an outlay of $35,000 he devised a subject index to his entire collection. More than twice this amount went into abstracting and note-taking. Going still further, he set some of his men to writing first drafts, and the less revision required, the better he liked it. Theoretically he made himself responsible for all that went finally into print, and in practice he did this sufficiently so that his 30,000-page, 12,000,000-word opus has unity of design and method and character. Oftentimes his personal contact was slight, for example with the chapters he read on the cable car between his library and his printery, yet the thirty-nine volumes are an integrated whole.[8]

When it came to promoting and marketing his works Bancroft was equally the businessman. Before releasing his first volume, he took proof sheets in hand and made a tour of New England and the eastern states, buttonholing Parkman, Lowell, Palfrey, Whittier, Emerson, Beecher, Wendell Phillips, Godkin, Higginson, and other arbiters of opinion to make clear to them the merits of his achievement. As reviewer for the *Overland Monthly* he personally selected Daniel Coit Gilman, president of the University of California, and when the review turned out to be "flabby" he tore up the manuscript and referred the editors to J. Ross Browne, then probably California's best-known writer. To avoid further mishap, Browne's review, a glowing tribute, was written for him by a member of Bancroft's staff.[9] All things considered, it is not surprising that this book got a rousing sendoff. "Never probably," Bancroft observed, "was a book so generally and so favorably reviewed by the best journals in Europe and America. Never was an author more suddenly or more thoroughly brought to the attention of learned and literary men everywhere."[10]

Foreseeing no likelihood that the ordinary channels of the book trade would provide a market for his voluminous works, Bancroft decided to be his own publisher and to sell the set by subscription. The campaign was carefully engineered. Canvassers were schooled in interviewing and selling, and the way was skillfully prepared for them through newspaper publicity, pamphlets and prospectuses, and letters of introduction.[11] The sales program roused some animosity. In the Prickly Pear Valley in Montana, for example, there was a mass meeting of disgruntled subscribers;[12] and, in San Francisco, Leland Stanford, who out of civic pride had agreed to take forty sets, lived to repent his generosity.[13] By subscription selling, however, Bancroft made this gargantuan publishing venture pay, made it yield a profit of something like half a million dollars. What is more important, he got enough of his books into circulation so that, though out of print for fifty years, the set has never been rare, but has been readily available to every library and every user wanting it. This is the real triumph of his marketing program.

The *Works* fall into four main divisions. The first five volumes are an excursion into anthropology wherein are tabulated all the facts that Bancroft and his staff could find recorded about the native races of the Pacific states. Anthropology has since become a science and, through utilizing archaeology and field work among living Indians, has corrected and extended the Bancroft description of the western Indians. But for its day, the 1870's, *Native Races* represents a creditable achievement, particularly interesting in its matter-of-fact, reportorial approach and in its tribal groupings, which approximate today's accepted culture areas.

Another segment, consisting of almost a score of volumes, relates the history of Spanish North America (Florida and Louisiana omitted). The organization is regional, with three volumes on Central America, six on Mexico, two on the north Mexican states and Texas, and so on. The treatment increases in exhaustiveness with progression northwestward and culminates in the five volumes devoted to California as a province under Spain and Mexico. Chiefly by resort to the archives of Spain and Mexico, which were neglected by Bancroft and all his contemporaries, this generation's scholars have remedied the Bancroft account through a series of spot studies and monographs. No one, however, has undertaken to redo the entire job, and Bancroft remains the largest and the basic contributor to the history of Spanish North America.

As historian of California his pre-eminence is even greater. This was where his library was richest and where he saw the climax of development in the Pacific states. To California's history, therefore, he allotted seven volumes, supplemented by two volumes of social analysis, *California Pastoral* and *California Inter Pocula,* and two, *Popular Tribunals,* on the history of vigilance. In recent years this field has been cultivated by a host of professional and amateur researchers. Yet our aggregate knowledge of California history derives less from these scholars than from Bancroft. Eventually the moderns must excel; theirs is the advantage of scientific training, of access to and recognition of the treasures in Hispanic archives, and of eligibility to investigate the remarkable growth of the state since 1890. Yet to date, the cumulative results of their efforts have not matched, let alone surpassed, Bancroft's contribution as historian of California.

Another nine volumes cover, almost as thoroughly, the Rocky Mountain and northwestern states from Nevada, Utah, and Colorado to Alaska. These volumes are less even, less exhaustive, and less happily organized, yet the persevering reader will get a detailed picture of the forces that went into the making of these ten states. Again, no modern writer has undertaken a reappraisal of this entire subject, and no one has essayed, on a like scale, to bridge the gap between the 1880's and the present. Here is another vast field of regional history where Bancroft stands alone.

As supplement to his histories Bancroft announced a set of biographies, the Kings of the Commonwealth, which before publication he toned down to *Chronicles of the Builders.* Following these seven volumes came two other subscription works, *The Book of the Fair* and *The Book of Wealth,* in five and ten volumes. The two latter are not of special interest except as examples of sumptuous bookmaking. The *Chronicles* were both better and worse. Together with supporting essays on such topics as agriculture, mining, and railroads, they presented biographies of some one hundred men, examples of the more successful bankers, lawyers, farmers, tradesmen, and industrialists who had built the West. These were men so much like Bancroft that in a sense he was writing variations on his own biography. Selection unfortunately was on a fee basis, the fees ranging from $500 to $10,000 and the take amounting to some $219,000.[14] The subscription character of this work put it under a cloud and had the further effect of casting suspicion upon the preceding histories. Intrinsically the *Chronicles* possess real usefulness. Yet it is clear that Bancroft's standing among his contemporaries and in the estimate of the historical profession would have been better if the idea of doing these biographies had never occurred to him.

Despite the magnitude of his achievements Bancroft receipted for much abuse. When his business house was gutted in a million dollar fire, he ruefully observed that the event was admirably calculated "to confer the greatest pleasure upon the greatest number."[15] Again he remarked that there were hundreds in California who damned him every day.[16] He was one of Ambrose Bierce's favorite targets,[17] and other journalists liked to berate him. A nephew sued him for libel,[18] and his librarian attempted blackmail against him.[19] The Society of California Pioneers also pilloried him. Infuriated by his findings on Frémont, the Bear Flaggers, and various pioneers — findings which present-day scholarship almost entirely confirms — the society with elaborate formality expelled him from honorary membership.[20] Largely because of this unpopularity the California legislature declined to purchase his library in 1892 and for the same reason the university regents hesitated in 1905. In 1903 and 1911 two papers by professional historians,[21] to date the most extended notices that have been accorded him, renewed the familiar charges, especially that he was not the sole author and, in fact, was not the real author of the volumes called his works.

This issue is far too complicated for satisfactory discussion in brief compass. Perhaps it will suffice here to offer the judgment that Bancroft's failure to credit his helpers, explicitly or semiexplicitly, on the title pages or in the prefaces, was the greatest mistake of his life. On the other hand, the substitution of any single name for his on any of the volumes would have been still more misleading. The question of authorship is the thing harped on in both these articles. Their long-term and cumulative effect has been to belittle Bancroft as a historian and to discredit his *Works*. Illustrative of the tenacity of this idea is the obituary item with which the *Oregon Historical Quarterly* in 1918 took note of his death. The editor was ready to grant that "Mr. Bancroft, the most voluminous of Pacific West historians, may have left a fame more enduring in the long lapse of time than that of any other person who has lived and wrought in this area," but he coupled with it reassertion of the Oregon doctrine that Frances Fuller Victor wrote Bancroft's northwestern volumes.[22]

The reputation of a historian seldom improves after his death. A few classical historians like Herodotus and Thucydides have a current repute that compares favorably with what they enjoyed in their lifetimes. Another few of more recent vintage, including mostly such brilliant literary craftsmen as Gibbon, Prescott, and Parkman, though less widely read today, have retained most of their original luster. More commonly, as new sources are uncovered, new techniques developed, new methods of evaluation devised, and new bases of interpretation discovered, the historians of a bygone era tend to depreciate. The saying is that for each generation history must be rewritten, and, to a considerable extent, this is what the reading public and the profession have demanded. It is, therefore, a matter of mark that Bancroft has been much more praised, in the quarter century after his death, than he was by his contemporaries.

Henry Morse Stephens, for example, hailed him as "the greatest of a half dozen great American historians, and the only one who had an adequate understanding of the historical West."[23] Charles Edward Chapman asserted that his *Works* "constitute the greatest single achievement in the history of American historiography."[24] The dean of Texas historians describes his *North Mexican States and Texas* as "the most satisfactory comprehensive history of Texas available," and the six volumes on Mexico as "perhaps the best work in its field in either English or Spanish."[25] Bernard DeVoto says, "I cannot imagine anyone's writing about the history of the West without constantly referring to Bancroft."[26] Franklin Walker, in his recent commentary on early California letters, though critical of the obscuration of authorship, praises the collection and the histories, pointing out that the latter "have to date maintained their preeminence as the basic authority on the half continent with which they deal." "One would not go far wrong," he continues, "in asserting that Hubert Howe Bancroft, the frontier bookseller who turned historian, accomplished the greatest feat of historiography since Thucydides."[27]

The explanation of this changed attitude is relatively simple. Time, though not the solvent for all undeserved aspersions, does tend to rectify. In the past quarter century researchers in ever increasing numbers have undertaken investigations of various parts of the Bancroft field. By experience this scholarly army has learned that for its purposes the Bancroft Library is the prime collection of materials, and that the Bancroft volumes are not merely the bulkiest but by all odds the most valuable reference. Thus by pragmatic test, the collection and the set, by proving themselves, have vindicated their creator and won him a belated recognition. Consequently, one who praises Bancroft today is on safer, or at least on more accepted, ground than those who had the wisdom and the courage to do so in the 1890's or in 1918.

Obviously the measure of Bancroft's achievement must be three-dimensional, embracing his work as businessman, as collector, and as historian. In each of these categories it is apparent not only that the fates smiled upon him but also that he fully earned his successes. Because of his lack of training and experience, it is doubtless most surprising that he succeeded as a historian. But he discovered a hitherto neglected subject, rich in human interest, which seemed to be the last great chapter in the transit of civilization from Greece and Rome to western Europe, across the Atlantic, and to continent's end on the shores of the Pacific. Wisely he chose to deal with this grand subject in its entirety rather than to be satisfied with the annals of some minor locality. Wisely he surrounded himself with a staff, because the task patently outreached his individual capacity. Wisely he chose to subordinate generalization and moralizing and to concentrate on presentation of ascertained and unadorned facts. It is of such stuff that the thirty thousand pages of the *Works* largely consist. Essentially they are a recital in endless detail of the particulars of Pacific slope history, for California unbelievably complete, for other areas only less so. They are the core around which every library of western history is built, and, though long since out of print, they are the most cited, the most used, and the most followed of all references in the field. In actual practice, therefore, Bancroft is honored above all other historians of western North America.

In the pattern of his career Bancroft may be thought of as the symbol of his generation. Other Westerners were creating businesses and amassing fortunes, some much larger than his. Others, though not so many, were using their wealth to bring cultural improvement to what had been a rough frontier: Adolph Sutro by collecting English pamphlets, Mexican imprints and manuscripts, and early Californiana; James Lick by endowing an observatory; and Leland Stanford by establishing a university. Still others were turning from the entertainment literature that had characterized the gold rush era to attempt more serious, scientific writing. Henry George's *Progress and Poverty* is the most famous example, but in the field of history the *Works* would qualify as an equally meritorious contribution. Bancroft's business success thus conformed to the West's economic pattern, his collecting expressed its cultural aspirations, and his publications illustrated its intellectual maturation.

In the fullness of time he may prove to have been the greatest of them all. Already he has eclipsed many of his better publicized contemporaries, including Thomas Starr King and E. D. Baker, the Union orators; William C. Ralston, once called "the man who built San Francisco"; the Big Four; the Kings of the Comstock; and Francis Bret Harte, Joaquin Miller, and Ambrose Bierce, once luminaries of considerably greater luster. The prominence of these men was based, it now appears, on a political cause, a bank, a mere accumulation of wealth, a style in poetry, or some other transitory factor, which, though impressive at the time, in the longer run has diminished or disappeared. Bancroft, on the contrary, in his library and his histories set up durable and viable assurances of lasting and growing recognition. A prodigious historian he certainly was; generations hence he may loom up as the most significant figure that the West has produced.

CALIFORNIA IN THIRD DIMENSION

Whoever reads history reveals a curiosity about what has happened. This curiosity often runs deeper, inquiring about causes and consequences and reaching toward understanding. More intently the reader wants the characters in the drama of history to come alive — to stand forth as human beings. And most readers no doubt regard this request as altogether reasonable. After all, the personages of history were actual pulsating individuals.

The ideal historian — and this is not just coincidence — is stirred by these same desires. He strives to find out what happened, what caused it, and what came of it. He is not content just to tabulate the data that is worthy of credence. He hopes also to interpret and, above all, to have real people walking the pages of his writing.

The materials of history often make it difficult to attain these goals. They may be so voluminous that they overwhelm, or so broken that they frustrate, and always there is the hazard that they will be erroneous or misleading. The rules of our craft offer some help. We know how to detect the unreliable. If the evidence is mountainous we know how to cut through by scientific sampling. If there are gaps we sometimes can reason our way across them. But the more antiseptic we render the evidence the less natural it becomes. The more scientific the sample the more impersonal it is apt to be. The places where we have had to patch or restore have an artificial cast, and all too often we end up with figures that are cardboard and a picture that is flat.

One way to make the picture live is to borrow the method of the stereoptican which achieves a third dimension by introducing a second perspective. For the purposes of the historian the added perspective most readily available is that of literature. I use the term in its standard meaning of "creative writing," bearing in mind, however, that professional novelists and poets do not monopolize this talent, that description and narration do not have to be figments of the imagination in order to qualify as literature, and snatches that are genuinely literary crop up in writing that is less pretentious. California will be a sufficient example. Certain chapters in its past have a special vitality because the approaches of literature and of conventional history both have been brought to bear. In others the picture is indistinct or distorted, often because the delineation has been left to one or the other of these perspectives.

The start, as in all western history, can be with the land and the Indians. On the land we have a wealth of attested facts. Cartographers no longer fancy California as an island or insert a Buenaventura River passing through from the Rockies to the Pacific. The state is charted with tolerable accuracy and the rivers are in their proper beds. Altitudes have been determined from Mt. Whitney down to Bad Water. The weather has been recorded over a period of several generations, and the natural resources have been inventoried systematically. True enough, the range of the weather is not yet fully determined — in 1958, for instance, Los Angeles had a hotter October than ever before recorded. As to resources, likewise, no one knows for sure whether the sardines will come back, and, to take another example, the oil companies still drill what they call discovery wells. Yet the sum total of what we know about our environment is enormous. Much of it derives from routine historical sources. A great deal of it comes from geography and the more recondite sciences. Much of it is statistical, and the whole of it is certified knowledge of the sort that historians in the Teutonic tradition have always preferred.

This is one way to know the land. Another is to meet it through the eyes and the emotion of literature, turning to Mary Austin for realization of the Land of Little Rain, to J. Smeaton Chase for an appreciation of the color of the desert, to Clarence King for the wonder of the giant sequoias, to John Charles Frémont for the lyric beauty of the flower-bedecked valley of the San Joaquin as seen after the ordeal of a winter crossing of the Sierra, to Robert Louis Stevenson for a rapturous description of the fog rolling in on Mt. St. Helena, or to John Muir's most apt phrase for the Sierra, "The Range of Light." With such companions we can go where most of us would not otherwise venture. We can sail with Cabrillo along the Big Sur, where, as he reported, "there are mountains which seem to reach the heavens, and the sea beats on them; sailing along close to land, it appears as though they would fall on the ships."[1]

Or with Muir we can go down into a crevasse of Black Mountain glacier, his pioneer discovery in the Sierra:

> A series of rugged zigzags enabled me to make my way down into the weird under-world of the crevasse. Its chambered hollows were hung with a multitude of clustered icicles, amid which pale, subdued light pulsed and shimmered with indescribable loveliness. Water dripped and tinkled overhead, and from far below came strange, solemn murmurings from currents that were feeling their way through veins and fissures in the dark. The chambers of a glacier are perfectly enchanting, notwithstanding one feels out of place in their frosty beauty. I was soon cold in my shirt-sleeves, and the leaning wall threatened to engulf me; yet it was hard to leave the delicious music of the water and the lovely light.[2]

The California Indians, as found by the Spaniards, were living in a state of such abysmal ignorance and simplicity that they made a very poor impression. Of the Diegueños at Coyote Canyon, for instance, Pablo Font remarked, "they are so savage, wild and dirty, disheveled, ugly, small, and timid, that only because they have the human form is it possible to believe that they belong to mankind."[3] The American pioneers heartily agreed. In allusion to their grubbing for roots and insects the Americans spoke of these people in disdain as the Digger Indians and moved callously toward exterminating them.

As early as 1852 B. D. Wilson pointed out that Indians were the backbone of the labor force of southern California and, despite all that was said against them, had skill and stamina enough to do what was required on ranch and farm and about town.[4] When anthropologists later came on the scene they too saw the California Indian in a better light, praising the dietary made possible by the acorn process, the highly developed art of basketry, and the kuksu and toloache fraternities.

Most fortunately for the ultimate reputation of these Indians they had a literature. Solely oral, it consisted of stories peopled by Coyote, Mouse, Eagle, and their brethren, all possessed with human qualities and characteristics. Some of the stories have a quiet moral, such as the one about Coyote who challenged the Los Angeles River to a race. He ran as hard as he could until he could run no more, looked over the bank, and saw the river running calmly on. He went off with tail between his legs and something to think about for many a day.[5] Others probed the most difficult problems — how the world began, where man came from, the question of good and evil. Others tackled history — how man got fire, how the languages originated, why buckeye wood makes a good fire drill. Nor was poetic imagery lacking, as we see in Mary Austin's translation from the Shoshone, beginning:

Neither spirit nor bird;
That was my flute you heard
Last night by the river.
When you came with your wicker jar
Where the river drags the willows,
That was my flute you heard,
Wacoba, Wacoba,
Calling, Come to the willows![6]

Helen Hunt Jackson, the anthropologists, and the Friends of the Indian may have helped, but this original literature probably goes farthest toward persuading us that the California Indian was indeed a human being with thoughts and feelings and responses very much like anybody else's. The other evidence that history has to go by might not have been persuasive on this most crucial point. Or at most this insight might have been left to surmise as in Robinson Jeffers' poem "Hands." It describes a cave near Tassajara painted with hands, "a cloud of men's palms," "signs-manual" that are like a "sealed message" saying:

"Look: we also were human, we had hands,
not paws. All hail
You people with the cleverer hands, our supplanters
In the beautiful country; enjoy her a season, her
beauty, and come down
And be supplanted; for you also are human."[7]

Next on the scene were the Spaniards. From the beginning they found California hard going. In the peninsula Cortés was rebuffed, and for a century and a half every other effort to gain a foothold failed dismally. The Jesuits then implanted Spanish control, yet none too securely as was illustrated by the wave of revolt in the 1730's, and not profitably enough to be a real incentive for extending the frontier farther northward. Those who went on to Alta California likewise had their share of drudgery and hardship. They were wracked by disease and often found themselves at the edge of starvation. Their heroism was in surmounting these hazards, or just in surviving them. Coldly inventoried, what they did was to establish hardly more than a token occupancy, which, as it happened, was all that imperial policy required. The keepers of the account would have to register all this as a quite modest achievement, except that it also had a value essentially literary.

As the first to spy out the land these men came on a great adventure that invited an aura of romance. As to some of them we know little more than that they were courageous, hard-bitten, and unlucky. So it stands for Melchior Díaz, who has the earliest credentials for setting foot on the soil of American California, for Sebastián Rodríguez Cermeño, and for Francisco Garcés. Assuredly these must have been men of spirit, but perhaps they were just stolid and phlegmatic, which is what Font says of Garcés. For a number of others including the founder of Alta California, Gaspar Portolá, the direct record attests nothing more.

Fortunately other chroniclers take us beyond the routine details and reveal some of the emotions that were stirred. Antonio de la Ascención's narrative of the Vizcaíno voyage is full of such passages, for instance in what he has to say about the stopover at Catalina and the Indian delegation that came aboard off Point Mugu. Font's diary on the second Anza expedition abounds in such entries. Juan Crespi's pen picture of the Los Angeles Plain at the moment of discovery in 1769 is another example, as is Engineer Miguel Costansó's commentary on California hospitality as experienced by these same pioneers of the Portolá expedition:

> The natives, not content with making us presents of their eatables, wished, furthermore, to give us a feast, thus manifesting the mutual rivalry and contention between the towns to excel each other in gifts and festivities. . . . The dancing continued all the afternoon, and we had hard work to rid ourselves of [our visitors]. Finally we sent them away, earnestly recommending them, by means of signs, not to come back during the night to disturb us; but in vain. At nightfall they returned with a large retinue of clowns or jugglers, playing whistles, the noise of which grated on our ears. It was feared that they would stampede our horses, and, for this reason, the commander, with his officers and some soldiers, went out to receive them. They gave the natives some glass beads, and intimated to them that if they came back to disturb our sleep, they would no longer be our friends and we would give them j bad reception.[8]

For at least one noteworthy figure of the Spaniard period the one fact securely established is that he was a romantic and fiction-minded. He is the man who gave California its name. We do not know who he was or when or where he did the christening. But as with President Roosevelt's favorite airplane carrier, the name came from a well-known book, in this instance Montalvo's *Las sergas de*

Esplandián, and California's anonymous benefactor had the genius and the sentiment to see its appropriateness.

Beginning with Lapérouse in 1786 a noteworthy succession of foreigners visited California. Instead of limiting themselves to matters that they might have classified as the stuff of history, they looked at the province with a wider curiosity.

Thus Lapérouse tells how the governor and the commander of the two corvettes at Monterey tried to outdo each other in making the visitors comfortable. He tells how at Mission Carmel they were received "as the lords of the parish making their first entrance into their lands." He comments on the two styles of architecture, Spanish and Indian, commends the missionary practice of whipping male neophytes in public and females in private, and marvels at the dexterity of the Indian women as with basket trays and open fires they toasted the grain for the daily ration of atole.[9]

At San Francisco in 1792 George Vancouver is struck by the confidence of the Indians venturing out into rough water in their tule balsas. For him the primitiveness of the commandant's quarters merely enhanced the quiet dignity of his wife and the decorous behavior of their children. As he summed up his impressions:

> Instead of finding a country tolerably well inhabited and far advanced in cultivation, if we except its natural pastures, the flocks of sheep, and herds of cattle, there is not an object to indicate the most remote connection with any European, or ot ter civilized nation.[10]

An entirely different set of circumstances prompted George W. Eayrs to write. He made port in 1813 to get supplies and incidentally to trade, as, in fact, he had done several times before. This time the Spaniards arrested him, took his ship, helped themselves to its cargo, appropriated a small Indian boy he had bought on the Columbia five years earlier, and made off with "a Young Female . . . with whom," Eayrs asserted, "I esteem equal the same as if I was lawfully marryed to hir." Eayrs' letter, dated "Sn Deago, October 8 — 1813," is easily the most eloquent of these writings on Spanish California. It begins:

> MOST NOBLE & EXCELLENT SIR, VICE ROY OF MEXICO —
> Being a Prisoner in this place and moste disagreeably situated, I have to deplore of Your Excellency as spedy relief as the nature of my captivity and difficulty of the times will admit of —[11]

Historians from Palou to Bancroft to Bolton have been at pains to get at the realities of the Spanish system as applied to California. In concert these historians of three centuries have given the political and economic history of the Spanish period lavish and discerning treatment. If the concern, however, is with the spirit of the times — an inward glimpse at the Californians — *The Journey of the Flame* (1933), by Walter Nordhoff, alias Antonio de Fierro Blanco, will prove more enlightening. Undeniably fiction, it utilizes an approach that none of the standard histories was in position to use.

On the Atlantic seaboard the colonies started under a regime of salutary neglect and only later was there a tightening of imperial controls. In California the restrictive system came first, and the neglect, salutary or otherwise, occurred in the Mexican period. The neglect was physical: government ships ceased to come with any regularity from Mexico. It was political: California was left much more to its own devices. The neglect also extended to the keeping of the record, with the result that the documentary materials on which the history of this quarter-century might be written are much less satisfactory. Partly as a consequence works of scholarship, numerous for the Spanish period, as the names Herbert E. Bolton, Henry R. Wagner, Charles E. Chapman, and Herbert I. Priestley suggest, are few indeed on California under Mexico.

In this period it is true, Americans and other foreigners began to infiltrate. Coming in private capacity, these people were under no obligation to report and most of them were most haphazard about building the record. Yet they were heralds of the next change of flag, and on the often fragmentary materials that are available historians and biographers have dealt quite elaborately with this troop of hide traders, beaver trappers, and overland pioneers. This is the subject matter that enabled Bancroft to match his two volumes on California under Spain with two on California under Mexico. Chapman's *History* has a more austere ratio: on Spanish California 454 pages and on the Mexican years 31, which was compensated only in part with Robert G. Cleland's budget in his companion volume of 200 pages to the preconquest phases of American contact. Given the archival inadequacy and the lack of officially certified statistics, any assist from literature would be all the more appreciated.

No one on the scene at the time was trying to write the great American novel. No one was writing any novel. A gallant caballero, it is true, was supposed to be able to improvise verses of romance as he strummed his guitar. So it is reported, but little of the product has survived.

Another genre of writing by participants does represent California before the conquest. In it the format is straight narration or description, usually quite unpretentious, and often far from literate, yet with memorable passages. James M. Clyman, for instance, after highly critical comment on California backwardness, went on to say:

> In speaking of the government of California I must say that it is the most free and easy government Perhaps on the civilized globe no Taxes are imposed on any individual what ever I saw nor heard of no requirement for Roade labour no Military tax no civil department to support no Judiciary requiring pay and in every respect the people live free you may support Priest or not at your pleasure and if your life and property are not Quite so safe as in some other countries you have the pleasure of using all your earnings.[12]

There are rewards also in Jedediah Smith on the Indians and bears of the Sacramento Valley, in Harrison Rogers on the customs at Mission San Gabriel, in Fred Walpole's picture of Frémont and his men trooping into Monterey, and in Carl Meyer's description of the *tertulia* and the fleas at Rancho Patrocinio de Alisal. Dancing and fleas were omnipresent in pastoral California. It remained for Meyer to establish the connection. "It is almost impossible," he wrote, "to rid the body entirely of these vermin during the day so these blood-related parasites also join in the pleasant entertainment of the *tertulia.*"[13]

Frémont, Robinson, and Dana offer more sustained literary effort. Frémont first entered California in the winter of 1843-1844, and before coming again in 1845 he filed a book-length report. An official account and published as a government document, it was much more: a story of adventure, a description of scenes new to American readers, and a commentary on unfamiliar types such as fur trade veterans, Indians of several different culture patterns, and the Californians as sampled at Sutter's Fort and southward. The literary quality matched the challenge.

Alfred Robinson's *Life in California,* published in 1846, had a quite different inspiration. Father Boscana's *Chinigchinich,* a treatise on the customs and beliefs of the Gabrielino, had come to his attention and he decided to prepare an English translation. As an afterthought he wrote an introduction describing the provincial culture. This essay became the main thing and some later editions omitted the *Chinigchinich.*

Richard Henry Dana, as is well known, wrote his *Two Years Before the Mast* (1840) to describe the lot of the workingman at sea. His book would have claimed many readers had it dealt with a voyage to Timbuktu or any other bizarre shore. To our great good fortune Dana also entered his picture of California and the Californians as seen by a hide drogher. For our comprehension of life as it was in this period we are in fact chiefly indebted to these works that are literary in quality.

A later generation of fictionists would discover this pastoral era as ineffably idyllic. Gertrude Atherton in her *Splendid Idle Forties* (1902) saw it in this perfection, and Stewart Edward White in his serials for the *Saturday Evening Post* was even more successful in evoking this image and bringing it to popular acceptance. There may be question whether this performance was a service to history, yet it was in tune with the mood of Bancroft's *California Pastoral* (1888) and Nellie van de Grift Sánchez' *Spanish Arcadia* (1929), and it was substantially confirmed in Cleland's *Cattle on a Thousand Hills* (1941).

As compared to the preceding decades the interval of the conquest seemed far more historic. From Commodore Jones's premature flag-raising at Monterey on through the Frémont-Castro imbroglio, the Bear Flag revolt, the American take-over, the southern California revolt, the protracted maneuverings of reconquest, the bickerings among the conquerors, the expostulations against military government, and the attainment of statehood, here was much bustle and excitement and in the end a most gratifying result.

The documentation is rich in state papers — the proclamations of Sloat and Stockton, the profusion of military orders through which the occupied province was governed, the multitudinous official reports, and as a crowning glory the constitution of 1849. As a gloss on this official record, another and in some respects a richer archive took shape in which would be numbered the more flowery proclamation that William B. Ide composed for the Bear Flaggers, the jottings in Walter Colton's diary, the first forays into journalism, the uninhibited fulminations of Philosopher Pickett, the better tempered narrative of Edwin Bryant, and the carefully composed reporting such as Bayard Taylor's on the closing scenes of the convention. The tone of what has become the standard treatment of this brief but critical interlude comes mainly from these personalized, intimate, literary sources.

Then, with no pause for adjustment to the great new fact of being part of the United States, California plunged into the more compelling excitement of the Gold Rush. Suddenly the state swarmed with adventurers from all the states and most of the nations. With this flood of new manpower, new initiative, and suddenly abundant purchasing power, the community rushed headlong into a social revolution that was at once a binge and a constructive advance.

The forty-niners had high consciousness that they were making history. That is one reason so many of them traveled to California notebook in hand and why they filled the mails with reports on their experiences. Their journals range from the bare bones of Sheldon Young's log to the wonderfully prolix testament of J. Goldsborough Bruff. Most of these accounts of travel and mining are at most the raw materials of history and quite appropriately they have been mined by researchers trying to sort out the facts. Other bits and pieces have meaning that can only be assayed if seen as literature. James H. Carson's report on the symptoms of the gold fever is not to be read as a clinical chart but as an attempt to communicate the emotional impact. Alonso Delano's pen picture of the Argonauts on the march, Bruff's reverie on the idyllic scene at Bear Valley, and Jacob Stover's rhapsody on the pure joy of emerging from the desert into the softness of California, although faithful in every detail, were composed to express considerably more.

The Gold Rush also gave Californians their first real opportunity to write for publication. Eastern publishers welcomed and even commissioned California manuscripts, and local newspapers, magazines, and book publishers vied for copy. The response was a florescence of writing, some of it exotic, but most of it focused on Gold Rush California. This degree of preoccupation with themselves and their time meant that such history as was written was introverted upon current events. Alongside this matter-of-fact chronicling we now encounter for the first time a companion venturing into fiction and poetry, most of which was directed to the selfsame scenes and themes.

This literature began with Old Block, John Phoenix, Dogberry, Dame Shirley, and Yellow Bird (pen names all), and later involved Bret Harte and Mark Twain. Among its characteristics two in particular stand out — broad humor and sentimentality. Neither is the surest avenue to immortality. George Derby's hyperbolic tales suited the taste of his day, but to many a modern reader seem hopelessly archaic. Our brand of sophistication balks at the mawkishness of "The Luck of Roaring Camp." Yet this literary legacy is as revealing as the tally of wagons passing Fort Kearney, the trail necrology of Bruff, the port records of San Francisco, or the tabulation of votes in the state elections.

To illustrate let me cite two outstanding modern works on California in its golden era. More thoroughly and perspicaciously than had ever been done before, Rodman W. Paul's *California Gold* (1947) inspects and analyzes the forty-niner as miner. G. Ezra Dane's *Ghost Town* (1941) looks almost exclusively at the miner when he was not at work. The one applies the method of the graduate seminar, the other of E Clampus Vitus. The one rests on data unexceptionably historical, the other derives from sources that are either literary or folklore. Each admirably accomplishes what its author set out to do. It is when these two are brought into conjunction that the Mother Lode prospector stands forth as the whole man.

Partly because the forty-niners were youthful and partly because their activities were so flamboyant, the Gold Rush era gave way only grudgingly. In time, however, the sons of the pioneers did take over, drafting a new constitution, gearing their life to the railroad, wheat, and the orange, and accommodating themselves to the tourist, the health-seeker, and the real estate promoter.

With an array of writers that included Ambrose Bierce, Frank Norris, and Jack London, not to mention Ina Coolbrith, Helen Hunt Jackson, T. S. Van Dyke, John Muir, Mary Austin, Will Irwin, Charles F. Lummis, George Wharton James, Herman Scheffauer, and George Sterling, this generation had literary brillance. And with Hubert Howe Bancroft, Josiah Royce, and Theodore H. Hittell as representatives, for the first time on the local scene history as a reflective study was also being pursued.

Bancroft the businessman, Royce the philosopher, and Hittell the lawyer had this in common, that as historians they were self-made men. Each exhibited strong-willed individualism: Bancroft as he broke through many of the conventions that had surrounded history writing; Hittell, as he worked away at his history with never a nod to Bancroft or so much as a visit to the Bancroft collection; and Royce as he decided that his history of California for the American Commonwealths series should be a monograph on just ten years out of the 350 that might have been covered.

Individualistic though they were, they all saw the climax of the state's history in the inauguration of the American period. Bancroft, to be sure, budgeted a great deal of space to prologue and setting — five volumes to the native races, nine or ten to Central America and Mexico, four or five to the states and territories eastward of California, and seven to the states and provinces northward to Alaska. That left, however, a dozen volumes for California. The space allocation within these California volumes is a good index to what he saw as important. He gave more than half to the period from 1846 to 1865, ten times as many pages as he reserved for the longer span from 1865 to 1890.

Hittell's pagination is somewhat different since he confined himself mainly to a recital of past politics, but his favorite also was the period from 1846 to 1865 and he saved no more than a tenth of his space for the next quarter-century. Royce, as mentioned, carrying the emphasis on American beginnings to an even greater extreme, began with the Bear Flaggers in 1846 and stopped with the Second Vigilance Committee in 1856.

These historians did not heap indiscriminate praise upon the midcentury Californians. Bancroft saw the Bear Flaggers as a blundering rabble and he belabored the pioneers for their cruelty to the Indians. Royce was unsparingly critical of Frémont and held the best people of San Francisco squarely to blame through their civic apathy for the abuses that the vigilance committees sought to correct. Yet in the value judgments made explicit, as well as in the space allotted, Bancroft, Royce, and Hittell underscored the primacy of the conquest and Gold Rush. Zoeth S. Eldredge's Exposition history in 1915 was cut from the same cloth and by the same pattern.[14]

All these historians, as is true of most today, were alert for signs of progress. Where struggle occurred they would record it, and as problems arose they carefully observed the efforts to solve them, but primarily they would tell the California story in terms of growth and development. For Royce it was the improvement of the body politic and social that mattered most, but that in all probability would contribute to economic growth as well. Within the narrow limits of his legalistic approach Hittell agreed. Bancroft was more catholic in his view. His heroes included a few men of the cloth and other idealists, but more often they were men of tangible achievement and wealth. Of such was the roster in his *Chronicles of the Builders*.[15]

The literary output of this intermediate period is less readily categorized. Some of it was essentially placeless or had the quality of apostrophe to Nature and little relevance to affairs of California past or present. Whatever the generalizations about these writers and their wares, Ambrose Bierce would have insisted on being an exception. In his favorite role as iconoclast he repeatedly deflated the image that the pioneers tried to give of themselves, the sentimental treatment by the Bret Harte school, and the glorification which the historians indulged in. As head-knocker he also paid his left-handed respects to the men of success and influence whom Bancroft identified as the builders. Bitter and caustic, Bierce offered little in the way of positive analysis. His pungent and electric prose reached a host of readers and often could be construed as rebuttal of the interpretation that was offered as standard history.

As a group the literati of this period were much less obsessed with bygone days than were the historians. Lummis crusaded to make his contemporaries aware of the quality of Indian culture and the magnitude of the Spanish heritage, but his *Land of Sunshine* even more vigorously played up the bustling growth from the eighties on. James wrote on antiquarian subjects such as Indian basketry and weaving, but principally to describe the scene as it then was. If Jackson's *Ramona* was nostalgic it was for the sake of calling attention to a problem that was current. Van Dyke hardly waited for the foreclosures before coming out with his lampoon of the boom of the eighties. Austin's period piece, *Isidro,* was less noteworthy than *The Flock* and *The Land of Little Rain,* both of which had immediacy. Irwin's most memorable writing was on San Francisco just before the Earthquake. Norris found his subject matter in the Mussel Slough tragedy of 1880 and in San Francisco of later date. London wrote of the University of California, the Oakland waterfront, and the fish patrol as of the very moment.

Another and more fundamental cleavage differentiated these historians and literati. In their appraisal of the age in which they lived the novelists and essayists identified issues and crises quite in contrast to those given prominence by the historians and developed an empathy for persons and types even more radically at variance. Muir's admiration certainly did not go to the enterprisers who would improve on Nature, or Van Dyke's to the real estate boomers. Austin's heroes were the shepherds of the desert and mountain pastures and the common people of Owens Valley. London's protagonists were as much the oyster pirates as the fish and game wardens and certainly not the swells with whom Martin Eden had to compete. In *The Octopus* the reader's sympathy is invited for the embattled farmers rather than for the magnates Bancroft had called the "Kings of the Commonwealth."

The contrast between historians and novelists is most dramatically epitomized in Royce, because he was both historian and novelist. His history, for all its philosophic overtones, was in consonance with Bancroft's and Hittell's. In his novel, *The Feud of Oakfield Creek,* published just a year later, Royce moved forward from the fifties to the eighties and took his stance with the rest of the fictionists on the side of the humble rather than the mighty.[16]

The creative writers, Royce to Norris to London, did not manage a complete documentary on what was going on and what was being achieved in California from 1875 or 1880 to 1906 or 1917. Their writings need to be supplemented by what historians contribute, as Glenn S. Dumke's *Boom of the Eighties* (1944) did for Van Dyke's *Millionaires of a Day* (1890). Obviously, however, this body of fiction is an important addition and corrective to the historians, Bancroft to Royce to Eldredge, for whom, to take another illustration, the Workingmen who rallied under Denis Kearney were a nuisance and a menace to reputable society. I know of no fiction centering on this movement of the Workingmen, but any reader of Norris and London will at least wonder if something should not be said in their behalf.

Early in the twentieth century the study of California history for the first time came to be university-centered. The initial impulse was the purchase of the Bancroft Library by the University of California. With F. J. Teggart in charge, the Academy of Pacific Coast History launched a program of documentary publication. Then in 1911 Herbert Eugene Bolton was lured across the bay from Stanford, and a beehive of historical studies soon sprang up. The resources of the Bancroft collection served as one support. Another, which for a time seemed more important, was the discovery of the archives of imperial Spain. With the Harvard device of the teaching assistantship to provide subsistence and with fellowships from the Native Sons of the Golden West to support archival pilgrimages, Berkeley soon came to be a formidable history research center.

Some of the students at Berkeley, among whom Cardinal Goodwin, William H. Ellison, Joseph Ellison, Owen Coy, J. Fred Rippy, William H. Binkley, LeRoy Hafen, Adele Ogden, Leland H. Creer, and P. K. Wyllys are representative, assigned themselves a reexamination of California and the American West. They concentrated their studies on the eighteen forties and fifties, the epoch that had held such fascination for the earlier free-enterprise historians. Their mentors at Berkeley were much more directly concerned with the Spanish period. The score or more of books by Bolton, Chapman, and Priestley that belong in a California bibliography all attach to the northward advance of the Spaniards. Another phalanx of their students labored in this same part of the vineyard, as these names, reading across the continent, will suggest: John Tate Lanning, Irving Leonard, Lawrence Kinnaird, A. P. Nasatir, Arthur P. Aiton, J. Lloyd Mecham, George P. Hammond, Charles W. Hackett, A. B. Thomas, Peter M. Dunne, W. L. Schurz.

This ferment of historical scholarship had broad repercussions, probably most significant in the stimulation of Latin American studies and in encouraging the broader perspective of Western Hemisphere history. Applied science was made to illuminate the history of California, but it was early California far more than recent. The Spanish approaches were more vigorously pursued than the American; more was written about California's temporary constitution than about its permanent one; stage lines and the explorations for railroads were more thoroughly reported than the building of the railroads; federal relations were analyzed mostly in their initial phases; the sea otter and hide and fur trades were more focussed on than the orange business or any element of twentieth-century economy. Preoccupation with a rather distant past thus was a marked characteristic of this school.

And what, we should inquire, were California's literary people doing during the nineteen teens and twenties? Austin was moving into mysticism. Lummis was promoting the Southwest Museum. Jeffers was beginning his introspections along the Big Sur. John Steven McGroarty, poet laureate, was intoning tributes to the romance of the mission period. No more influentially, but more durably, Atherton and White were singing the praises of the good old days when California was pastoral and contact with Spanish culture was modulating the rough Yankee newcomer into a more civilized person. These novelists were as retrospective as their parallel numbers in history, and more sentimental. That, however, is not quite the whole story. No generation of creative artists can be completely indifferent to what goes on around them.

Austin's *The Flood* (1917), though not the definitive epic on irrigation, captures the dazed frustration of the Owens Valley people, whose water rights were spirited away by the City of Los Angeles. A later novelist, Wallace Stegner, has come closest to doing justice to the Wobblies, who in these decades were treated as the worst of all menaces. And John Rorty's "Dissonance," slight though it is, is a most apt commentary on the booster spirit that pervaded the booming twenties. Any stanza will illustrate:

> There is a pewee bird that cries
> "La, sol, me,
> "La, sol, me."
> He is the only thing that sighs
> Beside the western sea. . . .
> It was a shock, I own, to see
> Sedition sitting in a tree
> Remarking plainly, "La, sol, me,
> "La, sol, me."
> . . . .
> I said, "My bird, you ought to know
> Enough to sing, 'Do, me, sol, do,'
> In major thirds, you see, for so
> You'll help to make the country grow."[17]

Since the twenties California has lived through the Great Depression and the Second World War and into the Cold War and the Atomic Age. It has experienced the automobile and the airplane, industry, smog, and fallout. Its population has almost trebled and the gravity of its problems has more than trebled.

Over these years the study of its history has gone on. Thanks in part to the Huntington Library its pursuit has become statewide instead of being concentrated at one center. Names such as Cleland, R. D. Hunt, John H. Kemble, William B. Rice, Dumke, Andrew Rolle, and Paul are suggestive on this score. Other names such as H. R. Wagner, W. W. Robinson, Carl I. Wheat, Oscar Lewis, Franklin Walker, George R. Stewart, Carey McWilliams, and Remi Nadeau point up that the happy partnership with avocational historians still persists.

With books such as Walton E. Bean's *Boss Ruef's San Francisco* (1952), George E. Mowry's *California Progressives* (1951), and Walker's *Literary History of Southern California* (1950), it is clear that today's historians have done more on the first quarter of this century than the historians of that period did on the last quarter of the nineteenth century. Here is some reduction of the time lag to which history is always prone. Yet a larger number of the best works of recent vintage deal with the more antique past of the Gold Rush and the fur trade and, with exceptions which almost come down to McWilliams and the textbooks, few studies have been attempted with subject matter in the nineteen thirties, forties, or fifties.

In national and international history no such reticence blocks the study of our times, witness the Roosevelt biographies now in progress and current titles such as *The Causes of World War Three*. On the local scene it is also true that the novelists and other creative writers are perfectly willing to deal with issues that are live.

Sometimes they write descriptively with no apparent intention to summon anyone to action. That is how most of Saroyan reads. He writes of people who are down but not quite out, and he is most vivid on what the Depression felt like and what it has meant in more prosperous times to belong to the depressed quarter or sixth or tenth of the population.

Stegner's *The Preacher and the Slave* (1950), as indicated, reaches back (just a little further than Norris did when he wrote *The Octopus*) to the criminal syndicalism hysteria. Another chapter in labor relations is the theme of John Steinbeck's *In Dubious Battle* (1936), followed shortly by *The Grapes of Wrath* (1939), the epic on the Dust Bowl refugees and their reception as migratory laborers in California agriculture. These Works breathe a strong social criticism. So does Budd Schulberg's *What Makes Sammy Run?* (1941), a novel on the drive for power, or, what Americans will do for success. It could have been set in Manhattan or the Pentagon, but no one has denied that Hollywood was an eligible choice. For a more refined treatment of the same theme one may turn to Libble Block's semi-allegorical *The Hills of Beverly* (1957) and for straighter reporting on the movie makers to Scott Fitzgerald's unfinished *The Last Tycoon* (1941).

Just one suburb away are Aldous Huxley's *After Many a Summer* (1940) and Evelyn Waugh's *The Loved One* (1948), excoriations of the necromantics, but also a gloss on other facets of southern California life. Orson Welles's *Citizen Kane,* not exclusively Californian, falls in this same context.

To the cultists Upton Sinclair paid his respects in *What Happened to Didymus* (1958), which might be read as a sequel to his What Happened to Upton, or, *I, Candidate for Governor, and How I Got Licked* (1934). On the techniques of manipulating people and particularly his majesty the voter Eugene Burdick discourses in *The Ninth Wave* (1956), an unbemused view of state politics.

Thanks mainly to colleagues in sociology and political science we do have a corpus of studies on the darkest blot on our war record, the mass removal of the Japanese, aliens and Americans alike. In a powerful novel, less adroit than Steinbeck or Huxley would have written, James Edmiston's *Home Again* (1955) goes with the Mio family on the hard road from Sunnyvale to Tanforan to Heart Mountain and back again.

The epoch of the Cold War offers an equally poignant theme in the machinations of the security program both official and unofficial. Of this vegetation California as is well known supported a particularly rank growth. In his opinion on *Pockman v. Leonard* Justice Jesse W. Carter analyzed and excoriated this folly, and several creative writers have examined its consequences: Martha Dodd in *The Searching Light* (1955) camouflaged with a Pennsylvania setting; Abraham Polonsky in *A Season of Fear* (1956), and John Beecher in *Land of the Free* (1956). With hardly more exception than proves the rule, historians have not applied their talent.

Similarly, on what must be counted the over-riding issue of our day — atomic fission, what to do with it, and how to co-exist with it — California through its scientists has had a leading rôle in giving dimension to this problem. On this grave issue the state's historians have touched most hesitantly if at all. Yet soon after Hiroshima, Jeffers courageously made it the theme of a poem in *The Double Axe* (1948).[18] Too long to recite and too tightly integrated to quote, this poem, although not the complete solution, goes unerringly to the heart of the problem.

Although monographic research on the California of our day is in its infancy, a forecast can be hazarded on the general treatment that historians will eventually give this epoch. As for the earlier chapters in the state's history the emphasis in all likelihood will go to growth and development. Ours has been a time of prodigious increase in population, industry, wealth, budgets, taxes, and almost everything else. Historians most certainly will be alert to this aggrandizement and will be intent on describing, measuring, and explaining it. That will be taken as the first assignment for the historian of these decades. And the figures given most prominence might well be the president of the biggest bank, the head of the largest airplane factory, the pacesetter in Hollywood, the federal official who contributed most to the Central Valley project, the state engineer who was the principal architect of the state's highway and freeway system, and the statesman who parlayed the little red schoolhouse and the College of California into the tremendous state system of higher, lower, and intermediate education.

In the creative writing already published on recent California these gentlemen, estimable though they may be, are not central. Instead, in the ancient tradition of their craft, Steinbeck, Saroyan, Stegner, Sinclair, and company have been attentive to individuals much more ordinary, not to say underprivileged. More than with the building of things and the making of money, they are concerned with human problems and human welfare. On that account when it comes to making the long-run apparisal of our era the future historian will certainly be appreciative of what we sometimes dismiss as the literary supplement.

California had been fortunate in its literary contributors. On a surprising number of topics what they have written stands as the best historical treatment. Examples would include *The Journey of the Flame, Two Years Before the Mast,* the *Shirley Letters, The Octopus, The Flock, The Preacher and the Slave, The Grapes of Wrath,* and *A Season of Fear.* Perhaps this suggests the exhortation that we go and write more novels. I do hope that the tribe of California novelists will increase, those who appropriate a California setting or hark back to the days of the dons, but more especially those who come to grips with the great current problems.

California also has been fortunate in its historians, perhaps even more so than in its roster of literary people. Nevertheless, it still stands in need of more and better history. There is work to be done all along the line and, to echo the most familiar of all complaints, particularly on the increasingly complex subject matter of the recent past.

That, however, does not pinpoint the most glaring delinquency. What is in shortest supply is the historical study that probes matters of the spirit and issues of human conflict. Emotion-packed and often controversial, these are precisely the topics most favored by the literary artists. But the literary treatment, however lively it may be, by itself cannot produce the roundness and balance that comes only when the perspective of history is also present. Such studies will have the happy effect of making the literary memorials more meaningful. Indeed, it is the two in conjunction that will provide the only means of doing justice to the still unfolding chapters of the California story. Meanwhile the addict of verse, the essay, and the novel would do well to read such history as is available, and the student of history neglects at his peril the works of literature.

THE LOCAL HISTORIAN: HIS OCCUPATIONAL HAZARDS AND COMPENSATIONS

The title of this paper implies that there is something about the local historian which sets him apart from the ordinary or real member of the profession. Perhaps it implies that in a gathering of historians, the practitioners of local research should be as readily distinguishable as, let us say, the poodles at a dog show. Whether the breed has identifying characteristics, such as a microscopic habit of the eye, or an untraveled look, I hesitate to affirm. Nevertheless, it is certain that the local historian is a well-known and established variety, and that he possesses traits, habits, possibilities, and limitations that are, at least in part, peculiar to him.

By local historian, incidentally, I mean to comprehend those who treat of state or region as well as those who deal with a fraction thereof. Purely quantitative considerations would seem to indicate such a course. A part of one state may well be larger than the entirety of another, and a single state may outbulk an accepted region. For example, the historian of Los Angeles, when he appears, will find that his subject dwarfs Rhode Island, and the historian of California must cover more ground than the historian of New England. Furthermore, there is a commonality of problem and method, of opportunity and danger, that all these less-than-national historians must face.

Those who confess to being local historians will probably insist that the occupational hazards outweigh the compensations, and that the pitfalls into which one may tumble are greater than the eminences to which one may aspire. I do not propose, however, to budget five minutes to rewards and twenty-five to penalties, or to attempt any other sharp segregation of pros and cons. The two are interwoven. Failure to grasp an opportunity is common cause for falling into error, and the attainment of success is often achieved by alert avoidance of hazards.

Of all the arguments for local research the most persuasive is doubtless that the materials for it are conveniently at hand. In California we have two great repositories, the Bancroft and the Huntington libraries, where one can consult almost every title listed in the bibliographies of California history. A half-dozen other libraries have notable collections, and scores of others are adequate for the investigation of wisely selected topics. Beyond this, anyone who possesses the thirty-nine volumes of Hubert Howe Bancroft's *Works* has the digested equivalent of a voluminous collection, superior to the best libraries available on several less fortunate states. The State Library and the Bancroft Library are strong in newspaper files; the Bancroft has a wealth of manuscript material on the Spanish, Mexican, and early American periods, and the Huntington Library, with some early manuscripts, is rich on the middle and late nineteenth century. Other manuscripts and newspapers are in humbler quarters. The only known file of the Inglewood *Star,* for instance, belongs to the Inglewood Historical Society; for the Coronel Papers one should go to the Los Angeles County Museum, and for the Bixby Papers to the Palos Verdes Library.

Furthermore, there are additional materials in county and city archives, in the possession of title companies, railroads, oil companies, land companies, and other business concerns, and in private hands. These materials are for the most part uncatalogued, and usually they have not been tagged as historical, yet it is from them that many chapters of the state's recent history must be written. The essential point is that a local researcher, though ordinarily he would do well to repair to the Bancroft or the Huntington, can usually find quantities of material closer at hand.

The hazard that attaches to this advantage is that one may forget that not all Californiana has been corralled within the state. The investigator of almost any phase of the Spanish period will find that the documentary trail leads to the archives in Mexico City, Seville, and Madrid. Forty-niner letters and diaries are constantly cropping up in the East, and eastern libraries often bid for collections which include important Californiana, as Yale University recently did with success for the superlative Mark Twain collection of the late Willard S. Morse.

A companion virtue of local research is that one can get close to the subject. A national or a world historian, if he has the traveling instinct of an Eleanor Roosevelt or a Wendell Willkie, may see much of the world. Yet it is doubtful that his knowledge of the natural setting of his chosen subject will compare with the local historian's. A Californian will be mindful of the climatic influences that hovered over the participants in local development. He can view the terrain on which they operated, and oftentimes can find it relatively unaltered. Since the more important action is crowded into the recent past, the chances are excellent that he will be able to interview some of the participants, or at least to get testimony from persons who knew them in the flesh. Thus Bancroft gathered hundreds of statements from forty-niners, from veterans of the War with Mexico, pioneer settlers, earlier American residents, citizens of Mexican California, and oldtimers who dated back to the Spanish regime. Similarly, today's investigator of the Epic campaign, of the Lincoln-Roosevelt reform movement, or of the Boom of the 'Eighties could gather firsthand information to supplement the manuscript and printed testimony.

The benefits of being close to the subject also include awareness of results. Modern California contains reminders of the Japanese problem of a generation ago, of the earlier and repeated demands for transportation improvement, and of the controversies between the sections of the state.

Inherent in this closeness to the subject is the hazard of bias. I am not sure that local historians are guilty of greater partiality than students of the Trojan War, the Spanish Inquisition, the conquest of Mexico, or the origins of the first World War, but the temptation is certainly present. Examples could be cited of colored accounts of the Spanish missions, of John C. Frémont, of the San Francisco Vigilance Committees, and of the Associated Farmers. The bias of which the local historian is most often accused is that of inordinate pride in his state or region. The California booster has long been a recognized type, and naturally his spirit has infected the writing of California history. Herein the damage may after all be slight. I do not argue that California merits boosting, but merely mention the standard antidote of ridicule, good-natured or otherwise, that is poured on promotional history, even when it is a sober recital of facts.

A more serious error to which the local historian is prone is that of provincialism, in my opinion his deadliest peril. Superficially the term "local history" may seem to call for concentration on the purely local, but in most instances it is totally unrealistic to look only as far as the county or state boundaries. For example, no one will understand the Spanish administration of California unless he considers it in connection with the practices and problems of the empire as a whole; no one can explain California's admission to statehood without integrating this step with the other elements of the Compromise of 1850; no one can get the full picture of the work of the California Fruit Growers Exchange unless he examines its nation-wide arrangements for marketing. California has had its quota of nearsighted chroniclers, who acted as though the state had existed in a vacuum. Bancroft, as the scope of his *Works* indicates, had a much broader view, and other writers, particularly in the last quarter-century, have shown awareness of the wide horizons that the subject demands. The local researcher who keeps this perspective will avoid the worst pitfall of provincialism and will find that local history, paradoxically enough, is broadening.

Local history is often used to illumine the course of national experience or world affairs. Thus one may study California politics of the 'fifties to learn about techniques of vote-getting and boss rule, or study the development of the Southern Pacific as an illustration of the rise of big business. Studies such as these yield a profit, but they do not provide a full view of local history. At the other extreme is the attitude that local history's essential function is to take note of local peculiarities, of deviations from the norm, and of elements that are unique. Rather more of our state history has been cut to this pattern, though occasionally with a reminder that Californians of a given generation shared in the experiences and aspirations of Americans in general. Since California history is written primarily for American readers, it may be proper to assume some understanding of the setting in national history. The local scene, however, is only partially reflected in a narrative that disregards so much that is orthodox American rather than peculiarly Californian. For example, we all know that Californians are often more concerned about the outcome of national rather than state elections, yet except for 1860 and 1912 our state histories cannot be counted on to record or analyze the presidential vote of the California electorate.

Between the definitions of local history as "a small-scale model of national or global history," and as "a narrative of peculiar and unique experiences," choice is neither easy nor comfortable. As with all dilemmas the solution seems to demand a bold grappling with both horns. Parts of local history move inexorably in the rhythm of the nation or the world. Thus the American acquisition of California was an expression of Manifest Destiny, and thus the problems of capital and labor in twentieth-century California dovetail with those of the nation. Other parts are unique — the gold rush, our Orientals, our motion picture industry, and much of our agriculture — and no attempt to treat them as average samplings of American experience will do them justice. The truth embraces both these definitions, and the local historian must weave his fabric with both warp and woof. Too often it has been only woof, or provincialism, or, so far as outlanders are concerned, triviality.

The sword of censorship is a greater menance to the local than to the national historian. In part this arises from proximity to his subject and from dependence upon local sources of support and upon a local printer. Furthermore, a local pressure group is more easily organized than a national one, and has greater prospect of success. There are a few famous instances of United States historians running afoul of censorship, but usually a censorship exerted by a local faction or chieftain such as Big Bill Thompson. I have never heard of a researcher being warned away from a national or larger topic because it was "loaded with dynamite." Within my limited experience, however, several such instances have occurred in the field of local research. I recall the phrase that research on the San Francisco Graft Prosecution would be "premature." I recall disapproval of a research proposal on the ground that it might offend a particular religious group. I recall a tempest over a historical document spread upon the pages of a local journal, a subsequent change in the editorship of that journal, and the suppression of the remaining installments of the document. In the realm of local history, censorship is an existent reality.

More significant than the fact of censorship are the impulses that promote it. One of these obviously arises because the readers as well as the writers of local history find themselves close to the subject, if not right in it. They have a natural desire that they, their fathers, their grandfathers, and their friends shall be given favorable and prominent mention. The usual expression and exploitation of this impulse is in the mugbook — the local history to which are appended biographical sketches that have been bought and paid for. The mugbook, of course, is an inversion of censorship, an application of external pressure to determine what shall be published, rather than a dictation of what must be suppressed. On occasion this same impulse has produced outright censorship; for example, when the choleric David S. Terry demanded certain changes in Bancroft's *Popular Tribunals*.

Another impulse to censorship derives from the fact that the average person, though chary of claiming expertness in medicine, engineering, law, or dentistry, can easily convince himself that he is an authority on local history. Living in a place supplies the observant person with bits of historical knowledge, and if family and friends help with traditive testimony, a certain amount of historical expertness can be soaked up from the environment. In community after community some oldster who "remembers when" is pointed out as knowing the entire history of the place.

The disingenuousness of the professional historian, the Ph.D. in history, contributes to this appropriation of authority. For history is the least mysterious and least cloistered branch of learning. It has no secret techniques of theory or apparatus; it has no special vocabulary. It is the one discipline whose most advanced findings are set forth in everyday speech and purport to be addressed to the multitude. This unpretentiousness requires the professionals to be better historians. It encourages them to sound reasoning and to clear expression. It also has opened the door to historical research and writing on the part of such gifted men as Francis Parkman, Theodore Roosevelt, James F. Rhodes, Albert J. Beveridge, George Fort Milton, and Carl Sandburg. Yet in the field of local history, there is at times an undue willingness on the part of the nonexpert to pass on the merits of historical studies. Our society has expressed in legislation its reluctance to have untrained persons build bridges, practice law, fill teeth, or doctor sick cats. Yet individuals with virtually no training in history volunteer to prescribe how local history shall be written.

The researcher in local history has the consolation that several publication avenues are open to him. California, for example, offers the quarterlies of the California Historical Society and the Historical Society of Southern California and the yearbooks and occasional publications of several county and local associations, all of which are devoted entirely to California history. Other historical journals, such as the *Pacific Historical Review*, the *Hispanic American Historical Review*, and the *Mississippi Valley Historical Review*, are more or less open to California contributions. In addition, there are journals of more popular vein, such as *Desert*, *Westways*, and the *Pony Express Courier*, which regularly accord some of their columns to local history. Eastern book publishers have developed a certain tolerance for California history subjects, and there are local publishers, such as the University of California Press, Stanford University Press, the Arthur H. Clark Company, the Grabhorn Press, the Colt Press, Ward Ritchie, and the Huntington Library, ready upon occasion to issue California books. A seminar of mine not long ago saw the majority of its reports into print, using such media as the Historical Society of Southern California *Quarterly*, the California Historical Society *Quarterly, the Pacific Historical Review,* the *Alumni Magazine* of the University of California at Los Angeles, and the Inglewood *Shopping News.* I mention this last, not only in genuine pride, but also in hopes that it will point the way to other stimulating outlets for student papers on local history.

Looking at the darker side, one notes that the circle of potential readers is more limited than for the national or world historian. California histories remind me of a remark attributed to one of the Marx Brothers turned author. "All my books," he ruefully reported, "are first editions." I happen to know that a high school text on the state's history, a work whose reputation is purely local, has sold more than 20,000 copies, which means several printings; but, so far as I am aware, no *History of California* has gone into a second edition.[1]

Also on the darker side is the limited market for the specialist in local history. California history is rather generally taught in the fifth grade and in high school. It is offered in most junior colleges and appears in the course list in several of the four-year colleges. Almost never does it constitute a full teaching program, and usually it is regarded as an incidental course to be handled by someone whose principal duty and specialization is in United States history, Hispanic American history, English, or physical education. The prospective teacher therefore should be warned to prepare to handle something in addition to California history. The Ph.D. candidate will not need that warning, for, even if his dissertation is in California history, most of the requirements for the degree will lie elsewhere. To the best of my observation, a dissertation in California history, though no great help, is no handicap when it comes to landing a job.

What effect continued specialization in local history would have on one's chances of rising in the profession is not so clear. The local specialist gives hostages to fortune. He forfeits any great likelihood of a call to Harvard, or Chicago, or any of the other seats of eastern learning. It is possible that this factor has something to do with the apparent reluctance of historians to devote themselves exclusively to research in California history. It is a curious and otherwise inexplicable fact that the leading authorities on our state's history and most of the professionals have been only part-time laborers in this vineyard. I can think of no other branch of history where part-time laborers are the rule.

Despite all these Cassandra-like warnings about the prospects for the researcher in California history, I extend a warm welcome to all who would dig in this soil. It is no private preserve. Anyone may enter. Much has been done, especially on the Spanish period and the early American era, but still more remains to be done. Portolá, Rivera, Neve, Borica, and Lasuén are as deserving of biographical study as were Serra, Crespi, Palóu, and Anza, on whom we have excellent appraisals. Chapman's thorough work on *The Founding of Spanish California* should be matched by a comparable work on the end of Spanish rule and on the secularization of the missions. Ogden's *California Sea Otter Trade* should have a sequel on the hide trade. Lives of Sutter, Marsh, Smith, and Reid should be followed by more adequate treatments of Larkin, Vallejo, Stearns, and Robinson. From Frémont and Starr King, we could profitably turn to such men as James E. Birch, David C. Broderick, and Sam Brannan; from the San Francisco Vigilance Committees to rural vigilante action.

Research possibilities are not yet exhausted on such familiar topics as the Spanish missions and the gold rush. The particular opportunity, however, lies in the American period and especially in its more recent portion. Works such as Daggett's *Chapters on the History of the Southern Pacific,* Stewart's *John Phoenix* and *Bret Harte,* Walker's *San Francisco's Literary Frontier,* Cleland's *Cattle on a Thousand Hills,* and Alexander's *Chaffey,* light up a few corners of this sprawling subject-matter, but the greater part is unexplored and uncultivated. There is room for good books on lumbering, on the cattle business after 1849, on whaling and fishing, on viticulture, on the grain ranches of Frank Norris' *Octopus,* on politics in the late nineteenth century. The mainstays of California's recent and current economy — oil, the citrus industry, moving picture production, the tourist business, and airplane manufacture — await their several historians. These and their companion social and cultural phenomena are perhaps less bizarre than the Franciscan friars, the red-shirted forty-niners, and San Francisco's volunteer firemen, but they go much farther toward explaining modern California, and they must eventually find recognition as the most significant chapters in local history. Their elucidation awaits researchers.

Lack of training in California history is no bar to entrance upon these tasks. The ideal perhaps is that most of this research should be done by Ph.D.'s whose dissertations were on California topics. I say "perhaps," because some doubts exist that professional training is essential, or even helpful. We still lack proof that there is a positive correlation between graduate training in history and effective research and writing.

California history, at any rate, has been written principally by individuals without training, or by individuals trained to do something entirely different. The first local historian, Francisco Palóu, made his preparation through missionary work, Franklin Tuthill through journalism, and Theodore H. Hittell through law. Josiah Royce took a sabbatical from philosophy to write the California volume for the American Commonwealths series, and Irving B. Richman warmed to the subject of the province under Spain and Mexico by doing a history of Rhode Island and a monograph on one of the Swiss cantons. Most prodigious of all these volunteers was Hubert Howe Bancroft, the San Francisco book dealer who turned collector, publisher, and historian. Among his staff there was nothing approximating a Ph.D. in history.

Among the moderns consider the leading authority on California history, who prepared for this career by writing a dissertation on the free Negro in the ante-bellum South and by seven years' teaching of medieval history. Consider also the retired mining engineer who has written authoritatively on Drake, on Spanish voyages of the sixteenth century, on West Coast cartography, and on the bibliography of the Spanish Southwest and the Plains and Rockies. Also, I might mention a past president of the Pacific Coast Branch whose specialty is Scandinavian history but who has found time to publish on California sheep drives and horse drives and on an early phase of the oil industry. Another illustration is afforded by a young instructor, fresh from New York by way of Harvard, who immediately upon arrival in the state began to supervise the writing of senior term papers in California history. Or — to make clear that these comments are not meant to be invidious — may I mention my own launching as a regional historian. Trained as a Spanish Americanist and innocent of any expertness in local history, I was, with one day's notice, placed in charge of three hundred students enrolled for a course in Pacific Coast history.

A field with such capacity for attracting and shanghaiing workers needs no sales talk. Nevertheless, I plead for more research all along the line and especially on the more recent phases of California development, that we may better understand our own position, and for the light that these local studies will throw upon national problems and world relations. California history has been rich in variety, in drama, in the ludicrous, in heroism and villainy. More than most local histories, it has influenced its bigger and more respectable cousins, national and global history. The researcher who elects this field will find that I have not exaggerated the pitfalls, obstacles, and hazards. I trust, however, that he will encounter correspondingly larger compensations.

Part IV

WESTERN JUSTICE

WESTERN JUSTICE

Until June 1949, John W. Caughey was preoccupied mostly with teaching, library research, and publication, though he also found time to speak frequently about California's political and social problems and serve on various state commissions. Then, in the late spring of 1949, he became involved in the famous oath controversy that rocked the University of California and gained national notoriety.

Faculty members first heard of the loyalty oath that was to be required of them when the secretary of the university's Board of Regents issued a notice in the *Faculty Bulletin* of May 9, 1949. In measured, official language, the notice stated that an oath of allegiance would be included with all 1950 contracts and that no salaries would be paid until it had been accepted. This news did not arouse alarm among the faculty until early June when the wording of the special oath was finally given. Now tempers of faculty members flared as they read the oath's peculiar language and realized that its announcement coincided with their summer departure from the campus.

These feelings John Caughey also shared. He questioned the legality of the regent's oath and worried about the harm it would do to the faculty's morale and institutions — especially the right of tenure which served as a buttress against political pressures and emotions. Thinking the state's traditional oath of a hundred years was sufficient to insure loyalty, he insisted that the constitutional proviso — "no other oath, declaration, or test, shall be required as a qualification for any office or public trust" — shielded citizens from any other oath. On further reflection he wondered whether oaths really guaranteed loyalty or served the interests of a university or of society. In a community of scholars where all were working to ascertain truth, he thought the traditional tests of competence, efficiency, and character were sufficient, particularly since they had been used during the life of the university to establish high standards of faculty employment and had been judged satisfactory. The regent's oath, he felt, added a new test for employment, a test imposed not by the state, but by the political overseers of the university. In short, the traditional methods of safeguarding the university and maintaining faculty quality seemed to be threatened by the imposition of outside standards.

When the university's president, Robert Gordon Sproul, suggested the oath to the Board of Regents in March 1949, he had simply been reflecting the temper of the times. Though he would later change his position, he was then worried about legislative interference, for he was living in an age of investigations and "vigilante justice," of Jack Tenney's shameless attempts at character assassination, of Martin Dies' unabashed techniques of guilt by association, and of Joseph McCarthy's audacious speeches from the floor of the United States Senate. President Sproul, hoping to shield the university from such demagogues, believed an exhibition of loyalty was all that was needed, a conclusion he had reached without consulting the organized faculty.

But the oath raised among professors emotional issues of tyranny, issues which Sproul and the regents could not allay. Through the succeeding school year they worked with the university Academic Senates, trying to find a wording for the oath that would satisfy everyone. With the aid of an alumni committee, the regents and faculty hammered out a compromise statement which imposed as a condition of employment the oath of allegiance and an affirmation of nonmembership in Communist and subversive organizations. Those who refused to sign could petition the Academic Senate Committee on Privilege and Tenure for a hearing, but the final decision on reemployment rested with the regents. So the nonsigners found themselves fighting for their professional lives before committees, the president, and the regents. The screening procedures were elaborate and thorough, and no Communists or "subversives" were discovered among the faculty. The regents, however, revealed that they were not interested in a clearance as much as they were interested in imposing their special test of loyalty. In that struggle for supremacy they brushed aside the committee reports and, on August 25, 1950, proceeded to fire the nonsigners, men like Caughey, Ernst Kantorowicz, Edward Tolman, and Jacob Loewenberg, who had served the university from eleven to thirty-five years. Though the nonsigners were relatively few in number, there were many others, like Louis Knott Koontz, Caughey's officemate, who were forced to take the oath against their better judgment because of compelling personal obligations and who bitterly regretted what they had done.

For a man of peace, this intense dispute was a traumatic experience, and John Caughey could barely believe that he would be forced to prove his loyalty after a lifetime of service to the university. The regents, he felt, had been arbitrary, had violated the ordinary standards of equity, and were undermining their announced objective of making the university safe for scholarship.

Two days after Caughey was released by the university, he joined with eighteen other nonsigners in a petition to the Third District Court of Appeal which, in 1951, found the regent's oath unconstitutional. To finance this fight and an appeal to the state supreme court, friends of the nonsigners began a campaign for voluntary contributions that could also be used for salary and other expenditures. In addition, attempts were made to rally the scholarly world and secure the cooperation of the American Association of University Professors. The nonsigners won university and nation-wide sympathy. The Rockefeller Foundation and the American Council of Learned Societies provided Caughey with fellowships, as they did some of the other nonsigners. Hundreds of colleagues in universities across the nation recorded their disgust over the oath, and a dozen or more eminent scholars refused appointments at the University of California. Meanwhile, the California legislature, still frightened by the menace of Communism and subversion, instituted its own oath of allegiance and required all public employees and defense workers to take it. The new oath was approved by the people of California when they voted in 1952 to add it to the state constitution. John Caughey, obeying state law, signed the new oath, not once but twice, in the process of serving the state in his multiple duties as a consultant. This new measure, popularly called the Levering Oath, was also required of the university faculty.

While the courts, legislature, and regents tried to harmonize their standards of loyalty, Caughey and other nonsigners were barred from their university positions. He was permitted, however, to retain his office in Royce Hall, where he edited the *Pacific Historical Review,* and the university continued to publish the *Review,* subsidize its costs, and provide editorial assistance. In the same office which he had occupied as a professor, Caughey conducted other professional duties, daily advising master's and doctoral candidates, handling business for the state Landmarks Commission, and doing his own personal research. Though often deeply depressed, sometimes lacking his usual smile, he refused to be discouraged for long. He revised his *California,* which remained the best selling history of the state and continued to be used by others in their courses held down the hall from his office; edited Benjamin Wilson's *The Indians of Southern California in 1852;* and completed a handful of articles for learned journals.

On October 17, 1952, more than two years after his release from the university, the Supreme Court of California affirmed the unconstitutionality of the regent's oath. Though the high court based its decision upon different reasons than those offered by the appeal court, the decision, nevertheless, achieved for Caughey and his conferees a victory of sorts, save that they had to struggle now for their lost salaries. The two years had changed most of the nonsigners; many felt bitterly the inequity of fighting the powerful Board of Regents. As individuals they had been pitted against an institution whose members and attorneys had used state funds and prestige to battle them in the courts and halls of the university. Most of them did not miss the meaning of this engagement as they returned to teaching and turned their minds to other matters.

Some years later Caughey tried to explain the price one pays as a freedom fighter. "To be a partisan of the freedoms entails genuine risk. It is a familiar concept that freedom is seldom free, that it must be bought with a price. In the United States, however, we had come to have the comfortable feeling that the heroes of the Revolutionary generation had won their rights for us and bequeathed them to us to enjoy. Even though Jefferson warned that eternal vigilance would be necessary, it comes as something of a shock that the freedoms are a legacy that requires our perpetual care. It is still more of a shock that to be a champion of freedom of religion, of speech, of the press, or of assembly, or an advocate of due process or equality before the law exposes one to criticism as a menace to society and un-American. Notwithstanding the weight of this antagonism, there are those who speak up for freedom."[1]

To speak up for freedom became John Caughey's preoccupation after 1949. Active in the American Civil Liberties Union, the American Association of University Professors, and in similar organizations, he has written papers against capital punishment, *de facto* segregation, and other societal encroachments upon human liberty. He has gained wide publicity for his public school texts in which he and associates have brought the Negro, Indian, Oriental, and other nondominant groups into the nation's history. *Land of the Free,* which he coauthored in 1967, was adopted in schools across the country as the standard text for eighth grade students, giving an exciting, appreciative view of the United States as a wonderful, though not perfect, place to live.

THEIR MAJESTIES THE MOB

In September, 1957, Little Rock, Arkansas, took the spotlight of world attention. Technically it was because the governor of the state defied the national government by calling out troops to block enforcement of a federal court order. Thereby he also called into action a mob of citizens determined to keep nine Negro children from entering Central High School. This was the living drama, and it was accentuated by a chorus of junior demonstrators chanting, "Two, four, six, eight; we ain't gonna integrate."

For groups to take the law into their own hands is an old American custom. It happened in colonial days and there was more of it at the time of the Revolution. The Boston Tea Party was such an incident. We remember it lightheartedly. But no one can be as complacent about the tarring and feathering, the riding on a rail, that our Revolutionary ancestors inflicted on their neighbors who persisted in loyalty to George III.

Another setting in which actions outside the law came naturally was the American frontier. Here life was turbulent and society only indifferently organized. The "western" in paperback or movie or radio or television serial may be assumed to exaggerate this violence, yet the truth often was as stark as fiction. Take, for illustration, the most voluminous of all western histories, the thirty-nine thick tomes that constitute Hubert Howe Bancroft's history of the Pacific states of North America. In the seventies and eighties when this most industrious of historians was compiling his monumental work, he thought it proper to devote two full volumes — an aggregate of more than fifteen hundred pages — to what he called the *Popular Tribunals*. Bancroft has been criticized for many things but not for this emphasis upon the committees of vigilance. They are recognized as one of the most characteristic institutions of the pioneer age.

The centennial of the most famous of these bodies, San Francisco's great committee of 1856, passed with practically no local observance. True, a laudatory book was published in New York and immediately excerpted in the historical magazine of widest circulation, *American Heritage*. For scholars this books was partly balanced by the appearance of a dispassionate biography of Judge David S. Terry, spectacular opponent of the 1856 committee. But a more significant observance of the centennial took place in Tennessee, Texas, and Kentucky.

In September, 1956, at Clinton, Tennessee, a dozen Negroes enrolled in the high school, and the first day passed without trouble. But then a stranger came to town, began to harangue on the street corners, and soon a crowd was threatening Negroes and smashing their cars. The next day citizens were out en masse in front of the school, and the Negro children could get in only under escort of national guardsmen with riot guns and fixed bayonets. Nearby Oliver Springs had a similar outburst of violence, with dynamite exploded near Negro homes, and reporters and cameramen hustled out of town at gun point. For a couple of days it was touch and go whether the guardsmen would be able to control or would themselves be run out of town.

At Mansfield, Texas, that same September, a crowd hanged a Negro in effigy at the high school and posted a sign, "Black Negroes Keep Out." The Rangers came to prevent a clash but left the effigy hanging. No Negroes entered. Meanwhile, Sturgis, Kentucky, population 2,500, had 500 at the schoolhouse to turn back nine Negro boys and girls. Here too the national guard provided armed escort, but the crowd threatened, "We'll get you niggers if it takes all year," and taunted the white children as "nigger-lovers." To these dramatics the governor of Arkansas added another dimension when he called out troops to prevent compliance with the law of the land.

In the fall of 1957 the television cameras picked up the action in a street scene in a southern city as a dozen whites cuffed and kicked a middle-aged Negro minister. Not long before that, another group of whites in Birmingham tortured and castrated an unoffending Negro. The only reason offered was that they wanted to prove their worthiness for higher station in the Ku Klux Klan. It was in Birmingham, also, early in 1956, that a group of men rushed on the stage and assaulted the popular musician Nat King Cole. A few months earlier, students and non-students drove Autherine Lucy from the University of Alabama.

Not much farther back in time there were bombings of Negro homes in the West Adams district in Los Angeles, the Trumbull Park housing project in Chicago was the scene of vicious demonstrations and violence, and as recently as the 1940's Detroit and New York had race riots that were even bloodier. The householders of Levittown, New Jersey, in 1957 did their best to drive away a Negro who had the "presumption" to move a few blocks up the street. Clearly the resort to mob violence is by no means a southern monopoly.

Nor is it confined to issues of race. In 1950, for example, there was the case of California's leading banker. He took exception to what he considered a softening on Communism by a state board of which he was a member. Angrily resigning, he promised if necessary to organize a band of twentieth-century vigilantes to do what the board would not do. Everyone understood what he meant. He was invoking the precedent of do-it-yourself justice which the historians of his state had established in the public mind as noble and heroic.

His allusion was primarily to the San Francisco committee of 1856. Incensed by a series of unpunished crimes, this committee enrolled and armed several thousand men and established and fortified its headquarters. Marching in force to the county jail it demanded and received two prisoners, who were taken to Fort Gunnybags, given the shorter shrift of vigilante trial, and hanged. The committee did the same to two others and assigned several lesser penalties. Throughout, it stood in armed defiance of the established local government. Indeed, the committee assumed the posture of an army of occupation interposing the substance and some of the forms of martial law.

This committee had to bear in mind the possibility that the state government would interfere. The Know Nothing governor, young J. Neely Johnson, did bluster, but in the face of the committee's determination he soon subsided. These vigilantes were also well aware that federal intervention could stop them in their tracks. Fortunately for them Washington was far away, overt challenge of federal authority was avoided, the Pierce administration preferred to keep hands off, and the army and navy commanders near the scene even went so far as to give covert assistance. For three months the committee dominated San Francisco through the combined tactics of civil insurrection and military occupation. Then it returned the city to the jurisdiction of the regular courts and peace officers.

The tradition of frontier vigilantism is much broader. San Francisco had an earlier, more boisterous committee. The habit in Los Angeles was intermittent, but involved several times as many hangings as in San Francisco. Throughout the diggings the miners meted out off-the-cuff trial and punishment. In the performance in 1849 that gave Hangtown its name, in the sadistic execution of Juanita at Downieville in 1851, and in a hundred other cases they, as Bancroft put it, left "the quiet oaks tasselled with the carcasses of the wicked." The vigilantes of Montana, incited by the atrocities of Sheriff Plummer's gang, operated expansively. In early Colorado and Nevada, in the Southwest and the Northwest, this same behavior was commonplace.

In our day the direct-action impulse crops up in the resistance to desegregation. It appears at Philadelphia where a pressure group seeks to force the Plymouth Meeting to fire its librarian, at Houston where another group uses irresponsible charges to get rid of a superintendent of schools, and in Hollywood where a conspiracy of blacklisters purges the employment rolls. In most phases of McCarthyism the impulse to go beyond the law is clearly visible. A vigilante-like approach is present also in much of the functioning of the loyalty-security program, in censorship drives, public as well as private, in the systematic discouragement of nonconformity, and in exposure as practiced by the congressional investigators.

Today's vigilantes bear some resemblance to those of a century ago, but it would be extraordinary if they turned out to be exact facsimiles. The analogies of ancient and modern, bucolic and sophisticated, may be worth exploring, but there is better promise in an analytical approach which will look at the causes and the rationale, the methods of holding trial and punishing, the associated attitudes, and the consequences to government and society.

Whatever else is said about vigilantism, it must be remarked that it is a subject afflicted with a sliding scale of labels. At the outset, therefore, it is advisable to pin down one basic definition. Vigilantism, lynch law, mobocracy — these are some of the variant terms. Each has an emphasis of its own, but in all of them the essence is the same. That essence is a group action in lieu of regular justice. Whichever synonym is used, that is the identifying character.

Vigilantism is a step removed from man-to-man retaliation. A one-man vigilance committee would be a contradiction in terms. Nor is the process to be confused with the control that a community can exert through social pressure. It is not a legislating or administering body like a folkmoot or a town meeting. Instead it is a group usually considerably smaller than the community as a whole. It is a group acting ostensibly in the interest of society. Indeed, the leading authority on lynch law, James E. Cutler, asserts that lynchings happen only when there is some substantial backing in public sentiment.

The characteristic group action is to sit in unofficial judgment on one or more persons and to visit a punishment likewise unofficial. The impromptu tribunal operates on a volunteer basis rather than through professional personnel. Its pace is much more rapid than the law's, partly because it spurns technicalities and disdains legalism in favor of what it calls judgment by common sense. At its best it is a short cut to the result that a regular court might reach. It may turn out to be a short cut through justice and to some other destination.

Impressed by the lengths to which some vigilance committees have gone to achieve the similitude of regular trial, historians on the whole have insisted that the frontier committees are not to be equated with lynch law or mob violence. A number of contemporary observers, on the contrary, saw the difference as more in manner than in substance. Senator David P. Barstow called the Downieville committee "the hungriest, craziest, wildest mob . . . that ever I saw anywhere." And Dame Shirley, the most perceptive of all commentators of life in the diggings, had withering scorn for the Indian Bar vigilantes she saw in action in 1852 — "Their Majesties the Mob," she called them.

Why does vigilantism arise? For the frontier the classic explanation is that it arose to fill a vacuum. People moved west more rapidly than did government. On the trail, in the mines, and in the scattered new settlements, the pioneers often found themselves beyond the reach of regular justice and stepped in to fill that gap.

The early West provides a number of examples that fit this description. One such instance was with the Donner Party in 1846. These emigrants left Missouri at the appointed season for the trek to California, but at Fort Bridger in the Rockies they turned off on a so-called cutoff that proved almost impassable. By much roping and double-teaming they managed to get through to Salt Lake, but almost a month behind schedule. In the salt and mire southwest of the lake they endured worse troubles. Frustrations as well as hardships brought nerves to the breaking point.

At Gravelly Ford, John Snyder began to whip James Reed's

team and, when Reed objected, brought the heavy whip down on him. Reed drew his knife, Mrs. Reed rushed in between the two men and was struck by the whip, and then Reed, half-blinded in his own blood, plunged the knife into his antagonist. Immediately he was as contrite as a man could be; he took the boards from his wagon to make the crude coffin in which Snyder was buried.

His companions now proceeded to pass judgment. Since they were several months out from Missouri, in a remote Mexican territory completely untouched by Mexican authority, they were not usurping jurisdiction. The recorded accounts, however, do not support their findings, verdict, or manner of holding trial. Reed claimed that he had acted in self-defense and in defense of his wife, and the evidence clearly indicates unpremeditated and justifiable homicide. The majority of his companions, however, saw it otherwise. They were not of a mind to hang Reed or to shoot him, but they decided to banish him empty-handed from the train. In that barren and Indian-infested territory they must have known that this was a probable death sentence. By night Reed's daughter smuggled a gun and ammunition out to him, and he got to California safely. After the others blundered into the terrible ordeal of being snowbound in the Sierra, with starvation and cannibalism, Reed was in position to come back and assist in the rescue. That he survived, however, was no indication of intended clemency on the part of those who had judged him.

Three seasons later, when the trail was crowded with gold-seekers on the march, an open-air court was convened at the Green River ferry. On June 20, near Devil's Gate on the Sweetwater, a man named Williams shot and killed a teamster who had repeatedly threatened his life. Williams went to several trains and offered to stand trial, but all were of opinion that he had acted in self-defense. Then on July 3 in another company a man named Brown, quite without provocation, killed one of his messmates. A volunteer posse set out in pursuit, failed to overtake their man, but brought Williams back to the Green River ferry to stand trial. A large crowd was on hand, waiting to be ferried and celebrating the Fourth of July. A court was convened and a jury impaneled. The lawyer defending Williams opened by challenging the jurisdiction of this impromptu court. That led to heated argument and to blows and a general melee, most of which one chronicler attributes to the "spirited" observance of the Fourth. Soberer heads separated the scufflers, but by mutual consent the trial was not resumed. The court was never adjourned but Williams took the cue and left, by inference having been cleared. Vigilante acquittals are seldom more explicit.

Later in 1849 in another company a thousand miles to the south in the dusty valley of the Gila two young men from Arkansas quarreled and fought. The stronger was pulled off, whereupon the other whipped out a knife and struck him dead. The company promptly chose a judge and jury which found the assailant guilty. The next morning the whole company confirmed the verdict. A firing squad was chosen by lot and handed six rifles with blank loads and six with powder and ball. Over the grave they posted a brief statement of what they had done.

Months out on the trail, these emigrants certainly were beyond the reach of regular courts. There even was question what government had jurisdiction. If society was to do anything about crime on the trail, it would have to be through improvised group action. In the mines the forty-niners asserted this same justification — that they had left regular justice a couple of thousand miles behind and that it had to be the vigilante response or none at all. Other parts of the frontier could also assert that they were remote or cut off from established courts.

Twentieth-century vigilantes are not in position to make any such claim. Our courts stand open for business. At most, these men may say that they propose to relieve the courts of part of their work by what might be called friendly usurpation. More often the mood is of sharp issue with the courts, and the direct actionists set out to do what the courts will not do or cannot be counted on to do.

In point of fact, most frontier instances were not so different. Most of them were carried out in close proximity to regular courts. Throughout 1849 there were courts no farther away from the mines than San Francisco and Monterey. At the close of that year the state government of California began to function, and presently its courts were stationed up and down the Mother Lode. The San Francisco committees rose up alongside regular courts and in defiance of them. The first committee's justification was that the courts were weak, the second committee's that they were corrupt. The Los Angeles vigilantes were well acquainted with the official court; indeed, they got most of their victims from the local jail. So it went quite generally in the frontier West. Initially the lack of lawful courts was real, but popular tribunals persisted long after the arrival of these agencies and reached a climax after courts were in good supply.

Frontier and modern experience both illustrate that the vigilante approach is habit forming. Once direct action is used, the tendency is to repeat. It is also contagious. After what happened at Clinton, violence was more in prospect at Oliver Springs; without the incident at Sturgis, there might have been none at Clay. After the San Francisco performance of 1851, committee action spread like a wave throughout California, and California veterans are identified as carriers of the virus or the inspiration to other parts of the West.

Still another reason for vigilantism is that many consider its law superior to that of the regular courts. The citizens of San Diego in 1912 who formed a gantlet and beat, tortured, and mutilated a number of unwelcome Wobblies could not claim that they were inflicting punishment which a regular court in due course would have assigned. Nor could the San Pedro volunteers who in 1924 kidnapped, beat, and tarred and feathered another set of I. W. W. members. Even in that politer exercise which is the power center of McCarthyism — the exposure before a legislative investigating committee — the trial is by methods and on evidence that no court would countenance, and the penalty of removal from employment ordinarily is far beyond what the law authorizes.

Yet the pioneers held that the standards enforced by their popular tribunals were the ones best suited to the time and place, not an obsolete carry-over from a distant and different past, but the code of the West. Today, the direct actionists in the South undertake to improve on the law that emanates from Washington. McCarthyism asserts that measures more extreme than those authorized by the statutes are needed to cope with the menace of domestic Communism. Out-of-court, beyond-the-law action is often preferred because it is quicker, simpler, less snarled in technicalities, more inexorable, and harsher in its penalties. This difference is not solely a matter of procedure; the preference also extends to the stern and retributive code that characterizes vigilantism.

In substituting themselves for a regular court, vigilantes, wherever they are, must hold trial. Usually the formality is much abbreviated. Modern practice, in fact, shortens it almost to the vanishing point. Yet the volunteer dispensers of justice cannot altogether evade this function. Explicitly or by inference they must include an accusation and a finding of guilty or not guilty.

If the crudest examples are selected, vigilantism affords a very poor substitute for regular trial. Back in 1846, surly old Lewis Keseberg opened the trial of James Reed by upending a wagon tongue for a gibbet. At Clinton, the crowd's verdict, "They shall not pass," stemmed from agitator John Kasper's anonymous phone calls, his street-corner tirades, and a one-sided discussion — if it can be called that — in the crowd. In 1950, when actress Jean Muir was deposed from her long-standing role as the mother in "The Aldrich Family," a few planted telephone calls were all that was needed to convene the agency, network, and sponsor and lead them to hand down this judgment.

At the other extreme stands San Francisco's second vigilance committee. Its dignity and decorum symbolized the fair trial that it sought to give. Counsel was provided for the accused and was respectfully heard. Even before this tribunal, however, the defendant was under severe handicap. He could ask witnesses to take the stand, but neither he nor the committee had any way to make them come or compel them to testify. They, on the contrary, had good reason to hesitate to appear before such a tribunal. The committee was not in a good position to try in open court and gave the public much less than full information on what went on. It operated under the pressure of time and sat far into the night. It could not consider a motion for change of venue, though with public sentiment as inflamed as it was, such a motion almost certainly would have been granted by a regular court. This committee, like all other vigilantes, sat as a court of first and last instance — there was no possibility of appeal and none for executive clemency. Thus in a number of particulars, notwithstanding the best intentions on its part, even this great committee could not accord due process as the courts and the legal profession construe it.

In the ordinary run of impromptu trials the position of the accused is even less favorable. Because the vigilantes always think they have their man, their trials begin with a presumption of guilt, the tendency is to take accusations at face value, and the alleged culprit has the uphill task of proving his innocence. Such was the plight of any number of suspects on the frontier, and of United States Senator Jacob Javits or anyone else "named" before an investigating committee. Vigilantes do not hesitate to try in absentia. A prime example was Attorney General Herbert Brownell's pronouncement against Harry Dexter White after the latter's death. This charge before the Jenner committee was subsidiary to another that had in it an element of absent treatment — the allegation that former President Truman had knowingly kept a Soviet agent in a key post in the government. The Montana vigilantes often completed a trial, sometimes at another town, before they bothered to notify the accused or make the arrest. In the second of two trials of the Mexicans at Hangtown in 1849, the defendents were still insensate from the lashes already inflicted.

The irregular court characteristically discourages testimony or pleadings for the defendant. Williams' witnesses were far ahead on the trail when he was brought before the Green River jury. The House Un-American Activities Committee under Chairman Walter would not hear the witnesses that the Plymouth Meeting or the Fund for the Republic wanted to present. Counsel is not permitted to argue or even address the investigating committees. The prepared statements that the Hollywood Ten as "unfriendly" witnesses offered for the record were haughtily rejected by Parnell Thomas of this same committee. Advocates of desegregation have been intimidated into silence at many of the demonstrations in the South. At San Francisco and Downieville in 1851, and at Columbia in 1855, admonition against hasty punishment was hooted down.

Vigilantes are not above extracting confession by torture. The frontier custom with an obdurate suspect was to put a noose around his neck and ease him off the ground a few times in hopes of making him more co-operative. A modern equivalent is to badger and browbeat unfriendly witnesses, to threaten their jobs, and often to maneuver them into the pillory of the Fifth Amendment.

In the frontier tribunals trial by jury was one of the vaunted adornments and the practice most calculated to give respectability. These juries, nevertheless, had certain defects. Sometimes the jury was the whole camp, or was chosen by lot and might be thought of as a cross-section of the community. More often it was drawn only from the vigilantes, not necessarily the majority element and assuredly not impartial. Yet only in the rarest instances was there any provision for challenging. These juries, moreover, were given little chance to deliberate, and frequently they were put under pressure to return a verdict of guilty. Thus, in several respects the average defendant was likely to find the jury rigged against him.

Furthermore, when we say "trial by jury," we actually have in mind trial by judge and jury; and in regular court, even in a jury trial, the judge may be the more important factor. It is the judge who decides what testimony and argument are admissible and what must be excluded. It is the judge who instructs the jury and, on occasion, declares a mistrial or dismisses a case for want of evidence.

The pioneer vigilantes set up someone to preside at their trials, but these judges could not invoke the majesty of the law and had only as much authority as their personal force could give. The result was that the prosecution ran the trials.

A similar criticism holds against most modern extralegal trials. For lack of an impartial judge in position to enforce standards, the congressional investigating committee when it sits as a kangaroo court falls far short of conducting a fair trial. The same is true of the cases decided by the Ku Klux Klan and other such bodies. This defect also appears in many of the administrative hearings that are the main functioning point in the loyalty-security programs of the federal and state governments.

What with presumption of guilt, inability to compel witnesses, acceptance of prejudiced jurors, carelessness about the rules of evidence, and lack of competent and watchful judges, trial as performed by vigilantes usually has been deficient in many of the safeguards against error and abuse. In addition, all too often such trials are conducted in anger. An upsurge of indignation is what brings the vigilantes together. Dispassionate resolve or ulterior design may keep them at their self-appointed task, but ill temper repeatedly shows in their work and all too often what they actually conduct is trial in passion.

After holding trial, vigilantes go on to punish, and of all their roles, this is the one in which it is most difficult to substitute for the state. One drawback is that, because of their unofficial character, they cannot use the stand-bys of regular punishment — fine and imprisonment. The pioneers could hold a man overnight. They were in no position to lock him up for life or for a term of years or even for thirty days. In rare instances they did assess something like a fine, a payment of so many ounces of gold to the person wronged, or the signing of a quitclaim to a piece of contested property. Almost always, however, they had to turn to a cruder and more direct reprisal. Today's vigilantes operate under this same handicap. In addition, in case after case, the vigilante court inflicts a punishment far more severe than the penalty, if any, that regular justice would impose.

Such punishment also entails a high degree of personal involvement. Even if the vigilantes put on masks, as in the Ku Klux Klan, they do what they do personally. No matter how formal and polite they may be, the punishment comes from them as individuals. A companion abuse often present is that vigilantes push personal grudges or operate for their private profit. Frontier and modern examples are legion. An Associated Press dispatch of March 2, 1957, will illustrate. It comes from Kampala, Uganda, and reads: "The Uganda government enlisted vigilantes to fight a crime wave in Kampala's suburbs but soon disbanded them. Prime Minister Michael Kintu said the vigilantes on nightly patrols assaulted and robbed people."

The frontier avengers commonly punished by whipping. Thirty-nine lashes well laid on were the most favored number, but sometimes they applied 75 or 100 or even 200. Some victims cowered abjectly; others bore the strokes with fortitude. To the more high spirited, this indignity was a fate worse than death. In *Two Years before the Mast,* the most graphic of all the accounts of the earlier California hide trade, Richard Henry Dana tells how one fellow seaman never recovered from the shame of a shipboard beating. And at Indian Bar on the Mother Lode a Spaniard begged a committee to put him to death rather than debase his honor with a whipping.

After applying the lash, the frontiersmen almost always added banishment. The San Francisco committees arranged passages to Australia and other distant parts and in other instances simply advised departure. The miners sometimes escorted a man out of camp but more often set a deadline such as, "Begone by sundown." With us, deportation and its obverse, denial of a passport, occur only with the connivance of the government, but blacklists have barred a number of persons from the entertainment industries, and extralegal pressures have excluded members of various professions from their careers.

The pioneers had an awareness that whipping was more apt to confirm a criminal than to cure one and that banishment was merely an invitation to such a character to go and sin elsewhere. They felt impelled, therefore, to put a mark on such a person. It might be done as part of the punishment, but with this added purpose of making the wrongdoer recognizable. Accordingly, they branded with the initial of the crime or, more commonly, they cut off an ear. This practice was so routine that one man who had lost an ear in a fair fight was advised to carry an affidavit that it had not been cropped by a vigilance committee.

The modern equivalent is by dossier-building, listing criticized activities and associations. The government may hold the dossier, but not to the exclusion of privately contributed entries. There are also privately held dossiers such as those used as the basis for blacklisting. Instead of snipping off an ear, the modern device is to cut a film or story credit, deny a speaker a platform, or ban a book.

Although the pioneers used several forms of corporal punishment, their trademark was the rope. Primarily they hanged, and it was this habit that gave a crispness to their proceedings. They hanged for murder, for assault, for robbery, and for thievery. Frequently they applied capital punishment when a regular court would have assigned a much lesser penalty. In one instance a committee was on the point of hanging a man for stealing a mongrel dog, but in the nick of time discovered that the cur had not been stolen after all. The pioneer vigilantes hanged on conclusive evidence; they also hanged on suspicion; and in a number of distressing instances they executed men who were innocent. The regular courts also make mistakes, but the impromptu tribunals, with fewer safeguards and no opportunity for review, are more prone to error, which becomes all the more deplorable when the punishment is irrevocable.

The pioneers often hanged with neat efficiency. At other times they bungled, failed to "give a good drop," and inflicted instead the agony of slow strangulation. Their work in such instances was harrowing even to watch. More often the defect was in making a carnival out of a hanging, preparing for it with heavy drinking, going about it boisterously, rough with anger, or sadistically.

But hanging is not the only way to lynch. Today's out-of-court punishments are more likely to be by exposure to contumely and disgrace, getting a man ejected from his job, or driving him from his career. The bald and direct economic consequence is serious enough. Upon certain individuals the result has been a total collapse of personality. With others, helplessness and fear of being caught in these toils has led to a reversal of character that is even more pitiable.

The beyond-the-law punishments of our day are marred by many of the same defects that characterize those of the frontier. There is the hazard that they will be amateurishly bungled; that they will be too much personalized; that the punishment will not fit the crime, if any; that they will be hippodrome performances played to the galleries; and that they will be done in passion. Even with the best of intentions vigilante punishment is subject to these drawbacks.

The outside-the-law character of vigilantism should preclude any participation by public officials. It is well known, however, that at its peak the Ku Klux Klan enrolled mayors, governors, state legislators, members of Congress, and judges. On the frontier most officials held aloof, but not all. A principal instance concerns Mayor Stephen C. Foster of Los Angeles. In October, 1854, he intervened to disperse a mob intent on hanging gambler Dave Brown, who had just perpetrated a killing. Foster's proposition was to let the regular court take charge. If it failed, he promised to head a vigilante group that would give Brown the punishment all felt he deserved. Brown was tried, convicted, and sentenced to be hanged. His lawyers at the eleventh hour got a stay of execution. True to his word, Foster at once joined with the vigilantes to break into the jail, take Brown, and string him up. With due regard for the proprieties, however, he first resigned from his office as mayor and did not resume that title until after the lynching was over.

Today's officeholders have fewer scruples about assisting in the application of extralegal trial and punishment. Senators and congressmen have used their immunity and their committee assignments as a cover to usurp powers that more properly reside in the courts. The activity which they call exposure invades the field of indictment better handled by the grand jury. When Senator McCarthy repeatedly attacked General Ralph Zwicker because he had signed the routine papers for the promotion of Eugene Peress, the army dentist who had invoked the Fifth Amendment before McCarthy's committee, the Senator was striving for something tantamount to an out-of-court conviction. So was Congressman Donald Jackson in his attacks on Bishop G. Bromley Oxnam for actions and associations by no means criminal. The hearings that Senator James O. Eastland conducted against the New York *Times* likewise were geared toward discrediting and intimidating if not actually fining its publishers. Upon learning that the respected Latin-American expert Lawrence Duggan had fallen from an office building window to his death, two members of the House Un-American Activities Committee made a midnight dash to the committee files to make a press release that would suggest that the committee had been Duggan's executioner. When the Canadian government held a Senate committee partly accountable for the death of career diplomat E. Herbert Norman, Senator Eastland thought it a sufficient response to say that his name "repeatedly came up." In actions such as these, members of the official class often spearhead today's substitutions for regular justice.

Vigilantism all too frequently has the mark of political motivation or personal ambition. Such considerations, of course, may infect regular justice. An attorney general may be overzealous because he wants to run for governor; a judge may warp his decisions to serve his party or his patron. There have been occasions also when the established courts have discriminated against the poor, the laborers, the foreign-born, or racial or other minorities. By its nature the extralegal approach is much more prone to all these abuses. Far more than the regular courts, vigilantism picks on the weak, the lowly, the unpopular, the people least able to resist or to retaliate.

On the mining frontiers in California and elsewhere punishments fell with special severity on Mexicans, Chileans, and Chinese. The San Francisco committee of 1851 specialized in punitive action against the Sydney "ducks" or "coves" from the penal colony of Australia. The stranger in camp was the particular candidate for the attention of the Mother Lode tribunals. The Indian often got more summary treatment than the white. In the South the violence has usually been against the Negro. Throughout the modern phases, too, vigilantism seems to be more at ease when it is pouncing on the underprivileged, the humble, and often the minority element. Many of the actors blacklisted were bit players, most of the witnesses pilloried by the congressional investigators were in the lower income brackets, the State Department thought twice about refusing a passport to a Nobel Prize winner, and presumably it was by inadvertence that red-baiters threatened a major studio's investment in a feature picture.

In almost every society the sad fact has been that, at least relatively, the little people have been expendable. Even the stony-hearted, however, cannot find much solace in the way in which vigilantes choose most of their victims from groups that are subordinate, looked down upon, or despised. On the frontier the whole community usually had to bow to the will of the committeemen. San Francisco's vigilantes took over the town and its second committee successfully defied the state government. There was a "better element" in the Wilson administration than the personnel carrying out the Palmer raids and deportations, but it did not block this action. Most of the nation's scientists were not in agreement with what was done to Edward U. Condon and J. Robert Oppenheimer, but they could not manage to stay either of these processes. And even though in most instances the individuals attacked have been relatively obscure, great universities, great corporations, and the entire Department of State have on occasion jumped to do the bidding of extralegal accusers who have spotted non-conformists or nonrespondents in the ranks of these agencies. The lowly station of the majority of the victims thus may be something of an illusion. Beyond-the-law trial and punishment have a way of being felt throughout the whole society.

On mining claims and water rights the pioneers improvised rules that subsequently were incorporated into state and federal law. Apologists for the frontier vigilantes insist that they likewise were architects of law and government, preparing the way for a regime of order and public safety. In the wake of the second vigilance committee, San Francisco did enjoy ten halcyon years of good government and good order. Elsewhere on the frontier a season of calm sometimes followed a vigilante performance. But not always. Dame Shirley saw the Indian Bar Committee as rousing more violence than it quelled. Vigilante action is too capricious to be a steady deterrent to crime. Its harsh punishments turn some first offenders into desperate men. And especially where it continued as a competitor against the regular courts, it retarded rather than advanced the attainment of lawful trial and punishment.

Like their frontier counterparts, the twentieth-century vigilantes have real power to hurt their victims and thus in most instances to intimidate. They almost never undertake to rehabilitate. Their work is repressive and retaliatory. As such it may supplement regular justice but cannot make much of a constructive contribution. By stretching matters we may say that the violence against the I. W. W. produced the rash of state criminal syndicalism acts; that out of the Dies committee came the bill of attainder against Lovett, Watson, and Dodd, which the Supreme Court promptly voided; that Tenneyism in California bore fruit in that state's special arsenal of repressive acts; that the monument to McCarthyism is the Humphrey Amendment; and that from the night-riders of the South stems the doctrine of interposition. Here and in such laws as the Smith, McCarran, and Feinberg acts are additions to the criminal code of which our regular courts must and do take notice. Yet, all told, this hardly establishes vigilantism as a creative force reshaping regular justice.

In its own time, the people's court of the frontier was greeted with a mixture of praise and criticism. The majority of correspondents, reporters, and editors complimented the ingenuity, aplomb, and dispatch with which a volunteer group could supply a substitute for regular justice. Others on the scene were more alert to the defects and abuses. These critics, however, were not numerous. In San Francisco in 1856 John Nugent's *Herald* was the only paper that opposed the committee. Its advertisers and most of its readers abandoned the paper forthwith, and the *Herald* dwindled and soon fell silent.

Because they were irregular and illegal agencies, most vigilante groups kept only fragmentary records. In letters and journals, nevertheless, they were far more articulate than their victims, with the result that the preserved source materials are one-sided. A further consequence is that historians, with their well-known penchant for following the sources, have in most instances put themselves on this same side. Hubert Howe Bancroft (for the most part), Theodore H. Hittell, Charles H. Shinn, John Steven McGroarty, Stewart Edward White, Robert Glass Cleland, Stanton A. Coblentz (with some reservations), James A. B. Scherer, Hoffman Birney, Wayne Gard, and Alan Valentine — all these, in what they have written about the pioneers, can fairly be classed as pro-vigilante.

In *The Forty-Niners* White compliments the San Francisco committees by giving them some 40 per cent of his space and by summing up the issue between the opposition and the vigilantes as a choice between law and justice. Cleland's tribute to these committees is that they cleared the city of undesirables and "put the fear of God" into the hearts of the lawless characters who remained. McGroarty saw the committee of 1856 as a "wonderful organization." "In the light of history," he went on, "the men who formed the organization stand entirely justified." The committee of 1856, says Hittell, was "one of the purest and best intentioned bodies of men ever assembled in San Francisco." He credits it with achieving "extraordinarily beneficent ulterior results," indeed, "the most remarkable municipal reforms ever known in the country." Bancroft gave the performance of 1856 this accolade: "One of the grandest moral revolutions the world has ever witnessed." And in that same frame of reference R. D. Hunt and N. V. Sánchez affirm, "The work of vigilance was one of splendor and permanence. . . . The motives of the men who willingly sacrificed private interest in order to discharge a great social and civic duty are unimpeachable."

A few historians have taken a more guarded position, either by being noncommittal or by noting the gains and losses for society and letting it go at that. If his conclusion alone is taken as the criterion, Josiah Royce appears to be of this group. The trouble in California of the fifties, as he sees it, was that "long-continued social apathy" and "treasonable public carelessness" had brought matters to such a pass that vigilantism was inevitable. The resort to direct action, he adds, "represented not so much the dignity of the sovereign people as the depth and bitterness of popular repentance for the past." The general tenor of his account, however, is much more critical, and he pointedly dissents from much of the extreme praise that by the eighties had become the standard comment on the popular tribunals of three decades earlier.

In their day the committees had more severe critics — Buffum, Barstow, and Shirley, for instance. One modern historian is unreservedly critical. He speaks of the 1851 committee's "parody of justice," detects only the most temporary and superficial improvement of the social body, and therefore judges this foray into vigilantism as "fundamentally a social and political failure." Similarly he notes the "surge of emotionalism" that swayed the committee of 1856. He points out that this committee was in truth a revolution. The execution of Brace and Hetherington, he says, was made "a sordid spectacle." Conceding that this committee did rid the state of some undesirables, he nevertheless concludes: "Not to any great extent did it lead the way to constructive reform. It was a menace to society; its formation was a tragic admission of failure. . . . It shockingly demonstrated the ease with which lawlessness in the form of mob or extralegal action rises when American citizenry are unwilling to control the destroying forces in social life by the successful operation of lawfully organized representative government." The historian I am quoting is William H. Ellison, in his *A Self-Governing Dominion: California, 1849-1860.* His appraisal relates specifically to the two San Francisco committees, in many respects the most polite and orderly of all the vigilantes, and in this judgment he stands almost alone.

Where historians have left off in their praise of the frontier vigilantes, the creative writers have begun. Bret Harte, for example, represents a genre of treatment which became current a little less than a generation after the fact. It is dominant in the reminiscences of the pioneers and still more so in the fiction. This school of thought attributes two qualities in particular to the impromptu tribunals. One is an implacable efficiency. An orator speaking in Buffalo as early as 1849 put it this way: "Woe to the felon upon whose track is the American borderer! Woe to the assassin before a self-impaneled jury of American foresters! No lie can help him, no eloquence prevail; no false plea can confuse the clear conceptions or arrest the judgment of a frontier court."

The companion quality attributed to the frontier vigilantes is that of good humor — that they were capable of a sentimental concern about the culprits brought before them, and that they were able to go about their grisly work with an air of jollity.

Actual incidents of rough humor are numerous and the fictionists have not hesitated to embellish them. There was the vigilante, hat in hand, telling the widow, "We've just strung up your husband, Ma'am. But the joke's on us; he wasn't guilty." Then there was the lad quite unperturbed by the sentence that his left ear should be cropped. When the factotum of the committee brandished his knife and reached under the shock of hair he found only a stump. With equal sangfroid the committee revised its sentence and claimed the other ear. Another condemned man implored, "Give a man time to pray." "Go right ahead," was the response, "and while you're praying we'll fit this rope around your neck."

The records of early official courts are even richer in anecdotes of uncouth and ribald humor. It stands to reason that the vigilantes would blunder into malapropism. Such lightheartedness as was present, however, was seldom intentional and never a genuinely ameliorating feature.

The romancers go further and endow the pioneer vigilantes with a soft-hearted sentimentality. Having given a thief the lash, they sometimes took up a collection and presented it to him before banishing him from camp. Or they are pictured as easily swayed by an eloquent and emotional appeal invoking the recreant's poor mother or the wife and children dependent on him for support. One story has a lawyer save a pockmarked client by spinning an imaginative tale about how he had heroically volunteered to nurse a stranger through the smallpox. As long ago as the eighties Josiah Royce effectively rebutted this allegation that the frontier committeemen would let sentiment hold them back from their appointed rounds. There is, I grant, a school of writing today, which *The Ox Bow Incident* represents, in which vigilantism is played as stark tragedy. Yet the short story, the western, the stage as in *Paint Your Wagon,* the movies as in *Jubal,* and most of the television serials still inject these elements of comedy and sentimentality and, for the most part, glorify this frontier institution.

In the fulness of time the modern equivalent will also be evaluated. For the part that expresses race hatred, the augury seems unfavorable. The documentation in current report and comment is mostly adverse, and these will be the principal materials for future generations of researchers. There are elements of principle that will have weight with historians, and again they are mostly against the racists. The aspect of heroism, furthermore, is emphatically not with those who would push down the already downtrodden or terrorize children who are doing no more than their duty in seeking an education. Rather, it is with the Negro children.

When it comes, however, to all the vigilantism that takes the name of anti-Communism, the outlook for the long view may be quite different. Here the bulk of current record and comment is much more favorable. A plausible argument is made that there is an end that justifies the means. Historians of a later generation will have at hand many pro-vigilante sources, will note that many persons of good will aided and abetted this activity, and that some of its announced objectives must be applauded. It is well within the realm of possibility, therefore, that a good many historians will give this anti-Communism vigilantism a seal of approval, as indeed some already have.

Furthermore, it is conceivable that the novelists, playwrights, and scenario writers, or whoever the troubadours of the next century are to be, will fulfil the analogy of our artistic and popular interpretation of frontier vigilantism. When they deal with the beyond-the-law practice of anti-Communism in America they may be most impressed with its tragic ludicrousness — the comedy of Cohn and Shine; the peripheral repartee of McCarthy and Welch; the banning, after all these centuries, of *Robin Hood*; the elephantine concern about alleged Communist infiltration of the Girl Scouts; and the wholesale collection of expurgatory test oaths from professional wrestlers in Indiana and from infant artists' models in California. Such material lends itself to burlesque. Or the treatment could be comic, edged with romantic idealizing, which is about what Bret Harte did for the vigilantes of the frontier. That interpretation, if it prevails, will be the saddest possible distortion of the travail of our times.

By friend and foe vigilantism has always been regarded as a strictly temporary institution. The emergency that calls it forth is always counted on to pass and then regular justice can take over. Given this expectation, the advice offered as practical has usually been to let the passion run its course, not to challenge it at once, but to wait for a more opportune time to re-establish a regime of justice under law. That is the formula of gradualism and of non-resistance to McCarthyism. A flaw in this complacency is that the emergencies of race and Russia have prospect of lasting a long time. The vigilantism that we are familiar with consequently may continue to the end of our days.

Furthermore, neither passivity nor martyrdom seems to be the best way to achieve a return to protection of the individual under the law. Much more has been gained by the resolution that succeeds. Thus Peter Zenger is a landmark in freedom of the press mainly because he won his case. Matthew Lyon, who went to jail under the Sedition Act, has and deserves less fame than the other Jeffersonians who won the election of 1800 and saw to it that this repressive law was not re-enacted. Autherine Lucy, for all the valor of her bid at the University of Alabama, accomplished less than the people of Louisville who integrated their schools.

If this analysis is correct, the ultimate responsibility for most of today's beyond-the-law practice of intimidation and coercion must be very broadly shared, with almost every American involved. An element of causation, to be sure, can be traced to the interpreters of frontier vigilantism. The historians and the less fact-bound narrators who have dealt with this topic have shaped a public memory that glorifies this part of the pioneer heritage. The current practice is thereby encouraged, but this consequence can be laid at least as much to the general timidity about opposing today's direct actionists.

For lack of a challenge, vigilantism stands by default. It gets an exaggerated appearance of popularity. Its leaders can posture heroically. And the whole movement, past, present, and perhaps future, gains a cachet of respectability which is indeed a strange accompaniment to its extralegal and antilegal character.

A UNIVERSITY IN JEOPARDY

Throughout the past year and a half the University of California has been riven by a faculty-regents dispute which has mushroomed to epic proportions.* It began as a debate over loyalty, which seems

*[This account of the oath controversy was written during the height of the dispute — in September, 1950 — and published two months later in *Harper's Magazine*.]

nonsensical because of course we all agree that only the loyal deserve faculty posts. But there was sharp difference of opinion about how to detect and keep out the disloyal — through an oath of non-membership in the Communist party, as the regents proposed, or through the traditional and tested routines of faculty self-inspection.

Intermittently there were indications that the drive against Communism was being used to cover other purposes. Finally, at the August 1950 meeting of the regents, this became quite clear. In connection with a motion to dismiss thirty-two members of the faculty this interchange occurred:

> "Do I understand," Governor Warren asked, "that we are firing these people merely because they are recalcitrant?"
>
> "It is not a question of Communism," said Regent Arthur J. McFadden, "but one of discipline."

Not disloyalty but discipline — these four words define the real issue. The tragic feature is that these men have been disciplined out of their jobs for following a course supposedly set up in good faith by the regents.

Inevitably there are overtones and consequences, some of which touch matters of vital concern to the existence of a true university. For example, when confronted with a so-called loyalty oath, which in reality was an oath of political denial set up as a condition of employment, the faculty opposition countered that it was completely and unreservedly loyal. It feels, moreover, a patriotic duty to safeguard a principle vital to Americanism and to the democratic republic in which we live. That principle goes under various names — freedom of speech, freedom of the press, and academic freedom. Academic freedom is usually taken to mean the right of a qualified scholar to teach and to speak and to write in the field of his expertness without interference. A fundamental thereto is that such a scholar shall not be censored out of eligibility to get or to hold an academic job.

On the loyalty front the oath and its sequel have not exposed a traitor or improved a patriot. Academic freedom, however, has been put in grievous jeopardy. Rights and guarantees that the faculty thought secure have been whisked away. A tradition of faculty self-government has been undermined, and faculty morale has been shattered.

Because this is the largest university in the land and one of the four or five most productive in scholarship, a narrative of how it happened here may have some intrinsic worth. For the same reasons, the California pattern is bound to be noticed by those who shape the destinies of other schools, and it may, for good or ill, set in motion other events of a similar kind. This possibility, in fact, explains why I have put down the following account. The perspective is admittedly personal; this is a report of the university's ordeal as I saw it develop.

The first intimation that the university would apply a political test came in June 1949. True enough, the Faculty Bulletin of the preceding month had a terse announcement of a loyalty oath. The sound, however, was that of a positive pledge of loyalty, and no one expressed, and I think no one felt, any reluctance about complying.

As unveiled on June 12, however, the regents' oath turned out to be a special one featuring a denial of belief. To it the faculty voiced a philosophical objection. We had all signed and we all preferred the straightforward pledge of loyalty written into the state constitution by California's founding fathers in 1849:

> I do solemnly swear (or affirm) that I will support the Constitution of the United States and the Constitution of the State of California, and that I will faithfully discharge the duties of my office according to the best of my ability.

For all state officers this oath had served well through the entire hundred years of statehood. For a number of years this oath had also been asked of the university faculty and had been taken with never a hint of reluctance. As men of integrity, furthermore, we have regarded this oath as a pledge of complete loyalty, with no loopholes left or wanted for unpatriotic action of any description.

Hindsight now makes clear that we should have held out for this constitutional oath and no other.

II

At the time, the more conciliatory approach seemed to be to suggest an additional general clause denying commitments contrary to the oath proper. On June 24, after the faculty had scattered for the summer, the regents accepted this suggestion, but vitiated it by inserting a phrase of specific denial — "I am not a member of the Communist party." This demand for a specific denial is the crux of all the subsequent trouble, for it most palpably sets up a political test. As amended the oath now read:

I do solemnly swear (or affirm) that I will support the Constitution of the United States and the Constitution of the State of California, and that I will faithfully discharge the duties of my office according to the best of my ability; that I am not a member of the Communist party, or under any oath or a party to any agreement or under any commitment that is in conflict with my obligations under this oath.

The objection to being made to say "I am not" is not confined to the minority that is under attack. A forced declaration of the obvious is equally distasteful. Thus when the Romans went around prodding men to deny that they were Christians, some good old pagans were incensed. When Catholic rulers at the time of the Reformation applied the same kind of pressure to root out Protestants, and when Protestant England used the device against Catholics, objection was not confined to the minority.

To Americans, because of a greater respect for individual rights and a greater awareness of the usefulness of minority opinions, test oaths have always been abhorrent. The fathers of our country took a strong stand against them. So did the fathers of our state; having spelled out the constitutional oath, they added this injunction: "And no other oath, declaration, or test shall be required as a qualification for any office or public trust."

Through the summer of 1949 there was official pretense that the special oath was requested but not required. It soon became apparent, however, that the only way to get a contract was to sign the oath. In the circumstances it is perhaps remarkable that any substantial number of the faculty refrained from signing.

From June to November the one reason assigned for the special oath was that Communists are victims of thought control and therefore cannot possibly carry out the impartial scholarship and honest teaching to which the university is dedicated. All along, the faculty has been aware that the whole strength of our foreign policy has been marshaled to resist the spread of Communism. In support of this program we, if anything, have gone further than the general public. If the peril to our nation becomes greater, if the federal government decides on more drastic measures, we stand ready to make any useful contribution that we can.

But if the concern of the regents is over an invasion of the university by charlatans and propagandists, we submit that no oath or declaration can be as sure a protection as the faculty's own method of selecting and screening its membership.

Since the early twenties the University of California has had a well-developed system of faculty self-government. The present members of the faculty are where they are because of a procedure of selection by their peers on the basis of character, competence, and performance. This selective process is not infallible; errors of judgment and of charity have been made. But we do maintain that the only trustworthy and effective means of building and maintaining a proper faculty is by reliance on the expert judgment of scholars. The alumni may be the best judges of football coaches. The regents may be better connoisseurs of capital investments. But just as we rely on the lawyers to decide who shall be admitted to the bar and on the doctors to say who may practice medicine, the only sound procedure is to have the scholars in the several disciplines decide who shall constitute a university faculty.

By resolution and by delegation the faculty several times reminded the regents of the cogency of this principle. We pointed to this method of selection as a main reason for the university's distinction. We expressed confidence that anyone sacrificing scholarly integrity on the Communist altar would be detected and disqualified through the regular faculty procedure. We reminded the regents that, although since 1940 they had had a standing rule against employment of Communists, not once had they had occasion to apply it against a member of the faculty.

Thus passed the first half of the year of the oath. The arguments so cogent to us seemed strangely ineffective with the regents. In November 1949 we got a hint as to the reason. The oath, we now were officially told, was traceable to State Senator Jack B. Tenney, the Martin Dies-J. Parnell Thomas-Joseph McCarthy of California. A measure he had ready for the state legislature early in 1949 so alarmed the university's legislative representative (or, in translation, lobbyist) that this worthy communicated his fears to the president, who, in turn, proposed to the regents in March 1949 the institution of the special oath.

This revelation put a worse cast on the matter. If the regents were concerned to protect the university against the fraudulent scholarship of a typical Communist, the faculty could collaborate on safeguards that would be both honorable and effective. If, however, the regents were playing politics, to what extent could the faculty go along?

A new faculty committee, nevertheless, was set up and sent, on January 4, 1950, to meet with a corresponding committee of the regents. The keynote of this conference was the regents' insistence on an explicit anti-Communist program. They had in mind the possibility of action for perjury against an oath signer who might turn out to be a Communist. Aware that special tests and restrictions surrounded the Radiation Laboratory and other government-sponsored secret activities in the university, they saw no reason why the same rigors should not be extended to all departments. More bluntly, they wanted to know why anyone who was not a Communist would object to saying so.

The faculty representatives insisted that under such restrictions a real university was impossible. They stressed the necessity of relying on the faculty to police its own ranks. They asked confidence in the faculty, and as one piece of evidence cited the president's statement that he knew of no Communist in the faculty. They expressed no love of Communists, but neither did they like the application of a political test which could easily become a precedent for further narrowing of the base of eligibility for the faculty.

We adjourned with the express understanding that the two committees would confer again before reporting to the board of regents or to the faculty. To our dismay, however, at the next meeting of the board of regents, their committee made its report and had itself discharged.

A month later the regents reiterated their anti-Communist policy. They added a proviso that before firing a Communist professor (if, as, and when one could be found) they would submit the evidence to the faculty for inspection. With heavier emphasis the regents affirmed an anti-non-signer policy. They announced that anyone who did not sign the special oath or an identical affirmation by April 30 would be dropped at the end of the semester. For such a person there would be no hearing whatsoever.

The charitable interpretation would be that it was by inadvertence that the regents set up a more considerate routine for Communists than for loyal and perhaps distinguished professors who balked at the special oath. Some observers were not so sure. Several of the regents, for example, had taken great umbrage at a faculty resolution reciting apparently unacceptable facts about the relative spheres of activity for faculty and regents in a well-ordered university. If the regents' main purpose was to bring the faculty to heel, then the February ultimatum was logical.

One ray of encouragement was that the action had not been unanimous. With eighteen of the twenty-four regents present, the vote had stood at twelve to six. Regents Earl J. Fenston, Farnham P.

Griffiths, Victor Hansen, and Edward H. Heller voted against the ultimatum. So did Governor Earl Warren and President Robert G. Sproul. The support of these six was most heartening. This was particularly true of the Governor, who, in an election year, was ready to brave an inflamed segment of public opinion, and of the president, who courageously admitted that he had changed his mind about the wisdom of the oath requirement.

III

Whatever its intentions, the ultimatum roused the faculty as nothing else had. The northern half of the Committee on Conference began a campaign of publicity and persuasion. It convened the Berkeley deans and department chairmen and got their support. It went to work to find a solution that would have the endorsement of the vast majority of the faculty. Similar steps, though more tardily, were taken at Los Angeles. Incidentally, it should be remarked that a major handicap to the faculty in this whole campaign has been its dispersal on eight widely scattered campuses. Here is an unexpected illustration of the Roman maxim *divide et impera.*

On March 7 and 8 the assembled faculties at Berkeley and Los Angeles considered resolutions condemning the sign-or-be-fired ultimatum and calling for rescinding of the special oath requirement. In the north the vote was a vociferous 900 to zero; in the south an estimated 400 to 10. The faculty then ordered a mail ballot on the committee's proposed solution. This proposal, in essence, was a return to the constitutional oath, plus a contract form placing the signer liable to, but not necessarily in endorsement of, the university's previously announced rules of employment. Nor was the contract to embody denial of a specific political membership. The proposal carried, 1,154 to 136.

In the preceding fortnight much else had happened. One regent, in an open letter to the president, extolled the special oath as a blow against "communism, of which socialism is the first step." He pointed to England where, he said, freedom had been destroyed by socialism. Herein was more than a hint that the anti-Communist policy could readily expand to bar other minority groups.

Another regent attacked the faculty as Communist tools, Communist dupes, and Communist-led. The whole opposition to the oath stemmed, he said, from a "dissident minority" to which the more stable faculty members had submitted. True enough, the various pressures applied had brought the non-signers down to a small fraction. But many had signed under protest, and the faculty votes, one after another, had been by thumping majorities. At no time did it appear within the faculty that opposition to the oath was monopolized by a "hard core" or a "dissident minority."

Another plaint of this same regent was that the faculty was actually and purposely shielding Communists. In the light of his repeated attacks, many of us were not surprised to find in a newspaper report of one of his statements a passing reference to "seven admitted card-carrying Communists" in the faculty. By the time this report reached Los Angeles the number was twelve. Actually the regent's statement had been a hypothetical one that "even admitted card-carrying Communists" would or would not do thus and so. By typographical error an "s" was added and "even" became "seven"!

We were, as a matter of fact, under the handicap of having to wage this campaign in the realm of pure theory. Lacking a flesh-and-blood example of the group under attack, our argument had to be on the off chance that such a person whom we would consider eligible by competence and loyalty might sometime show up. Possibly no such person existed. If that were so, our argument still was that the regents' method was not the proper means of insuring exclusion, that it was inherently inefficient, and that it was a most dangerous precedent. But for lack of a live specimen in our ranks, we were restricted to intangible and theoretical resistance.

This circumstance, together with the urging of the most vocal of the regents, seemed to account for the faculty's motion on March 7 to send another proposition to mail ballot. It stated that proved members of the Communist party, by reason of their anti-scholarly commitments, are not acceptable to the faculty. This statement, of course, is a direct contradiction of the stand of the American Association of University Professors. Curiously, some members of the faculty argued that the statement did not affirm guilt by association but was an individual rather than a group condemnation. Others, influenced by the temper of the times, cast a politic affirmative vote. In the university-wide poll this proposition carried, 1,025 to 268.

Subsequently a faculty leader revealed that there had been a bargain. This proposition, in his words, was "put over" after assurances that the regents would be satisfied with it as a substitute for individual oaths of denial.

In the June-to-March palaver over the special oath, the faculty reminded me — and I hope I am Irish enough to be allowed to use the anecdote — of the Russian family dashing through the snow with the wolves in hot pursuit and saving itself by throwing out a baby whenever the wolves got too close. We also had been making sacrifices at regular intervals. In this second proposition I thought we had thrown out one baby too many.

Wiser tacticians thought not. And the sequel seemed to bear them out, for on March 31, when the board of regents, slightly revised through two new appointments, took up the faculty proposal of liability through contract, the motion to rescind the special oath failed by ten to ten.

No one took the tie vote as final. All looked forward to reconsideration at the next meeting of the regents.

IV

The faculty campaign, some weeks since, had been entrusted to a new committee which, by chance or otherwise, was more cautious than its predecessor. The policy it followed was one of limited publicity, almost no response to attacks in the Los Angeles and the Hearst press, co-operation with the president, and reliance on finding an additional vote somewhere in the board. The grapevine — how reliably I do not know — had it that a vote or two could be counted on and that the faculty proposal would squeak through.

At almost the eleventh hour the president and his immediate advisers decided that such a margin was not enough. In order to increase it they invited the Berkeley Alumni Council to appoint a special committee to investigate and, as it developed, to mediate.

The alumni committee took the task seriously. By private plane they flew from one end of the state to the other, interviewing most of the regents, consulting at length with three members of the faculty, and more briefly with a few others. As mediators they found it difficult, if not impossible, to understand that the faculty had already made every concession consistent with principle. They looked for a solution somewhere between the last stand of the faculty and that of the regents. This was the settlement which the alumni proposed and the regents adopted:

(1) The regents would escape from the untenable position of the ultimatum by withdrawing the special oath and with it the sign-or-be-fired stipulation.

(2) Although the oath as such was no more, as an "equivalent affirmation"* it would transmigrate to the annual contract.

(3) Every new appointee would have to sign this affirmation.

(4) Any member of the present faculty, however, could appeal for review by the Committee on Privilege and Tenure, including investigation and full hearing on his reasons for not signing. Recommendations of the committee would be subject to review by the president and final decision by the board of regents.

The board welcomed this "solution" by a vote of twenty-one to one, with the lone dissenter bewailing a Communist victory that would set the bells to ringing in the Kremlin. If there was any rejoicing in the faculty I did not hear about it. A few optimists hailed the new order as the first step toward a settlement. Many heaved a sigh of relief that the controversy could now be committed to history.

Others recognized a complete defeat for the faculty. The political test as a condition of employment is, if anything, more effectively enshrined in the contract than it had been in the oath. Ordeal by oath had given place to ordeal by inquisition.

A committee to act as a court of last resort for those who are on the point of dismissal is standard equipment in most universities. Almost always, however, those who appear before it are there to answer charges of gross neglect of duty, incompetence, or moral turpitude. When I joined the UCLA staff twenty years ago, the last thing I expected was that I should ever appear before such a committee.

Under the alumni formula anyone who objects to the political test is liable to dismissal unless cleared, not merely by his committee, but also by the president and the regents. This three-fold ordeal, furthermore, was to be an annual rite, and since my life expectancy in the university ran another twenty years before retirement, my professorial head would be on the block sixty-three times in the years to come.

A reasonable question, I believe, is whether a moderately sensitive person could be expected to do his best in the classroom and in research under this routine of multiple jeopardy.

*This clause reads: ". . . that I am not a member of the Communist party or any other organization which advocates the overthrow of the government by force or violence, and that I have no commitments in conflict with my responsibilities with respect to impartial scholarship and free pursuit of truth."

V

After April 21 the faculty had little choice but to submit to the formula worked out by the alumni and adopted by the regents. Now it was left to each individual to consult with his conscience whether to sign the contract statement or to appeal for a hearing. Those non-signers whose worry had been solely in terms of a special oath now could sign without a qualm. Others, measuring their resources against the dire threats by certain of the regents, reluctantly let prudence lead them to signing. A remaining few showed confidence that the board of regents' authorization of the route of appeal was made in good faith. These executed the constitutional oath and appealed for a hearing on their reasons for not signing the statement.

Full and careful hearings were held, the president reviewed the reports, and on June 23 the regents met to take final action. After hours of spirited debate they voted (a) to defer action on all these reports so that they could study each case individually, and (b) to fire 157 employees who had neither signed the new contract for the period to June 30, 1950, nor requested hearings. According to the press reports, most of these 157 were nonacademic employees and few if any were regular members of the faculty. According to the press reports, most if not all the 157 were leaving the university as of June 30. Firing them was thus an empty gesture, though it certainly was not intended as a compliment.

Practically all the discussion concerned those who had chosen the alternative of a committee hearing. Certain of the regents expressed great displeasure that so many had appealed and had been approved. One said he had understood that the hearing avenue was only for Quakers. The attitude of one was, "They have had their hearings, now let us discharge them." The reasons for not signing were attacked as "the flimsiest excuses."

Other regents, notably the Governor, the president, Fenston, Griffiths, Hansen, Heller, and (recently appointed) Jesse Steinhart, took the stand that under the formula of April 21 appeal to the committee was a perfectly legitimate move. It was authorized in the plain reading of the regents' resolution. They would not admit that mere recourse to the appeal route constituted grounds for dismissal.

They also argued that arbitrary disregard of the recommendations of the committees and the president would play havoc with the university.

After a month in which to study the committee reports, the regents met again on July 21. Once more, the bone of contention was whether to countenance any use of the appeal route. The argument did not touch on the loyalty or disloyalty of any individual. Instead, it had to do with the intent and meaning of the regents' resolution which had set up the hearings option.

The faculty was not in position to testify as to intent, but it did try to clarify the meaning as received. A professor who had been one of the first to sign, two non-signers, several members of the Committee on Privilege and Tenure, and, most eloquently, Provost Emeritus Monroe E. Deutsch made statements to the board, either in writing or in person. All agreed that the entire faculty understood and had been given to understand that appeal was legitimate and presumably safe for anyone not a Communist.

Finally the regents voted. In the first quarter of the roll call the votes were almost all to fire, in the middle they were more evenly divided, and it took every vote toward the end of the alphabet — Nimitz, Simpson, Sproul, Steinhart, and Warren — to carry the day, ten to nine. One regent, elderly and invalid, had to leave just before the vote. He had been consistently in the opposition.

Without debate and without dissent the regents then voted to accept signatures, resignations, and clerical corrections which brought the 157 fired in June down to 83. In similar fashion they voted to fire six members of the faculty as recommended by the president on the basis of committee reports, not as Communists but for refusal to co-operate with the examining committee. On any other day this action would have made the headlines. In the context of the debate that had preceded, it was eclipsed by the "rehiring" of those who had committee endorsement. All the papers treated this as the chief news of the meeting.

Just before adjournment the chief campaigner against the faculty went back to the previous question, changed his vote to "aye," and announced his intention of moving reconsideration at the next meeting. But in answer to a reporter's question, the secretary of the regents said he would send contracts to these men.

He did not do it. Early in August we read in the papers that, pending possible reconsideration, we who had refused to sign but had been recommended by the committee and the president would get no contracts and no salary payments. We were not told to stop working, but in effect the message was, "You may be fired on August 25, therefore your pay is stopped as of last June 30."

The August meeting, by all accounts, was as heated as any of the others. This time, the long debate was on the motion to reconsider the hiring of the group recommended by the committee and the president. Governor Warren as presiding officer ruled the motion out of order and further that the action it proposed was illegal. On the latter point the university attorney agreed. Ably supported by Regents Steinhart and Hansen, Governor Warren argued this point at length, citing a Los Angeles City Council case as providing an analogy that would hold. Undeterred by this legal opinion, the nine opponents of the previous month, plus three men then absent, voted to overrule the chair. By the same tally, twelve to ten, the board voted to overrule the recommendations of the faculty committee, to turn down the recommendations of the president, to reverse its own action of July, and discharge the appeal-route professors.

Before the vote to dismiss, Regent Heller demanded to know, for the record, if any regent had any charge of Communism or any evidence of disloyalty to lodge against any of the persons whose fate was about to be decided. No such charge or evidence was brought forward. It was at this point that one of the hostile regents said, "It's not a question of Communism, but one of discipline."

After the vote to discharge, the leader of the twelve turned magnanimous. He proposed that the dismissed in all categories, whether the findings had been favorable or not, should have another ten days in which they might sign and be rehired as of July 1 last, with no questions asked. Further, he proposed that anyone who now chose to resign could claim up to a year's severance pay — proportionately reduced if he found an academic job sooner.

Regents Steinhart, Hansen, Fenston, and Warren, I'm told, hit the ceiling at this proposal, saying that the men involved were either fit for employment and should have been retained, or unfit for employment and should be cut off entirely. They did not approve of using the taxpayers' money as rewards for resignations.

Some regents undoubtedly voted for this proposal out of compassion for those who otherwise were so suddenly deprived of work and income. It carried.

As of early September, when this is written, the latest development is a suit for writ of mandamus to compel the issuance of the contracts voted in July. If it succeeds some of us will be allowed to teach and to draw pay until next June.

Meanwhile, the number of contenders has been reduced to a

token. As of April 21 there were said to be about 280 who had refused the special oath. Of these 69 went through committee hearings and were on the regents' docket in June. Signatures and resignations cut the number hoping for clearance in July to 40, in August to 32, and as of today to perhaps 25, some of whom will be moving to other jobs no matter what the outcome of the suit may be.

As one of those summarily dismissed, after half a lifetime of service to the university, I find it hard to be sent into exile, and all the harder because the action of the regents has been arbitrary and in bad faith.

Along with every other member of the faculty I was perfectly willing to take the constitutional oath of loyalty, which I have done. I was and am perfectly willing to give additional positive assurances of my loyalty to the United States, my preference for its basic institutions, my devotion to its historic ideals, and my willingness to serve it without stint in time of peace and without question in time of war.*

I stand ready to answer any charges brought against me and to submit my whole record to inspection and all my actions to investigation. In going through the hearings procedure, this in effect is what I have done.

My concern, however, is not just personal. I am distraught at the damage that this action of the regents does to the university and to its students. Through the course of this controversy the university has suffered incalculable loss in disturbed teaching, interrupted research, emotional exhaustion of many persons involved, and indelible distrust within and between the faculty and the regents.

The tragedy is the greater since in many respects the University of California faculty-regent relationship had been a model of excellence. It is true that certain regents sometimes verged on a proprietary attitude in matters such as the architectural decoration of new buildings, or the question of who might speak on the campus. In the epoch of the New Deal, too, the regents had been adamant against acceptance of PWA money, with the consequence that students to the third and fourth academic generations are still crowded into classroom, laboratory, and dormitory space that is much less than adequate. Yet until the hysteria of the oath, our regents on the whole had an exemplary record. The university was able to attract good men to its ranks, not simply because of fair

*[Caughey apparently did not mean that he would serve without question in *any* war. See his comments on the Vietnam War in "Our Chosen Destiny".]

salaries, not simply because of a bonus in climate, but more significantly because it had the reputation of being effectively safeguarded from political interference by a devoted and disinterested board of regents.

The long-term record of the board offers hope in the present crisis. Within the board, too, there is a strong determination to restore the university to its proper condition. Within the faculty there is a corresponding will. These forces, backed by the unwillingness of the people of California to have less than a first-rate state university, are capable of rescuing the university from the jeopardy in which it now is.

Perhaps it will be by pumping the original meaning back into the April formula. More probably it should be by improving upon that formula. Ideally it should involve cancellation of the whole requirement of a political denial. Certainly it must include removing the stigma of the recent dismissals.

More broadly and basically there is the necessity of restoring the old climate of mutual confidence that used to prevail between regents and faculty. Even more fundamentally there is the need to redefine the university as a community of scholars dedicated and free to pursue the truth wheresoever it may lead. This is no small task. For myself, for the university, and for the nation I hope California has men who are equal to it.

A PLEA TO THE REGENTS OF THE UNIVERSITY OF CALIFORNIA

GOVERNOR WARREN, PRESIDENT SPROUL,
MEMBERS OF THE BOARD OF REGENTS:

I am one of those who took the route of appeal to the committee on privilege and tenure, the president, and the regents. I am here not so much to enter a plea for myself as for the group which chose this harder way, and not so much to plead for this group as for the welfare of the university as a whole.*

*[This "Plea to the Regents" was spoken at the regents' meeting July 21, 1950, while they were considering the dismissal of the nonsigners.]

Some of you know me, but let me introduce myself briefly. After graduate work at Berkeley I went to UCLA, where I have been for twenty years. I am an American historian with special interest in California history. I have a dozen books to my credit and have worked with thousands of undergraduate students and a hundred or more graduate students. I am editor of the *Pacific Historical Review,* general editor of the Chronicles of California, a member of the California State Landmarks Committee, and consultant for the California State Lands Commission in the Tidelands litigation. At forty-eight I am, statistically, at the halfway point in my career in the university. The gods willing, I have another twenty years before retirement.

My specialization in California history is an extra tie binding me to our university. But I am not unique in having a great devotion to the university. The whole faculty has this feeling, and so, I am sure, do you.

Men who have the interest of an institution so much at heart as you do and as we do ought to be able to find an area of agreement. We should be able to find a way out of this great and tragic misunderstanding.

I have no illusions that we can argue our way out of it. I am here not to argue, but to try to explain why some of us chose the route of appeal and why we count on being continued in the university family through that route.

First, let me make clear that there is no conspiracy among us. We have not, for example, tried to get before you a group of men all equipped with military records, FBI clearance, the right religious connections, and long tenure in the university. I, for example, because of physical disability was ineligible for military service. My specialization being what it is, I have not come under FBI scrutiny. Having been brought up a Presbyterian rather than a Quaker, I do not rest on religious scruple. All these factors, however, seem to me extraneous. We appellants acted individually, impelled by reasons of conscience and principle. We did so in spite of the fact that we recognized that the route we were choosing, as compared to simple and automatic clearance by signature, was a much harder course.

Second, we are loyal Americans. We gladly took the constitutional oath. To us it meant a pledge of full and unqualified loyalty. Furthermore, our loyalty, along with our competence and character, has been carefully investigated by the committee on privilege and tenure, and the committee reports have been carefully weighed by the president. In these reports and recommendations you have evidence that is worth more than a mere assertion by a possible suspect and an interested party.

The reasons why we prefer not to sign the statement of denial of membership in a designated political party vary, person to person. Mine include the following:

The political test as a condition of employment seems to me to infringe on tenure as we have known it.

To sweep through the university and demand of every employee a political denial seems to me to violate the spirit of the state constitution.

The political test, by oath or contract, seems to me very much like the tactics of totalitarianism, which I abhor. I could not help noticing the alarm of several colleagues who had seen the same sort of thing happen under Hitler.

Required denial, by oath or affirmation, is a farcical way to insure loyalty or to exclude Communists. I don't believe it has exposed a traitor or improved a patriot. Committee investigation and presidential review can give a much sounder certification of loyalty, and it was partly on this account that I chose this route.

As an American historian I have a special awareness that a democratic republic such as ours needs to have functioning and vocal minorities. The majority endangers itself and the country when it attempts to silence them. As a historian, too, I am well aware how an action of this sort can easily become a precedent justifying another such step. I see involved the principle of minority rights, or rather of the wisdom of permitting minorities to exist and operate.

Along with other members of the faculty I have dedicated my life to the pursuit of knowledge. I try to make my classes a place where my students and I constantly try to learn. I take seriously the university's dedication to the free pursuit of truth and its full exposition. The political test as a basis for eligibility in the faculty seems to me to violate this vital principle — that a university must rely on truth to combat error.

In a totalitarian state there may be logic in having a party-line university. For us I do not believe there is logic or safety in having less than a free university. Academic freedom is usually taken to mean the right of a qualified scholar to teach, speak, and write in the field of his competence without interference. A fundamental thereto is that such a scholar shall not be censored out of eligibility to get or to hold an academic job.

These arguments against the special oath and the special contract still seem to me to be valid.

In April the board of regents announced two methods of qualifying for continuance in the faculty. One was simple and automatic: the other more complicated, full of hazard for an incompetent scholar or a traitor, but presumably safe for a good patriot and good scholar. To the faculty policy committee on April 19 and to the faculty as a whole on April 22 and 24 and May 6 and 7 the formula was explained in this fashion. It also is the clear reading of the document itself, which sets forth two ways to stay in the university — one easy and broad, the other awkward and tortuous, but still a route advertised as open.

It was with this understanding that the faculty accepted the formula and that a few score men chose the route of appeal. It is in this spirit that a few of us still count on this establishment of our eligibility. We think we acted within the clear authorization of the regents.

In the last couple of weeks some of my colleagues who went through the committee hearings have found reason to abandon that route and to switch to the other. Personally, I cannot see my way clear to make such an about-face.

To do so now would imply lack of sincerity in my original stand.

To do so now would look like an act of fear.

To do so now would indicate loss of confidence in the committee on privilege and tenure and in its action in clearing me.

To do so now would be a similar desertion of the president. I cherish a couple of letters of commendation from him written in quite different contexts and prior to this whole controversy. I also am proud to know that his approval is on the favorable report of the committee on privilege and tenure. I don't see how I could run away from my present position without betraying lack of trust in the wisdom and efficacy of his recommendation.

Also, for me to sign now would indicate no confidence in the good faith of the board of regents.

My wish is that the regents, with confidence in the faculty restored, would cancel the whole requirement of a political denial. My immediate plea, however, is merely that the board honor its word of April 21, that the road of appeal be treated as a legitimate pathway, and that the reports and recommendations of the committees and the president be received by the board with the respect that they deserve and which the faculty had every reason to expect would be accorded.

Such action will be a long step toward the reëstablishment of that concord within and between the faculty and the regents which we all recognize our university must have.

TRUSTEES OF ACADEMIC FREEDOM

There is not an academic person in America who does not think himself entitled to academic freedom.* The triteness of the things most necessary to say about it also points up its basic importance. It is a subject which Mr. Arbuthnot, the *New Yorker's* cliché expert, would relish. Academic freedom, I can hear him say, is one of the finer things in life. Like health, it is taken for granted when you have it. Like youth, it is appreciated only when it is gone.

Yet for all the familiarity of the phrase, even among scholars academic freedom does not have one clear, unmistakable meaning. Too often the definitions voiced, written, implied, or felt break off in the middle. They may, for example, stress the right to teach, without apparent recognition of the equally vital right to learn. Or they may narrow academic freedom by undue emphasis on the word "right." A right it is, but it is also a privilege and a responsibility. The individual scholar should understand this meaning of academic freedom, and should claim it as inherent in scholarship and essential to the delivery of scholarship's full service to society.

The significance of academic freedom and its rationale are well stated in the preamble to the 1940 Statement of Principles on Academic Freedom and Tenure which was formulated and agreed upon by representatives of the American Association of University Professors and of the Association of American Colleges. This statement reads as follows:

> The purpose of this statement is to promote public understanding and support of academic freedom and tenure and agreement upon procedures to assure them in colleges and universities. Institutions of higher

*[This address was delivered in December, 1950, to a joint meeting of the American Historical Association and the Mississippi Valley Historical Association.]

education are conducted for the common good and not to further the interest of either the individual teacher or the institution as a whole. The common good depends upon the free search for truth and its free exposition.

Academic freedom is essential to these purposes and applies to both teaching and research. Freedom in research is fundamental to the advancement of truth. Academic freedom in its teaching aspect is fundamental for the protection of the rights of the teacher in teaching and of the student to freedom in learning. It carries with it duties correlative with rights.

Tenure is a means to certain ends; specifically: (1) Freedom of teaching and research and of extramural activities, and (2) a sufficient degree of economic security to make the profession attractive to men and women of ability. Freedom and economic security, hence tenure, are indispensable to the success of an institution in fulfilling its obligations to its students and to society. . . .

I

Most frequently, academic freedom is taken to mean simply a sort of on-the-job protection, a guard against invasion of the classroom and censorship of textbooks. When censorship takes either of these forms, realization of common interest makes scholars aware that it is a present or potential loss to them all. Particularly so, if there is a dismissal.

Curiously, however, if the dismissal is divorced from texts and classes — if it comes, say, through an arbitrary change in the conditions of employment — the violation may go undetected. This calls to mind a method of duck hunting practiced by the California Indians. Hiding under a decoy-like helmet, the hunter would wade quietly into a covey of sitting ducks. Then he could pull one bird under without alarming the rest, then another, and another. If there is no gunfire of classroom invasion, scholars may be bagged in somewhat similar fashion while some of their colleagues, with honest imperception, do not realize that academic freedom is being flouted.

Realistically approached, academic freedom is more than a matter of on-the-job protection. Its very cornerstone is what is called tenure — the right of the employed scholar, after he has demonstrated his qualifications and proved his worth, to count on security in his job. Without tenure, the inviolate classroom is only an illusion.

The bare essentials of the meaning of academic freedom offer valid reasons to cherish it. They indicate a happy mixture of values, personal, professional, and patriotic.

II

One impelling reason for the observance of the principles of academic freedom is that these principles are inherent in the scientific method in which we are trained and to which we are habituated and deeply committed. The scientific method means the sifting and the weighing of evidence before reaching conclusions. The scientific method requires open-mindedness and resistance to biased or preconceived views, whether the bias or the preconception of views be one's own or be ordered by some governing authority.

Scholars, furthermore, work in a tradition of intellectual freedom which is older than the scientific method and older also than our constitutional freedoms. This tradition reaches back to the Renaissance and even to Aristotle and Socrates. Thus the more history-minded scholars are the more they feel an obligation of loyalty to intellectual freedom and to the unfettered university which institutionalizes this concept of freedom as an essential of scholarship.

As Americans, moreover, we stand committed to a philosophy of government which in essence is the scientific method set to politics. We begin with no postulates superior to reason, such as the divine right of kings or a pedestalled ruling class. Our dogma comes nearer to being that, in Lincoln's phrase, "you can't fool all the people all the time." I take this to be a way of saying that, in the long run, in a free competition of ideas those which are sound will prevail. We take it for granted that governmental forms and practices shall be subject to change. We stand ready to experiment. We try to keep the the door open for suggestion of improvements. We encourage minorities, at least to the extent of promising them a chance to be heard. And for that purpose we announce, and to a fair degree we foster, freedom of speech and freedom of the press.

In American practice freedom of worship got early enunciation. It did not become universal in the colonies, but there were conspicuous examples. Freedom of the press appeared as an ideal and a principle almost before there was a press. Freedom of speech also has respectable antiquity. But in view of the state of early American education, of the elementary quality of the curriculum, the emphasis on rote learning, and the stress on training for the ministry, it is understandable that academic freedom was less emphasized. The schools, to begin with, were not the prime intellectual force, and well into our national period editors, poets, and public men, rather than professional scholars, took the lead in formulating ideas. In the Declaration of Independence, in the Bill of Rights, in Wilson's Fourteen Points, and in Roosevelt's Four Freedoms, academic freedom did not make the grade.

Yet the more fundamental truth is that these several freedoms are merely different facets of one central freedom. Freedom of religion is a variety of freedom of conscience, freedom of the press a printed version of freedom of speech, and so on. On the relationship of academic freedom to this cluster a regent of the University of California, the late Chester Rowell, wrote as long ago as 1921: "I think it is the central liberty of civilization without which no other liberty could long survive or would be worth keeping."

III

Notwithstanding all these powerful arguments in its favor, the principle of academic freedom, or the integrity of scholarship, is recurrently in danger. The historic examples unfortunately are legion. They have exhibited much variety. They have run through cycles, such as the one in which the highest crime was to be at variance with the prevailing religion, and a later pattern in which the most dangerous heresy was to advocate economic reform.

At one time or another scholars have been in jeopardy for such diverse sins as favoring or opposing the abolition of slavery, favoring or opposing segregation, advancing the Darwinian hypothesis, defending progressive education, making honest report on the nutritive values of oleomargarine, withholding outright condemnation of the New Deal, and admitting that San Francisco had been visited by an earthquake. Despite the miscellaneous sound, this is not just hit or miss. A safe generalization is that no one has jeopardized academic freedom by endorsing the status quo or by siding with the vested interests. So far as academic freedom is concerned, the safest place to march is not quite abreast of current public opinion, but a few steps back and to the right.

Teachers have alleged and no doubt have experienced derogation of academic freedom at the hands of department chairmen. In other instances deans and presidents have appeared to be the prime agents in making it wither. In still other instances, a militant newspaperman, a mortgage-holding banker, a past or prospective benefactor, or a political demagogue has spearheaded the attack. Yet, the organization of our colleges and universities being what it is, no drive on academic freedom, at least none so violent as to produce a dismissal, can carry through without the consent and usually the active support of the institution's board of trustees. The board thus looms as the focal point in such issues. For almost every curtailment of academic freedom it gets the blame. Perhaps this view exaggerates the actual role of the board. It does help to explain why proposals in behalf of academic freedom so often dwell exclusively on reforming boards of trustees.

The companion question is more vital: Characteristically, who comes to the defense; *who are the trustees of academic freedom?*

In a Latin American university one would count on the students. Our undergraduates north of the border can, on occasion, be as ebullient. They have been known to rally several thousand strong to urge a college head not to go to another job, or to reason with the authorities that a coach's tenure should be lengthened or shortened.

Do the alumni rush to the rescue? They, as is well known, have an expansive goodwill toward alma mater. They could be a doughty phalanx in academic freedom crises, yet their more natural métier seems to be through participating in homecoming, providing scholarships, reducing the mortgage, or recruiting athletes. They are rarely concerned with academic freedom.

Then there is the impressive array of presidents, chancellors, provosts, registrars, bursars, comptrollers, business managers, vice-presidents, deans, subdeans, and archdeans with which every reputable school is now equipped. This hierarchy wields an effective veto power and sometimes has been a stalwart line of defense. An example is the recent discomfiture of free-charging investigators in Springfield, Illinois.[1]

Or, as the defensive platoon, what of those who bear the title overseers, fellows, directors, regents, trustees? It has happened; for example, when the president of Harvard University could delegate to a member of the institution's Corporation the responsibility of replying to Alumnus Ober.[2]

But are any of these the real trustees of academic freedom? There may be times when an editor, the students, the alumni, a public official, a university administrator, or the governing board will bear the brunt of the defense. Yet any of these, or all in concert, can hardly guarantee academic freedom unless scholars buckle on their armor. It will be very difficult to save academic freedom unless the academicians want it saved.

More bluntly, if academic freedom is lost, who ultimately will get the blame? The answer of posterity is easy to predict. It almost certainly will be the academicians. The inevitable questions will be: Where were the professional scholars during the years 1948-1951? Why did they let it happen?

IV

Instead of theorizing about the behavior of scholars as trustees of academic freedom, I should like to turn to an actual example at the eight-campus University of California. Even if it should happily prove to be abnormal rather than typical, it involves the largest and strongest university in half a continent, with a faculty of about two thousand scholars equipped with the Ph.D. or its equivalent, and by its very dimensions claims a prominent place in the intellectual history of our times.

Fortunately, there is no need to recite the whole story. Such an account would only be repeating what may be read in detail in George Stewart's *Year of the Oath* and in articles in *The Saturday Review of Literature, The American Scholar, Pacific Spectator, Harper's,* the *Bulletin of the Atomic Scientists,* and the *Bulletin of the American Association of University Professors.*

At the close of the spring semester of 1949 the faculty of the University of California was suddenly confronted with a request, soon revealing itself as a requirement, of a special oath denying membership in the Communist party. There were objections that the requirement was a slur on the loyalty of the faculty, that it was unnecessary, that it would be ineffective, that it constituted a political test for university teaching, that it employed the unscientific criterion of guilt by association, that its effect, if not its design, would be to silence minorities and to intimidate the unorthodox, that it would be used as a precedent for other encroachments, that it was unconstitutional, that it nullified tenure rights and thereby infringed on academic freedom, that it ran counter to the ideal of a free university, and that it violated the principles of proper relationship between the university's faculty and regents.

Some members of the faculty felt none of these compunctions and signed at once. Others, on a variety of grounds within and beyond the list just given, were convinced that the requirement was unwise and should be opposed. Arguments, circumstances, and pressures induced most of these individuals to make personal compliance. With varying degrees of protest and delay they signed the oath or its later equivalent as a contract statement. Still others held out.

Meanwhile, there was a counterplay of faculty resistance and regential insistence, sometimes expressed in cool reasoning, sometimes in warmer debate, at times in hot temper. One crisis came in February, 1950, when the regents issued a sign-or-be-fired ultimatum. Two months later, in April, at the suggestion of an alumni committee, they voted to rescind the oath requirement and offered two ways of continuing on the faculty. One was by signing a revised annual contract incorporating the essence of the oath. The other was by submitting one's self and record to scrutiny by a faculty committee, review by the president and final decision by the regents.

A sharper crisis arose in August, 1950, when the regents by vote of 12 to 10 broke faith with their April proposal, rescinded contracts voted in July, refused to accept any favorable recommendations from the faculty committee and the president, and dismissed all who were trying to qualify for retention through the second announced avenue — that of committee inspection.

Earlier in August the salaries of all in this category had been stopped as of the preceding June. In mid-September they were ordered to stop work. Later that month a state court took under advisement a plea by a score of these professors for delivery of the contracts promised in April and voted in July and for recognition of the tenure rights which had been traditional in the university.

In April, 1951, the District Court ruled in favor of the petitioners, basing the decision on California's constitutional ban against test oaths for officers of public trust and on the constitutional requirement that the university "shall be entirely independent of all political or sectarian influence" and "kept free therefrom . . . in the administration of its affairs. . . ."[3] At successive meetings in April and May the regents voted, 11 to 10, not to appeal to the State Supreme Court. On its own motion, however, that court has taken the case under review.

Pending its verdict the dismissed professors remain dismissed and for the faculty as a whole the contract form for 1951-1952 is the one which the District Court declared to be in violation of the state constitution. Nor has it fazed the hostile regents that dismissees have willingly subscribed to the new oath enacted by the legislature in the fall of 1950 in which all state employees are required to deny treasonable or disloyal record, intent, or affiliation.

Whatever character the dispute may have had in its early stages, since August, 1950, it has had crystal clarity as a disciplinary action, a question of confidence or lack of confidence in the faculty and the president, and a test of tenure. Back of tenure lie the larger ramifications of academic freedom and the integrity of scholarship.

At several points along the way the faculty unequivocally recorded its sentiments: in June and September, 1949, asking repeal of the oath requirement; in March, 1950, denouncing the regents' sign-or-be-fired ultimatum; in September, 1950, censuring the regents for the dismissals of the preceding month; and, more recently, in subscribing a considerable sum for grants in lieu of salary to those dismissed and to press home the fact that the faculty must have a recognized role in the control and direction of a well-ordered university.

Actions such as these bespeak a strong and consistent wish to preserve academic freedom. Yet so insidious was the attack, so difficult the defense, that this veritable army of well-intentioned scholars found itself confuted. And this despite the stalwart support of the governor of the state, a famous admiral, enough other regents to add up to almost half the board, and the scholars' professional organization, the American Association of University Professors.

V

Why was the defense of academic freedom in the University of California situation so difficult? There are many answers: among them the hyperindividualism that is the scholar's occupational disease; the hostility of most of the California press; and the California climate, which has encouraged the hostile regents to believe that no matter what happens, they can have the pick of the nation's brains. These factors are self-explaining. Two others are less obvious. One is a matter of auspices, the other a matter of hostages.

As to the first, this drive on academic freedom came beautifully camouflaged and with all the panoply of innocence by association. Customarily the attacks on the freedoms are in the name of orthodoxy, loyalty, or Americanism even unto the hundredth per cent. This one took the unassailable ground that the faculty should be loyal. All the faculty, as a matter of fact, had pledged full loyalty to state and nation through California's century-old constitutional oath.

The announced target, as is also customary when civil liberties are being abridged, was the minority element currently the most feared and hated. The proposal, moreover, was offered as a necessary safeguard for impartial scholarship and honest teaching. It came, in other words, in the guise of academic freedom. It came, furthermore, from a governing board of excellent repute, and through a president whose strongest point had been his record as a supporter of academic freedom. Although the proposal had the earmarks of a political test for teaching, it was first presented so politely that it seemed to be optional and even with explicit denials that it had any connection with contracts and salaries. It thus was surrounded and encrusted with almost every good auspice.

Still other compelling arguments were used in its behalf, openly and privately, and at the outset and later: that it was a necessary element in the cold war, that it was requisite to success in Korea, that it was needed to save the university, that without it the president would be lost, that anyone who took an opposite stand was being incredibly naïve. Thus, as to arguments as well as to tactics, the advocates of academic freedom were thrown completely on the defensive. Whoever proposed to joust for academic freedom found himself up against a host bearing the banners of sweetness and light.

The second observation that this California experience has underlined is the appalling degree in which scholars have given hostages to fortune. The reference is not to wives and children and other dependents, although this is a factor that has made many a man cautious, even though his family shared to the full his awareness of responsibility to academic freedom.

The reference is rather to other hostages such as the one in the pattern of the scholar's earning. Its elements are a long period of preparation and training at heavy cost, then an apprentice-like starting wage, and gradual increase. A professor in midcareer probably has three-quarters of his income still to collect. This pattern of delayed compensation impels toward caution.

In a category less mundane, the professor in midcareer almost certainly has ahead of him more than half of his opportunity with advanced and graduate students. Concern about the immediate welfare of a group of students can be a potent reason for hedging in the defense of academic freedom.

Another type of hostage, less tangible yet real, is a sentimental attachment to a region or state, to a school, to a department, to a group of colleagues, or even to a course. Or it may be in a rational and sentimental devotion to a specific career in which the achievements of necessity will be cumulative.

A university faculty is fantastically irreplaceable. Yet certain factors dull this weapon almost to uselessness. One is that most scholars are very low in mobility. Modern higher education may look like an assembly-line process, but its parts are not interchangeable. Instead they tend to be geared to a particular library or laboratory, to the program of a particular school, to the needs of a particular student body, and to the service of a particular community. They are not tied to the soil like medieval serfs, but they are not migratory laborers either.

Their immobility shows itself in another more embarrassing fashion. Everybody knows that when a baseball team such as Connie Mack's old Athletics is broken up by sales and retirements, it usually takes years to rebuild to championship caliber. Scholars know that when retirements and departures take sudden toll of a top-flight department it may be just as difficult and just as expensive to rebuild to the original luster. Yet so much of what they do is recondite, so much is gauged for long-term results, that when a school declines in whole or in part, the public may not find out until much later, many students may not realize it, and the regents are not necessarily impressed. This is a peculiar hostage that scholars have given to fortune.

So far as I was concerned the thought of hostages given was far more arresting than all the sound and fury of arguments for compliance. Some of the latter seemed clearly fallacious, others were at least doubtful, and still others seemed to betray lack of understanding of the essential purpose and nature of a university. Furthermore, in so far as I am a historian, my conscience works in terms of the probable decision before the bar of history. And as I reflected on history, especially American history, I found it difficult to think of instances in which authoritarian stoppage of thought, silencing of criticism, and hounding of minorities escaped an ultimate verdict of condemnation.

For my colleagues en masse my information is more fragmentary. Clearly there is a paradox in the behavior of so many who condemned the oath yet signed it, and who deplored the infringement of academic freedom yet did less than they wished to in its defense. My impression, for what it may be worth, is that most of the explanation lies in the hostages to fortune which expose modern scholars to fear and force.

True enough, among the reasons given for ceasing to resist there were some that reflected the good auspices, but a much more formidable list of reasons for giving in was the one in which the element of fear and compulsion was paramount. This list, compiled from actual examples, included: to hold onto my job, to protect the family income, to avoid confiscation of retirement annuities, to ward off personal attacks, because of ill health, because of going or being about to go on sabbatical, because of being summoned to military duty and wanting assurance of a job to come back to, to preserve eligibility for government work, because of being a dean or a department chairman, so as not to imperil or handicap the work of one's department or school, so as not to become unemployable, because of youth, because of old age, or, worst of all, because of middle age. Add all these and the result is Irving Stone's phrase "Twisted Arms among the Ivy."

VI

I know of no panacea that can be invoked to safeguard academic freedom from all the dangers to which it is exposed. One suggestion is to insert a professor or two in every board of trustees. A far better alternative would be to keep the boards strictly lay bodies, but bring them to recognize that their proper function is the supervision of the financial and business aspects of institutional operation. These reforms would be steps in the right direction; they are not a complete cure.

A more basic suggestion is that academic freedom, the reasons for it, and the necessity of it for our national welfare must be adequately explained to the public, to the alumni, to the students, to trustees, and even, it would appear, to the professional scholars themselves. To this task the American Association of University Professors has been and is dedicated.

Many other channels for explaining academic freedom are open. Bill-of-Rights Week is one; speeches of welcome to an entering class or of parting advice to graduates are another. In certain philosophy courses the theory of academic freedom would be appropriate subject matter. Indeed, in all college courses it should have a place, perhaps most often under the denominator of scientific method. For the presentation of the concept to young Americans, no courses are better suited than the ones which historians offer, especially those in American history. Every such course is an invitation to stress how our nation and people have benefited by encouraging open-minded inquiry, by insisting on a free competition of ideas, and by pursuing the truth wheresoever it may lead.

An educative program such as this has the cardinal virtue that it can go on constantly. Too often, the friends of academic freedom have been roused to action only when there was a full-scale attack to repel, a last-ditch stand to make, or a salvage job to do. They have been like the shiftless man with the leaky roof. Between rains they saw no need to fix the roof. When it rained they could not fix it, and usually all they did was to set a bucket to catch the drip.

As an element in an educative program designed to put a proper roof over scholarship, it would obviously help a great deal if it were clear that, like the doctors and the lawyers, scholars have a code of professional standards to which they owe adherence, and that this code exists for the good of society. There is general recognition of the secretness of the confessional, of the lawyer's obligation to respect the confidences of his client, and of the code of the physician, but there is no such clear awareness of the existence of an ethics of scholarship.

Perhaps what is needed is a Hippocratic Oath with the Ph.D.

This oath of the scholar would consist of ideas already familiar, though some have fallen into neglect. It should have the clarity of simple wording. It should set forth the nature of the scholar's calling, the obligations that scholars assume, the reciprocal duty of society to scholarship, and the fundamental requirement of scholarly integrity.

Such an oath might properly be administered to claimants of the Ph.D. as part of their initiation into the full privileges and duties of the profession. In time the ritual might be judged a more useful exercise than publication of the dissertation or defense of the thesis.

Such a credo would be a standard to repair to in time of stress. It would be a weapon to fight with, a succinct statement of principles affording inspiration, a yardstick for self-measurement, an explanation that would persuade the public, an avowal that would earn the confidence of students, a guide to presidents and regents, and a warning to those who at times are tempted to limit or destroy academic freedom. The content of such a credo has already been developed by the American Association of University Professors. What is still needed is a more succinct and specific statement of this credo in the form of a professional commitment that might be required of all who enter the academic profession. The modern Hippocrates who puts this credo into clarion words, along with those who have developed the principles of academic freedom, will deserve the endless gratitude of his fellow scholars and of society at large, which will be equally benefited. The reason can be stated very simply:

The world today, as never before, stands in need of honest and untrammeled scholarship, for the preservation of what is known, for the extension of the boundaries of knowledge, and for improved understanding of the problems of mankind. Totalitarian dictatorship prefers a limited, captive scholarship. But our nation, as a democratic republic, depending in the last analysis upon an alert and informed citizenry, cannot afford to limit inquiry or to restrict the interchange of ideas. Thus in true patriotism, those who enter the profession of scholarship are under obligation, to the best of their abilities, to strive to deliver impartial research and honest teaching. The profession is under equal obligation, in season and out of season, to remind itself, to remind the public, and to insist that the establishment and maintenance of academic freedom are absolute requisites for rendering to society the benefits of scholarship. This is the first duty for those who claim the name of scholars, and who are, above all others, the trustees of academic freedom.

THE PRACTICAL DEFENSE OF ACADEMIC FREEDOM

I

. . . Since the summer of 1949 I have been involved, to the best of my lights and capacity, in trying to defend academic freedom on a certain front.* In this effort I was so impractical as to get myself fired, or — in the terminology preferred by those who did the firing — to get myself severed, detached, and dissociated from the job I had held for twenty years. Such a result is not the acme of practicality.

Experience, nevertheless, is a remarkable teacher. In this unenviable experience there was insistent tutelage on how and how not to defend academic freedom. That is the burden of this essay — not why to defend academic freedom, but how. The ideas I shall offer are mostly old, but for me at least they are ideas that recent experience has sharpened and tempered and given new point.

The first of these practical hints is that to ourselves we scholars

* [This address was delivered in March, 1952, at a meeting of the American Association of University Professors.]

need to clarify the meaning of academic freedom. In view of the torrents of spoken words and the barrels of printer's ink that have been spilled in attempts to analyze and define the concept, and in view of the sustained program of enlightenment carried on by the American Association of University Professors, it is fantastic that uncertainties still prevail. But prevail they do. This was one of the more humiliating disclosures in the California controversy. Again and again the the academicians gave academic freedom a working definition that narrowed it, curtailed it, and deteriorated it into something hardly worth defending. In so doing, they brought themselves down to a value hardly worth defending.

The most common example was reducing this freedom to a mere personal property. "*My* academic freedom," said one colleague, "has not been infringed." What he meant, no doubt, was that *his* classroom had not been invaded. No one had told *him* what text to use or not to use. The special oath demanded did not offend *his* conscience. In this pattern of thinking there appeared to be no awareness of academic freedom as a guaranty to the whole community of scholars and still less recognition that it is something ordained by and for society.

Another all too common warping of the meaning was to regard academic freedom simply as a generality rather than as something for specific application. A general principle, I was surprised to discover, could be so bright and glittering as to blind the eye to even the most flagrant violation. This was not the mere lag so often encountered between theory and practice, between the ideal and its realization. It was not an instance of human frailty but of rationalizing; its form a retreat into nebulous theory. By refusing to recognize the concrete instances of academic freedom violated, or by glossing them over as inescapable exceptions, one could proclaim, and apparently feel, complete devotion to the glorious principle. I had hoped that this flight from reality was a strictly local phenomenon and not widespread among scholars. I am told, however, that the professional staff of the American Association of University Professors is frequently asked, "Why don't you stick to the *principles* of academic freedom? Why do you concern yourselves with specific cases?" I find little comfort in academic freedom's existence in the ethereal realm of the abstract — in fact, I wonder if it really has that existence — unless it also reaches down into the mundane realm of actual experience.

Examples could be multiplied of academic freedom shrunken

and distorted by inadequate definition. These two, excessive personalizing and generalizing, are perhaps enough to suggest how even scholars fail to see it in the whole.

Substandard definition leads inevitably to an equally inadequate grasp of the reasons for defending this freedom. If it is nothing more than an abstract theory, logic would limit the defense to theoretical arguments such as are alleged to have been the principal joy and occupation of medieval scholars. For this world at least, the outcome of such speculations has only theoretical importance. Perhaps this draws the bow too far — it is not always predictable when theory will suddenly exert a resounding impact upon practice; witness Einstein's formula, $E = mc^2$, and its translation into the atomic bomb. Nevertheless, to defend what is merely a fine-spun abstraction often seems just an idle exercise.

At the other extreme, if this freedom is strictly a personal right, the motivation for guarding it will also be strictly personal, which is to say, selfish. Selfish motivation can be powerful. Looking out for No. 1 is the oldest and most prevalent of human impulses. As a ground for persuading others, however, our purely selfish interests rank near the bottom of the list. Particularly for professional people, who to a degree at least have dedicated themselves, the argument of selfish interest is least calculated to win friends and support.

Yet, as I have observed it, the scholars' defense of academic freedom has suffered greatly by the attitude that the concept is just a generality, and by giving the impression that the actual motivation is strictly selfish.

For the practical defense of academic freedom the issue must be elevated above the personal. In the imbroglio in which I am a casualty, certain regents acted as though personal motivation was paramount. The board's minutes, recently opened to public gaze, have a refrain, "We must salvage the prestige of the Board." On the other side, the faculty too often gave an equally unfortunate impression of being out to guard the personal prerogatives of tenure and the other personal dividends of academic freedom.

II

Part of the trouble, I believe, is that too much of the time we view academic freedom through the wrong end of the microscope. It does entail advantages for the individual scholar. But these are means toward a larger purpose which is not just for the benefit of the researcher or the teacher. We talk too much about the place of honor and influence that the faculty must have in a well-ordered university and not enough about the kind of intellectual experience that the enrolled students are entitled to have. We talk too much about the conditions necessary if a university is to operate to best advantage and too little about how a free university is vital to the general welfare. We talk too much about our personal and professional interests and too little about the public interest.

Reliance on reason and intelligence is the essence of academic freedom. The force of the mind, rather than of emotion or superstition, is our problem solver. Modern man is actually in pretty thorough agreement with this doctrine. As to most branches of science he fully accepts it. For example, in medicine, agriculture, the development of bigger and better weapons, and the devising of more ingenious and intriguing gadgets, Americans are committed to unrestricted, all-out study and research. History and the social sciences often are subjected to superpatriotic pressure to hedge on uninhibited study and on absolutely impartial teaching. Still, modern man is toughminded. He does have respect for facts. Though not unswervingly logical, he believes in reason. He has confidence in the scientific method. The thing he frequently has not grasped is that academic freedom is an integral and necessary component in the application of intelligence to our problems. Once aware that academic freedom does precisely that, the average person today would be much more inclined to line up in its support.

In the United States there is a very special reason for supporting a freedom dedicated to the increase of knowledge, the ceaseless sifting and winnowing of the facts and generalizations presumed to have been established, and the spread of this knowledge without hindrance or distortion. For the United States, to our great good fortune, is one of those countries in which the people have the final say. We are the ultimate authority. In last analysis we are sovereign. In so simple a thing as an airplane no one would choose to have part of the dials and gauges blacked out from the pilot's view. In an automobile no one would choose to have the driver blindfolded. In our government We the People sit in the driver's seat. By itself academic freedom cannot make all the people paragons in knowledge and wisdom, but it is the enabling factor for putting the electorate into position to act on the basis of knowledge and understanding. Its defense therefore is an act of patriotism.

Let us suppose that an academic freedom crisis arises. Faced by such an emergency, the advocates and defenders of this freedom will have to decide whether to try to explain the issue to the public or to maintain a studied silence. On this matter the California faculty was neither unanimous nor consistent. At certain stages there was much spontaneous and miscellaneous comment by members of the faculty. At other stages a more concerted and systematic effort was made to inform the public through prepared releases to the press and even with formal press conferences. At other times the predominant attitude was that no public comment of any sort should be made. This last policy is well exemplified in one professor's assertion to the regents: "The moment I got into control of that situation we layed off all publicity. . . . We have suppressed telegrams, cablegrams from all over the world."[1]

The arguments for silence are that it is much more dignified, that issues such as these are hard to explain to the uninitiated, that our vocabulary of academese is not much good in the marketplace, and that anyhow the immediate issue will be settled within the college or university and not by the electorate.

Yet the opponents can be counted on to be vocal. Their side or version of the affair will get publicity. Academic silence will be taken to signify absence of valid arguments to the contrary, and public opinion is almost certain to go along with what has been heard and read. After the verdicts in the Insular Cases half a century ago, Mr. Dooley observed that "the Supreme Court follows the election returns." It is equally natural, and on the whole a good thing, that men on boards as well as on the bench are swayed by public opinion. This patent fact casts considerable doubt upon the wisdom of disregarding the public. The spirit of academic freedom, the appeal to reason, also would seem to call for candidness in its defense.

III

Another question sure to arise is whether to compromise. If two men quarrel about a property line, perhaps they can split the difference. If labor and management are at loggerheads, by give and take they may be able to reach a mutually tolerable solution. The whole pattern of mediation and conciliation rests on mutual concessions, and so does much of the actual procedure in our lawmaking. But academic freedom controversies are seldom solved by maneuvering, bargaining, haggling, or horsetrading.

One consideration cautions against resort to such a method. As I elaborated in another paper,[2] scholars go into any such negotiations hampered by a long list of hostages that they have given to fortune. Across the table they will face men who are much more experienced in arguing cases, lobbying, and making business deals, and whose incomes and careers are not at stake. The California experience — and I say this without special rancor against the regent negotiators — was that bargaining was a good way for the faculty to concede points and to retreat, but not a reliable means of improving the position of academic freedom.

A corollary to this warning against depending on negotiated concessions for the protection of academic freedom is that there should be caution about assuming that time is on the side of the scholars. Over the long run I have no doubt that it is, but not in terms of several years of prolonged uncertainties as against a quick decision. In the California difficulty one school of thought was that anything that kept the negotiations open or that prolonged them was favorable. But when there is delay, all the factors that hamper scholars as negotiators, all the hostages that they have given, work against the chances for salvaging academic freedom.

More fundamentally, the fallacy of the negotiating method is that academic freedom is not a proper subject for compromise. It may not be an absolute, but I am inclined to believe that the only tenable method for its defense is to deal with academic freedom as an absolute as we do with such concepts as bills of attainder, trial by jury, celibacy, and virginity. As to bills of attainder, for example, we would not condone a relaxing of that ban so as to create a special hazard for, let us say, Pennsylvanians. Nor would we countenance a tampering with the guaranty of trial by jury even to exclude cases where a most revolting crime is charged. If academic freedom is compromised its devaluation is almost complete, almost as the ethics and standing of a physician are undermined by one illegal operation.

The defense of academic freedom must be pitched on the level of high principle. Indeed, I mean highest principle. In the California controversy we took the high ground that the special oath requirement was unnecessary, unwise, and ineffective. The response was that at most this objection meant there might be a better means of implementing the basic purpose of the regents. We took the higher ground that the special disclaimer oath was unconstitutional. The response was that that was for the courts to decide. In April, 1951, the District Court so ruled but, pending review by the State Supreme Court, the lower court's decision is not operative.

These were reasonably high grounds for objection, but not high enough to be effective.

Incidentally, I have a lingering doubt whether resort to the courts is the best means of ensuring academic freedom. When the violation of the law seems crystal clear, legal action is a great temptation, and if the action is successful the position of academic freedom will be substantially buttressed. On the other hand, no layman can be sure, nor the lawyers either, what meaning the judicial mind will find in the law. Furthermore, a decision contrary to public opinion can easily touch off new legislation or a constitutional amendment. More serious, it is difficult almost to the point of impossibility to get the whole issue of academic freedom before a court. Some of its facets, such as a question of contracts being irrevocable, or whether professors as public officers or holders of public trust are entitled to equality before the law, may be included in the statutes, but not academic freedom in its entirety. In submitting it to litigation, therefore, there is a hazard that the right as a whole may be lost on a technicality and that a faculty may find itself legally the chattel slaves of a governing board. Certainly all the possibilities should be considered before going to court.

IV

In seeking the high ground on which its defense of academic freedom should rest, the California faculty had difficulties. Because of the way in which the oath requirement was presented, it was not easy to divine the real purpose behind it. For a long time we were given to believe that the basic intention of the pronouncement against employment of Communists and of the oath was to protect the university against dishonest scholarship and propagandizing teaching. Months later we were told that primarily it had been a move for better accord with the legislature and the public. At times there were hints that the concern had been to exclude spies and saboteurs from the vicinity of secret research projects contracted to the university. Still later it seemed that the real issue became one of authority in the university. That certainly was not the issue in the beginning, but the firings that eventually occurred were technically for insubordination. As an aside I might remark that a good case can be made out that there was no act of insubornation until after the dismissals.

The minutes of the regents' meetings, recently made public, suggest a different motivation. They do not reveal why the president surprised the board with his oath proposal in March, 1949. They are informative on the frame of mind of the regents in accepting it and on why the regents displayed such zeal for it in the summer of 1949 and, some of them, long afterwards. Judging by these minutes it appears that at the outset the animations of ensuring impartial scholarship, currying favor with the legislature, guarding against spies and saboteurs, and subordinating the faculty were secondary and perhaps incidental. Instead, the banning of Communists seems to have been regarded not as a means toward other goals, such as the improvement of scholarship, but as an end, the end, in itself. It appears to have been the ruling motive.

Such an attitude characteristically arises when a minority group or sect becomes increasingly an object of suspicion, distrust, and hate. For example, in the 1870's it happened in California with regard to the Chinese. Itemized charges that they were immoral, uneconomic, unsanitary, and unassimilable led to, and then were supplanted by, the fixed idea that the Chinese must go just because they were Chinese.

Had there been awareness in the faculty that the anti-Communist policy pronouncement had so much of this quality, quite a different case history might have developed. But it was hard for the faculty to know this at the time, and it would have been hard for the faculty to believe it. One reason is that since 1940 the regents had had a ruling against Communists being on the faculty. So far as the records go there had been no violation of this rule, no occasion to invoke it against any individual, and no candidates for eviction under this rule at the time the oath requirement was set up. In the midst of the controversy the president stated categorically that he knew of no member of the Communist party employed as a member of the faculty. Against this decade-long background there was no visible logic in sounding a sudden alarm that Communists must go and accompanying it with wholesale application of a test oath.

Pared to the bone, the issue was the question of guilt by association. It is true that Martin Dies and his successors and imitators, the Smith Act, the Taft-Hartley Act at least in part, and the McCarran Act have used the doctrine. The courts also have given guilt by association a measure of support. But to me it seems that there is better history and more wisdom in the policy statement of the American Association of University Professors, in what Francis Biddle has said on the subject in his *The Fear of Freedom,* and in Justice William O. Douglas' recent dictum that guilt by association is "repugnant to our society." As Douglas goes on to point out, "The very threat of such a procedure is certain to raise havoc with academic freedom."

The alternative is to measure an individual in terms of his own acts and performance. Credit thus will be on a personal basis, and guilt likewise. As concerns the latter, the time-honored American practice is that there shall be presumption of innocence until through due process an accusation to the contrary is sustained. The formula of guilt by association has the temptation of ease of application. It can dispense with endless individual investigations, and appraisals by substituting attention merely to the particular stigmatizing label.

V

In the climate of opinion that now prevails there is no label so baleful as Communist. It carries at least the reproach that attached in the first century to Christian, in the eighteenth century to Jacobin, in the South to carpetbagger, and in Nazi Germany to Jew. Communism is anathema because of its linkage to Russia, our most obvious enemy in the cold war. It is anathema because of its totalitarian methods. It is anathema because it is regarded as the antithesis of free enterprise and capitalism. It would be hard to say which of these is the most heinous. Denunciation of Communism thus comes easily, not merely to our politicians, but to a great many other Americans. An opinion poll in this country would show hardly a trace of sympathy for Communism. Since by latest reports attributed to the F.B.I. the number of Communists in the United States is set at between 31,000 and 32,000, their ratio is only about one to 5000 of our population. Never, one might be tempted to paraphrase, have so many been thrown into panic by so few. Yet, small though this group is, I view Communism with alarm and I look upon Communists with suspicion.

Nevertheless, I do believe it important to bear in mind that these people are Americans and, according to the law and tradition of the land, they are covered by the same guaranties of rights and freedoms as apply to you and me. To be sure, it is frequently suggested that somehow these guaranties ought to be withdrawn from this unpopular minority and reserved for regular, true, majority-minded, conforming Americans. The start might be to deny these people of the unpopular minority the rights of free speech and press. But once started along this line of thought, it is very difficult to find a logical stopping place, and already there have been urgings that Communists be denied the rights of habeas corpus, trial by jury, the right to have counsel and witnesses, and of protection against excessive bail and cruel and unusual punishments. There are two reasons why we and our courts should recoil from this full measure of discrimination. One is the patent unfairness. The other is that such breaches undermine and weaken the guaranties of rights and freedoms for us all.

The more realistic suggestion, therefore, is along the line advanced recently by a California congressman. Irritated by uncooperative and perhaps Communist witnesses called before the House Un-American Activities Committee, who invoked the Fifth Amendment, he raised the question of closing this loophole by repealing the Fifth Amendment. To deprive Communists of this protection he would have us all surrender it. As a matter of fact, that is about what it comes down to, whether the guaranty is cancelled just for the minority or for all.

The question, it seems to me, is not so much, Do we view Communism with alarm? but, Do we view our American system with alarm? In the face of the threat represented by these few thousand dissenters, is our American way inadequate? Does the existence of this fringe of disagreement make our traditional and constitutional guaranties of due process and of equality before the law a menace to the nation? Answering these questions on their substance, I would record an emphatic conviction that our democratic-republican approach and method are equal to the emergency. Furthermore, because of what I know about the consequences of action by frontier vigilance committees, impromptu tribunals, and lynch law, I particularly question the extra-legal approach to stripping from an individual or from a minority the protection of the laws.

VI

In point of fact, the Congress and the courts have stopped short of outlawing Communists and the Communist party. The decision in the *U. S. v. Dennis* did not do so. Attorney General McGrath, certainly no apologist for Communism, commented immediately afterwards that this decision affected the eleven defendants and perhaps other party leaders, but not the party members all the way down the line. It did not outlaw the party.[3]

The California regents, however, considerably outrunning the lawmakers and the courts, pronounced the Communist party a conspiracy to overthrow our government by violence; they denied its existence as a party; and, upon every person thus associated, they were ready to apply the sentence they had pronounced upon the group as a whole. Repeatedly in their discussions voices were raised to require from every member of the faculty an endorsement of blanket disqualification of Communists.

The faculty, it is true, saw that this issue of guilt by association was involved. It never, however, had an awareness of the degree to which this thought actuated the regents. Assuming that other motives were dominant, the faculty focused too much of its effort on them. Led down various by-paths by these side-issues, the faculty was less sound and effective than it might have been on the real issue, guilt by association.

In June, 1949, when the oath itself seemed to be the menace, the faculty addressed itself to analyzing its wording. In September, 1949, though still concentrating on the oath as such and on how to ensure honesty in scholarship, the faculty did take a robust stand against blanket disqualifications based on mere label or affiliation — in other words, against guilt by association. This stand was reaffirmed later in the fall, and was emphasized to the regents by a faculty committee in January, 1950. Previously, however, certain faculty leaders had condoned group proscription and another faculty committee had consented to the idea.

In March, 1950, intrigued by a "deal" whereby a faculty resolution endorsing group proscription would be substituted for the requirement oaths from every individual, the faculty recanted on its September stand. What followed was a more prolonged pressure on individuals to sign the oath or its equivalent. The deal fell through, and the faculty was left with its recantation echoing on and on. The latest development, illustrating how insidious surrender of principle can be, is a new set of tenure rules, which a faculty committee has proposed. In them the grounds for dismissal are listed as: incompetency, neglect of duty, dishonesty, moral turpitude, and membership in the Communist party.

I tarry on this point so long because I believe it is today's chief menace to academic freedom. At least in the foreseeable future the major drives against the free pursuit of truth are almost certain to come in the guise of an America-protecting insistence on proscribing Communists. Some persons think these drives play right into the hands of the Communists. I would concede that in a bungling sort of way they may inconvenience that party's program. But they have a far greater potential for damaging the American way of life, for sabotaging the freedoms that are basic to our system, and particularly for destroying the freedom to learn and to use our minds — the freedom we call academic.

Too late it became evident in California that, once guilt by association was admitted, then there was hardly any sort of implementation that could be objected to. Presumption of innocence was out, because suspects were already judged guilty and had become, in effect, fugitives from justice. Disclaimer oaths now had the appearance of legitimacy. The faculty, perhaps without intending it, now had assumed a moral responsibility to ferret out members of the proscribed group just because they were members. To perform this duty, an F.B.I., a *Faculty* Bureau of Investigation, and an Inquisition were in the offing. In fact, the screening process actually used on the nonsigners did not satisfy the regents in the end, precisely because it had not been sufficiently inquisitorial. In March, 1952, the university observed the third anniversary of the oath by appointing an officer to act as liaison with the State Senate Committee on Un-American Activities in, as the papers reported it, "ascertaining what the Reds are up to on the campus and in preparing to meet the infiltration."

Had it held out against guilt by association, the faculty might have suffered a number of dismissals for insubordination, uncooperativeness, and the like, such as actually occurred. But it would still have possessed a basis for continued protest on grounds not just of procedure but of fundamental principle. The likelihood of ultimate restoration of genuine academic freedom would, I think, be considerably greater. The faculty would have been in far better position to rally general professional support, though it is true that the profession has rallied nobly and effectively. It would have been in better position to recruit nonprofessional allies, though here also a substantial support was forthcoming.

This brings me to the suggestion that no body of scholars should try to perform a solo defense of academic freedom. There are reservoirs of assistance in the nationwide and international community of scholars that ought to be tapped. And properly so, because defense on any sector is important not only for that sector but for academic freedom everywhere. In a sense, academic freedom is geographically indivisible. Likewise, there are battalions of supporters outside the profession, and these should be enlisted. The most obvious are the particular beneficiaries and custodians of the other freedoms — the gentlemen of the press, of the speaking platforms, and of the cloth — because instead of being separate, the freedoms are all interrelated and integrated. Still more broadly, if properly approached, the people at large can be stirred to uphold the freedoms, which in last analysis are theirs and for them.

VII

The last of my practical hints is that the defense of academic freedom must not be limited to mere covering up and counterpunching. It must take the aggressive and carry the battle to the foe. Or, in language that may seem more appropriate, it must be continuous, preparatory, preventive, and prophylactic. Let me prove this point by example. Over the years the University of California had produced a prodigious number of alumni. Into our environs too had moved probably an equal number of alumni of eastern and midwestern schools and colleges. Some of these direct and adopted alumni saw the issue as clearly as any of the faculty and were towers of strength in fending for academic freedom. Others — and often it seemed that these were a majority — exhibited no real comprehension of the meaning of this freedom and no awareness of the menace to the university that lurked in the application of the fallacy of guilt by association. We scholars and teachers are presumably the chief defenders of academic freedom. Yet when we had the chance in the classroom, apparently we had negelcted or failed to transmit an understanding of the concept, much less a conviction and a devotion in and to it. Our mistake, I believe, was that too generally we postponed any concern about it until the attack came.

The points I have tried to make run something like this: The defenders of academic freedom would do well to clarify its meaning and the reasons for defending it. They should elevate the issue above the personal and stress the interest possessed by our society and nation. Academic freedom deserves to be defended in the spirit of academic freedom; that is, by applying reason and intelligence, by spreading out all the facts rather than concealing them; not by conniving, bargaining, and compromising, but by resting the case always on grounds of highest principle. The defense should not be just by a few beleaguered scholars, but by the profession as a whole. Scholars should enlist the aid of other professions and the recruiting of allies should be carried much farther, since all these freedoms were created by and for society and all of them have a very special relevance to a democratic republic such as ours. Finally, the defense should be taken out of the rearguard classification and made continous, educative, and preventive.

If the defense can be marshalled on such a basis, I have every confidence that it will succeed. Indeed, even with far less spirited and coherent action the defense is by no means hopeless. As a casualty and a displaced person I may have some trouble being convincingly optimistic. We California nonsigners are still completely outside the pale; we have not been reinstated to our positions and tenure. Yet even our experience holds much that should be encouraging to the friends of academic freedom.

As soon as the gravity of the situation became apparent, messages of encouragement and support began to come from individuals and from groups of scholars all over the land. A number of organizations, particularly the American Association of University Professors, exerted potent influence toward getting the university back on the right track. A number of scholars declined appointments in the institution pending a restoration of proper conditions. Colleagues and friends subscribed a considerable sum for legal expenses and for advances in lieu of salary to the dismissed nonsigners. Tangible expressions of confidence came also in invitations to joint the teaching and research staffs of institutions such as Harvard, Wesleyan, Princeton, Johns Hopkins, Oberlin, Carnegie Institute of Technology, Chicago, Tulane, Kansas State, Pomona, the Huntington Library, and the Institute for Advanced Study. Several foundations awarded research grants, and government agencies welcomed still others of the nonsigners. This record of employment and support is a clear demonstration that academic freedom has a host of staunch friends.

It is heartening too that late in 1951 the Board of Regents, by that time somewhat revised in membership, voted to abolish the special requirement of a disclaimer oath or declaration. In future appointments the loyalty statement required of university personnel will be the same as for other holders of office or public trust in the state. The special oath and its equivalent, therefore, are no more.

I am also cheered by reflecting on American history. In the long run, it seems to me, the American people do not condone roughshod violations of the freedoms, whether by the witch hunters of Salem, the authorities who moved against Peter Zenger, the authors of the Alien and Sedition Acts, the hooded terrorism of the Ku Klux Klan, the excesses of the Palmer raids, or the internment of the Japanese Americans. It may not come in our time, but unless the American people become totalitarians, I count on eventual recognition of academic freedom for what it is — the prerequisite to a rational and intelligent way of life. A conviction that it can succeed may well be the best morale builder and the most practical of all encouragements to the defenders of academic freedom.

Part V

CAUGHEY'S CREED

CAUGHEY'S CREED

To a select number of scholars is given each year an opportunity to deliver a presidential address. The ceremony among historians is a coveted honor, usually woven with the ritualistic considerations of outstanding research, teaching, and service that would be appreciated only by the committee who weighs and balances his qualifications with other eminent candidates. The address, with overtones of a farewell pronouncement and a sermon upon the mount, takes the professional audience through time, exhorts it, and finally leaves some distillation of truth as a kind of historical manna.

Occasionally historians like John Caughey have enjoyed the extraordinary privilege of traveling the plateau of honor more than once. As president of the Pacific Coast Branch of the American Historical Association in 1957 ard as president of the Organization of American Historians in 1965, he had the opportunity to speak on California and the West and American traditions of liberty. These threads of his career were well illustrated in his 1965 address, "Our Chosen Destiny," when he revealed his deep commitment to American history and his abiding concern for libertarian principles.

Neither address puts more sharply his concern for the nation, the individual, and progress than does the concluding chapter of *Land of the Free,* of which he is the senior author. This exhortation, entitled "Unfinished Business", gives the eighth grader a final word as he concludes his first course in American history. It has, too, the overtones of a farewell address, with the important difference that it is an address to the young who have the future of the nation in their hands.

UNFINISHED BUSINESS

This study of the United States and its history must break off rather than close. Modern Americans, more than can be said of certain earlier generations, live in an on-rushing world.

Toward meeting the challenges of these times, today's Americans have tremendous assets. In world affairs the United States is in position to exert the largest influence. It leads the world in industrial plants, skilled workers, and able management. The economy is at the point where the gross value produced in a single year exceeds the total for the entire colonial and revolutionary period.

Now more than ever before the nation is concerned for the welfare of every American. Now it offers the broadest educational opportunity, thus enabling every person to make the most of his abilities. Along with this momentum, past generations of Americans have handed on a set of institutions and ideals, inspiring and fortifying.

We do, however, have unfinished business. A fifth or more of American families earn too little for decent food, clothing, and housing. In a nation so rich, such a condition should not exist. Nor should the cities where most Americans live be slum-ridden and inadequate in transportation, schools, and public services. And the countryside, a precious heritage for future generations, is being stripped of its resources and beauty at a prodigal rate.

While the drive for civil rights has scored heartening gains, there is a long way to go before the constitutional guarantees of equal rights and fair treatment have full effect. The First Amendment freedoms, meanwhile, have been cut back in the supposed interest of better security.

Over the world ever since 1945 has hovered the specter of an all-out nuclear war which could destroy mankind. Since that date we who invented the bomb and others who now possess it have held back from using it. That good record must be preserved.

Great responsibilities thus remain — to combat poverty, to make our cities better places in which to live, to make equal rights a reality, to bring the United States closer to being, in full truth, the Land of the Free; to preserve the small planet on which we live; and to save succeeding generations from the scourage of war.

If the past is at all a guide to the future, this list of unfinished business is itself incomplete. When a new problem becomes crucial, American history may not offer a ready-made answer. Those on hand will do well, however, to review past experience for what it may provide toward a solution.

OUR CHOSEN DESTINY

To ask an individual his purpose in life leads only to confusion. The pressure of our society prompts us almost always to overstate or understate our aims. Our asserted goals, furthermore, tend to become the goals of our self-delusion.

For a group a more realistic definition is possible, especially if there is a record of performance. For the people of the United States many attempts have been made to define the national goals, and there are 358 years of behavior against which this posturing may be checked.

To Jamestown the first Virginians came in a spirit of adventure. They also hoped to get rich, or at least to better their lot. That attitude has characterized America ever since. Though inconsistent on other matters, Americans have remained true to the cult of economic progress. Last November, when the landslide of votes came in, the President agreed that it amounted to a mandate. When asked, "For what?" he had a ready answer. "Why," he said, "I believe everybody understands — Peace and Prosperity."

The Pilgrims came to Plymouth hoping to make a better living. They also hoped to have greater freedom than they could count on in England. In particular they sought religious freedom, by which they meant escape from the tyranny of an established church. John Winthrop and his companions in the Massachusetts Bay Colony envisioned a New Canaan where they might erect a Light to the World. Roger Williams and Anne Hutchinson challenged the enforced orthodoxy of the Massachusetts Puritans. Williams made Rhode Island a model of religious freedom.

Freedom of religion in America benefited because Charles I granted a colony to a Roman Catholic and Charles II used land to settle a debt to a Quaker. Lord Baltimore's policy of toleration was a necessity if his fellow Catholics were to have a refuge they could depend on. William Penn clearly believed in freedom in religious belief and practice for non-Quakers as well as for Quakers. Throughout the colonies toleration was hastened because there were many sects and not simply one heresy challenging what was orthodox.

Concern for freedom of religion persisted. In drafting the Bill of Rights, James Madison led off with the words now familiar, "Congress shall make no law respecting an establishment of religion, or prohibiting the free exercise thereof." That provision, as part of the supreme law of the land, has not kept Americans from crusading against certain organized churches, particularly when it seemed that these churches were taking to themselves functions that belonged to government. On this ground, at times, the Roman Catholic Church has been criticized. On this ground, war was waged on the Church of Jesus Christ of Latter-day Saints. On this ground, there is complaint that the Southern Christian Leadership Conference is engaged in work quite removed from Christian duty.

We have succeeded almost too well in absolving all churches of fear of government interdict or control. The present hazard is from a government eager to strengthen churches by financial support. Government support, we are prone to forget, is half the battle in breaking down separation of church and state and creating established churches.

Massachusetts in the 1630s was a theocracy in which church and state were thoroughly interwoven. Thus everything that Anne Hutchinson did may be interpreted as a challenge to the church. Viewed more secularly, she was raising questions of freedom of speech and freedom of assembly. Roger Williams, just as clearly, was protesting arbitrary government as well as the monolithic church.

In many other ways the colonists showed concern about liberties other than religious. The Massachusetts Body of Liberties of 1641 is an instance. Its twelve enumerated "Capitall Lawes" separate this code from standards acceptable in twentieth-century America. We no longer are prepared to hang witches — at least not those of the old definition. We can more readily appreciate other parts of this Body of Liberties, limiting the powers of government, and revealing the intention of its authors to write a Magna Carta brought up to date and pertinent to this English colony.

Other colonial events spelled out other particulars, as in 1735, when John Peter Zenger's forthright publishing, Andrew Hamilton's unorthodox pleading, and the jury's disregard of instructions from the bench produced a landmark decision on freedom of the press.

More significant than the episodic build-up of an American pattern were the molding forces of the colonial experience. Geography and meager transportation set the colonists apart from England.

On the piedmont frontier of the latter part of the era, the settlers were further insulated from the mother country. On the firing line at Deerfield, Schenectady, or Boonesborough, they had to rely mainly on their own efforts. Imperial neglect encouraged the colonists to manage some of their own affairs. Before long, the intermingling of non-English and the numerical majority of the American-born loosened the tie to England.

The authorities do not agree whether the political sagacity and ambition of the 1760s to 1780s were by inheritance from England, out of reading the classical and modern political philosophers, or as the fruit of American prosperity, geographical separation, or the special stimuli given by the frontier. Multiple causation is a more acceptable explanation.

Many of the great steps and great documents in political development have been generated by a crisis, among them the Charter of the United Nations, the Emancipation Proclamation, the Thirteenth, Fourteenth, and Fifteenth amendments, the English Bill of Rights, Magna Carta, and the Ten Commandments.

The same is true of the formulation of an American position. Had not George III and his ministers pulled in a bit on the apron strings, American protestants might not have been inspired to hammer out in debate the specifications of the rights of Americans as Englishmen, the arguments for independence, and the statement of purpose for the new nation. In ideology, therefore, we as a people, besides being descendants of the colonists, are more particularly children of the Revolution.

Yet there is a hazard in depending on political debate as the means of formulating a purpose. Much of the real American Revolution was by pamphleteering, much of it in public speech. Occasionally there was opportunity for a prepared paper, but almost always the tone was forensic. Many of the utterances and some of the papers in this debate are marred by overstatement. The line between a regulatory tariff and a revenue tariff was not as sharp as the colonists claimed. Some of Tom Paine's arguments for independence made less sense than he claimed. George III did not deserve all the abuse heaped on him in paragraphs 2-29 of the Declaration of Independence. In a calmer atmosphere the statesmanship might have been better.

Clearly the men of the Revolutionary generation were working under difficult conditions. They were struggling for union as well as for independence. They had to make some concessions to region, to race, to religion, to employments, and to political attitudes. They compromised, not only in the Constitution, but in many other of their pronouncements and enactments.

Americans have not always distinguished between the first principles laid down by the founding fathers and certain acts of expediency. An instance is the notion of a bicameral legislature, with one house chosen popularly and the other chosen unpopularly. This shibboleth long made the United States Senate particularly susceptible to control by special interests. In imitation, many a state still operates with an unrepresentative state senate. The authors of the Constitution set this system going, not on its merits, but in order to achieve consensus on union. Another element of compromise, the Constitution's twenty-year blessing on the slave trade, no one now condones. What is remarkable is that our Revolutionary forefathers, working under such pressure, formulated such an excellent set of animating principles.

In their day these men were not able to make the practice of their generation match all the high principles they enunciated. They capitalized on intimidation by mobs, such as in the Boston Tea Party and the sacking of the house of Thomas Hutchinson. They asserted the right of revolution but were not tolerant of counter-revolution. They, the patriots, more than the British and the loyalists, made use of tar and feathers, the rail, and confiscation.

They spoke of consent of the governed and intoned that We the People established the government of the United States. Yet they were not ready to give the vote to every person irrespective of property or taxpaying, and certainly not irrespective of race or sex.

They proclaimed equal justice, but denied some of the most elementary protections to Negroes, Indians, and women. They accepted as inevitable that there would be a continuation of slavery.

Yet the wonder is that, although the nation was so weak and the hazards were so great, Washington, Franklin, Jefferson, Hamilton, Madison, and their associates erected a system which provided a remarkable degree of freedom of religion, freedom of the press and of speech, and freedom of assembly.

Later generations have improved upon some of the imperishable words. Lincoln did in his Gettysburg Address. Later Americans also improved upon some of the guarantees — for instance, by adding the Thirteenth, Fourteenth, Fifteenth, and Nineteenth amendments, by the Civil Rights acts of 1875 and 1964, and by Supreme Court decisions such as *Gitlow* in 1925, bringing the states under the reach of the First Amendment; *Brown* in 1954, outlawing school segregation; and *Baker* in 1963, declaring the rule of one man, one vote.

To a greater extent, succeeding generations have done well if they could keep alive the guarantees of freedom specified by the founding fathers.

The main tenets in America's announced purpose include these three points: a government answerable to the people, a government showing equal respect for every individual, and a government limited by certain guaranteed freedoms.

True, the checks and balances designed to thwart a would-be dictator or a runaway legislature are also a check on popular sovereignty. Indirect voting such as that through the electoral college was intended as a curb on direct democracy. The people, as the out-group in government, are at some disadvantage as compared to the in-group consisting of the elected officers and the bureaucrats. Yet fundamentally our government is answerable to the people.

Respect for the individual begins with equal treatment at law, the guarantees of due process and fair trial, provision of public education, equal voting rights, and a shoring up of the floor under the least well off. The guaranteed freedoms begin with religion, the press, speech, and assembly. Our announced purpose is admirable. Our practice has included so many deviations as sometimes to reduce the principle almost to a mockery.

One important category in the lapses from the ideal is in governmental favoritism. There is no trouble getting a historian's verdict that Rockefeller should have been restrained from using the rebate to eliminate competition. The pools and trusts of the J. Pierpont Morgan era captivate certain historians, but the prevailing opinion is that these pools and trusts should have been abated.

Athletes, artists, and other short-span performers have a running vendetta against the 27½ percent depletion allowance that is the peculiar blessing of the oil industry. These persons assert that their resources are also subject to depletion. They find some intellectual support, but no effective lobby. Few citizens realize that the 27½ percent favoritism discriminates against all other taxpayers.

Estes Kefauver found the American public receptive to the coonskin cap. But when he tilted a lancet against what he asserted were unethical procedures and pricing in the drug industry, he got little action.

Walter Prescott Webb had a similar experience. His readers

followed along avidly as he discussed barbed wire, windmills, and the American desert. They paid little attention when he attacked the regional inequities of discriminatory freight rates and monopoly through patent licensing.

Just over twelve years ago Eisenhower brought to Washington equanimity in the face of monopoly, acquiescence in the dismantling of regulation, and indifference about giveaway of natural resources. A few voices cry out. The Sierra Club, for instance, although it lost Glen Canyon, saved Dinosaur Monument and hopes to save some of the Giant Redwoods. But the modern temper as to the special interests is more permissive.

Far more serious lapses from our high purposes are to be seen in the realm of human relations. Heading the list was the continuation of slavery, long after it had been renounced almost everywhere else in the civilized world. Besides slavery itself, there was the legalizing of the slave trade to 1808 and a large amount of slave running thereafter.

Briefly, after the Civil War, the Negro expected equal rights, but the dream was mostly shattered in 1877. After that, Jim Crow laws legislated his position of inferiority. The nation, it should be remembered, authorized this action. Although a few of the more awkward Jim Crow devices were voided, the Supreme Court enunciated the doctrine of separate facilities in *Plessy* v. *Ferguson* in 1896, and that decision stood for fifty-eight years. It was controlling, not merely in the jurisprudence of the southern states, but in federal jurisprudence as well.

Nor is that the whole story of less than equal rights for Negroes. Ninety-five years have not been time enough for the Fifteenth Amendment to penetrate the Black Belt. Negroes are being shortchanged as to education, employment, income, housing, and government services. As a group, Negroes are grossly underrepresented in our college populations and overrepresented in the poverty census. The phrase "last to be hired, first to be fired" has grisly reality. Negroes draw the worst housing but have to pay premium rents. In many places and in most crucial respects Negroes cannot count on equal treatment at the hands of government.

The Negro American enters life with a higher expectancy of suffering violence than does the white American. Part of the explanation is that the United States as an organized society gives him less protection. The annual tally on lynchings is an evidence in point. The headlines on conspicuous violence in the South tell part of the story. What is published, however, is nothing like a full report on the attacks and killings that occur, without follow-up of trial or conviction and often without even becoming a matter of police record. Much publicity has attended recent bursts of violence in Mississippi, Alabama, and Georgia against Negroes or friends of the Negroes. Yet few if any of us could give accurate count of the number of such homicides.

Our system of justice metes out much harsher punishment to accused Negroes. A recent tabulation of convictions and sentences in one southern state disclosed that, in practice, criminal rape is actionable only if it is interracial, and interracial in one direction. In many states in all parts of the country, the death penalty, as it works out, is reserved mainly for the poor rather than the well-to-do and for minorities, particularly the Negro.

In American society the Negro for a long time has been a neglected stepchild. The present drive by blacks and whites together, though distasteful to some of our sages, is long overdue. It aims to correct the most glaring betrayal of this nation's heralded purpose.

The Negro, of course, is not the only victim of discrimination. The American Indian stands among us as one dispossessed as well as subjected to discrimination. A hundred years after the founding of the United States, Helen Hunt Jackson looked back on American Indian policy and called it "a century of dishonor." Her title had a flaw in that it omitted the colonial record. It also could not look ahead to the period after 1876. But it was correct that exploitation of the Indian began early.

The enlightened territorial policy of the Northwest Ordinances, under which the blessings of cheap land and self-government spread across the continent, was based on taking the land away from the Indians. This dispossession was followed up by a program of segregation. We called it, to be sure, the reservation policy, but the reservation more often than not was a ghetto — a ghetto purely American. In the 1965 march on Montgomery, by the way, I was delighted to see that one of the delegations identified itself by a banner "The American Indian."

Americans have on their consciences a period of anti-Chinese agitation, when a handful of western states persuaded the national government to negotiate and enact an exclusion program. Later, the animosity was against Japanese-Americans. The Pacific states, California in particular, prodded the national government into a series of actions. The climax was to herd this entire racial group into concentration camps east of the Sierra Nevada. Californians spearheaded the agitation, but what began as a local aberration became national. The Army and the Department of Justice fell in line, the President gave his approval, and the Supreme Court rationalized what was done. In retrospect, this court decision is seen as one of the most flagrant instances on record of limiting the constitutional guarantees to mere fairweather protections.

Today the overriding issue is equal rights for the Negro and thereby for all Americans. Such is our concentration on this issue that it is most unfashionable to turn from civil rights to civil liberties, from equal rights for minorities to the freedoms of the First Amendment — the familiar concepts of freedom to worship, to publish, to speak, and to assemble, or more significantly, freedom to exercise one's conscience, to read, to hear, and to protest.

Last year the American Civil Liberties Union of Southern California deliberately budgeted 90 percent of its effort to a civil rights issue — a vain endeavor to defeat the constitutional amendment guaranteeing the real estate owner's asserted right to be a racist. This is one of many illustrations that civil rights today have priority over civil liberties. Another illustration, higher placed, is in the President's program to bring better education to the disadvantaged child. Because a great many of these children are Negroes, the bill is part of the present civil rights program and has urgency. To get the necessary consensus for quick passage, the backers of this bill have thought it necessary to sacrifice a fundamental civil liberties guarantee, separation of church and state.

It is indeed time to push for equal rights. Yet if civil liberties are lost — if the guarantees of the Bill of Rights are cancelled out — the Negro may be no better off when he achieves equal rights in a downgraded society.

Over the years the First Amendment freedoms have suffered periodic attack and blight. The Sedition Act and prosecutions that were the last gasp of the Federalist party were one instance. The anti-Catholic crusade resulted in strictures on the freedoms, as did the antiabolition drive with its purpose of silencing the abolitionist reformers.

During the Civil War, Unionists from ordinary citizens up to the President used the war as cover for severe repressions of speech and press. Threats and hanging in effigy drove Rev. William A. Scott, secessionist sympathizer, from his San Francisco pulpit. Off-duty soldiers led the mob that destroyed the press and type of the pro-Confederate Visalia *Expositor*. When the Los Angeles *Star* persisted in anti-Unionism, the postmaster general excluded it from the mails and thereby forced it to cease publishing. California was one of the many states in which such incidents occurred.

Before and after World War I, there were attempts to silence the IWW radicals. The methods used included beatings, making these men run the gauntlet, scalding their children with hot coffee, applying tar and feathers, and assassinating. Criminal syndicalism laws simplified the getting of convictions. All that was needed was to show that the accused carried a card or had attended a meeting. By such devices, the Wobblies were put beyond the reach of the standard protections.

In the 1920s the rejuvenated Ku Klux Klan applied its sanctions against other kinds of nonconformists. The Klan, for the most part, was operating outside the law, but at times with the cooperation of the established authorities. The Palmer raids were an official denial of the right of assembly. They made a travesty of fair trial. In the same category falls the unseating of the duly elected Socialist members of the New York legislature.

This frenzy subsided, for reasons not altogether identifiable, only to rise again in the late 1930s with the Communists as the certified menace. The House Un-American Activities Committee dates only from 1938, and its state counterparts from only slightly later. It would be unfair to minimize the work of Martin Dies and his early imitators, but the more sensational outbursts came after World War II. They included the interrogation of the Hollywood Ten and the setting up of the blacklist, Richard Nixon's encounters with Alger Hiss and Helen Gahagan Douglas, and Joseph R. McCarthy's personal reign of terror, beginning in 1950 and reaching its climax in 1954.

These crestings of the flood get automatic attention. More significant is the long-run and enduring blight to the freedoms. The overarching cover, of course, has been the Cold War, which set up a permanent emergency and made anti-Communism the talisman for judging all persons and all endeavors.

American Communism had a tincture of totalitarianism that was antithetical to democracy. But many of its announced aims were clearly much more in the neighborhood of the New Deal than of the Liberty League, more akin to liberalism than to conservatism. These facts made the Communist target a most convenient one for the political dart game. The chances were high that a dart would puncture a bystander, who in all probability would be a New Dealer, a Fair Dealer, or a liberal.

Equally significant is the degree to which the attitudes and mechanics of McCarthyism have been institutionalized and still operate. Along with Martin Dies, Parnell Thomas, Patrick A. McCarran, and Francis E. Walter, local luminaries such as Frank B. Ober, Paul Broyles, Jack B. Tenney, and Albert F. Canwell are usually credited with this achievement. In fact, the responsibility must be more broadly shared. Our present elaborate network of test oaths, security checks, and dossiers had more respectable authorship than these names suggest. The machinery and the system owe much to pleadings by the heads of the AEC, the CIA, and the FBI, and to the loyalty and security program initiated by Truman and extended and elaborated by Eisenhower.

The degree to which we have sacrificed the freedoms on what we were told was the altar of security is often lost sight of. Yet it is a commonplace that a student who joins or participates in the work of today's protest movements picks up marks on his dossier that may well handicap him in the fellowship market and in the job market.

It is not settled whether this bundle of principles that I identify as our chosen destiny is supposed to control in our relations with other countries. Substantial evidence suggests that it should have this reach. The Declaration of Independence not only was addressed to the world but, in its affirmative passages, was phrased in universals. Benjamin Franklin insisted that the free society Americans were striving to achieve was to be available for export. "God grant," he said, "that not only the love of liberty, but a thorough knowledge of the rights of man may pervade all the nations of the earth, so that a philosopher may set foot anywhere on its surface and say: This is my country."

Monroe, in his most famous pronouncement, promised the Old World that it was exempt from intervention by the United States. Lincoln's Emancipation Proclamation, important though it was in the internal operations of the United States, was more immediately calculated to ensure continuation of British neutrality. Hay's policy of the Open Door intimated a fair-play protection that the United States would extend to China. The intervention that Roosevelt, Taft, and Wilson practiced in the Caribbean was represented as being for the good of these neighbor nations. A few years later, Wilson summoned Americans to a crusade to make the world safe for democracy. As a corollary, he hoped to endow as many peoples as possible with the right of self-determination.

Franklin D. Roosevelt's leadership was more suave. Ours then was a partnership role in a titanic struggle against totalitarian aggressors. He called on the American people to put forth a superlative effort to win the war and to reshape the world. At the same time, bearing in mind our good neighbors in the Americas, whenever possible he stressed defense of the hemisphere rather than just of the United States. Furthermore, acutely conscious of how fortunate we were to have allies, he consistently stressed not just the war aims of the United States but the team effort and the aims of the allied powers.

Since the war, Presidents Truman, Eisenhower, Kennedy, and Johnson and the American people have behaved differently. The United Nations at its best has been a looser association than the wartime alliance. Britain and France sustained shattering losses, while the United States emerged with a flourishing economy. With the Bomb, the United States stood tall in singular grandeur. Naturally, our Presidents of the next twenty years, and the American people, have seen the United States as protector of the free world. That is the posture we have taken.

From 1776 to 1965 American professions to the world have had a sustained high tone, but our actions have not always conformed. With Andrew Jackson at the head of the foragers, we relieved Spain of western Florida. Under the rationalization of manifest destiny, we, on meager provocation, went to war with Mexico, occupied her northern provinces, and retained the entire expanse from Texas to California.

In the 1890s we elected the course, but not the sinister label, of imperialism. We imposed our will on the Filipinos; we took Panama; we wielded the Big Stick of intervention in Central America and the Caribbean. Wilsonian idealism was matched by a pietistic interventionism. Harding and Coolidge represented an equally self-righteous turning of the cold shoulder to the rest of the world.

Our present claim to unlimited oversight — not just in the western hemisphere, but all the way to outer space — again has a seamier side underneath the altruism. Repeatedly, and with little evidence of displeasure, we have given abrazos to dictators — to Franco, Pérez Jiménez, Somoza, Duvalier, Trujillo. Thus the list begins.

We were the ones who broke through the moral barrier and dropped nuclear bombs on enemy cities. We began the nuclear arms race. We also, so long as we had marked superiority, disregarded all appeals to halt nuclear testing. We have been the major contributor of nuclear fallout. It was our secretary of state who was the chief apologist for nuclear saber rattling, better known as brinkmanship.

Failure at the Bay of Pigs saved us from an interventionist program that would have appeared far more cynical than the early twentieth-century use of the marines to take over the customs houses and make neighbor nations solvent in spite of themselves.[1] All these matters and the talk of unleashing Chiang and the Seventh Fleet to liberate mainland China now seem ancient history.

What of the present? What of Vietnam? We began by sending military advisers and supplying conventional equipment. Now more frankly, Americans are sent to fight, and the weapons and tactics include helicopter transport and strafing, amphibious personnel carriers, a grenade launcher highly accurate at 700 yards, greatly improved landing craft, million candlepower flares to simplify the work of night bombing and strafing, a shell or bomb that erupts into thousands of steel darts lethal at a hundred feet, three kinds of sublethal gas, napalm firestorm applied to defoliate the jungle as well as to cause direct casualties, and air support from the decks of the *Coral Sea*. The analogy seems very close to the Nazi and Fascist try-out of weapons and tactics in the fighting against the Spanish Republicans, but apparently what is happening in Vietnam carries no such reminder to Americans. On the contrary there are rumblings about escalating the military tryout and the half-declared war.[2]

These selections from the record indicate that in our dealings with other nations we have departed from idealism perhaps as often, and as far, as we have in our domestic affairs. Despite this foreign and domestic record, our good intentions as announced have a certain amount of survival.

Slavery is ended and with it the slave trade and the fugitive slave law. Jim Crow laws are on their way out. The class action against the Japanese-Americans is now regretted. Parts of the Smith Act have been held unconstitutional, as have certain parts of the witch hunt against alleged security risks. Discriminations against Negro Americans have not been eliminated — nor have they been confined to the Black Belt — but they have been reduced.

Sometimes abuses create a revulsion of feeling and therefore a reversal of action. So it was with Bull Connor's police dogs and cattleprods and Jim Clark's whips, clubs, and gas. Sometimes the courts drag us back to first principles. Sometimes an impassioned voice — Martin Luther King's from the Birmingham jail, or Lyndon B. Johnson's after Selma — pulls us onto the right track. Interpretive history also can fortify the will to put things to right.

Our chosen destiny is in the form of a compact with ourselves. We may pretend that at our pleasure we can subtract from our stated aims or can renege. In fact, we do not really have that option. Having repeatedly announced these aims to all mankind, we cannot cavalierly pretend that they never existed.

On several scores I doubt that the American people will renounce this commitment. Our chosen destiny has compelling uses. It is a comfort in time of stress. It actually gives comfort to those who wish to abridge the freedoms. They can rationalize that, after the emergency is over, the constitutional protections can be reactivated. In a few widely scattered instances, such a restoration has occurred. Our chosen destiny is an arsenal for political pleadings. It puts the burden of justification on those who would deny the freedoms. Our chosen destiny is a guideline of first principles for our courts. It is a core element in education — the most inspiring part of American history. Our chosen destiny is a standard inevitably applied in historical evaluation. With it as the meeting ground, we are all conservatives; we are all humanitarians.

American history, thus viewed, is a dreary recital for which I can claim no originality. Indeed, the essence of what I have been saying was published in last Sunday's paper in Charles M. Schulz's "Peanuts":

"Brush this guy back, Charlie Brown! Give 'im the ol' beanball!"

"No, I can't do that . . . it wouldn't be right . . ."

"It wouldn't be RIGHT?!" "Listen to who's gone moral on us all of a sudden! Ol' Wishy-Washy here is too moral to throw a beanball!"

"What about the way the early settlers treated the Indians? Was that moral? How about the Children's Crusade? Was that moral?"

"Yeah, and how about those awful movie ads you see nowadays?"

"Do you call those moral, Charlie Brown?"

"Do you think that incident at Harper's Ferry was consistent with morality?"

"Define morality!"

"Our whole system of freeways is a perfect example of what I'm trying to say!"

"Have you listened to radio lately?"

"How about this whole conservation situation?"

"We never win any ball games, but we have some interesting discussions!"

American history is a paradox if not a contradiction. Ours was the first nation to dedicate itself at the outset to a regime of freedom. As a people we have consistently endorsed the principles upheld by the Pilgrims, the Puritans, Williams, Hutchinson, Penn, and Zenger; codified by Jefferson and Franklin, the founding fathers, and the authors of the Bill of Rights; and proclaimed anew by Lincoln, Wilson, Roosevelt, and Warren.

Yet as a nation and as a people we have all too often strayed from this path. We have betrayed our tradition and our heritage. That is the inescapable verdict on much of our domestic history and on much of our behavior in foreign affairs. What we have done is enough to make scoffing hecklers of our neighbors and cynics of our citizens.

Even so, the will for freedom persists. The American people still choose to make this the land of the free. Acceptance of the principle of freedom will not down. We as a people struggle toward it.

Over the past twenty-five years, I am not sure that we have made any real progress toward fulfillment of this chosen destiny. But in the past fifty years, yes; in the past one hundred, decidedly; and in the past two hundred, absolutely.

NOTES

INTRODUCTION

[1]"Their Majesties the Mob," *Pacific Historical Review*, XXVI (1957), 218-219.

[2]This incident was recounted by Caughey in *Returning a Salute* (Los Angeles, 1962), 3-4.

[3]"Herbert Eugene Bolton," *American West*, I (1964), 38.

[4]See Powell's comments in Phil Townsend Hanna, *Libros Californianos* (revised and enlarged by Lawrence Clark Powell; Los Angeles, 1958), 75-76.

[5]*Mississippi Valley Historical Review*, XXIII (1946), 466; *San Francisco Chronicle*, September 29, 1946, p. 10; *Oregon Historical Quarterly*, XLVII (1946), 387-388.

[6]Though details a plenty can be found in David P. Gardner's *The California Oath Controversy* (Berkeley, 1967), the book fails to capture the tension and excitement of the incident, and some critics feel that it betrays an ignorance about the purpose of a university.

[7]Quoted in *ibid.*, 150. See also Caughey, "A University in Jeopardy," *Harper's Magazine* (November, 1950), 68.

[8]"A University in Jeopardy," *op. cit.*, 68-70.

[9]*Ibid.*, 70; Caughey, "How to Fire a Communist," St. Louis *Post-Dispatch*, April 6, 1956.

[10]See Caughey's reflections on the Levering Oath in *Law in Transition Quarterly*, IV (September, 1967), 176.

[11]*In Clear and Present Danger* (Chicago, 1958), 192.

[12]*Their Majesties the Mob* (Chicago, 1960), vii.

[13]*Ibid.*, viii.

[14]*UCLA Daily Bruin*, October 30, 1967.

[15]This quotation and much of what follows can be found in Caughey's "The politics of Adoption," *California Social Science Review*, VI (June, 1967), 34-40. For an analysis which reveals the spurious nature of the criticisms of *Land of the Free*, see California Teachers Association, *"Land of the Free" and Its Critics* (Burlingame, Calif., 1967).

[16]"California in Third Dimension," *Pacific Historical Review*, XXVIII (1959), 111-129.

[17]"The American West: Frontier and Region," *Arizona and the West*, I (1959), 7-12; "Toward an Understanding of the West," *Utah Historical Quarterly*, XXVII (1959), 7-24.

[18]*Returning a Salute*, 12.

PART I: THE WEST

INTRODUCTION: THE WEST

[1]From Caughey's remarks during the session on "Training Western Historians," October 14, 1967, at the Western History Association convention in San Francisco.

THE AMERICAN WEST: FRONTIER AND REGION
Reprinted with permission from *Arizona and the West*, I (1959), 7-12.

TOWARD AN UNDERSTANDING OF THE WEST
Reprinted with permission from the *Utah Historical Quarterly*, XXVII (1959), 7-24. This address was delivered at the joint convention of the American Association for

State and Local History and the Society of American Archivists held on August 20, 1958, in Salt Lake City, Utah.

[1]Quoted in Lawrence Clark Powell, *Philosopher Pickett* (Berkeley, 1942), 144-145.

[2][Both Hawaii and Alaska were admitted to statehood in 1959.]

THE SPANISH SOUTHWEST: AN EXAMPLE OF SUBCONSCIOUS REGIONALISM
Reprinted with the permission of the Regents of the University of Wisconsin from Merrill Jensen, ed., *Regionalism in America* (Madison: University of Wisconsin Press, 1951), 173-186.

PART II: THE OLD SOUTHWEST

LOUISIANA: A SPANISH OUTPOST, 1763-1783
Reprinted with permission from John W. Caughey, *Bernardo de Gálvez in Louisiana, 1776-1783* (Berkeley: University of California Press, 1934).

[1]The interpretation in William R. Shepherd, "The Cession of Louisiana to Spain," *Political Science Quarterly,* XIX (1904), 439-458, is revised and supplemented by Arthur S. Aiton, "The Diplomacy of the Louisiana Cession," *American Historical Review,* XXXVI (1931), 701-720.

[2]Charles Gayarré, *History of Louisiana,* 4 vols. 2nd ed. (New Orleans, 1879), II, 141.

[3]This biographical sketch is based on the following: Gayarré, II, 141-152, 173-178; Herbert Eugene Bolton, *Athanase de Mézières and the Louisiana-Texas Frontier, 1768-1780,* 2 vols. (Cleveland, 1914), I, 127-128n; Benjamin Franklin French, ed., *Historical Collections of Louisiana,* 5 vols. (New York, 1846-1853), V, 151-152n; Marc Villiers du Terrage, *Les Dernières Années de la Louisiana française* (Paris, 1903), 228.

[4]Gayarré, *op. cit.,* II, Lectures 3 and 4.

[5]Grimaldi to Ulloa, May 24, 1766, Archivo General de Indias, Seville: Papeles procedentes de la Isla de Cuba (hereafter cited as A. G. I., Cuba), 174.

[6]Villiers du Terrage, *op. cit.,* 236-238.

[7]Royal cédula, May 3, 1768, Archivo General de Indias, Seville: Audiencia de Santo Domingo (hereafter cited as A. G. I., Sto. Dom.), 1215; Grimaldi to Loyola, June 20, 1768, A. G. I., Cuba, 2357.

[8]Alcée Fortier, *A History of Louisiana,* 4 vols. (Paris and New York, 1904), I, 190-195: Vera Lee Brown, "Anglo-Spanish Relations in America," *Hispanic American Historical Review,* V (1925), 348; James E. Winston, "The Cause and Results of the Revolution of 1768 in Louisiana," *Louisiana Historical Quarterly,* XV (1932), 188-190.

[9]Villiers du Terrage, *op. cit.,* 235; David K. Bjork, "The Establishment of Spanish Rule in the Province of Louisiana, 1762-1770," (Ph.D. dissertation, University of California, Berkeley, 1923), 94.

[10]Bucarelli to Ulloa, June 7, 1768, A. G. I., Cuba, 1054.

[11]French, *op. cit.,* V, 158; Gayarré, *op. cit.,* II, 185.

[12]Gayarré, *op. cit.,* II, 184; French, *op. cit.,* V, 151-152.

[13]Gayarré, *op. cit.,* II, 173-186.

[14]Ulloa to Grimaldi, December 4, 1768, A. G. I., Sto. Dom., 2542; Nota de Personas de que se componía la familia con que se transportó á España dn. Antonio de Ulloa, December 14, 1768, *ibid.;* Account of the Louisiana Insurrection, 1768, A. G. I. Sto. Dom., 2543; Villiers du Terrage, *op. cit.,* 255-257; Gayarré, *op. cit.,* II, 190-191.

[15]A summary of the written opinions of the members of the Council is given in Gayarré, *op. cit.,* II, 249-264.

[16]Bucarelli to Arriaga, July 7, 1769, A. G. I., Sto. Dom., 1220.

[17]Relación de Como D. Alejandro O'Reilly Pacificó la Ciudad de Nueva Orleans, August 30, 1769, in Manuel Serrano y Sanz, ed, *Documentos Históricos de la Florida y la Luisiana, Siglos XVI al XVIII* (Madrid, 1912), 299-301; O'Reilly to Arriaga, August 31, 1769, *loc. cit.*, 307-308; Gayarré, *op. cit.*, II, 295-299.

[18]O'Reilly to Munian, August 31, 1769, A. G. I., Sto. Dom., 1220.

[19]Affidavit by Rodríguez, October 29, 1769, A. G. I., Sto. Dom., 2543; Testimonio sacado por . . . Rodríguez, A. G. I., Cuba, 81. See also Winston, "The Cause and Results of the Revolution of 1768 in Louisiana," *Louisiana Historical Quarterly*, XV (1932), 198-213; and Gayarré, *op. cit.*, II, 315-343.

[20]The latter part of O'Reilly's administration is described at greatest length in Bjork, *op. cit.*, 150-255.

[21]French, *op. cit.*, V, 254.

[22]O. Garfield Jones, "Local Government in the Spanish Colonies as Provided by the Recopilación de Leyes de las Reynos de las Indias," *Southwestern Historical Quarterly*, XIX (1915), 88.

[23]O'Reilly, Instrucción del modo de substanciar y determinar, November 25, 1769, A. G. I., Cuba, 1055, and printed in French, *op. cit.*, V, 269-288.

[24]Quoted in Villiers du Terrage, *op. cit.*, 319-320.

[25]O'Reilly (list of appointees), February 4, 1770, A. G. I., Cuba, 1055.

[26]O'Reilly to Arriaga, October 17, 1769, No. 3, A. G. I., Sto. Dom., 1221.

[27]Deposition of Oliver Pollock, June 8, 1808, in James M. Wilkinson, *Memoirs of My Own Times*, 3 vols. (Philadelphia, 1816), II, appendix I.

[28]O'Reilly to Arriaga, October 17, 1769, No. 4, A. G. I., Sto. Dom., 1221; Bucareli to Arriaga, April 1, 1770, Archivo General de Indias, at Seville: Indiferente General (hereafter cited as A. G. I., Ind. Gen.), 1630; O'Reilly to Bucarelli, April 3, 1770, No. 93, A. G. I., Cuba, 1055; Grimaldi to Bucareli, June 23, 1770, A. G. I., Ind. Gen., 1630.

[29]Bolton, *Athanase de Mézières*, I, 70.

[30]The description which follows is based on O'Reilly to Arriaga, October 17, 1769, No. 3, enclosure B, A. G. I., Sto. Dom., 1221.

[31]O'Reilly to Arriaga, December 10, 1769, No. 18, A. G. I., Sto. Dom., 1223, quoted in David K. Bjork, "Documents Relating to Alexandro O'Reilly," *Louisiana Historical Quarterly*, VII (1924), 21-22.

[32]In 1769 St. Ange listed twenty-three tribes that were accustomed to come to St. Louis annually for presents. A dozen of them resided east of the Mississippi. Louis Houck, *A History of Missouri*, 3 vols. (Chicago, 1908), I, 44-45.

[33]*Ibid.*, I, 77-82.

[34]Herbert Eugene Bolton, *Texas in the Middle Eighteenth Century* (Berkeley, 1915), 378-383.

[35]French, *op. cit.*, V, 289-291; O'Reilly to Arriaga, February 14, 1770, A. G. I., Cuba, 1055.

[36]Gayarré, *op. cit.*, III, 44, 102-104; Bolton, *Athanase de Mézières*, I, 136-137, *n*.

[37]Clarence E. Carter, *Great Britain and the Illinois Country, 1763-1774* (Washington, D.C., 1910), 142-144.

[38]Unzaga to Grimaldi, June 8, 1770, A. G. I., Sto. Dom., 2543; Bucareli to Arriaga, August 17, 1770, *ibid.*; O'Reilly to Grimaldi, September 30, 1770, *ibid.*; Grimaldi to Unzaga, October 24, 1770, *ibid.*; Carter, *op. cit.*, 182-183.

[39]Gayarré, *op. cit.*, III, 49-65, 83-85, 90-91; Houck, *op. cit.*, I, 114-120.

[40]Clarence Wyatt Bispham, "Contest for Ecclesiastical Supremacy in the Valley of the Mississippi, 1763-1803," *Louisiana Historical Quarterly,* I (1917), 184-185; Para el Consejo, March 15, 1775, A. G. I., Sto. Dom., 2583. Cyril later became Bishop of Louisiana.

[41]Unzaga to the Bishop and to Torre, quoted in Gayarré, *op. cit.,* III, 84-91.

[42]These terms are used in the sense of "one who sits beside" and "one who hears"; in other words, a legal adviser. Laura L. Porteous, ed., "A Suit for Debt in the Governor's Court, New Orleans, 1770," *Louisiana Historical Quarterly,* VIII (1925), 240-241.

[43]Laura L. Porteous, ed., "Index to the Spanish Judicial Records," *Louisiana Historical Quarterly,* VI- (1923-), *passim;* Joseph Loppinot vs. Juan Villeneuve, April 15, 1774, *ibid.,* X (1927), 438.

[44]Laura L. Porteous, ed., "Torture in Spanish Criminal Procedure in Louisiana, 1771," *Louisiana Historical Quarterly,* VIII (1925), 5-22.

[45]Albert Phelps, *Louisiana, a Record of Expansion* (Boston, 1905), 136-137; Francois-Xavier Martin, *The History of Louisiana,* 2 vols. (New Orleans, 1827-1829), II, 26-27.

[46]Unzaga to De Mézières, October 4, 1771, Bolton, *Athanase de Mézières,* I, 254-255; Ripperda to Unzaga, September 8, 1772, *ibid.,* I, 344-349.

[47]De Mézières to Unzaga, February 16, 1776, *ibid.,* II, 120-121.

[48]Philip Pittman, *The Present State of the European Settlements on the Mississippi* (London, 1770), ed. by Frank Heywood Hodder (Cleveland, 1906), 95-96; Houck, *op. cit.,* I, 85-107.

[49]Census of Louisiana, September 2, 1772, A. G. I., Cuba, 2357.

[50]Justin Winsor, *The Westward Movement* (Boston, 1897), 110.

[51]Unzaga to Torre, February 27, 1772, No. 18, A. G. I., Cuba, 1145.

[52]Unzaga to Arriaga, June 19, 1776, No. 160, A. G. I., Sto. Dom., 2547.

[53]Unzaga to José de Gálvez, June 19, 1776, No. 159, *ibid.,* 2656.

[54]Lee to the Governor of New Orleans, May, 1776, *ibid.,* 2596.

[55]Unzaga to José de Gálvez, September 7, 1776, No. 181, *ibid.;* Winsor, *op. cit.,* 147-148.

[56]Unzaga to José de Gálvez, September 30, 1776, No. 184, *ibid.*

[57]O'Reilly to Unzaga, June 15, 1776, A. G. I., Cuba, 181.

[58]Herbert Ingram Priestley, *José de Gálvez, Visitor-General of New Spain, 1765-1771* (Berkeley, 1916), 9-10.

[59]Cuellar to José de Gálvez, April 28, 1769, No. 342, copy, Huntington Library, Gálvez Papers.

[60]José de Gálvez to Cuellar, May 17, 1769, No. 2, copy, *ibid.*

[61]Relación que en Extracto . . . , November 23, 1770, Archivo General de Indias, at Seville, Audiencia de Guadalajara (hereafter cited as A. G. I., Guad.), 416.

[62]Croix to Arriaga, September 19, 1771, No. 1090, *ibid.*

[63]Gálvez to Bucareli, November 29, 1771, No. 512, *ibid.*

[64]Bucareli to O'Reilly, October 27, 1771, draft, mentioning the request of José de Gálvez and the designation of Hugo Oconor to relieve Bernardo de Gálvez, Archivo General de Indias, at Seville, Audiencia de Mexico (hereafter cited as A. G. I., Mexico), 1242.

[65]Gálvez to Bucareli, November 1, 1771, copy, A. G. I., Guad., 512.

[66]*Appleton's Cyclopaedia of American Biography,* II, 584-585.

[67]Quoted in De la Torre to José de Gálvez, December 1, 1776, No. 1282, A. G. I., Sto. Dom., 1211.

[68]The French text of the regulations is given in Villiers du Terrage, *op. cit.*, 353-354.

[69]Gayarré, *op. cit.*, III, 106.

[70]Proclamations of Gálvez, April 18, 1777, A. G. I., Cuba, 1232; July 15, 1777, *ibid.*; November 21, 1777, Louisiana Collection, Bancroft Library, University of California, Berkeley.

[71]Gayarré, *op. cit.*, III, 117-118.

[72]*Ibid.*, 107.

[73]Proclamation of Gálvez, June 15, 1777, A. G. I., Cuba, 1232.

[74]Bucareli to José de Gálvez, September 25, 1777, No. 3325, A. G. I., Mexico, 89-4-9.

[75]*Ibid.*; Gayarré, *op. cit.*, III, 107.

[76]Houck, *op. cit.*, I, 158-159.

[77]Proclamation of Gálvez, November 21, 1777, Louisiana Collection, Bancroft Library.

[78]Census report, May 12, 1777, certified copy, A. G. I., Cuba, 2351.

[79]Proclamation of Gálvez, February 19, 1778, in Houck, *op. cit.*, I, 155-157.

[80]Gálvez to José de Gálvez, January 15, 1779, A. G. I., Sto. Dom., 2574.

[81]Mattie Austin Hatcher, "The Louisiana Background of the Colonization of Texas, 1763-1803," *Southwestern Historical Quarterly*, XXIV (1921), 170; Gálvez to José de Gálvez, January 15, 1779, No. 233, A. G. I., Sto. Dom., 2574; James Alexander Robertson, ed., *Louisiana under the Rule of Spain, France and the United States*, 2 vols. (Cleveland, 1911), I, 248; Martin, *op. cit.*, II, 46.

[82]"Ramao de Población y Amistad de Indios: items as usual, augmented by the extra expenditures on account of the arrival of settlers, transportation of Indians, Indian gifts, etc. . . . 1,028,544 reales de plata." (A peso was worth eight silver reales.) Charles H. Cunningham, ed., "Financial Reports Relating to Louisiana," *Mississippi Valley Historical Review*, VI (1919), 385.

[83]S. C. Arthur and G. C. H. de. Kernion, *Old Families of Louisiana* (New Orleans, 1931), 414.

[84]Deposition of Oliver Pollock, June 8, 1808, in James M. Wilkinson, *Memoirs of My Own Times*, 3 vols. (Philadelphia, 1812), II, appendix I.

[85]Wilkinson, *op. cit.*, II, 150.

[86]Except as otherwise noted the account of Clark's work is drawn from James Alton, *The Life of George Rogers Clark* (Chicago, 1928) and his edition of the *George Rogers Clark Papers, 1771-1781* (Springfield, Illinois, 1912).

[87]Clark to Mason, November 19, 1779, in James, *George Rogers Clark Papers, 1771-1781*, 122.

[88]James G. Randall, "George Rogers Clark's Service of Supply," *Mississippi Valley Historical Review*, VIII (1921), 254.

[89]*Ibid.*, 251*n*; H. J. Eckenrode, *The Revolution in Virginia* (Boston, 1916), *passim*; James, *Clark Papers*, 327, p. lxxxii.

[90]*Ibid.*, p. lxvii; Clark to Pollock, August 6, 1778, *ibid.*, 64-65.

[91]*Ibid.*, p. xcvii.

[92]Deposition of Oliver Pollock, June 8, 1808, in Wilkinson, *Memoirs of My Own Times*, II, appendix I.

[93]James Alton James, "Spanish Influence in the West during the American Revolution," *Mississippi Valley Historical Review*, IV (1918), 207.

[94]Pollock to Gálvez, December 18, 1779, copy, A. G. I., Cuba, 112.

[95]Summary of a report by Governor Bernardo de Gálvez at New Orleans on October 24, 1778, in Arthur Preston Whitaker, ed., *Documents Relating to the Commercial Policy of Spain in the Floridas* . . . (Deland, Florida, 1931), 11-21; summary of a representation by Gilbert Antoine de St. Maxent, October 4, 1781, *ibid.*, 22-29.

[96]The cédula is printed in Spanish and in translation in Whitaker, *op. cit.*, 30-39; see also Rafael Antúnez y Acevedo, *Memorias Históricas sobre la Legislación y Gobierno del Comercio de los Españoles con sus Colonias en las Indias Occidentales* (Madrid, 1797), 37.

[97]See his letter to José de Gálvez relative to the Indian trade of the Floridas, December 20, 1783, in Whitaker, *op. cit.*, 38-41.

[98]From February 4 until the last of April, 1785.

[99]Miguel de Corral to José de Gálvez, June 2, 1785, A. G. I., Mexico, 1512; the audiencia of Mexico to José de Gálvez, June 28, 1785, No. 197, *ibid.*

McGILLIVRAY OF THE CREEKS

Reprinted with permission from John W. Caughey, *McGillivray of the Creeks* (Norman: University of Oklahoma Press, 1938).

[1]Albert James Pickett, *History of Alabama and Incidentally of Georgia and Mississippi* (Sheffield, Alabama, 1896), 345. Ames is quoted in John B. McMaster, *A History of the People of the United States*, 8 vols. (New York, 1910), I, 604.

[2]Absalom H. Chappell, *Miscellanies of Georgia* (Columbus, Georgia, 1874), 28.

[3]Little Tallassie, or Otciapofa as the Creeks called it, was on the Coosa near its junction with the Tallapoosa to form the Alabama. During the French period Fort Toulouse had stood here; present-day Montgomery is not far from the site.

[4]On the early history of Fort Toulouse see Alfred Wade Reynolds, "The Alabama-Tombigbee Basin in International Relations, 1701-1763," doctoral dissertation, University of California, Berkeley, 1928; and Pierre Heinrich, *La Louisiana sous la Compagnie des Indes, 1717-1731* (Paris, 1908).

[5]Louis (LeClerc) Milfort, *Mémoire ou coup d'oeil rapide sur mes différens voyages et mon séjour dans la nation Crëck* (Paris, 1802), 23.

[6]Marriage customs are described in John R. Swanton, "Social Organization and Social Usages of the Indians of the Creek Confederacy," *Bureau of American Ethnology, Forty-Second Annual Report* (Washington, 1928), 368-384.

[7]Described in John W. Caughey, *Bernardo de Gálvez in Louisiana, 1776-1783* (Vol. 4 of the University of California at Los Angeles Publications in Social Sciences: Berkeley, 1934), 187-214.

[8]*Ibid.*, 215-242. James Colbert had lived for forty years with the Chickasaws, had a rich lodging and about fifty-five Negroes, and several sons by Chickasaw women. He made a quixotic effort to get the release of the leaders in the Natchez uprising in 1781 by seizing Spanish travelers on the Mississippi, among whom was the wife of Governor Francisco Cruzat of St. Louis. The scheme failed, chiefly because Colbert relied on the pledged honor of his prisoners to return to captivity unless the Natchez leaders were released.

[9]William Bartram, "Observations on the Creek and Cherokee Indians," *Transactions of the American Ethnological Society*, 3 vols. (New York, 1845-1853), III, 31-32.

[10]The Spanish campaigns are described in Caughey, *Bernardo de Gálvez in Louisiana*, 149-214.

[11]William Panton was the principal figure in Panton, Leslie and Company, with whom McGillivray concerted for carrying on the Indian trade. This British company had traded at St. Augustine and St. Marks during the English period. After the transfer of Florida to Spain, it was permitted to continue business temporarily. This permission was extended, and, largely through McGillivray's influence, the company was permitted to expand its monopoly to Pensacola (1785), Mobile (1789), the Cherokee country (1792), and Chickasaw Bluffs (1795). See Marie Taylor Greenslade, "William Panton, 1745-1801," *The Florida Historical Society Quarterly*, XIV (1935), 107-129.

[12]Panton to Miró, July 12, 1790, in Caughey, *McGillivray of the Creeks,* 268. Estevan Miró was Gálvez' right hand man in Louisiana during the American Revolution. He was sent to Havana in 1780 to persuade the captain general to support the campaigns against Mobile and Pensacola, and two years later he was assigned the important task of suppressing the Natchez rebellion. He became acting governor of Louisiana in Gálvez' absence and succeeded him in the office, which post he held until 1792.

[13]Arturo O'Neill was the Spanish official in closest contact with McGillivray. Born in Dublin in 1736, O'Neil emigrated to Spain with his parents. In 1762 he served in military campaigns in Portugal and Algiers, and subsequently in Brazil.

[14]Benjamin Hawkins left the senior class at the College of New Jersey at the outbreak of the Revolution to join Washington's staff as French interpreter. He was a member of Congress, 1781-84 and 1786-87, and United States Senator from North Carolina, 1789-95. Then he became agent to the Creeks and general superintendent of the Indians south of the Ohio. For sixteen years he kept them at peace, instructed them in agriculture and animal husbandry, and earned for himself the name, "Beloved Man of the Four Nations." He was, in a way, successor to McGillivray in dominant influence over the Southeastern Indians.

[15]Andrew Pickens was a pioneer on the South Carolina frontier. He fought with distinction in the Revolution, especially at Cowpens. Hopewell, his plantation on the Oconee, was the scene of treaties with the Chickasaws, Choctaws, and Cherokees in 1785 and 1786. McGillivray came to have an excellent opinion of him.

[16]Joseph Martin, a veteran of the French and Indian War, of Dunmore's War, and of the Revolutionary War, was also an experienced Indian negotiator, having been commissioned by Patrick Henry to deal with the Cherokees in 1777 and again in 1783 to treat with the Southern Indians.

[17]McGillivray to Pickens, September 5, 1785, American State Papers, Indian Affairs, I, 17-18.

[18]McGillivray to Zéspedes, April 25, 1786, Library of Congress, East Florida Papers 114 Jg.

[19]McGillivray to Zéspedes, January 5, 1788, in Caughey, *McGillivray of the Creeks,* 165-166.

[20]John Miller was senior partner of the Providence firm of Miller and Bonamy. He was a determined foe of Panton, Leslie and Company. John Murray, fourth Earl of Dunmore, the famous Governor Dunmore of New York, 1770-71, and of Virginia, 1772-76, known also in connection with Dunmore's War, was a member of the House of Lords, 1776-87, and a governor of the Bahama Islands, 1787-96.

[21]McGillivray to Leslie, November 20, 1788, in Caughey, *McGillivray of the Creeks,* 207.

[22]Pickens and Osborne to the Creeks, April 20, 1789, Archivo General de Indias, at Seville, Papeles de Cuba, 182.

[23]President Washington appointed Benjamin Lincoln, Cyrus Griffin, and David Humphreys to act as commissioners. They sailed from New York on August 31, reached Savannah on September 10, and set out at once for Rock Landing. They carried on a correspondence with the governor of Georgia and with their predecessors as commis-

sioners, Osborne and Pickens. Benjamin Lincoln of Massachusetts was one of Washington's most trusted generals. He was severely wounded at Saratoga. At Yorktown he received Cornwallis' sword. Besides this Indian commission, he was sent in 1793 to try to arrange a treaty with the Indians north of the Ohio. Cyrus Griffin's chief claim to fame is that he was president of the Congress under the Articles of Confederation in 1788. David Humphreys had a reputation as a poet and a friend of Washington. He had been an aide-de-camp to the general during the Revolution and then accompanied him to Mount Vernon. From 1784 to 1786 he was in London and Paris as secretary of legation for Franklin, Adams, and Jefferson.

[24]Marinus Willett is well characterized by McGillivray as a man of experience, enterprise, and honor. Willett's revolutionary activities were chiefly in western New York, at Oriskany and Oswego in particular. He was for a time sheriff of New York and subsequently mayor. See *A Narrative of the Military Actions of Col. Marinus Willett, Taken Chiefly from his own Manuscript,* ed. William Marinus Willett (New York, 1831).

[25]For a description of the ceremony see Caughey, *McGillivray of the Creeks,* 278-279.

[26]Quoted in McMaster, *op. cit.,* I, 604.

[27]McGillivray to Leslie, November 10, 1790, Spanish translation in Archivo Nacional de Havana, Expedientes de Intendencia, 3889 bis.

[28]Francis Hector, Baron de Carondelet, has been characterized as the worst possible successor to Miró as governor and intendant of Louisiana. He did know French and he was a brother-in-law of Las Casas, the captain general at Havana, but he did not understand the border problems that he would have to face, and he was not temperamentally suited to meet them. His impetuosity in plunging into action frequently threatened Spain's position with the Americans and with the Indians. Arthur Preston Whitaker discusses Carondelet in his *The Spanish-American Frontier: 1783-1795* (Boston and New York, 1927), 153-170.

[29]McGillivray to Panton, November 28, 1792, Caughey, *McGillivray of the Creeks,* 348.

PART III: CALIFORNIA

CALIFORNIA AND THE NATION: A TALLY OF TWO HISTORIES
Reprinted with permission from the *California Historical Society Quarterly,* XL (1961), 193-202. This paper was presented at the first meeting of the California Historical Society at its southern California headquarters, El Alisal, on May 25, 1961.

[1]Chapman, *History of California* (New York, 1921), 492, citing Fita y Colomé, "*Noticia de la California,* obra anónima del P. Andrés Marcos Burriel," Real academia de la historia, *Boletín,* LII (Madrid, 1908), 396-438.

GOLD IS THE CORNERSTONE: AN ASSAY
Reprinted with permission from John W. Caughey, *Gold is the Cornerstone* (Berkeley: University of California Press, 1948), 291-299.

[1]John Bidwell "noted not merely the methods they [the miners] were using, but the kind of soil they were working, which reminded him strongly of gravels near his rancho at Chico, north of the Buttes. Returning home, he organized an expedition, prospected several locations along the Feather, and went to work with his Indian retainers at a spot soon named Bidwell's Bar."

DON BENITO WILSON: AN AVERAGE SOUTHERN CALIFORNIAN
Reprinted with permission from the *Huntington Library Quarterly,* II (1939), 285-300. A version of the paper was read before the Pacific Coast Branch of the American Historical Association, at Stanford University in December 1938.

[1]"Observations on Early Days in California and New Mexico", a manuscript dictated for Bancroft in 1877; printed, apparently from an imperfect copy, in R. G. Cleland, *Pathfinders* (Los Angeles, 1929), 371-416, and more satisfactorily edited and annotated

by Arthur Woodward in the Historical Society of Southern California, *Annual Publication for 1934,* 74-150.

[2]Big Bear Lake was so named because on one occasion Wilson and twenty-two companions lassoed twenty-two bears there.

[3]Compare Caughey's later textbook account of Wilson's career in his *California,* 2nd ed. (Englewood Cliffs, New Jersey, 1953), 214, 234, 264, 326, 418.

[4]An uncatalogued collection, consisting of several hundred letters. About one-third consists of correspondence with the family; most of the rest are letters received from political and business associates, with an occasional draft or copy of Wilson's reply. The present paper, though it represents the first utilization of this collection, is in the nature of an introductory appraisal rather than an exhaustive exploitation.

[5]The principal source is Wilson's "Observations," MS, as above. See also J. Albert Wilson, *History of Los Angeles County, California* (Thompson & West, 1880), 36-37; Hubert Howe Bancroft, *History of California,* 7 vols. (San Francisco, 1884-90), V, 777.

[6]Last will and testament, signed Benjn. Davis Wilson, and witnessed by Horace G. Wheeler, K. H. Dimmick, and W. G. Dryden. (All manuscripts cited in the paper, except as otherwise noted, are from the Wilson Papers in the Huntington Library.)

[7]Bancroft, *California,* V, 777.

[8]"Report on the Indians of Southern California," *Los Angeles Star,* January 15, 1853; reprinted, *ibid.,* July 18, 1868. Long extracts are given in Wilson, *Los Angeles County,* 87-90.

[9]E. F. Beale to B. D. Wilson, August 19, 1854.

[10]B. D. Wilson to [Wiley R. Wilson], April 12, 1854.

[11]"The Indians of Los Angeles County," serially in the *Los Angeles Star,* 1852, reprinted in book form, Los Angeles, 1926.

[12]E.g., see Scott & Sander to B. D. Wilson, June 2, 1857.

[13]William Anderes to B. D. Wilson, February 12, 1856.

[14]See various letters from Benjamin Hayes and H. R. Myles, 1855 and 1856. See also Harris Newmark, *Sixty Years in Southern California,* 3d ed. (Boston, 1930), 189-190.

[15]Tho. Foster to B. D. Wilson, January 1, 1856.

[16]B. D. Wilson to S. C. Foster, March 16, 1853.

[17]S. H. Willey to Mr. & Mrs. Wilson, December 30, 1854.

[18]Archi. H. Gillespie to Benj. T. [i. e., D.] Wilson, August 4, 1859.

[19]See various letters from W. B. T. Sanford and others.

[20]Wm. Marsh to B. D. Wilson, July 13, 1854.

[21]Wm. M. Gwin to B. D. Wilson, December 25, 1858; same to same, February 2, 1861.

[22]J. Earl to Wilson, April 30, 1857.

[23]J. Lancaster Brent to Wilson, November 2, 1858.

[24]Adolf Eberhart, a Swiss, "a hard working & honest man of good habits, and has been for Years in business, where he had to oversee Wines of all Descriptions, so that he knows not only the making of Wines but also how to keep it well." (Kohler and Frohling to B. D. Wilson, October 2, 1857).

[25]H. R. Myles to B. D. Wilson, February 22, 1856.

[26]James Wise to Wilson, May 4, 1857.

[27]Hobbs, Gilmore & Co. to B. D. Wilson, July 5, 1862.

[28]Carmick & Co. to B. D. Wilson & Son, October 17, 1865; J. H. Lyman to Wilson, February 25, 1873.

[29]Hobbs, Gilmore & Co. to B. D. Wilson, August 24, 1863.

[30]Sue [Wilson] to Father, February 27, 1864.

[31]A. Eberhart to B. D. Wilson, August 5, 1863.

[32]John B. Wilson to B. D. Wilson, September 6, 1865; George F. Hopper to B. D. Wilson, September 18, 1865.

[33][?] to B. D. Wilson, September 7, 1863.

[34]J. Phelps to B. D. Wilson, December 27, 1864.

[35]A. M. Campbell to B. D. Wilson, November 13, 1877.

[36]Nichols, Blum & Co. to B. D. Wilson, August 27, 1877.

[37]J. De Barth Shorb to President U. P. Rail Road, December 18, 1876, San Marino Rancho Papers, Huntington Library.

[38]Various letters in the late sixties and seventies.

[39]Jno. B. Wilson to Father, October 1 [1865].

[40]J. De Barth Shorb to J. D. Whitney, February 28, 1874, San Marino Rancho Papers. Professor Whitney incorporated this opinion in his article on California for the *Encyclopedia Brittannica.* For doing so he was roundly upbraided by Charles F. Lummis, in an installment of "The Right Hand of the Continent," *Out West,* XVIII (1903), 139-167.

[41]E. E. Hewitt to B. D. Wilson, December 17, 1871.

[42]T. H. Rose to Wilson, January 8, 1872; M. Kramer and H. D. Barrows to B. D. Wilson, T. D. Mott, and Asa Ellis, January 7, 1872. See also Newmark, *Sixty Years,* 418-419.

[43]J. W. North to B. D. Wilson, January 29, 1872.

[44]L. J. Rose to B. D. Wilson, January 19, 1872.

[45]J. De Barth Shorb to B. D. Wilson, January —, 1872.

[46]J. De Barth Shorb to President U. P. Rail Road, December 18, 1876, San Marino Rancho Papers; J. Strelitz to J. De Barth Shorb, February 12, 1878.

[47]Doolittle, Webster & Co. to B. D. Wilson & Co., February 14, 1878.

[48]J. P. Widney to B. D. Wilson, January 12, 1872; Phineas Banning to B. D. Wilson, October 26, 1872.

[49]Fred W. Mitchell to Wilson, October 17, 1872.

[50]J. W. Dallas to Wilson, December 2, 1872.

[51]C. G. Blauvett to Wilson, April 11, 1873.

[52]J. C. Masser to B. D. Wilson, January 29, 1876.

[53]Wm. H. Ross to B. D. Wilson, May 2, 1876.

[54]Ezra S. Carr to B. Wilson, February 2, 1873.

[55]J. De Barth Shorb to C. Cooper Spencer, May 8, 1870, San Marino Rancho Papers.

[56]J. De Barth Shorb to Herman Glass, January 9, 1877, *ibid.*

[57]Several examples in the Wilson Papers, including F. W. Wood to B. D. Wilson, January 4, 1878. As early as 1876 the company had issued an illustrated folder, *Description of Orange and Vine Lands in Los Angeles County.*

[58]Jno. D. Thorne to B. D. Wilson, July 30, 1877.

[59]Jeanie Spring Johns to B. D. Wilson, January 22, 1876.

[60]J. De Barth Shorb to Wilson, March 25, 1870, San Marino Rancho Papers.

[61]T. H. Rose to B. D. Wilson, February 9, 1872.

[62]R. C. Stoneman to B. D. Wilson, March 29, 1876.

[63]J. De Barth Shorb to Wilson, March 27, 1870, San Marino Rancho Papers.

HUBERT HOWE BANCROFT

Reprinted with permission from the *American Historical Review*, L (1945), 461-470. A version of the paper was read at the Mississippi Valley Historical Association (Organization of American Historians) meeting in St. Louis on April 20, 1944.

[1]For example, Carl L. Cannon, *American Book Collectors and Collecting from Colonial Times to the Present* (New York, 1941), 96-102; Oscar Lewis, "The Launching of Bancroft's 'Native Races,'" *Colophon*, new style, I (1936), 323-332; William A. Morris, "The Origin and Authorship of the Bancroft Pacific States Publications: A History of a History," *Oregon Historical Quarterly*, IV (1903), 287-364; Rockwell D. Hunt, "Hubert Howe Bancroft: His Work and His Method," Historical Society of Southern California, *Publications*, VIII (1911), 158-173.

[2]Principal among his published works are the following: *Native Races*, 5 vols., (New York, 1874-75), reissued with *History of the Pacific States* (28 vols.) and with six supplementary volumes as the *Works*, 39 vols. (San Francisco, 1882-90); *Chronicles of the Builders*, 7 vols. and index (San Francisco, 1891-92); *The Book of the Fair*, 5 vols. (Chicago and San Francisco, 1893); *The Book of Wealth*, 10 vols. (New York, 1896-1908); *Vida de Porfirio Díaz* (San Francisco, 1887); *A Popular History of Mexico* (San Francisco, 1887); *Resources and Development of Mexico* (San Francisco, 1893); *The New Pacific* (New York, 1899); *Retrospection, Political and Personal* (New York, 1912); *History of Mexico* (New York, 1914); and *In These Latter Days* (Chicago, 1917).

[3]The chief source on Bancroft's early career is his *Literary Industries* (San Francisco, 1890), 47-167, wherein the rise of the business house is likewise described. On the latter point see also "A. L. Bancroft & Co.," *Pacific Printer*, June, 1877, and "A Cosmopolitan Publishing House," *Printers World*, March, 1881.

[4]On his collecting consult *Literary Industries*, *passim*, but especially pp. 168-217, 365-445, 468-561, and 618-649; his "Journal While in Europe, 1866-1867," a 240-page manuscript in the Bancroft Library; [Hubert Howe Bancroft], *The Bancroft Historical Library* (San Francisco, 1886); [*id.*], *Evolution of a Library* (n.p., [1901]); and Reuben Gold Thwaites, "Report on the Bancroft Library," *University* [*of California*] *Chronicle*, VIII (1905-1906), 126-143.

[5]*Ibid.*

[6]In conversation with the writer.

[7]Bancroft, *Literary Industries*, 228-229.

[8]Bancroft's own description of his literary workshop and method appears in *Literary Industries*, 230-276, 562-617. See also Henry L. Oak, *"Literary Industries" in a New Light* (San Francisco, 1893), and Morris, in *Oregon Hist. Quar.*, IV.

[9]Oak, 57.

[10]Bancroft, *Literary Industries*, 361; or, as a modern writer has paraphrased it, "No budding historian before or since ever launched his maiden effort with a greater splash," Lewis, in *Colophon*, new style, I, 327.

[11]See in particular [Nathan J. Stone], *Information for Agents to Assist in Selling the Works of Hubert H. Bancroft* (n.p., n.d.).

[12]Reported in the Helena, Montana, *Daily Independent*, October 14, 1885, and the Bozeman, Montana, *Weekly Avant Courier*, May 13, 1886.

[13]George T. Clark, "Leland Stanford and H. H. Bancroft's 'History,' a Bibliographical Curiosity," Bibliographical Society of America, *Papers*, XXVII (1933), 12-23.

[14]Harry B. Hambly, "List of Subscribers to 'Chronicles of the Builders of the Commonwealth,' Stating Amount Subscribed and Paid," October, 1936, MS., Bancroft Library.

[15]Bancroft, *Literary Industries,* 777.

[16]*Ibid.,* 310.

[17]In particular see his column in the San Francisco *Examiner,* January 22, 1893.

[18]*Ibid.,* September 19-October 8, 1893.

[19]Henry L. Oak to H. H. Bancroft, April 3, 1892, printed in Oak, 66-67.

[20]Society of California Pioneers, *Misrepresentations of Early California History Corrected: Proceedings of the Society of California Pioneers in regard to Certain Misrepresentations of Men and Events in Early California History Made in the Works of Hubert Howe Bancroft and Commonly Known as Bancroft's Histories* (San Francisco, 1894).

[21]Morris, in *Oregon Hist. Quar.,* IV, and Hunt, in Hist. Soc. of Southern California, *Publications,* VIII.

[22]*Oregon Hist. Quar.,* XIX (1918), 74-75.

[23]San Francisco *Examiner,* March 3, 1918.

[24]Charles Edward Chapman, *A History of California, the Spanish Period* (New York, 1921), 499.

[25]Eugene C. Barker, *The Life of Stephen F. Austin* (Nashville, 1925), 532, 534.

[26]Bernard DeVoto, *The Year of Decision, 1846* (Boston, 1943), 525.

[27]Franklin Walker, *San Francisco's Literary Frontier* (New York, 1939), 302-315.

CALIFORNIA IN THIRD DIMENSION
Reprinted with permission from the *Pacific Historical Review,* XXVIII (1959), 111-129. This paper was John Caughey's presidential address to the Pacific Coast Branch of the American Historical Association (delivered at Whittier College in December, 1958).

[1]Henry R. Wagner, *Spanish Voyages to the Northwest Coast* (San Francisco, 1929), 90.

[2]John Muir, *The Mountains of California* (New York, 1894), 33.

[3]Herbert E. Bolton, ed., *Anza's California Expeditions* (Berkeley, 1930), IV, 145.

[4]John W. Caughey, ed., *The Indians of Southern California in 1852* (San Marino, 1952), 21-23.

[5]As reported in Hugo Reid's letters, serialized in the Los Angeles *Star* in 1851, and collected in book form as *The Indians of Los Angeles County* (Los Angeles, 1926), 33. See also Edward W. Gifford and Gwendoline Harris Block, eds., *California Indian Nights Entertainment* (Glendale, 1930).

[6]Mary Austin, *The American Rhythm* (New York, 1923), 91.

[7]*Dear Judas and Other Poems* (New York, 1929), 128.

[8]Frederick J. Teggart, ed., *Diary of Miguel Costansó* (Berkeley and Los Angeles, 1911), 42-43.

[9]*Voyage de la Pérouse autour du monde* (Paris, 1797), I, 249-283.

[10]George Vancouver, *A Voyage of Discovery to the North Pacific Ocean* (London, 1798), II, 4-9.

[11]Reproduced in Charles F. Lummis, *Flowers of Our Lost Romance* (Boston, 1929), 147-152.

[12]Charles L. Camp, ed., *James Clyman, American Frontiersman* (San Francisco, 1928), 187.

[13]Ruth Frey Axe, ed., *Bound for Sacramento* (Claremont, 1938), 64.

[14]Zoeth S. Eldredge, *History of California,* 5 vols. (San Francisco, 1915).

[15]Eight volumes, San Francisco, 1891-1892.

[16]*California* (Boston, 1886); *The Feud of Oakfield Creek* (Boston, 1887).

[17]James Rorty, *Children of the Sun and Other Poems* (New York, 1925), 57-59.

[18]The poem is strikingly and patly entitled "The Inquisitors." but the allusion is not at all to the Dies-Tenney-McCarthy variety.

THE LOCAL HISTORIAN: HIS OCCUPATIONAL HAZARDS AND COMPENSATIONS
Reprinted with permission from the *Pacific Historical Review,* XII (1943), 1-9. This paper was read before the History Guild of Southern California, at Pasadena, on December 30, 1942.

[1]Since 1940 Caughey's *California* has had two editions and over a dozen printings.

PART IV: WESTERN JUSTICE

INTRODUCTION: WESTERN JUSTICE
[1]John W. Caughey, *In Clear and Present Danger* (Chicago, 1958), 164-165.

THEIR MAJESTIES THE MOB
Reprinted with permission from John W. Caughey, *Their Majesties the Mob* (Chicago: University of Chicago Press, 1960), 1-25.

A UNIVERSITY IN JEOPARDY
Reprinted with permission from *Harper's Magazine* (November, 1950), 68-75.

A PLEA TO THE REGENTS OF THE UNIVERSITY OF CALIFORNIA
This statement was read at the July 21, 1950, meeting of the regents while they were considering Caughey's dismissal. These remarks later appeared in pamphlet form and, under a different title, in *Frontier,* on August 15, 1950.

TRUSTEES OF ACADEMIC FREEDOM
Reprinted with permission from the *Bulletin of the American Association of University Professors,* XXXVII (1951), 427-441.

THE PRACTICAL DEFENSE OF ACADEMIC FREEDOM
Reprinted with permission from the *Bulletin of the American Association of University Professors,* XXXVIII (1952), 245-260.

[1]Transcript of the minutes of the Board of Regents, University of California, March 31, 1950.

[2]"Trustees of Academic Freedom," *Bulletin of the American Association of University Professors,* XXXVII (1951), 427-441.

[3]In 1954, two years after Caughey published this paper, Congress did outlaw the party when it passed the Communist Control Act.

PART V: CAUGHEY'S CREED

UNFINISHED BUSINESS
Reprinted with permission from John W. Caughey, John Hope Franklin, and Ernest R. May, *Land of the Free: A History of the United States* (Pasadena: Franklin Publications, Inc., 1967), 618-619.

OUR CHOSEN DESTINY
Reprinted with permission from the *Journal of American History,* LII (1965), 239-251. This paper was Caughey's presidential address to the Organization of American Historians (delivered at Kansas City, Missouri, on April 22, 1965).

[1]At proofreading time, ninety days after these words were spoken, it is clear that the failure at the Bay of Pigs merely brought a reprieve from interventionism. Following the pattern of the Eisenhower-administered overthrow in Guatemala and the Kennedy attempt in Cuba, the Johnson administration moved with unprecedented might into

the Dominician Republic. The cost shows clearly in the depreciation of the Organization of American States and the devaluation of the Good Neighbor.

[2]By the end of July the American "advisers" have become outright combatants and the early commitment of American personnel is estimated at 200,000.

BIBLIOGRAPHY
OF CAUGHEY'S WRITINGS

CHRONOLOGICAL BIBLIOGRAPHY

BOOKS

The Emigrant's Guide to California, by Joseph E. Ware. Edited, with notes and introduction, by Caughey (Princeton: Princeton University Press, 1932).

History of the Pacific Coast (Los Angeles: The Author, 1933; New York: Prentice-Hall, Inc., 1938).

Bernardo de Gálvez in Louisiana, 1776-1783 (Berkeley: University of California Press, 1934).

McGillivray of the Creeks (1st ed., Norman: University of Oklahoma Press, 1938; 2d ed., 1959).

California (1st ed., New York: Prentice-Hall, 1940; 2d ed., 1953).

Hubert Howe Bancroft: Historian of the West (Berkeley: University of California Press, 1946).

The Los Angeles Star, 1851-1864, by William B. Rice. Edited by Caughey (Berkeley: University of California Press, 1947).

Gold is the Cornerstone (Berkeley: University of California Press, 1948).

East Florida, 1783-1785: A File of Documents Assembled and Many of Them Translated, by Joseph B. Lockey. Edited, with a foreword, by Caughey (Berkeley: University of California Press, 1949).

Robert Owen: Social Idealist, by Rowland Harvey. Edited, with a foreword, by Caughey (Berkeley: University of California Press, 1949).

Rushing for Gold. Edited, with an introduction, by Caughey (Berkeley: University of California Press, 1949).

Seeing the Elephant, Letters of R. R. Taylor, Forty-niner. Edited, with an introduction, by Caughey (Los Angeles: Ward Ritchie Press, 1951).

The Indians of Southern California in 1852, by Benjamin D. Wilson. Edited, with notes and introduction, by Caughey (San Marino: Huntington Library Press, 1952).

America Since 1763: A Survey of Its History (México: Instituto Panamericano de Geografía e Historia, 1954).

In Clear and Present Danger: The Crucial State of Our Freedoms (Chicago: University of Chicago Press, 1958).

Six Months in the Gold Mines, by E. Gould Buffum. Edited, with an introduction, by Caughey (Los Angeles: Ward Ritchie Press, 1959; 2d ed., 1965).

Their Majesties the Mob (Chicago: University of Chicago Press, 1960).

California Heritage: An Anthology of History and Literature. Edited by John and LaRee Caughey (Los Angeles: Ward Ritchie Press, 1962).

California's Own History. By John and LaRee Caughey (San Francisco: Century Schoolbook Press, 1963).

Windows on the Pacific. By John Caughey, LaRee Caughey, and Katherine Peter (San Francisco: Century Schoolbook Press, 1963).

A History of the United States. By John W. Caughey and Ernest R. May (Chicago: Rand McNally & Company, 1964).

Land of the Free: A History of the United States. By John W. Caughey, John Hope Franklin, and Ernest R. May (Pasadena: Franklin Publications, Inc., 1965; rev. ed., 1966, 1967; 2 vols., 1966; New York: Benziger Brothers, 1966).

Turner, Bolton, and Webb: Three Historians of the American Frontier. By Wilbur R. Jacobs, John W. Caughey, and Joe B. Frantz. (Seattle: University of Washington Press, 1965).

School Segregation on Our Doorstep: The Los Angeles Story. By John and LaRee Caughey. (Los Angeles: Quail Books, 1966).

ARTICLES AND PAMPHLETS

"The Panis Mission to Pensacola, 1778," *Hispanic American Historical Review,* X (1930), 480-489.

"Willing's Expedition down the Mississippi, 1778," *Louisiana Historical Quarterly,* XV (1932), 5-36.

"Bernardo de Gálvez and the English Smugglers on the Mississippi, 1777," *Hispanic American Historical Review,* XII (1932), 46-58.

"Alexander McGillivray and the Creek Crisis, 1783-1784," in *New Spain and the Anglo-American West* (2 vols., Los Angeles: Privately printed, 1932), I, 263-288.

"The Natchez Rebellion of 1781 and Its Aftermath," *Louisiana Historical Quarterly,* XVI (1933), 57-83.

"The Value of History in Modern Life," *California Daily Bruin,* July 7, 1933.

"A Survey of the Field for Research in Local History," in *Social Science Research in the Los Angeles Area* (Los Angeles: University of California Institute for Social Science Research, 1936), 95-113.

"Southwest from Salt Lake in 1849," *Pacific Historical Review,* VI (1937), 143-164.

"The Jacob Y. Stover Narrative," *Pacific Historical Review,* VI (1937), 165-181.

"Don Benito Wilson: An Average Southern Californian," *Huntington Library Quarterly,* II (1939), 285-300.

"Shaping a Literary Tradition," *Pacific Historical Review,* VIII (1939), 201-214.

"Current Discussion of California's Migrant Labor Problem," *Pacific Historical Review,* VIII (1939), 347-354.

"A Criticism of the Critique of Webb's *The Great Plains,*" *Mississippi Valley Historical Review,* XXVII (1940), 442-444.

"Life in California in 1849 as Described in the 'Journal' of George F. Kent," *California Historical Society Quarterly,* XX (1941), 26-46.

A Tribute to William B. Rice (Inglewood, Calif.: Richard Jones, 1942), 9 pp.

"The Local Historian: His Occupational Hazards and Compensations," *Pacific Historical Review,* XII (1943), 1-9.

"William B. Rice," in *William Money, A Southern California Savant,* by William B. Rice (Los Angeles: Dawson's Bookshop, 1943), 60-61.

"Hubert Howe Bancroft, Historian of Western America," *American Historical Review,* L (1945), 461-470.

"Flag of the Bear," *Westways,* XXXVIII (June, 1946), 8-9.

"The Conquest," *Westways,* XXXVIII (July, 1946), 10-11.

"California's First Newspaper," *Westways,* XXXVIII (Aug., 1946), 8-9.

"Comic Opera Conquest," *Westways,* XXXVIII (Aug., 1946), 9.

"The Great Battle of Chino," *Westways,* XXXVIII (Sept., 1946), 12-13.

"California Marathon," *Westways,* XXXVIII (Sept., 1946), 13.

"Tragedy in the Sierra," *Westways,* XXXVIII (Oct., 1946), 14-15.

"Across the Continent With Kearny," *Westways,* XXXVIII (Nov., 1946), 14-15.

"The Battle of San Pasqual," *Westways,* XXXVIII, (Dec., 1946), 16-17.

"The First Inhabitants of the Coast Ranges," in Roderick Peattie, *The Coast Ranges* (New York: The Vanguard Press, 1946), 23-43.

"Headlands in California Writing," in Roderick Peattie, *The Coast Ranges* (New York: The Vanguard Press, 1946), 165-185.

"The Mosaic of Western History," *Mississippi Valley Historical Review,* XXIII (1947), 595-606.

"The Mill that Ground Out Gold," *Westways,* XL (Jan., 1948), 10-11.

"California's Naturalization Papers," *Westways,* XL (Feb., 1948), 4-5.

"The Little Red Schoolhouse Comes to California," *Westways,* XL (May, 1948), 14-15.

"A Yankee Trader in the Gold Rush: Letters of Walter Gardner, 1851-1857," *Pacific Historical Review,* XVII (1948), 411-428.

"California's Intellectual Centennial," *California Library Bulletin,* X (1948), 55-58.

"Gold Fever and How It Spread," *Westways,* XLI (March, 1949), 8-9.

"Rocket Men on the Mexican Border," *Westways,* XLI (July, 1949), 12-13.

"The Steamboat Era," *Westways,* XLI (Aug., 1949), 12-13.

"Samuel T. Farquhar," *Pacific Historical Review,* XVIII (1949), 315-317.

"California's Founding Fathers," *Westways,* XLI (Sept., 1949), 10-11.

"The Race to Discover Humboldt Bay," *Westways,* XLI (Nov., 1949), 6-7.

"Legislature of a Thousand Drinks," *Westways,* XLI (Dec., 1949), 8-9.

"There's History in Those Files," *California Librarian,* XII (1950), 19-20.

"California After 100 Years," *Westwood Hills Press* (Feb. 9, 1950), 1, 6.

"A Statement of Principles," *Frontier,* I (Aug., 15, 1950), 7-8.

A Plea to the Regents of the University of California (Los Angeles: Privately printed, 1950), 4 pp.

"The Editor's Page," *Pacific Historical Review,* XIX (1950), 349-350.

"A University in Jeopardy," *Harper's Magazine* (Nov., 1950), 68-75.

"The Teaching of Southwestern History," in *A Conference on Teaching and Research in Southwestern History* (Los Angeles: Occidental College, 1950).

"Louis Knott Koontz," *Pacific Historical Review,* XX (1951), 327-329.

"Trustees of Academic Freedom," *Bulletin of the American Association of University Professors,* XXXVII (1951), 427-441.

"The Spanish Southwest: An Example of Subconscious Regionalism," in Merrill Jensen, ed., *Regionalism in America* (Madison: University of Wisconsin Press, 1951), 173-186.

"Rare Books and Research in History," in *Rare Books and Research* (Los Angeles: University of California Library, 1951), 31-36.

"Hubert Howe Bancroft," in *The Handbook of Texas* (Austin: The Texas State Historical Association, 1952), I, 104-105.

"Rival Methods of Colonization," in Richard W. Leopold and Arthur Link, eds., *Problems in American History* (New York: Prentice-Hall, inc., 1952), 1-43.

"Academic Freedom: Bulwark of Democracy," *Bulletin of the Bureau of School Service,* XXIV (March, 1952), 27-37.

"The Practical Defense of Academic Freedom," *Bulletin of the American Association of University Professors,* XXXVIII (1952), 244-260.

"Historians' Choice: Results of a Poll on Recently Published American History and Biography," *Mississippi Valley Historical Review,* XXXIX (1952), 289-302.

"Herbert Eugene Bolton," *Pacific Historical Review,* XXII (1953), 109-112.

"The Decline and Fall of the Fifth Amendment," *Frontier,* IV (Aug., 1953), 14-15, 18.

"Trends in Historical Criticism," *Mississippi Valley Historical Review,* XL (1954), 619-628.

"California's Fling at Dueling," in *Theater Arts* (Los Angeles: University of California Theater Arts Department, 1954), 7-11.

"Aid to Education: F.O.B. Detroit," *Frontier,* VII (April, 1956), 5-6.

"How to Fire a Communist," St. Louis *Post-Dispatch,* April 6, 1956. [Reprinted in *Frontier,* VII (May, 1956), 27.]

"A Bagful of Bad Little Boys," *Western Folklore,* XV (1956), 289. [Written with LaRee Caughey.]

"A Program Note for the Crucible [A play by Arthur Miller]," in *Theater 170* (Los Angeles: University of California Theater Arts Department, 1956).

The Section on United States History, in R. R. Palmer ed., *Atlas of World History* (New York: Rand McNally Co., 1957).

"Under Our Strange Device: A Review of the 'Review'," *Mississippi Valley Historical Review,* XLIV (1957), 519-535.

"Their Majesties the Mob," *Pacific Historical Review,* XXVI (1957), 217-234.

"Toward an Understanding of the West," *Utah Historical Quarterly,* XXVII (1959), 7-24.

"The American West: Frontier and Region," *Arizona and the West,* I (1959), 7-12.

"California in Third Dimension," *Pacific Historical Review,* XXVIII (1959), 111-129.

"Major Issues on the Home Front," *Social Education,* XXIII (1959), 254-257.

Foreword to John E. Baur, *The Health Seekers of Southern California, 1870-1900* (San Marino: Huntington Library Press, 1959), vii-ix.

"California and the Nation: A Tally of Two Histories," *California Historical Society Quarterly,* XL (1961), 193-302.

"Wilderness and the American Dream," in David Brower, *Wilderness: America's Living Heritage* (San Francisco: Sierra Club, 1961), 32-34, 40-41.

"Robinson Jeffers," *Pacific Historical Review,* XXXI (1962), 105-106.

Returning a Salute (Los Angeles: Privately printed, 1962), 13 pp.

A Call for Integrated Schools. By LaRee and John Caughey (Los Angeles: American Civil Liberties Union of Southern California, 1963), 23 pp.

Keepers of the Heritage. The Edith M. Coulter Lecture (Los Angeles: California Library Association, 1963), 17 pp.

"Herbert Eugene Bolton," *American West,* I (Winter, 1964), 36-39, 79.

"Young Californians and Their History," *Southern California Quarterly,* XLVI (1964), 1-10.

"Our Chosen Destiny," *Journal of American History,* LII (1965), 239-251.

"The Long Transition," *Westways,* LVIII (Oct., 1966), 45-48.

"The Midas Touch," *Westways,* LIX (May, 1967), 54-55.

"The Politics of Adoption," *California Social Science Review,* VI (June, 1967), 34-40.

Segregation Blights Our Schools (Los Angeles: Quail Books, 1967), 20 pp.

Opportunities in American Indian History Study (Los Angeles: Privately printed, 1967), 42 pp.

"Endless Crisis," in Jack Lyle, ed., *The Black American and the Press* (Los Angeles: Ward Ritchie Press, 1968), 15-22.

"Segregation Increases in Los Angeles," *California Teachers Association Journal,* LXIV (Oct., 1968), 39-41.

"On Leaving the Editorship," *Pacific Historical Review,* XXXVII (1968), 373-379.

INDEX

INDEX

Academic Freedom, 207-214, 222-235
Academy of Pacific Coast History, 148
Acadians, 47, 67. *See also* Louisiana
Adair, James, 74-75
Adams, John Quincy, 7
Alaska, 6, 11, 15, 16, 24, 25, 32
Alvord, Clarence W., 102
American Association of University Professors, xii, 170, 209-210, 219-220, 222, 228, 234
American Civil Liberties Union of Southern California, xii, xx, xxvi, 170, 248
American Civil War, 21, 118, 248-249
American Council of Learned Societies, xiii, xviii
American Dental Association, xxii
American Frontier, xii, xxiv-xxv, 11, 16, 17; as Region, 3-8 passim, 25-27; Historians of, 25. *See also* Bolton, Turner, Webb
American Historical Association, Pacific Coast Branch, xiii, xxiv, 239
American Revolution, 48, 68, 74, 78-79, 171, 243-244; Spanish activity in, xiii-xiv, 41-42, 61-62, 67-71; in Southwest, 261-262 *n 23*, 262 *n 24*
American West, 11, 19, 23-25, 27; discriminated against, 18, 21, 23
Ames, Fisher, 72
Apalache, Florida, 86
Apaches, 63-64, 73
Arizona, 10, 32-38 passim, 114; mining in, 111
Arizona and the West, xiii, xxiv, 25
Armijio, General Antonio, 20
Arriaga, Julián de, 58
Arrington, Leonard, 25
Atherton, Gertrude, 143
Aubry, Philip, 45-50 passim, 52
Austin, Mary, xxiv, 107, 136, 138
Austin, Moses, 12
Austin, Stephen F., 8, 22
Austin, Texas, viii
Australia, 110, 185

Baegert, Johann Jakob, 105
Bahama Islands, 86-87, 261 *n 20*
Balize, Louisiana, 46, 47
Bancroft, George, 105, 106
Bancroft, Hubert Howe, xiv, xv, 13, 25, 106, 114, 115, 141, 143, 145, 146, 148; life and works of, 126-135 passim, 155, 157, 158, 162, 171, 187, 265 *n 2*
Bancroft Library, x, 101, 128, 132, 133, 148-149, 154-156
Banning, Phineas, 116, 126
Barcelona, Cyril de, 57, 58
Barstow, David P., 175, 188
Baur, John, xii
Bay of Pigs, 252, 267-268 *n 1* (Part V)
Beale, Edward F., 115
Bear Flag Revolt, 143, 146
Becerril, Diego, 63
Biddle, Francis, 228
Bidwell, John, 110; Quoted on Gold Rush, 262 *n 1* (Part III)
Bieber, Ralph P., 28
Bierce, Ambrose, 107, 131, 134, 145, 147
Bingham, Edwin, xii
Bloom, Lansing, 27-28
Bobb, Bernard, xii
Bolton, Herbert Eugene, viii-xi, xiii, 13, 101, 106, 128, 141, 148; Students of, 148-149
Boone, Daniel, 6
Boscana, Gerónimo, 142
Boston, Massachusetts, 16
Boston Tea Party, 78, 171, 244
Boulder Dam, 8, 18, 37
Bouligny, Francisco, 67
Bowles, William Augustus, 87, 88
Bradford, William, 105
Breen, Patrick, 105
British Colonies in North America, ix, xix, 3, 6, 9, 10, 41, 57, 61, 71, 102, 241-242, 254; Historians of, 103, 105. *See also* Bahama Islands
Brown, Edmund G. (Pat), 100
Brown, Thomas, 87
Brown v. Board of Education, xx, 245
Browne, J. Ross, 129
Brownell, Herbert, 179
Bruff, J. Goldsborough, 144, 145
Bryan, William Jennings, viii
Bucareli, Antonio María, 53
Buffum, E. Gould, xv
Buntline, Ned, 5, 13
Burriel, Andrés Marcos, 105
Butler, Father, 68

Cabeza de Vaca, Álvar Núñez, 30
Cabrillo, Juan Rodríguez, 3, 12, 30, 136
Cahüenga, Battle of, 115
California, 14-15, 28-29, 32, 36-37, 108 118, 178, 193; Agriculture, 17, 36, 116-119, 121-126, 157, 162; Politics, 22, 98, 117; Industry, 23, 34, 37, 98-99, 124-125, 162; Transportation, 32-33, 109; History, 97-99, 101-113, 126-134, 145-146, 148-150, 153-156, 159-163; Literature, 107-108, 135-153; Gold Rush,

108-113, 115, 144-145, 185; Descriptions of, 116, 120, 122-125; Name of, 139-140; Under Mexico, 141-143; Vigilantees in, 156, 171, 173-178, 182-183, 186; Loyalty and Communism, 167-171, 178, 190, 227-235; Oath Controversy in, 191-209, 214-215, 221-235
California Historical Society, 101, 159-160
California State Board of Education, xxi-xxiv
Capital Punishment, 104, 247
Caribbean, 7, 31; United States Intervention in, 250-251
Carondelet, Francis Hector, Baron de, 92, 262 *n 28*
Carpenter, Edwin, xii
Carr, Ezra S., 122
Carson, James H., 144
Carson, Kit, 16
Cattle Frontier, 6, 17, 32, 33
Caughey, Emily Walton, viii
Caughey, John Walton, passim, but especially: Personality, vii, xi, xxvi-xxvii, 160, 169, 247, 253; Early Life, viii-x; Education, viii, ix, x; Reputation, viii, xix, xx, xxi, 239-240; Teaching Career, viii, x-xiv passim, 169-170, 200, 206-207, 221, 239; Students of, xii, xxvi; on History, 97-108, 135-136, 154-163, 160; on Vigilantism, 189-191; on Religion, 206, 241-242, 248, 254; on Bay of Pigs, 252, 267-268 *n 1*
Caughey, John Walton, and University of California Oath Controversy, 167-171, 191-205, 208, 221, 228, 231; his Plea to Regents, 205-209; on Control of Communism, 207, 228-229, 233-235; on Academic Freedom, 207-208, 210, 221, 231-233; on the Faculty, 217-218, 233-234
Caughey, LaRee, xv, xx, xxiv-xxvi
Caughey, Rudolph Weyerhaeuser, viii
Central High School, Little Rock, Arkansas, 171
Cermeño, Sebastián Rodríguez, 139
Chaffey, George, 8, 22, 161
Chandler, Raymond, 13
Chapman, Charles E., 105, 106, 133, 141, 161
Charles III of Spain, 28, 41-43 passim, 49, 51, 62
Charleston, South Carolina, xiv, 75, 78
Chihuahua Frontier, 64
Civil Liberties, vii, xviii-xx, xxiii, 146, 152, 158; for Negroes, 171-173, 181, 246-248; in Early America, 241-243. *See also* Vigilantees
Clark, Arthur H., 28, 102, 159
Clark, George Rogers, 68-70, 102
Clavigero, Francisco Javier, 105
Cleland, Robert Glass, 106, 141, 143, 150, 187
Clinton, George, 90
Clinton, Tennessee, 172, 179
Clyman, James M., 142
Coe, William Robertson, 101
Colbert, James, 79, 260 *n 8*
Colorado, 21, 23, 28-29, 32, 111
Colton, Walter, 143
Committee for Representative University Government, xviii
Communism, xvi-xix, xxii, xxiii; Investigated, 168-169; Anti-Communism, 190-191, 228-229, 249-250; Spread of, 194-196, 207, 229
Comstock, Henry Thomas Paige, 111-112
Condon, Edward U., 185
Cooper, James Fenimore, 5, 106-107
Corle, Edwin, 107
Costansó, Miguel, 105, 139
Council of Indies, 48-49
Creeks, xiv, 73, 78; Customs, 76-77, 80; Tribal lands, 79-80; Relations with Spain, 81-85, 87-92 passim; Relations with the United States, 81-82, 84-86, 88-91, 261-262 *n 23*
Crespi, Juan, 139, 160
Crisis Magazine, xxiv
Cuellar, Lope de, 62-63
Culture in West, 22, 133-134, 135-163 passim

Dana, Richard Henry, 12, 105, 107, 142-143, 182
Dane, G. Ezra, 145
Davis, William Heath, 97
Delano, Alonso, 144
Derby, George, 144-145
Deutsch, Monroe, 202
De Voto, Bernard, 133
Días, Melchoir, 139
Dies, Martin, 186, 195, 228, 250
Dobie, J. Frank, 28
Donner Party, 175
Doris Duke American Indian History Study Project, xii
Douglas, Donald, 8, 22
Douglas, William O., 228-229
Du Bois, W. E. B., xxiii
Duggan, Lawrence, 184
Dumke, Glenn S., xii, 148, 150
Dunmore, John Murray, Lord, 86-87, 261 *n 20*

Eastland, James O., 184
Eayrs, George W., 140

Eberhart, Adolf, 263 *n 24*
Echevarría, Santiago José, 57-58
Eisenhower, Dwight, xix, 246, 251
Elbert, Samuel, 78
Eldridge, Zoeth S., 106, 146, 148
Ellison, William H., 148, 188
Emerson, Ralph Waldo, 107, 129
European Expansion into West, 6-11, 16, 19, 28-32, 35. *See also* Immigration, Louisiana
Explorers in West, 6, 16, 28, 30-31

Falkland Islands, 57
Fergusson, Erna, 28
Fisher, Vardis, 13, 17
Florida, 30, 41, 71, 72, 79, 81-87 passim, 251; Trade with Louisiana, 57, 59
Font, Pablo, 137, 139
Forbes, Alexander, 106
Fort Bridger, 175
Fort Toulouse, 75, 260 *n 4*
Franklin, Benjamin, xxi, 106, 250, 254
Franklin, John Hope, xxi-xxiv passim
Frémont, John C., 12, 16, 132, 136, 142, 143, 156
Freneau, Philip, 106
French America, ix, 6, 9, 19, 31; Louisiana colony, 42-49
Fur Trade, 8, 10, 11, 16, 23, 32

Gadsden Purchase, 29
Gage, Thomas, 57
Gálvez, Bernardo de, xiii-xiv, 67, 81, 261 *n 12*; Early Career, 62-63; Indian policy, 62-66; Evaluation, 67-68; Aid to Americans, 70; Close of Career, 71-72
Gálvez, José de, 62
Gálvez, Matías de, 62, 72
Garcés, Francisco, 139
Gardner, David P., 255 *n 6*
Gardner, Walter, xv
Geiger, Maynard J., 104
George III of England, 243
George, Henry, 134
Georgia, 74, 78, 79, 90-92; Attitude toward Creeks, 84-86, 90-91, 261-262 *n 23*; Indian Policy, 89-92 passim
Giannini, A. P., 8, 22
Gibault, Father, 69
Gibson, George, 61
Gilman, Daniel Coit, 129
Gold is the Cornerstone, xv, 98
Gold Rush, 13, 18, 32, 98, 108-113, 115, 144-146; Violence during, 174-178, 186; Trails West, 175-177, 180; Orientals in, 185
Grand Coulee Dam, 8, 18, 22
Great Britain, 74, 78-79, 81, 87
Greeley, Horace, 13, 126
Greenwalt, Emmett, xii
Gregg, Josiah, 12
Grey, Zane, 5, 13
Griffin, Cyrus, 88-89, 261-262 *n 23*
Griffin, Dr. John S., 116
Grimaldi, Marqués de, 48
Gwin, William, 117, 126

Hafen, LeRoy, 13, 28, 148
Haldimand, Frederick, 57
Hargraves, E. H., 110
Harte, Francis Bret, 107, 134, 188, 190
Havana, Cuba, 48, 53, 56, 68, 71-72
Hawaii, 7, 11, 15, 16, 21, 23, 24, 256 *n 2* (Part I)
Hawkins, Benjamin, 84, 89, 261 *n 14*
Health-seekers in West, 7, 17, 18
Hearst, George, 112
Henry, Patrick, 69, 261 *n 16*
Hereford, Dr. T. A., 115
Hide Trade in West, 17, 23, 32
Historical Society of Southern California, xiii, 159
History, ix, x, 25, 253-255; Beginning with Indians, 3, 15, 30; Research Opportunities in West, 4, 101, 114, 134, 152-163; Publishing in West, 28, 38, 101-102, 159-160; Local and Regional, 99-113, 154-163; Censorship of, 158
Hittell, Theodore H., 106, 145-146, 148, 187
Hollywood, California, 4, 12, 18, 33-35 passim; Communist Investigation, 174, 179, 180
House Un-American Activities Committee (United States Congress), 180, 184, 186, 230, 249
Hudson's Bay Company, 16, 111
Humphreys, David, 88-89, 261-262, *n 23*
Huntington Library, 28, 38, 101, 102, 114, 150, 154-155, 263 *n 4*
Hutchings, James M., 12
Hutchinson, Anne, 241, 254
Hutchinson, Thomas, 244
Huxley, Aldoux, 107
Hydroelectric Power, 8, 18, 22, 33-34, 36-37. *See also* Irrigation in West

Ide, William B., 143
Illinois Country, 60, 69-70
Immigration, 9, 11, 19, 34, 104-105; to Florida, 60-61; to Louisiana, 66-68
Indians, xii, 15, 17-19 passim, 21, 30-34 passim, 97, 98, 185, 247; Creeks, xiv, 41-42, 72-93; Reservations for, 34, 104, 115, 247; In Louisiana, 46, 52-55, 59-60; Apaches, 62-64; United States

Relations with, 84-92, 115, 247, 261 *n 11, 14, 15, 16*
Invention and the West, 8-10, 18, 23, 32
Irrigation in West, 18, 19, 22, 32-33, 36-37, 123, 124, 152
Irving, Washington, 106, 107
Irwin, Will, 107

Jackson, Helen Hunt, 13, 107, 138, 247
Jackson, James, 91
Jamestown, Virginia, 6, 30, 241
Jeffers, Robinson, xxiv, 107, 138
Johnson, Hiram, 22
Johnson, J. Neely, 173
Johnson, Lyndon B., vii, 251, 253
Johnson, Sir William, 74, 81
Jones, Idwal, 107
Jones, Thomas ap Catesby, 143
Jordan, David Starr, 8, 22
Jordan, Fred, xvii
Judah, Theodore, 8, 22

Kaiser, Henry J., 8, 22
Kantorowicz, Ernst, 168
Kaskaskia, 69
Kearney, Denis, 148
Kearney, Stephen, 20
Kemble, John H., 106, 150
Kentucky Frontier, 6, 10, 41
Kerrville, Texas, viii
King, Clarence, 136
Knox, Henry, 88, 90, 91, 92
Koontz, Louis Knott, 168
Ku Klux Klan, 172, 181, 183-184, 234-235, 249

La Follette, Robert M., 18
Land of the Free, xxi-xxiv, 170-171, 255 *n 15;* Quoted 239-240
La Pérouse, Jean François Galaup, Comte de, 140
Lee, Charles, 61
Levering Oath, xviii-xix, 169-170
Lewis, Oscar, 107
Lewis and Clark Expedition, 12, 13, 16
Lick, James, 134
Lincoln, Abraham, 244, 250, 254
Lincoln-Roosevelt League, 22
Lincoln, Benjamin, 88, 89, 261-262 *n 23*
Lincoln, Nebraska, viii
Little Tallassie, 74-75, 92, 260 *n 3*
Loewenberg, Jacob, 168
London, Jack, 107, 145, 147
Los Angeles, California, x, xx, xxi, 15, 33, 118, 120, 121, 124, 126, 173, 184, 248; Education in, 120, 121, 126; Owens Valley Water, 149
Los Angeles Board of Education, vii
Los Angeles Dodgers Baseball Club, vii, 23
Los Angeles Pioneer Oil Company, 119
Los Angeles and San Pedro Railroad Company, 119-120
Louisiana, xiii-xiv, 29, 41, 42; Smuggling in, 45, 51, 53, 56, 59, 65; Legal Institutions of, 52, 58-59; Indian Policy of, 52, 53-55, 59-60, 71; Relations with Britain, 53, 56, 261 *n 12;* Defense of 57, 61; Trade of, 59, 71; Population of, 66-67
Louisiana Purchase, 7, 20
Lucy, Autherine, 172, 191
Lummis, Charles F., 27, 97, 102, 147, 149
Lyon, Matthew, 191

McCarthy, Joseph, 168, 178, 184, 186, 190-191, 195, 249
McCarthyism, xvi, 178-179, 183, 184-186, 190-191, 250. *See also* Vigilantees
McGillivray, Alexander, xiv, 42; Fame, 72, 92-93; Health, 72-73; Parents, 73-77, 81; Education, 77-78; Creek Leader, 83-93, 261 *n 11, 13, 14, 15;* Negotiations in New York, 90-92; Death of, 72, 92-93
McGillivray, Farquhar, 75, 78
McGillivray, Lachlan, 74-77 passim, 79
McGillivray, Sehoy Marchand, 75-77, 81
McGrath, James Howard, 230
McGroarty, John Steven, 149

Malin, James C., 14
Manifest Destiny, 7, 17, 25, 29, 32, 157 251
Marchand, Captain, 75
Marion, Kansas, viii
Marsh, John, 16
Marshall, James, 17
Marti, Werner, xii
Martin, Joseph, 84, 261 *n 16*
Massachusetts-Bay Colony, 241-242, 254
Mather and Strother Company, 84
Mathews, Indian Agent, 86, 88
May, Ernest R., xii, xxi-xxiv passim. *See also Land of the Free*
Mexican-Americans, xxi, 34
Mexican-American War, 16, 20, 32, 251. *See also* Manifest Destiny
Mexico, xv, 9, 20, 28, 29, 30-32, 67, 72, 130, 155
Meyer, Carl, 142
Mezerik, E. G., 28, 29, 36. *See also* Webb
Mézières, Athanase de, 55, 59-60
Miller, John, and Miller and Bonamy, 85-86, 261 *n 20*
Miró, Estevan, 67, 68, 83, 85, 88, 92, 261 *n 12*, 262 *n 28*

Mississippi Valley, 3, 6, 8, 9, 12. *See also* Illinois Country
Mississippi Valley Historical Association. *See* Organization of American Historians
Mobile, 79, 83, 84, 92, 261 *n 11, 12*
Monrovia, California, xxii
Montalvo, Ordóñez de, 139-140
Monterey, California, 140, 143, 177
Morales, Juan, 70
Morgan, Dale, 13, 25, 106
Mormons, 12, 13, 20, 22, 32, 33, 242. *See also* Irrigation in West, Utah
Morris, Robert, 68-69
Morse, Jedidiah, 78, 105
Mortensen, A. Russell, xii, 25
Muir, John, 107; Quoted, 136-137
Mulford, Prentice, 107
Murdock, R. K., xii

National Association for the Advancement of Colored People (NAACP), xxiv
Natchez Rebellion, 45, 60, 79, 260 *n 8*, 261 *n 12*
Natchitoches, 46, 53, 55, 59; Description, 60
Native Sons of the Golden West, x, 148
Negroes, 9, 75; Education, xx-xxiv, 170-172 passim; in Louisiana, 52, 59, 60, 65, 66; Discrimination, 171-173, 185, 191, 248, 252-253; Post Civil War, 246-247
Nevada, 23, 32, 36, 112
New Mexico, x, 10, 20, 28, 30, 31-34 passim, 46. *See also* Santa Fé Trail
New York City, 90-91, 262 *n 23*
Niagara Movement, xxiii-xxiv
Nixon, Richard, 249
Nolan, Philip, 31
Nootka Sound Dispute, 90
Norris, Frank, 13, 17, 107, 145, 147, 148, 161. *See also* Culture in West
Norris, George W., 22
Nordhoff, Walter, 141
North, J. W., 120
Northwest States, xiv-xv, 16, 17, 25, 134; Historians of, 25
Nueva Vizcaya, 62, 63

O'Neill, Arturo, 83, 85, 88, 92, 261 *n 13*. *See also* McGillivray (Alexander)
O'Reilly, Alejandro, 41, 49-57, 62, 68; Revolt in Louisiana, 49-50; Indian policy, 54-55
Odoardo, Cecilio, 58
Ohio Valley, 29, 69, 70, 261 *n 14*
Oklahoma, 29; Indians of 33-34, 38
Old Southwest, ix, x, 27-29, 42. *See also* McGillivray (Alexander) and Gálvez (Bernardo de)
Old Spanish Trail, 13, 114
Oppenheimer, J. Robert, 8, 185
Oregon, 7, 12, 113; Missions in, 17. *See also* Northwest States
Organization of American Historians, xiii, xxvii, 239
Orientals in West, 9, 10, 18, 19, 35, 122, 123, 185, 228, 247
Owens Valley Aqueduct, 36
Oxnam, G. Bromley, 184

Pacific Historical Review, xiii, xxvi, 159, 160, 206. *See also* American Historical Association, Pacific Coast Branch
Paine, Thomas, 106
Paloú, Francisco, 104, 141, 161, 162
Panama Route to California, 32, 113
Panis, Jacinto, 67
Panton, William, 83, 84, 86-87, 90, 91, 261 *n 11*
Panton, Leslie and Company, 87, 261 *n 11*
Parkman, Francis, ix, 103, 129, 132
Paul, Rodman W., 145, 150
Pawnee City, Nebraska, viii
Peace of Paris of 1763, 41, 43, 81
Pensacola, 57, 79, 82, 84, 85, 261 *n 11*, *n 12*
Pickens, Andrew, 84, 86, 88, 90, 261 *n 15*
Pickett, Albert James, 260 *n 1;* Quoted, 72
Pickett, Charles E., 143; Quoted, 20-21
Pico, Andrés, 117
Piedmont Frontier, 6-9 passim, 13, 102
Pike, Zebulon M., 12, 16, 31
Pitt, Leonard, xii
Pierce, Franklin, 173
Plessy v. Ferguson, 246. *See also* Negroes
Polk, James K., 16, 32
Pollock, Oliver, 53, 61, 68-70
Portolá, Gaspar, 100, 139
Powell, Lawrence, Clark, xv
Priestley, Herbert I, 141
Proclamation Line of 1763, 81
Public School Desegregation, xix-xxi, 170-172

Railroads in West, 11, 12, 13, 21; Pioneers, 8, 22, 119; Rate Discrimination, 17-18, 24, 157; Aid to Travel, 32, 33, 113, 119-120, 121, 124
Ralston, William, 22, 112, 134
Ramsay, David, 105
Regional and Local History, 4, 5-11, 14, 15, 19-28, 154-163
Reid, Hugo, 116

Rezánov, Nikolai, 31
Rice, William B., xii, xxvi, 150
Ripperdá, Juan María de, 56
Robidoux, Antoine, 12
Robinson, Alfred, 142-143
Robinson, W. W., 106, 150
Rockefeller Foundation, xiii, xviii, 28, 169
Rogers, Fred, 106
Rogers, Harrison, 142
Rolle, Andrew, xii, 150
Rose, L. J., 121, 126
Roswell, New Mexico, viii
Roman Catholic Church, 31, 57, 138, 242; Sisters of Charity, 116-117; in Louisiana, 50, 57-58
Roosevelt, Franklin, 139, 151, 251, 254
Rorty, John, 150
Rowell, Chester, quoted on academic freedom, 212
Royce, Josiah, 145, 162; on Vigilantees, 188-189
Rubí, Marqués of, 56
Russian-American Company, 16
Rydell, Raymond A., xii

St. Louis, Missouri, 25, 60
Ste. Geneviève, 60
Salt Lake City, Utah, 17, 18. *See also* Mormons, Utah
Sánchez, Nellie van de Grift, 143
San Bernardino, California, 166-117
San Bernardino Junior College, x
San Diego, California, 178
San Francisco, California, xviii, 13, 18, 22, 23, 33, 36, 115, 127, 134, 140; in Gold Rush, 109, 110, 112-113, 144-145, 161-162; in Wine and Oil Business, 117-119, 121; its Vigilantee Committees, 156, 158, 171-179 passim, 182, 185-189
San Francisco *Chronicle,* xviii
San Pascual, Battle of, 20, 108
Santa Fé, New Mexico, 7, 16, 17, 114
Santa Fé Railroad, 121
Santa Fé Trail, 6-7, 12, 13, 16-17, 28, 32, 114. *See also* Railroads in West
Santo Domingo, 45
Saroyan, William, xxiv, 107, 153
Savannah, Georgia, xiv, 78
Scarborough, Dorothy, 17
Schreiner Institute, viii
Serra, Junípero, biographies of, 104
Shaler, William, 31, 105
Shirley, Dame (Louise Smith Clappe), on Gold Rush violence, 105, 107, 175, 186; on the Vigilantees, 188
Shorb, J. De Barth, 119, 122-124, 126
Sharon, William, 112
Sinclair, Upton, xxii, 151, 153, 156
Slavery, 104, 123, 252; in Louisiana, 47, 53, 66, 260 *n 8*. *See also* Louisiana, Negroes
Sloat, John D., 143
Smith, Henry Nash, 14
Smith, Jedediah, 13, 142
Smith, Captain John, 6, 102, 105
Southern Pacific Railroad, 120-121, 124, 157, 161. *See also* Santa Fé
Southwest, 27-31, 34-38. *See also* Old Southwest
Southwest Museum, 101
Southwestern Historical Quarterly, 28
Soviet Union, xvi. *See also* Communism
Spain, 6, 9, 27; Borderlands of, xiii-xiv, 41, 42; Colonization of, 28, 30-31; Trade Restrictions of, 65-66; Part in American Revolution, 68 passim, 81-82; Indian Policy of, 71. *See also* Louisiana, McGillivray (Alexander)
Spanish-American War, 21, 108
Sproul, Robert Gordon, in University of California Oath Controversy, 168, 197, 201, 202, 205, 228-229. *See also* University of California, Loyalty Oath Controversy
Stanford, Leland, 129-130, 134
Stanford University, 8, 22, 101, 159
Stearns, Able, 126
Stegner, Wallace, 150, 151, 153
Steinbeck, John, xxiv, 13, 107, 151, 153
Stewart, George, 107, 161
Stevenson, Robert Louis, 107, 136
Stockton, Robert F., 143
Stonehouse, Merlin, xii
Sutter's Fort, 142
Stover, Jacob, 144
Sutro, Adolph, 112, 134

Taylor, Bayard, 13, 143
Teggart, F. J., 148
Tennessee, 6, 10, 41
Tennessee Valley Authority, 22
Tenney, Jack, Loyalty Oath Controversy in California, xvi, 168, 186, 195, 250
Tenneyism, 232. *See also* McCarthyism
Terry, David S., 158, 172
Texas, 7, 11, 22, 23, 28, 37, 60; Annexation, 20, 32; Spanish Frontier, 30, 46; in Southwest, 32-38 passim. *See also* University of Texas, Webb
Texas State Historical Association, 28
Thomas, J. Parnell, 180, 195, 250. *See also* McCarthyism
Thwaites, Reuben Gold, 128
Tobacco Trade, 65-66
Tolman, Edward, 168
Tolman v. Underhill, xviii

Toole, K. Ross, xii
Tourism in West, 7, 12, 17, 18, 22, 33
Transportation in West, 34, 37, 113, 119-121, 124. *See also* Railroads in West
Treaty of Guadalupe Hidalgo, 32, 115
Treaty of New York of 1789, 88-92
Treaty of Paris of 1783, 41, 81, 83
Treaty of Pensacola, 84-85
Treaty of San Lorenzo, 29
Truman, Harry S., xix, 179, 250, 251
Turner, Frederick Jackson, viii, ix, xxv, 13, 25, 32
Twain, Mark, 13, 101, 107, 144, 155

Ulloa, Antonio de, 41, 43-49, 52, 54, 62; Marriage of, 47; Revolt against, 47-49
United States Congress, 23, 32, 34, 88, 90-91
United States Reclamation. *See* Irrigation in West
United States Relations with Western States, xiv, 35, 68-70, 82-84
United States Supreme Court, xix, xx, 186, 230, 244-246
United States v. Dennis, 230
University of California Board of Regents, xvi-xix, 168-170, 191-205
University of California, Loyalty Oath Controversy: Origins, vii, 167, 191-197, 208, 214, 228-229, 231; Academic Senate, 168, 226, 231; Committee of Privilege and Tenure, 168, 200, 202; in the Courts, 169, 215, 226; Results of Oath Controversy, 192, 204-205; Wording of Oaths, 193-194, 208, 228; Communism at, 194-199, 206, 216, 228-229, 231-232; Regent's Opposition to Oath, 196-197, 201, 202, 203, 215; Faculty Votes on Oath, 197, 198; Press and Oath, xviii, 198, 199; Alumni and Oath, 199-200; Dismissed Faculty, 201-204 passim; Academic Freedom and Oath, 214-217, 224-225; Study of Controversy, 255 *n 6*
University of California, Berkeley, ix, x, 122, 148-149, 199, 206, 214. *See also* Bancroft Library, Bolton
University of California, Los Angeles, x-xiv, xxv, xviii, 101, 115, 200, 206, 214; Faculty Promotion in, vii, x, xi
University of Texas, viii, ix
University of Washington, xvi
Unzaga, Luis de, 56-62, 68
Utah, 13, 17, 22, 23, 25, 29, 30, 33, 175. *See also* Mormons
Utah Historical Quarterly, xxiv

Vallé, Francisco, 60
Van Buren, Martin, 102
Vancouver, George, 140
Van Dyke, T. S., 145, 147, 148
Vietnam, the War in, vii, xxv, 252
Vigilance Committees, vii, 173-178 passim, 179, 180, 182-186 passim; Historical Evaluation, 187-191
Villard, Henry, 13
Vincennes, 69, 70

Wagner, Henry F., 106, 141, 150
Walker, Franklin, 133, 150, 161
Walpole, Fred, 142
War of 1812, 7
Ward Ritchie Press, 102, 159
Warren, Earl, xix, 254, 192, 197, 201-205 passim
Washington, George, 244; Negotiations with Spain, 29; in Revolution, 61, 69-70; Relations with Creeks, 83, 88, 90-92; Works on, 104
Webb, Walter P., xxv; at University of Texas, viii-ix; Geographical Determinism, 13-14, 28, 36, 245-246; the West in American History, 25; on Bancroft, 133
Webster, Noah, 105
Weintraub, Hyman, xii
White, Stewart Edward, 143; on Vigilantees, 187
Whitman, Marcus, 12
Wichita, Kansas, viii
Wilkinson, James, 68
Willett, Marinus, 89, 262 *n 24*
Williams, Roger, 241-242, 254
Wilson, Benjamin, xv, 97, 137, 170; Career, 114-115, 117, 120, 126; Family, 115-116, 121, 122, 125-126; Property, 115, 116, 117; Agriculturalist, 117-119; California Promoter, 122-125
Winn, Richard, 88
Wister, Owen, 5, 13

Yale University, 155
Yazoo Land Grants, 89, 90, 92
Young, Brigham, 8, 22. *See also,* Mormons
Young, Sheldon, 144

Zenger, Peter, 191, 234, 242, 254
Zéspedes, Manuel de, 85, 87
Zwicker, Ralph, 184